WITHDRAWN

# FABLES OF SUBVERSION

# FABLES OF

# Subversion

## SATIRE AND THE AMERICAN NOVEL,

## 1930–1980

## STEVEN WEISENBURGER

The University of Georgia Press  *Athens & London*

© 1995 by the
University of Georgia Press
Athens, Georgia 30602
All rights reserved
Designed by Richard Hendel
Set in 10.5 on 14 Berkeley
Oldstyle Book
by Tseng Information Systems, Inc.
Printed and bound
by Thomson-Shore, Inc.
The paper in this book meets the
guidelines for permanence and
durability of the Committee on
Production Guidelines for Book
Longevity of the Council on Library
Resources.
Printed in the United States of America
99 98 97 96 95 C 5 4 3 2 1

Library of Congress Cataloging in
Publication Data
Weisenburger, Steven.
Fables of subversion : satire and the
American novel, 1930–1980 / Steven
Weisenburger.
    p.  cm.
Includes bibliographical references and
index.
ISBN 0-8203-1668-7 (alk. paper)
1. American fiction — 20th century —
History and criticism.   2. Satire,
American — History and criticism.
3. Postmodernism (Literature) —
United States.   4. Modernism
(Literature) — United States.   5. Black
humor (Literature)   I. Title.
PS374.S2W4   1995
813'.50917 — dc20   94-15268

British Library Cataloging in
Publication Data available

FOR RACHEL & JAMES

# Contents

Acknowledgments [ ix

1   Introduction [ 1

2   Late-Modernist Disruptions: West, O'Connor, and Hawkes [ 30

3   What Was Black Humor? [ 80

4   The Sixties and After: Social and Political Satire [ 139

5   Encyclopedic Satires: Gaddis and Pynchon [ 199

6   Conclusion: Defining Satire, Reading Postmodernism [ 257

Notes [ 263

Bibliography [ 295

Index [ 315

# Acknowledgments

This book was researched and partly written during a sabbatical leave made possible by a fellowship from the National Endowment for the Humanities. I am deeply grateful for that assistance. Thanks also go to the University of Kentucky for enabling me to take that leave, and for encouragements to this project since then.

Portions of chapter 2 were adapted from previously published essays: on Nathanael West, in *South Atlantic Review;* on Flannery O'Connor, in *Genre;* and on John Hawkes, in *Delta* (Montpellier, France). Part of the discussion of John Hawkes in chapter 3 appeared, in different form, as an essay for *The Review of Contemporary Fiction;* portions of chapter 5 dealing with William Gaddis are adapted from essays published in *Genre* and *The Review of Contemporary Fiction,* and material on Pynchon for that chapter was adapted from an essay in *Texas Studies in Literature and Language.* I wish to thank the editors of those journals for their permission to use these materials here.

In various connections, a number of colleagues have read particular chapters or the whole draft of this book. All along, I have been greatly aided by their wise suggestions, their keen and helpful readings. Particular thanks go to John Cawelti, David Cowart, Jerome Klinkowitz, John Kuehl, Steven Moore, Patrick O'Donnell, and Susan Strehle. Karen Orchard and the staff at the University of Georgia Press made the transition from manuscript to book easy and enjoyable, and Mark Pentecost did a masterful job of copyediting. Blessings to you all.

# FABLES OF SUBVERSION

# 1

# Introduction

One of the remaining, unchallenged shibboleths of formalist New Criticism is that the satirist cannot "speak for the
twentieth century" because satire itself has allegedly "gone
stale and mouldy." This is Northrop Frye's claim in a 1944
essay; versions of it influence every major study of satire
published since then. Readers have confidently understood
satire as a rationalist discourse launched against the exemplars of folly and vice, to rectify them according to norms of
good behavior and right thinking. In what follows, I call this
the "generative" model of satirical practice. In this view the
purpose of satire is to construct consensus, and to deploy
irony in the work of stabilizing various cultural hierarchies. Particularly with the rise of modern capitalism, satirists have been expected to sustain the dominance of ideal
over merely commodified being; they have been under-

stood, in other words, as writers working to sustain the dream of "original" signifieds standing in clear relation to signifiers, thus to retell the fable of a utopian, transcendental goal for capitalist production. Satire in this generative mode does not participate in the oppositional, subversive work of much twentieth-century art. Doubtless this is why theorists have often dismissed satire as, in Alan Wilde's recent phrase, "a minor form in modern times."[1] Put simply, satire could not address the central anxieties of modernity and even seemed complicitous with the worst forms of modern, propagandistic consensus-building.

This book is about the rise of a radically subversive mode of satire from 1930 to 1980, an epoch bracketed, in the chapters that follow, by the novels of Nathanael West and Thomas Pynchon. During these decades the remarkable outpouring of satirical fictions, their inscriptions of a new satirical heritage, and the centrality of those writings to any view of American postmodernity tell us not only that Frye's negative prognosis for satire was dead wrong but also that we need to reexamine the generative model behind that prognosis. I began to question standing ideas of satire mainly through reading the likes of West, John Hawkes, William Gaddis, and Robert Coover. The following chapters grew from my sense that their novels, so obviously produced and received as satires, lacked a clearly recognizable place in the literary genealogy that scholarship has defined.

In time this made sense to me. As a number of theorists have argued — most powerfully Bakhtin and his followers — satire has played a crucial role in shaping the novel from its beginnings. Especially in our own time, however, the ubiquitous collisions of satire and the novel contribute decisively to the shift away from modernism. Thus one might take up any of various studies, like Frederick Karl's encyclopedic *American Fictions, 1940–1980,* and call the roll of novelists hailed as vital to the postmodern turn: one common denominator will be their uncertain but general reception, whether for one or two novels or their whole body of writings, *as satirists.*[2] In fact there once was a sense, prevalent in the sixties and dependent then on powerful sociopolitical forces, that American culture was unfolding a new "age of satire." Yet even from the first, critics regarded it as satire with a difference: the new novels simply would not square with formalist models of satiric activity. The broad front of these texts appeared to attack so far "beyond satire" as to redraw the boundaries of genre and mode alike, thus to necessitate new names. Among them, "Black Humor" once was the popular cognomen, although in retrospect it seems more academic and marketing hype than identifiable literary type. If anything, the idea of Black Humor was too limiting. It said very little about the wholesale redirecting of satiric aggression in contemporary novels, still less about the function of satire in refocusing the American novel.

This book argues for a mode of "degenerative" satirical writing that stands in crucial opposition to the generative satires of a Pope or Twain. The purpose of satire in the degenerative mode is delegitimizing. Loosely in concord with deconstructionist thought, it functions to subvert hierarchies of value and to reflect suspiciously on all ways of making meaning, including its own. Still more, it suspects that any symbolic practice may entail incursions of power whose logic tends toward either total domination or the final chaos of reciprocal violence. In this book I argue, moreover, that the concept of a degenerative satire can begin to map the landscape of contemporary American fiction in meaningful new ways, tracing lines of descent and differentiation that were previously fuzzy and indistinct. Such a concept best spotlights the subversive cultural work of these writers.

I also see the development of a degenerative satire as a postmodern phenomenon, and here one needs a working definition. To date, the modalities of postmodern perceiving and thinking have been graphed by Jean-François Lyotard as the rise of an "incredulity toward metanarratives" and mapped by Ihab Hassan around the seven collapsed imperial hills or "rubrics" of high modernism. Its hesitations between the poles of modernist metonymics and antimodernist metaphorics have been traced by David Lodge, as Brian McHale has plotted its centerings on a "dominant" strain of ontological simulations. Among these and numerous other surveys, the most powerful and encouraging definitions locate postmodernism as a survivable middle ground between the self-canceling polarities of modernist thought. Thus Andreas Huyssen argues that postmodern art has erased the modernist split between high art and a mass culture that was always derogated (in Flaubert, Joyce, Eliot) as the abject, usually feminine "other" of modern times. Similarly, Alan Wilde argues for the "suspensiveness" of postmodern fictions, his term for the writer's acceptance of contingency, along with the nontotalizing rhetorics needed to constructively deal with it. Particularly encouraging in such recent forays (see also Fekete, Klinkowitz, Tyler) is the idea of a postmodernism that began by deconstructing the unresolved modernist cruxes of reflexivity, nihilism, and authority, yet which now entails a less negative, more values-oriented inquiry. Now the agendas are less deconstructive than deconstrictive.

Nevertheless, both aspects are vital to any understanding of the postmodern satirical novel. Postmodernism certainly begins with the final breaking of the mirror, the onset of a radical doubt toward representation in general and Lyotard's "master narratives" in particular, those enabling and legitimizing myths of (for example) enlightenment or emancipation, plots by which the modernist seeks to westernize and totalize all of history. This does *not* mean that one can't *do* representation, just that one now does it doubtfully and, as the following chapters claim, subversively. Therefore postmodernism continues as the long overdue, carnivalesque gleanings of what had been marginal to that mirror, gleanings characteristically represented by pastiche, salmagundi, or random listing of all that modernist thought indexes as "other": speech and orality, the feminine, the folkloric, the mass-cultural, the ethnographically "strange," even the truly monstrous. Furthermore, if the aim of modernist writing was mostly transitive, its idea being to move from the signifier (or "work") to its signified (or "meaning") and thus to isolate it from discursive processes that include authorial intention, the errancies of signifiers, and their ideological reading, then postmodern writing may be defined as intransitive, as Barthes and Derrida foretold. Now the signifier plunges back into radiant flows of signifying moments (Barthes's *signifiance,* the schizoid flux of Deleuze and Guattari). The "work" gives way to "text" and "intertextuality," frustrating the desire for a stable and objective meaning, and reading doubles back to discursive processes in all their contingency.

Postmodernist thought fantasizes no quests for a displaced or mystified "arche-writing," that idea of an originary difference between what represents and what is represented.[3] The novels examined in the following chapters characteristically disrupt, by means of pastiche and parody, our dreams of a regressive "progress" toward such a millenium. They expose what Nietzsche suspected all along: representation is inherently violent, a business of exclusion, expropriation, abstraction, self-replication, monologue, and closure. The best of these satires exemplify how postmodern culture has broken the spell of various binary, "othering" dualisms common to modernism: not only the signified and its signifier but also such thought-pairs as higher/lower, mind/body, conscious/unconscious, subject/object, male/female, nature/culture. Postmodern art doubts these polarities in profound yet playfully degenerative ways, and thereby reenergizes the universe of contingent, undecideable, immanent, and pluralistic speech. Despite all their apparent negativity or nihilism, then, the subversive carnivals of postmodernism bear witness to the opening of a "pagan" discourse that was always at the heart of modern darkness.

"Pagan" is Lyotard's recent cognomen for the postmodern, in his dialogue entitled *Just Gaming* (1985). By it he indicates all that is restlessly subtended by the discursivity, contingency, and plurality described above, yet he also stabilizes it by an ethics whose principal hope is that we shall no longer perpetuate the forms of mastery and violence coded into the cultural logics of Enlightenment and modern thought. Lyotard's is an ethics, in other words, whose only imperative is unfettered exchange, a free play or "just gaming" in the fields of discourse. The very concept occasions a tantalizing observation from Lyotard's respondent, Jean-Loup Thébaud: "All that you have said concerns me a great deal because one is led to think that what you call paganism is a sort of satire, in the Latin sense of the word, namely, that all the known language games are maintained. If none is privileged, none is dropped either."[4] Lyotard assents to this connection to the Latin *saturae*, then details the contingent norms on which it relies: in essence, values without "truth-value" and justice without doctrine. He concludes the dialogue by arguing that the "capital issue" facing postmodern thought is that "the social bond, understood as the multiplicity of games, very different among themselves, each with its own pragmatic efficacy and its capability of positioning people in precise places in order to have them play their parts, is traversed by terror." This "terror" he further defines as any attempt to regulate and thus to kill the games, not only by murder but also by seemingly endless means: "imprisonment, unemployment, repression, hunger, anything you want" (99). *Fables of Subversion* argues that precisely this concern forms the ethos of American postmodernist satire.

The common thread will be the contemporary suspicion of *all* structures, including structures of perceiving, representing, and transforming. Narratives, especially, are among the most problematic of such structures, and satire becomes a mode for interrogating and counterterrorizing them. Yet postmodern satire is stuck with the very simulacra of the knowledge it so distrusts — stories. This is why the satirist often turns metafictionist and parodist, seeking out "intramural" and self-referring ways of striking at the aesthetic rules hemming us in. Such moves are decidedly not an outgrowth of the modernist project for salvaging high culture through self-reflexive, parodistic play with conventions. The new satires involve much more than mere "inter-art discourse," and in many cases readers must ask just what, if very much, the satirist means for one to salvage.[5]

The postmodern satirist suspects *all* kinds of codified knowledge as dissimulations of violence, and all of us as potential victims during their exchange. Contemporary, degenerative satire is itself a discourse of violence. It is a means of exposing modalities of terror and of *doing violence* to cultural forms that are overtly or covertly dedicated to terror. Especially in postmodern America, degenerative satire is realist narration backlit by fantastic outrage. As a provisional definition, this will also do. Still, it should already be clear that what subsequent pages call satire is not simply "the ridiculing of human vices and follies in order to correct them," as countless textbooks and critical studies would have us understand.

Narrative satire is a major form by which the postmodern writer interrogates and subverts authority. With contemporary philosophy, it wants to discover "who decides what knowledge is, and who knows what needs to be decided" (Lyotard 9). Its historical context is no longer bourgeois society, that old target of modernist satire (see Wyndham Lewis's 1934 *Men without Art*). Instead its conditions (note: *not* its "target") involve a contemporary mega-bureaucracy and its blindly progressive "information society," including what Jean Baudrillard and others define as an "ecstacy" or frenzy of semiotic exchange — the "fast-image" world of advertising, politics, electronic media, and the like. Some of the postmodern satirist's most powerful metaphors rely on the cybernetic formula for "noise," ideas of entropy, molecular Brownian motion, metamathematical demonstrations of "incompleteness" in any complex sign system, formal paradox, relativity, and catastrophe theory. At first glance these decidedly postmodern figures suggest a world where the individual subject cannot be heard and has ceased to matter. The human subject seems merely a site occupied by various discourses before being swept aside by terrifying, impersonal forces. The initial picture is of an amoral landscape, an axiological wasteland where all the monuments to rectitude have been leveled. One need only recall the apparent difficulty of locating any coherent narrative voice and viewpoint in *The Cannibal* (1949) or *Gravity's Rainbow* (1973) to see another ramification of the satirist's skirmishes with authority: the "author" slides between modes of discourse like a sniper amid the trees. Yet these strategies also begin to suggest how postmodern satirical novels aren't the negativistic, absurdist pictures they seem at first. The best of them demonstrate that no one, not even the least privileged among us, is ever really stripped of her power over those messages that continually relocate one as sender, referent, and addressee. In short, there *are* norms operating in these texts. Their values may only be nomadic and conditional, at best: no longer held aloft as universals of conduct, they are, as Barbara Hernnstein Smith argues, values "without truth-value."

A brief illustration. In *Gravity's Rainbow* the reader finds an episode that, along with Uncle Sam's buggering of Richard Nixon in Coover's *The Public Burning*, seems "one of the most disagreeable in all Postwar American fiction."[6] That episode concerns the coprophagy of Brigadier General Ernest Pudding, in the fourth episode of part 2.[7] So gross were the alleged "incomprehensibility and obscenity" of this and similar scenes that the Pulitzer board revoked the decision of their judges and denied Pynchon (on the eve of his thirty-seventh birthday, as it happened) a 1974 prize for fiction.[8] The scene itself is introduced by the musings of a behavioral psychologist, Dr. E. W. Pointsman, whose Pavlovian conditioning of old Pudding increases his (Pointsman's) control over research funding. He begins by thinking of a quotation from Pavlov's *Lectures,* then the action spins into a dramatic monologue Pointsman has composed in the style of T. S. Eliot, turns next into a dialogue between Pointsman and his assistants on the difficulties in Pudding's operant conditioning, and then jumps into a fantasy that may (or may not) occur in the mind of research assistant Webley Silvernail, where laboratory rats and dogs arise to jazzily croon a song entitled "Pavlovia (Beguine)." Enter Brigadier Pudding, veteran of The Great War and its bloody, muddy battle at Passchendaele. In the dead of night he makes his way through seven "antechambers" leading to a ritualized assignation. Each room contains "a test," in the form of objects planted by Pointsman and connected, either symbolically or metonymically, to deviant sexuality (Sacher-Masoch and Krafft-Ebbing) or The Great War. In the last chamber Pudding bows to *Domina Nocturna,* a witchy, Valkyrie-like figure snatched from Jakob Grimm's *Teutonic Mythology.* There, as "goddess of the night," she is pictured roving over battlefields to embrace the souls of fallen warriors. In Pointsman's version she appears dressed in furs and sitting on a thronelike chair. She receives the general, whips him in a ritual of pain, displays and as quickly denies him her sex, then orders Pudding to drink her urine before obliging him, in the climax of this highly formalized degradation, to swallow her excrements as she passes them. Pudding "bravely clamps his teeth shut" on each turd, thinking of them as ritual "bread" and recovering through shit that smell of mud and the putrefied corpses of soldiers he once commanded in the Flemish "Valley of Passion."

It is a fantastic moment, disgusting and yet impressive in the obliqueness of its satirical allegory. For this entire sequence of actions hangs together by structurally imitating and subverting not only the Mass but more particularly the Kabbalistic myth of a soul's ascent to the Merkabah, or Divine Throne. The first sign of this parallel comes when Pudding begins his journey and hears the call of "blessed Metatron," foremost among the Kabbalistic angels and keeper of Jahweh's throne. Gershom Scholem, whose *Major Trends in Jewish Mysticism* was Pynchon's source, summarizes the "ascent" as a sevenfold progression through "antechambers" where an aspirant's holiness is tested before he stands "erect with all [his] might" before Jahweh.[9] Pudding's "tests" precisely invert each of these until in the end he stands (sexually) erect before *Domina Nocturna,* skillfully acted for him by a former Dutch spy, her accent a reminder of actual "women of the night" he'd known in Flanders. Indeed, the whole scene has that look of a tacky bawdy house and its plotting the feel of some archetypal pornographic text, with Katje taking the role of maternalistic disciplinarian. The allusions to Sacher-Masoch's *Venus in Furs,* to Krafft-Ebbing's *Psychopathia Sexualis,* to the brute historical realities of Passchendaele, to Germanic and Hebraic myth, to the strategies of high modernist art (Pointsman's Eliotic poem) and to the tactics of "objective" science (Pavlov) — taken together these indicate not a progression toward divinity but a nightmarish *regression* into primordial, obsessive violence. Yet the root of it all, we remember, is money, Pointsman's need for "Funding" to keep his "show" going (227). At stake are questions of control, of domination, of "reality" itself as performance, and finally of the degradation of symbols as they are exchanged in each new "script." Pudding's very being is crisscrossed by messages that have positioned him, over and over, as victim. *He* knows it, but more significantly so does Katje, as actress in Pointsman's script. Indeed, Katje had played victim in analogous scripts composed by the Nazi Lieutenant Weissman, one of the novel's most pathologically demonic characters. It is precisely that recognition of the whole exchange, and of her power within it, that spurs Katje to turn the tables on Pointsman and his ilk, in the last part of *Gravity's Rainbow.*

Among recent examples, this one not only seems most in need of defense but also illustrates many aspects of postmodern satire. Besides the extreme grotesqueness of its imagery, there is the carnivalesque instability of its narrative viewpoint as Pynchon slides imperceptibly from cartoonlike fantasy to zero-degree description to the inner speech of characters. There is of course the juxtaposition of high culture with vernacular stuff, as well as the structural inversion of a mythic progress — two old satiric devices. Yet there is also the headlong play of quotation, allusion, and parody, until the fiction seems to disintegrate in "transtextuality" — that complex of manifest and latent relationships between prior texts and the one a reader holds.[10] There is in particular the *deformation* of narratives themselves, both familiar ones and those which even the most attentive reader finds obscure. And finally there is, from the distant perspective of such a reader, *laughter,* although not everyone will make the long walk to get there.

Postmodern narrative satire needs new maps. Individual books have been criticized, or dismissed, as "obsessively detailed . . . angry and cruel" (the

*New York Review of Books* on Coover's *The Public Burning*), "excessive" (*Time* on Gaddis's *J R*), and "eccentrically plotless" (the *Hudson Review* on O'Connor's *Wise Blood*). Such comments are surprisingly common; they are still more vehemently stated by defenders of "realism" and "morality" in the novel (Robert Alter, Saul Bellow, John Gardner, and Richard Price, for example). While their comments might have been useful judgments of the texts as novels in the Great Tradition, we can now take them as nothing more than descriptions of the novels *as satires*. Perhaps such confusions persist because no practicing satirist with the stature of a Wyndham Lewis or a John Dryden has yet stated the case for these grotesque fables of subversion. What's clear is this: just as Augustan satirists such as Dryden and Pope defended their work against charges of perversity and libel by stressing its reformative powers and historical moment, or as modernists like Wyndham Lewis defended their disregard for normative judgment in satire by pointing to the bourgeois stranglehold on "norms," so the postmodern satirist would answer that the obsessive deformations of narrative plot, the grotesque violence, the transtextuality, and excessive detailing are contemporary versions of the form.

A more powerful source of confusion has been the negative prognosis for satire. According to this view the satirist could "not speak for the twentieth century," and his forms had "gone stale and mouldy." That (once again) was Northrop Frye's dismissal, in his 1944 essay, "The Nature of Satire," but it reappears in almost every major study published during the quarter-century after David Worcester's pioneering 1940 book, *The Art of Satire*. Echoing the opinions of G. K. Chesterton and Bliss Perry, Worcester had pronounced the death of satire, and subsequent critics generally nodded their assent.[11] There were a few exceptions: in the mid-sixties Kernan perceptively singled out Nathanael West as an influential modern instance, and Paulson addressed the persistence of satirical energies in modernist fictions. Still, Worcester's pronouncement had a remarkable staying power, even into more recent studies, and despite mounting evidence that the last rites were prematurely spoken.[12]

How could it happen, when its newest avatars were reshaping the American novel, that satire was dismissed as "a minor form in modern times," or that satire was believed to only "slip in [a novel] unobtrusively" because satire and fiction "do not mingle well"?[13] Answers have much to do with the nature and aims of the American literary establishment and the complex way it receives new forms.

American scholarship on satire has for too long been charged by the desire of formalist New Critics to generalize its elements by comparing masterworks from selected epochs. Critics assumed this approach would produce a transhistorical definition. Frye's archetypal method, in his "Third Essay" of *Anatomy of Criticism* (1957), is representative. Finding a "pregeneric" pattern in irony and satire (the "Mythos of Winter"), Frye argues that its impetus is the attempt "to give form to the shifting ambiguities and complexities of un-idealized existence" and that, as such, its central principle is the "parody of romance" (the "Mythos of Summer").[14] Already there are problems. For one, every age will clearly discover its own "ambiguities and complexities"; yet Frye never addresses the potential of such discoveries to alter not only the content but also the formal elements he associates with satire. For another, by treating it as a "parody of romance" Frye establishes satire as a posterior form; it is inconceivable save as the disfiguration of a prior, original (hence authoritative) mythos with its previously pictured ideal. Now, no one would deny that many satires do conform to that analysis. Parodic satires, like Fielding's *Shamela,* are exemplary, but the Brigadier Pudding episode of *Gravity's Rainbow* illustrates the tendency of many satires, especially those of the post-modern era, to disfigure any type of narrative and, at its extreme verge, any rationalized knowledge. The reason, however, Frye defines *all* satire as an epigonal form of romance becomes clearer when he spells out its essential features. Chief among them is the preexistence of "moral norms." Satire, he states, "assumes standards against which the grotesque and absurd are measured" (223). Those normative standards or universals are present in the mythos of romance that precedes satire, and they underwrite its grotesque fantasy and the "militant attitude toward experience," which Frye enumerates as satire's other essential elements (223–24). To Frye, the universalist norms of satire are so crucial that he spends the remainder of his analysis specifying the range of its types, from "Low Norm" to "High Norm Satire," a system of hierarchical categories carried over from earlier critical studies by David Worcester and Ian Jack.

In fact, however, P. K. Elkin has traced that hierarchical analysis, as well as the normative assumption on which it rests, to neoclassical writers like Casaubon, Dryden, Pope, and Addison, who elaborated the "Augustan defense of satire." Still more interestingly, Elkin shows that the Augustans understood satire as "historically relative": different ages had different ideas about it, just as the Augustans themselves differentiated their own satires from what they saw as the harsher, more unrefined and overtly punitive forms of satire in Elizabethan writing.[15] While they might find precedents in classical writing, the Augustans even recognized the hierarchical conception of satire's types as peculiar to their worldview. (The high-low division of satire in Pope's *Peri Bathous* is consistent with the Great Chain of Being in his

"Essay on Man.") Nonetheless, in seeking a transhistorical model of satire, the formalist critics disregarded that relativistic definition at the same time they accepted the Augustan hierarchy. It was accepted with the full bulk of normative requirements on which it depends.

This critical heritage still predominates. Indeed, in singling out Northrop Frye's analysis I have only selected the most representative and powerful example of a tradition that claimed satire to be a therapeutic, generative practice. That claim, however, emerged from a particular context. For decades, theories of satire have been developed by scholars who specialized in British Neoclassicism and its backgrounds in Greco-Roman literature. No doubt this has much to do with the formalist bias and historicist organization of English departments in the modern university. This system was quite effective at inculcating that textbook definition of satire, so familiar to us all: ridicule of human follies and vices with an eye on their reform. Given its great interpretive power when applied to the age of Swift and Pope, the weakness of the definition when it was deductively turned on postmodern fictions was taken as a sign, not of something new in literary satire, but of satire's demise and so of writers having packed their tents for a territory "beyond satire." That territory was called "Black Humor" for a time, and English departments colonized it through a minor academic industry of scholarly articles, books, dissertations, and courses dedicated to hunting down and describing its wildlife.

These phenomena are subjects for the following chapters. Beginning from a critique of the theory of satire, this study works through the novels themselves, isolating their important contributions to an emerging postmodern satire. My focus will necessarily be on the satirical fictions of a definable age in our national literature and on the context of their reception within that culture. This book therefore sets aside right now any pretense of transhistorical validity for the understanding of the satire it describes. Its chapters work against the formalist practice of a critic like Frye, and are warily mindful of a warning that has held up very well since the Romantic era: "art and literature react against the norms of prevailing aesthetic theory in a manner that is often ruinous to that theory." [16]

*Fables of Subversion* treats narrative fictions as manifestations of intertextuality or "dialogism" in the Bakhtinian sense, thus as counterpositionings not only of different voices in the narrative itself but also of anterior texts and the codified elements of language or culture in general. That approach coincides with the provisional definition adopted earlier: degenerative satire as a form for interrogating and subverting codified knowledge and revealing it as a dissimulation of violence. Yet Bakhtin's methodology is notoriously diffuse. From other theorists (such as Barthes, Todorov, Genette, Culler, and Jameson), I have therefore borrowed interpretive tools that bring textual dialogism into sharper focus. These will be clearer in the chapters that follow. The dangers of such tools, however, are in their tendency to still provide relatively stabilized, closed readings of individual texts.[17]

The Cannibal, Lolita, The Free-Lance Pallbearers, Gravity's Rainbow, J R, The Public Burning: these novels demand an opening out of our interpretive practices. With a narrative satire, the author's intent, the competence required for readers to participate in encoding and decoding the novel, the awareness of contextual elements (necessary to the satiric aggression), ever-changing conventions, the influence of previous generic examples and their promotion and reception in a media-induced culture, and the effect of all these upon the reader, are dynamic aspects that have always seemed to be more pronounced in satire than in other kinds of writing. Formalist approaches to satire sometimes recognized their presence but never made them part of a conscious and organized interpretation. To do so would have been heretical. It would have meant acknowledging that a text may also spread its disruptions into previously disreputable (because very contingent) places in literary scholarship — author's intent and reader's response. Perhaps this is still another reason why criticism reached an impasse with the postmodern satirical novel, for when we speak of it we do not mean simply the ridicule of human failings as against some identifiable, universal codes. We mean the intent to ridicule and disfigure the codes themselves and, in addition, we mean both a recognition of that intent and the competence to find and interpret the other "texts" conspiring in the disfiguration.

Returning to the example from Gravity's Rainbow, Brigadier Pudding's midnight journey is a parodic inversion of the Kabbalistic ascent to the Merkabah, perhaps with suggestions of a Black Mass woven through it, but its satire gathers support from other "texts," such as historical narrative or the gestural system and topos of pornography. Were any of these recognized by readers who rejected the novel as incomprehensible and obscene? If not, could they still read the episode as Pynchon's satire on the pornographies of mastery and warfare? They certainly could, and did, for satire may be announced in many ways. For example, it may be signaled through the author's labeling the work a satire or by establishing its satiric pedigree either directly or indirectly in allusion or quotation, as well as through the author's utilizing a diction and stylistic texture which makes the absurd or grotesque especially vivid and blends feelings of amusement and contempt in the shock it delivers.

As Gilbert Highet points out, these have long been accepted criteria for most critics.[18] And in his use of a Rabelaisian, Swiftian scatology, Pynchon's scene seems typical. A cross-disciplinary comparison of it to other contemporary phenomena (the satiric monologues of Lenny Bruce, the underground comic books of R. Crumb, the outrages in some contemporary artistic "happenings" like those conducted by Rudy Schwarzkogler, even finally the novels of Ishmael Reed) would show that its satire was by no means extreme.

In sum, this approach to satire involves not only the discursive moves of the text but the entire satirical action, which includes the author of the text, its reader, its time and place, and discourses anterior and posterior to it, among them discourses revealing its public reception. Chapter 2 traces a coherent lineage of satire in novels by Nathanael West, Flannery O'Connor, and John Hawkes, whose intentions for their work reveal them here (for the first time that I know of) as close kin. Against the background of their radical project for satirical fiction, those developments associated with Black Humor (taken up in chapter 3) seem modest, but very instructive about the curious ways that the new satire was received. During the sixties Black Humor was also associated with social and political criticism, a more familiar territory for satire, and chapter 4 takes up some representative texts, most notably by Ishmael Reed, Norman Mailer, Philip Roth, and Robert Coover, where we see postmodern satire operating on that rough terrain. Chapter 5 turns to the most radical projects of postmodern satire: the so-called encyclopedic novel that holds all codified knowledge suspect, with examples by William Gaddis and Thomas Pynchon.

Far-reaching and unstable as is the territory of contemporary American fiction, satire remains one of the most obvious and effective lenses through which to study it. Postmodern satire is "radical" in both of the best senses of that word. Satire is a category known for traditionally formal qualities, indeed a deep-running conventionality that should disturb those who harp on the newness of postmodern fiction as if it were some nuclear mutation. At the same time, postmodern satire also invites definitions of truly disruptive effects on both the mode of satire and the novel as a genre. See the postmodern satirical novel, then, as a test case. As an example of modal conventions (for satire) intersecting those of genre (the novel), it provides chances to study how such a confluence may change both sets of conventions. Genres, such as the lyric or the novel, are conventional forms for literary production and reception that are, as Stephen Mailloux points out, deeply traditional, founded on past literary practice, and quite resistant to change. By comparison, in the general sense modes such as "realism," "modernism," or "postmodernism" involve cultural conventions pertaining to the worldview of writers and readers; within that culture, satire is more particularly a discursive or literary mode of producing and receiving texts. As Frye puts it, mode is "a conventional power of action" that one assumes about the world; or, as Paul Alpers claims, it is "the literary manifestation, in a given work, of the writer's and putative reader's assumptions about man's nature and situation." [19] Modes cut across genres, affecting both the mimetic and the diegetic strategies of individual works. Not only traditional, modal conventions are also "constitutive," in the sense of setting "the conditions under which a certain action has meaning." [20] They thus do not merely regulate literary practice, as do the conventions of genre, they also create and define new cultural practices. The intersections of mode and genre therefore assume particular importance to scholars who want to understand *how forms change*.

In postwar America, satire has certainly altered our sense of what the novel can be. Long-standing assumptions about "plot," "character," "scene," and "theme" had already been undercut by 1950, in satirical fictions by Nathanael West and John Hawkes. Yet those changes would not have come without, in the first place, a radical challenge to traditional (that is, formalist) assumptions about satiric activity. In the traditional view, satire has always been a closely targeted, normative, and corrective aggression. And one way of summarizing these traits is to say that, despite all its surface disorder or its outright meanness, the traditional satire was both written and read in hopes of a return to order and grace. Its aggressions were meant to be generative. In the degenerative mode, however, the American postmodernist satire enacts the return of a repressed horror or violence, an unbridled outrage spreading irrevocably through signification in general and hence, in particular, through its own narrative practices. Still worse, it identifies no stable, totalizing center for the shifting terms of that outrage. It lacks a steady narrative voice, specific "targets," and fixed norms or corrective goals. While this change to a degenerative satire is not new — one can find examples scattered in the writings of Petronius, Rabelais, and Swift — its general spread after 1945 is remarkable. Moreover, these changes occurred in connection with the realist novel, in which the new satire has seemed to ride like a parasite. Thus, if the decades of American fiction since Nathanael West can begin to make historical sense, it may well be along lines that are thrown into sharpest relief by the black-lighted, subversive fables of a Hawkes or a Pynchon.

Before launching this survey it will be useful to critique that formalist theory which was so influential, because so useful. One can imagine it as a tightly knit system of primary elements and secondary features. To address one element, therefore, is of necessity to take up all the others. Indeed, its unity gives this theory a real interpretive power but is also the source of its greatest vulnerability: put pressure on one part and watch the whole collapse. In effect this is what five decades of American literary practice accomplished, although in the early decades it did not seem so to critics like Worcester and Frye. An interpretive strategy developed to contain the great ages of Classical and Neoclassical satire, and believed to have transhistorical validity, simply would not enclose contemporary works at even the most fundamental points. Something needed readjustment, and one can take it as an example of the intransigence of literary critics that they clung to formalist definitions, deductively applying them while deporting the new satirical novel to vaguely drawn territories of "humor."

The primary elements of the formalist theory were four in number. First of all, satire in its purest forms was held to be a profoundly *rhetorical* mode, a persuasive literature at least and at most an openly polemical discourse. Second, it followed that satire would be unthinkable without some *target of attack* in the "real world." Third, in opposition to that target, the satire was defined as proposing a *corrective* or ameliorative course of action. Finally, this course was unthinkable without reference to some absolute moral code; in short, satire had to be universally *normative,* for this last element would legitimize the unleashing of aggressions that followed from the other three. One could begin with any of these; I will take them in the order listed.

1. *Satire is rhetorical.* This is certainly the most untested pillar in the critical literature on satire: that it must be rhetorical in the limited sense of putting forth a rational argument. Worcester's statement sets the standard: satire, he claims, "is the most rhetorical of all kinds of literature . . . it must practice the art of persuasion and become proficient with the tools of that art."[21] Subsequent critics have either echoed this claim verbatim or varied it only slightly.[22] But Worcester's definition is by no means the extreme. Some critics have gone so far as to describe satire as only "pretending" to be literature while being in fact "a propagandist distortion" or, among other literary kinds, "a department of rhetoric" or a mode for "imitations of rhetorical structures."[23] Even Worcester, who always seems to delight in the eccentricities of satiric literature, gloomily speaks of it as "painless philosophy," an easy means for "imparting ideas, propaganda, criticism" (51). Such statements clearly depend on a view of rhetoric as the coercion of audiences in order to reaffirm *endoxa,* common opinions held by a majority of people. The New Critics distrusted such direct appeals, such demands for a bourgeois acqui-

escence before, instead of a close participation with, just the literary text. So it seems unusual for them to make an exception with satires. One reason was that some did not regard satire as literature *per se,* another was that others were willing to entrust its "direct appeals" to an ethos of bygone times when faith in objective reason hadn't crumbled. For instance, T. S. Eliot's introduction to "The Vanity of Human Wishes" is almost wistful in its admiration for Johnson's use of rhetorical arts in "castigating the vices of his time and place."[24]

The definition of satire as rhetoric is typically evident in Harry Levin's 1978 essay, "The Wages of Satire." He opens with a caveat, granting that satire "has never been easy to pin down."[25] But then, like many authors of longer studies, Levin spins through a historical survey, from Robert C. Elliott's primitive satirists through the Greeks, Romans, British Neoclassicists, and ending with selected moderns like Waugh and Orwell. This survey leads Levin to a summit that even he implied was unattainable: a transhistorical definition. Satire, he says, is a didactic, rhetorical form, "purposeful comedy." It aims to correct, according to universal norms. It may "scourge" as well as "purge"; it is a moral "therapy" (8). Therefore, Levin concludes, when interpreting satire the critic must confront "questions regarding the efficacy of satire as a means of signalizing and attaining definite objectives" (12), for such are the "wages" a satirist desires to collect. Levin's idea of satire's "extra-literary" purpose is, in fact, widespread.[26] By these lights satire is rather like a Department of Propaganda, a means to some rationalist end; formalism thus accorded satire a responsibility it imposed on no other art — to work demonstrable change in the world. So the formalist critic might say of a poem that it must not mean, but be. Interestingly, however, that is a luxury he denies to a literary satire.[27]

The contradictions of this approach are readily apparent. One might say that while *some* satirists are writers with a mission, just as some first basemen conceive a missionary purpose for baseball, that fact in no way compels us to define *all* satire (or baseball) as propaganda. More typically, however, critics have tried to mitigate these side effects of a rhetorical definition by reclaiming some of satire's imaginative, especially its mimetic, scope. Paulson, for instance, argues that while "satire originates as rhetoric, or attack, it only matters — or survives as literature — as mimesis." Later he claims that satire becomes less effective as it becomes more rhetorical, seconding Frye's argument that "at least a token fantasy," or fiction, is necessary to make the rhetoric more palatable.[28] This echoes the conception of satire as "a distorting mirror" widely held among the Augustans. In his preface to *The Battle of the*

*Books* (1704), Swift wrote: "Satire is a sort of glass, wherein beholders do generally discover everybody's face but their own, which is the chief reason . . . that so few are offended with it." This is still a widely quoted passage.

To many, this means defining satire as writing that moves in an ellipse whose foci are argumentative rhetoric and narrative mimesis.[29] Still, that avoids the central issue: there is no compelling argument behind either the didactic *or* the mimetic definition of satiric activity. Indeed, as Michael Seidel wisely suggests, the rhetorical-mimetic definitions of some critics are just the latest attempts in a centuries-long effort to dodge satire's radical ethos and make it "less noticeably profane." Confronting satire's pandemic violence against all forms of signification, theorists ever since the Renaissance have argued for its "rhetorical, forensic, and moral justification."[30] In doing so they too easily dismiss the power of satire to contaminate both the satirist and the reader with its aggression. According to Seidel's argument, a new theory would first have to locate the power of satire not in mimesis — for it mimes, simply, violence itself — but in aspects of *diegesis*: those strategies of discourse that encourage us to create, as well as to deform, a fiction. Second, the theory would have to acknowledge a definition of rhetoric that involves, beyond persuasion and polemics, playfulness and intertextuality. There have already been a few tentative moves in this direction, suggesting that criticism is ready to cope with a kind of satiric literature that systematically defies the imposition of argumentative rhetoric.[31]

2. *Satire requires an object of attack.* If it is aggressive, rational rhetoric, then there must be a target — or so the theory goes. Frye holds that "an object of attack" is one of "two things" that are "essential to the satire," the other being humor based on a grotesque or absurd fantasy. Paulson adds that along with its fantasy or "fiction" satire must "make the reader aware of a pointing finger, an ought or ought not, that refers beyond the page." Thus he also links the "target" with the corrective and normative purposes of satire. The formalist critics all assent to Paulson's claim that the target must be external to and universal for the work in question. Of late that claim has also become a principal means of differentiating parody from satire. Margaret Rose holds that, in deforming some anterior text, parody "makes the object of attack part of its own structure," whereas satire does not. And despite her disagreements with Rose on other points, Linda Hutcheon concurs: "The difference between the two forms lies . . . in what is being made into a 'target.' In other words, parody is not extramural in its aim; satire is."[32]

But in what sense can any extramural satiric target or "object of attack" be said to exist? Both Neoclassical and formalist theories accepted the idea that the target exists outside the book, as an objective fact or universally accepted proposition. In what sense, however, does "Richard Nixon" exist as an "object of attack" for the reader of Coover's *The Public Burning* (1977)? No one — perhaps least of all a Cambodian villager — would deny his existence and its objective historical consequences, although that is not in question. The answer must be that, *for readers,* "Richard Nixon" exists as the subject of reports in *Time* or various other periodicals, as the subject of biographies and autobiographies, of anecdotes and jokes, of histories, of radio and television news bites, and so on. These are exactly the materials from which Coover's satire invites us to reconstruct the character. He comes to us, then, as a representative from the "real world" to which the *story* refers; but *discourse* cannot actualize a "Richard Nixon" except as the (tentative) subject of other conceptual structures, other discourses. This condition is by no means unique to literary satire: in semiotic theory it is shown to hold for reading in general. Eco convincingly argues that readers would be incapable of making their "inferential walks" through a text without carrying along a vast baggage of knowledge, metaphorically described as an "encyclopedia" (with systematically coded information and overcoded correlations, as well as various intertextual and interpretive frames). In the same vein, Iser concludes that the "meaning" of a fictional text is never "a given external reality nor a copy of an intended reader's own world." Instead the work's meaning "is something that has to be ideated in the mind of the reader," and this would be impossible without an "existing stock" of coded information. Such an approach defines the "world of reference [as] an encyclopedic construct" unique for each reading subject.[33] One could never hope to exhaustively describe it for everyone, but for communication to occur it obviously must overlap the "real world" in myriad ways.

This is decidedly not a way of treating all reality as textual, and so of merely seconding the motto of some deconstructionist speculation: *il n'y a pas de hors texte.* Nor is it a pat way around the charges of libel that have perennially dogged literary satires, *The Public Burning* among them. It *is* a pragmatic and decidedly constructivist way of defining the satiric "target." No longer conceivable as simply an objective, "extramural" fact, the target is mediated by those intersubjective processes of representation in general. It is a cultural construct available synecdochically, so to speak, *in* the satiric diegesis. Think of the target as a representation stripped of some clothing and made the subject of another representation, and perhaps still another, in infinite regression. Yet this presents problems for conventional ideas of satire. For instance, can it suffice to define parody as the "usually comic representation of a 'modelled reality,'" and satire as the "critical representation of a 'non-modelled reality,' i.e., of the real objects"?[34] In the pragmatics of reading, the distinction between "modelled" and "non-modelled" seems quite blurred. Indeed, if satiric aggressions are "targeted" in any way, it may well be that they take aim at the very problems of "modelling" or "representing." Therefore the search for an "object of attack" should send us first and foremost into the discursive practices of the satire itself, in particular its intertextual energies.

In the postmodernist novel this difference is essentially one of degree and not of kind. The postmodernist satire is still, in an important way, a targeted aggression. But its infections erupt *mainly within,* amid discursive activity itself, and are therefore identified with semiotic practices of which the text is itself an instance. Again, here is that reflexivity so essential to postmodern thought. By contrast, generative satire ridicules subjects thought to be specific and extramural, as most critics point out. And indeed there are instances of contemporary American satire, like Roth's *Our Gang* with its ridicule of Richard Nixon, that still aspire to that goal. However, contemporary satire characteristically looks inward and says less about specific persons or human vices than about the general slide of discourse into violence. If these fables of subversion can be said to target anything, it is fiction making, the very strategies of dissimulation by which the nuclear age seeks to mask its violent being.

3. *Satire is corrective.* Again, this follows directly from the first proposition: if satire is rhetorical (in a logico-didactic sense), then it must be corrective. This claim also comes from a desire to ameliorate the aggressiveness involved in "attacks" or "targets" — for one doesn't "correct" out of sheer meanness. And like (1) and (2) it comes widely recommended. Worcester, for example, refers to the necessity of believing that readers will "adopt [the criticism] as their own," and Highet claims that satirists write "in order to benefit society as a whole," indeed that some write for the purpose of "awakening and instructing a mindless public."[35] A version of this claim appears even in Kuiper's recent attempt to ground a "scientific" theory of satire in readerly "perception."[36] And then there is the curative impulse that is another form of the satirist's "wage," for example in the anthropological claim that "cultures institutionalize ridicule for the health of their communities," or in the familiar proposition that irony, "unlike satire . . . does not pretend to cure."[37] However, P. K. Elkin has shown how subsequent generations have inherited this corrective-curative view from the Augustan defenders of satire. In an age of burgeoning print media, and fearing stricter censorship on all writing in order to control libel, the Augustans agreed that satire was an ideal remedy

for cultural ills, to point out knavish scribblers, to indict vice, and so on.[38] The idea seems ill-suited to twentieth-century culture, yet it lives on in the critical literature.[39]

There are other problems. Disagreeing with Morton Gurewitch, D. C. Muecke points out that *all* ironies (including modes of irony like satire) are correctives in a general sense because they supplant, or invalidate, a naive meaning with a more experienced one.[40] Moreover, it is probably invalid to make any special claims about satire's power to operate on a reader. In semiotic theory it is axiomatic that any exchange of signs modifies the experience of exchanging signs. Or: that semiosis is always altered, its trajectory changed, by further acts of semiosis. This is what Eco (following Peirce) refers to as an "energetic response" to any sign. His example is a piece of music, and he concludes that, "after having received a series of signs and having variously interpreted them, our way of acting within the world is either transitorily or permanently changed."[41] Reader-response theorists have been equally clear about the universality of these factors. Iser, for example, argues that any reader open to a literary text and its effects will be compelled to reformulate his understandings. Reading literature thus involves "an experience which entails the reader constituting himself by consituting a reality hitherto unfamiliar." It is in this way, he argues, that literature "significantly changes" its readers.[42] The theory involved here is only pragmatic. It has no idealistic basis and nothing to say about how humans in general *ought* to behave, an important consideration as we move into (4) below. So a photograph could be as useful as a satire in "correcting" a malign world. One can therefore see no reason why this function of satire ought to be regarded as in any way unique.

In fact, in chapters 3 and 4 I will argue that the idea of satire's sanative or corrective purpose led to one of the more revealing quirks of its recent literary history. In seeking to justify their own non-traditional practices, some of the new novelists — the Black Humorists — claimed that they had been forced to seek new means because (what they called) satire had been "usurped" by documentary forms. They argued that documentary photography and film had assumed the corrective powers of satire ever since the thirties, and they pointed out that the very purpose of documentary, like satire as formalist critics defined it, was after all to identify social ills, to suggest possible cures, and by directing (targeting) readers' emotions to inspire corrective action. Now all of this may have been so, but it is neither a unique trait of documentary or satire, nor is it therefore useful in defining satire. As such, the fear that this power of satire had been "usurped" reveals less about the new fictions than about the narrowness of a critical framework increasingly unable to circumscribe them.

4. *Satire is normative.* "There is no prejudice so inveterate, in even the educated mind," wrote Wyndham Lewis in 1934.[43] There is also more disagreement about this proposition than about any of the prior three. Still, it persists. Dooley, for example, holds to "a firm moral stance" as "the *sine qua non* of satire."[44] A number of critics agree that it is essential for satire "to take a moral stand, make a judgment, and place or distribute blame"; in short, satire must be normative in a positivist or universalist sense.[45] Thus to many critics the satirist has been at best a conservative — and at worst a fascist — working "within the established framework of his society, accepting its norms. . . . He is the preserver of tradition."[46] Paradoxically, though, nothing seemed more farfetched to the archconservative (and sometime fascist) Wyndham Lewis, who argued that "the greatest satire *cannot* be moralistic at all: if for no other reason, because no mind of the first order, expressing itself in art, has ever itself been taken in, or consented to take in others, by the crude injunctions of any purely moral code."[47] This counterclaim was designed to knock the traditional view of satire down to its foundations. Lewis's greater purpose, however, was to restore to satire its stature *as an art* by detaching it from morals and propaganda.

Why should any of the formalists have disregarded that goal? It was, after all, a cornerstone of modernist aesthetics that the work of art, although its subject may be human conduct, should not argue a brief for one or another moral statute. In particular this was a cornerstone of the New Criticism. John Crowe Ransom, in an influential 1941 essay, condemned the moralistic biases of writers and critics as "the immoral recourse of thinkers with moral axes to grind."[48] Even latter-day moralists like John Gardner argue that the moral energies of art must operate unobtrusively, like some natural force, for "the artist who begins with a doctrine to promulgate, instead of a rabble multitude of ideas and emotions, is beaten before he starts."[49] If one had followed through on such claims the result would have been a *purely* formalistic definition: satire as only an empty vehicle that can be filled with a variable content, and thus driven by the partisans of *any* morality. Yet even the best of formalist critics (Frye, Highet, Kernan) were unwilling to go that far in the case of satire: its universal norms had to be "relatively clear" or at least "implicitly" stated.[50]

There were probably several reasons for this apparent shortcoming. Again, there was the deep attachment New Critics felt for Neoclassical writers who, as P. K. Elkin shows, overemphasized the moral-didactic role of satire to legitimate their own practices. To them, satire might be "a shining supplement to publick laws," but to Wyndham Lewis that view turned satire into the mere "insignia of a sheriff or a special constable" who, ironically, had to patrol a "lawless" territory.[51] Still more profound was the attachment New Critics felt for theories of irony handed down from Romanticism. As Muecke demonstrates, Romantic philosophers like Schlegel and Kierkegaard were quick to distinguish between "specific" and "general" irony. The former was defined as a "normative irony, the kind employed in the service of satire or controversy" and against particular, individual exemplars of folly or vice. In contrast, general irony was defined as operating amid "those contradictions, apparently fundamental and irremediable, in a universe that seems to be utterly alien, utterly purposeless."[52] Irony in this new, "general" sense was to Schlegel a kind of "never-ending satire," a disturbance without the stop of unwavering moral judgment. It admitted varieties of paradox to which satire, if one accepted Neoclassical definitions, could never accede. As René Wellek observed, for Schlegel irony had thus become a "recognition of the fact that the world in its essence is paradoxical and that an ambivalent attitude alone can grasp its contradictory totality."[53] Romantic (or general) irony was the vehicle of that ambivalent, irreverent attitude. It was defined as less didactically rhetorical and no longer satirical, while being more subjective and ambiguously witty. Supposedly, it had pushed beyond the traditionally normative field of satire, a claim that was repeated, as chapter 3 will show, by the promoters of Black Humor.

This is why critics continue to insist that "satire is, relatively speaking, a minor form in modern times." It is because satire's "notion of a correctable error or folly" had evidently been "superseded" by what recent scholars of Romanticism have seen as a paradoxical humanity living in an unfathomable cosmos, and best approached through still-evolving forms of irony.[54] It was clever: with one hand literary theory denied satire the rights of mutability and ambiguity, while with the other it granted those rights to irony.

No doubt Wyndham Lewis was right. This "inveterate" prejudice, so much involved with the Romantic revolt against the normative foundations of Neoclassical art, continues to skew our definitions of satire. However, from a poststructuralist and pragmatic standpoint there are indeed no "norms" in satire, only discursive structures, or "devices," by which readers decode the ideological gestures of a work.[55] Just as with any other kind of writing, there is room in satire for widely divergent readings. In this regard it is instructive to consider the example of Flannery O'Connor (see chapter 2). By every indication she intended to write satire according to the moral precepts of a Christian theology. Yet to one of her most astute readers, John Hawkes, the devices of her prose succeeded in turning her fictions in a diametrically opposite direction.

Finally, it is worthwhile to consider recent semiotic approaches to irony. As a trope, it has always been seen as crucial to the strategies of satire. Traditionally, it is defined as *antiphrasis*, the marking of a contrast between stated and real meanings, or as inversion, when a latent message overturns the manifest one.[56] In either case it is important to understand these as semantic functions within the text. However, irony also has a pragmatic function: to signal judgment. Whether "specific" or "general," irony is a trope that situates a speaker's evaluative attitudes in the text and, in turn, spurs the reader to interpret and evaluate them.[57] So irony is another of Eco's "inferential walks." Moreover, all ironies have a "corrective" function, and not only those "simple or "specific" forms which the Romantics thought they had transcended. Thus it would be just as accurate to say, "Irony is normative," so long as one understood that, as with satire, its norms are "situated" by aspects of production, structuration, and reception. In short, the norms are cultural constructs.

According to Anglo-American formalist theory, these are the four primary elements of satire. Over the years, their broad acceptance has seemed to grant them a kind of diplomatic immunity from interrogation. They are confidently reasserted in textbooks and handbooks, though none of the four wholly withstands either a theoretical critique or, as these chapters argue, the problematizing onslaught of postmodern writing. Yet formalists often also mentioned, almost in passing, a range of secondary, background features common to satire. Never part of an organized description in the critical literature, these features are nonetheless foregrounded in recent fictional satires. This change, perhaps more than any other, enables one to begin understanding satire's contemporary evolution.

Most important is the presence in satire of the grotesque. Worcester aptly sees it as a "hinge into irony," because grotesque technique "makes the ugly seem fascinating"; it manages to caress the very "subject it feeds on" (65). Moreover he sees the grotesque as "satire by description," a strategy common to narrative instances of the form. Wolfgang Keyser provides a historicist definition of the grotesque that links its aims to those of satire, as formalist theories were then defining it. Like satire, he writes, the grotesque stems from a desire to identify and exorcise what society perceives as abnormal, demonic, evil. Yet the grotesque is also, according to Keyser, a "fundamentally ambivalent" way of actualizing "the deep absurdities of existence." It mixes horror and humor, the monstrous and the ludicrous; indeed it threatens to emerge as a "comprehensive structural method" of achieving an absurd, disorienting heterogeneity — a subversive intermixture of human, bestial, even the inanimate.[58] If anything this definition would seem to link the grotesque more closely to the "general irony" situations of Romantic and modernist aesthetics than to the "specific" ironies identified with traditional satire. Nevertheless, Anglo-American critics have only marginally included the grotesque in their definitions of satire. Again, there is Frye's glancing "sense of the grotesque or absurd" which he holds central to satiric "wit or humor," and other critics concede its role in satire's "distortion" or "exaggeration" of the familiar.[59] Still, to many critics its role is limited to ridiculous depictions of specific characters and settings. Probably this is because more general and ambivalent versions of the grotesque (as in Keyser's formulation) would not square with the proposition that satire must have a clear "object of attack" and be "normative." For what did a monstrously grotesque work seem to assault, except our very ways of signifying (on) being itself? Worse, it appeared to actually celebrate disorder, a categorical disarray anterior to semiosis. For these reasons the grotesque could only be subordinate to the (supposedly) more focused aggressive and normative aims of satire.

Postmodern fictional satire forces us to reconsider the role played by its grotesques. Now they are readymade allies, both semantically and pragmatically, because only the grotesque can inscribe, in a mere figure, those disruptions of codified knowledge peculiar to the new satire. Semantically, the grotesque style intermixes categories of being that the systems of language, and thus of representation, normally keep discrete. In the work of Flannery O'Connor, for example, the host of animate, often insectlike objects, juxtaposed to the host of less-than-human, often insectlike characters, composes the image of a terrestrial pandemonium. Like ridiculous monsters out of demented, schizophrenic consciousness, her grotesques seem to rebuke the very idea of category. This is precisely the point: grotesque art assaults, not existence, but the categorical imperatives through which we shape experience. Semantically, the grotesque is an atavistic, disruptive game played with the differential order of signifiers. Pragmatically, it implicates the reader in that atavism. This is probably the most obvious but neglected aspect of the grotesque. To read, for instance, of the circuit-preacher in *Wise Blood* who "rode all over three counties with Jesus hidden in his head like a stinger," is first of all to laugh, the initial response to a trope whose vehicle and tenor are pulled from such distant lexical fields. It is also to be enlisted in a conspiracy of laughers who have the interpretive competence to participate in O'Connor's disfiguration, thus to read this trope against the outrageous backlighting of an accumulating narrative structure.[60] Responding to the clusters of grotesque tropes the writing shadows forth, we also draw inferences about O'Connor's satirical intent.

Two other features associated with grotesque satire, again only marginal in formalist approaches, are its carnivalesque setting and its regressive plotting. Carnival is, simply, the *topos* of the grotesque figuration. Kernan, working from Pope's examples of the "variegating" and "confusing" tropes in the *Peri Bathous,* calls it the "Mob Tendency" and traces it through the crowd scenes common in Dryden's "MacFlecknoe" and Pope's *Dunciad,* as well as in the novels of Evelyn Waugh and Nathanael West.[61] Frye, generalizing from these and similar examples, identifies carnival with "low-norm satire," where "gaiety predominates" in "an upside-down world dominated by humors and ruling passions"; and other critics reiterate these connections without developing them.[62] However, in American postmodern satires the *topos* of carnival looms as a much fuller and more disturbing image. We find it throughout the period: in the mob scenes of *The Day of the Locust,* the lunatic asylum of *The Cannibal,* in Vonnegut's novels, and most powerfully of all in *Gravity's Rainbow* and *The Public Burning.* In these fictions it emerges as a popular, folkloric, or mass-cultural phenomenon that is decidedly antirepresentational: during carnival, nothing *is* what it *seems.* As in postmodernity generally, so during carnival characters move in a space *only* of surfaces, where fictions of the "internal man" bear no significance. Instead, human subjects are just their simulacra or roles, and in playing them they discover the freedoms of the radical "other," in absurd, monstrous opposition to a society of rigid stereotypes. Such freedoms extend, moreover, to language itself. The "open" ethos of carnival fosters a heterogeneous flux of discourse types: for example, of underworld slang, cant, professional jargon, popular slang, standardized English, obscenities, versions of lyric, and ethnic expletives. This dialectical clash of languages is central to European theories of satire, especially in Bakhtin. There, the harassment of the "literary" by extraliterary language, of the formal by informal and even obscene speech, is seen opening the field of permissible discourse. Carnival definitively illustrates the semiotic processes of dismantling and exposure of which satire is a part. Amid its disorder, one discovers points of view, specific orderings that are suppressed by or in sharp opposition to authorized representations.[63] This is why Bakhtin and his followers take carnival as the controlling ethos of the genre that carries it: Menippean satire. Their further step, not yet fully acknowledged amid the remarkably positive reception of Bakhtinian theory in America, is to make satire the enabling condition of novelistic discourse.

If carnival is the *topos* of grotesque satire, regression is often the principle of its action, its plot. To recall *The Satyricon,* the *Encomium Moriae, Gargantua and Pantagruel,* "MacFlecknoe," *The Dunciad,* or *Don Juan* is to evoke images of mobs swirling around figureheads of foolishness and atavistic physicality, all in a loose succession of scenes whose only rationale is the confirmation — and perhaps the crowning — of those central figures. Formalist theory often commented on this regressive principle of satiric plots, whether they were shaped in verse satire or prose narrative.[64] But the disorder of fictional plotting has remained a persistent problem. Kernan stops short of labeling as antirepresentational the disjunctiveness, digression, and atavism of the form. His position is that satire requires a reader to suspend the Aristotelian rules for imitative, well-ordered, unitary action, *because that is what "Dullness" does.* The regressive plots of satire imitate the motives of "Dullness," which "drives toward a dismemberment of form"; it "strives in spite of nature to create Progress yet always produces the opposite."[65] This solution to the problem of satiric plotting is ingenious. It depends on a commonsense rejection of stupidity, but still more significantly on a universalized normative judgment: Dullness is *unnatural* ("in spite of nature"), therefore reprehensible and in need of correction. This certainly has explanatory power in the context of Neoclassicism. (Kernan's authority was the "reversing trope" in Pope's essay, *Peri Bathous.*) Yet that power is sharply curtailed in the context of postmodern knowledge, where ideas of "Nature" as progressive evolution are countered by the restrictions of entropy, undecidability, and incompleteness. It is also curtailed by our recognition, through Roland Barthes and other poststructuralists, of just how pervasive is the "naturalization of the cultural" for purposes of ideological control and mastery. More specifically, it loses force in an age that has carried the subversion of continuity and authority over into language. Now, revealing anything about the dissimulations of violence in human discourse, satire disrupts "Progress." It "suspects the very nature of language in fostering hypocrisy," as Michael Seidel so aptly puts it. Thus satiric plots require a "double action, a regress in the form of a progress."[66] Here is the key paradox: by moving onto degenerate ground, the satirist reveals language as a great cover-up, but it is only with language that one keeps moving at all.

This paradox was a main force in shaping the satirical novels of American postmodernism. The contemporary narrative satire, far from being an imitation of the chaos and disorder of "Dullness," is concisely ordered by the possibilities, in atavistic times, for a regressive diegesis: satire, then, as degenerative, subversive fantasy. If anything, the obsession with violence in postmodern satire has produced overdetermined plots, a structural counter-pointing so articulated as to seem an intensely reasoned hysteria. The satiric "double action" is plainly evident in early instances: West's *The Day of the Locust*, O'Connor's *Wise Blood*, and Hawkes's *The Cannibal*. Yet it continues as a powerful force. An encyclopedic satire like *Gravity's Rainbow* deploys the double plot as a vastly articulated structure of mirrorings, digressions, and regressions (the Brigadier Pudding episode, for example), all contained by an inwardly spiraling motion whose controlling idea seems to be that the only stop humanity creates for incompleteness is atavistic violence.

As a form for the degenerative exposure of language and its systems of representation, a regressive progress for fictional plot is one of those features, like the grotesque style and the *topos* of carnival, that postmodern satire foregrounds, even as its practitioners challenge or simply disregard those four elements that formalist theory once held up as primary and totalizing. It is one way that postmodern narrative satire resists "naturalization," defying those processes of reading that seek to integrate the text with social and aesthetic norms or with consensus-building metanarratives. For the student of literary types, there is a tale here. It involves new practices and possibilities for both satire and the novel, as well as some curiosities of literary reception in an age when, after T. S. Eliot, criticism became a mostly academic profession.

Again, however, one is speaking of differences and changes of degree. The broad front of American postmodernist fictions certainly includes a large group of satires, but even among them there are important variations. Some writers (like Mary McCarthy, Philip Roth, or Terry Southern) adhered to an idea of satire that is decidedly *generative;* they took for granted satire's power to punish vice and uphold liberalist norms. Others (like Coover, Hawkes, or Pynchon) can only be described in terms of a *degenerative* satire that poses incisive and counterbalancing challenges to previous theories about satirical work. Yet some of the most engaging instances, in addition, are of individual texts or literary careers where the pull of one or another submodality of satire, the generative or degenerative, is telling. In *Cabot Wright Begins* (1964), James Purdy cuts off a stunning release of degenerative aggressions to end on a note of corrective-normative ridicule; in *Wise Blood* (1952), O'Connor's technique runs away with what had been intended as a normative satire. An important Black Humorist like Kurt Vonnegut turns out, by these lights, and despite all contrary hype, to have been attempting a quite traditional satire; while the career of Ishmael Reed can be understood as a movement away from the wildly degenerative satire of his first novel, *The Free-Lance Pallbearers* (1967), and toward the more stabilized, normative aggressions of his later work. In comparison, writers like John Hawkes, William Gaddis, and Thomas Pynchon have increasingly undermined the normative-corrective conventions of traditional satire. In such instances the tensions of satirical practice and postmodern thought can also be seen as central to recent American writing, for example in several of its most obvious contributions to narrative fiction: the Black Humor novel and the encyclopedic fiction. The tensions are also very much a part of so-called experimentalist challenges to the conventional realist novel. All are, quite clearly, modal expressions of an uncertain age always bristling with threats of unappeasable terroristic violence.

This study therefore initiates a revision of satirical theory even while a full critique of theoretical issues lies beyond its scope. My main intention is to compose a literary history. Its organizing theme is that the really seminal American postmodernist fictions can best be interpreted, and differentiated from their predecessors, by the kind of satires they write. This shift can be understood as a foregrounding of those features — the grotesque style, carnivalesque *topos,* and regressive plotting — mentioned in formalist analyses but never integrated with an organized theory of satirical writing. At most, critics acknowledged that some satires tended to assume a destructive power. Elliott, for example, refers to a kind of satire that, like black magic, operates on a "dark and fearsome side," setting in motion "disturbing and subversive influences" that may spin out of control until "the local attack cannot be contained"; and Frye speaks of that rare satire, for instance by Petronius or Rabelais, that "plunges through to its final victory over common sense," reaching a chaos whose sign is "the verbal tempest."[67] In general, however, the critics have all agreed with Elliott that the true "art of satire" consists of distancing one from its degenerative power by various logico-rhetorical devices. Degenerative satire was the exception and not the rule. But the satirical novels of contemporary America fly in the face of that received knowledge so often, and with such a widely shared poetics, that a revision of the theory seems necessary. The historical focus of these chapters is both a call to and a preliminary brief for that revision.

The key satirical novels of postmodern America are texts that sacrifice the human, sign-producing world on the altars of its own degenerative, violent consciousness. As such, these subversive fables ask to be seen as both antithetical to *and* the precondition of any regenerative or emancipatory work. Again, these traits sharply distinguish postmodern satires from those of prior ages. One may clearly graph the shifts, not only away from the normative, rationalist satires of Enlightenment writers, but also away from the antibourgeois, general irony situations of Romantic and modern thought. With the main currents of postmodernism, then, the recent satires refuse to "naturalize the cultural," as Roland Barthes phrased the challenge. Having given up the quest for universals of conduct, for the originary signified, they concentrate a vision of the reflexive, deconstructive, but also radiant play of signifiers, a game that still entails pragmatic concepts of justness.

Satire is certainly a complex, still-evolving mode, in its form and ethos. One ought to reckon with it in that spirit. Still, to write of satire at all is to situate oneself in the midst of irresolvable but irresistible paradoxes. It is to deal with meanings that assail the processes of making meaning. It is to gaze into what these fables of subversion identify, again and again, as the terror of the ridiculous. No doubt, what attracts writers and readers to satire is just that intractable, madcap seriousness. As Mark Twain once put it: "When we remember that we are all mad, the mysteries disappear and life stands explained."

# Late-Modernist Disruptions

## West, O'Connor, and Hawkes

Throughout the forties and fifties literary critics were pro-
nouncing the death of satire, arguing that a satirist could
"not speak for the twentieth century" because satirical
forms had "gone stale and mouldy."[1] Yet a metamorpho-
sis of satire was already under way. The satirical novels of
Nathanael West, practically unread when they were published during the thirties, were reprinted and well received
from 1946 on. Then two remarkable first novels by John
Hawkes and Flannery O'Connor, *The Cannibal* (1949) and
*Wise Blood* (1952), radically shifted the functions and form
of satire. Later, both writers would acknowledge the importance of West's writing on their own fictions. In turn,
their novels became touchstones for a generation of satirists
whose work began appearing in the sixties. So the critics
had been dead wrong. Their terminal prognoses for satire,

like those "death of the novel" predictions common to the sixties, were greatly exaggerated.

An old axiom of historiography holds that decisive shifts of temperament are difficult to perceive, except retrospectively. It is the same in literary scholarship. Only years later, sometimes only after a movement or period-bound practice has exhausted itself, do we recognize the key texts, figures, and collaborations conspiring in its development. The analeptic view is always privileged, in both history and narrative art. During our time, this is seen as a highly problematic yet unavoidable proviso that understanding imposes on itself, particularly in the study of contemporary culture. Popular reception and practical criticism identify powerful new texts and movements, then, mindless of the paradox, solid scholars stamp their imprimatur on the new by appraising it in the light of what is already old. Moreover, these appraisals are often based on little more than nebulous themes. This is what happened, for example, with phenomena like "Black Humor" or — what is the blackest of texts — *Gravity's Rainbow*. The reviewers' blurbs printed on book jackets, generally a reliable gauge in these matters, were quick to make connections with the recent past: "Heller, Barth, Vonnegut, and Now PYNCHON," proclaims the 1974 Bantam paperback copy of Pynchon's novel, linking its world to his predecessors' "ghastly, fantastic" vision of our age. Introductory anthologies of Black Humor fiction (by Davis and Friedman) cast farther back. These editors were quick to make the obligatory thematic connections between contemporary works, with their "antihero" moving in an "absurd cosmos," and similar figurations in earlier fictions by the likes of Céline, Sade, and Swift. During the last quarter-century, literary scholarship has done little to question these popular claims of parentage.

Yet imagining chains of causal events has not always been, and in particular is not now, the most reliable means of defining and appraising cultural practices. Indeed it is something that the satirists of postmodern America vehemently mock. Better, then, to seek historical understanding with associative logics in addition to causal determinations. Or still better, to recognize a range of possibilities at work in culture: causal, associative, subversive, even that which may be *sui generis*.

Something like that range of possibilities shaped the emergence of new satire in contemporary American literature. In retrospect, the decisive coincidences occurred in the years immediately following 1945. The posthumous reissue of Nathanael West's novels, with the publication of *The Cannibal* and *Wise Blood* from talents that seemed to have come out of nowhere — these can now be taken as decisive indications of the changing temperament. Yet this is not all, for in the subsequent effort to understand their own writings, O'Connor and Hawkes frequently spoke to audiences about their work, discussed it with each other in a long correspondence (during the five years before O'Connor's death in 1963), and even (in Hawkes's case) ventured a scholarly assessment of their fictions in relation to West's. Beyond that, while reconsidering his own early fiction Hawkes became more certain of its subversive energies: for him the very conventions of narrative were, by 1962, the "enemies" he had once set out to assail. Theorists would later identify that kind of struggle as a distinctive element of literary postmodernism.

Such coincidences of emergence, of inclusion and exclusion, involving transformations of both mode and genre and subsequently involving both the attempts of writers to define their own emerging practices and the general — that is, scholarly *and* mass-cultural — reception of their work, are the strongest reasons we have for composing the literary history of an age. The canons of British Romanticism or Anglo-American modernism are always being negotiated on such terms. Scholars of American culture should therefore begin to recognize satire as an important aspect of the postmodern temperament. Like parody and metafiction, satire is a crucial means by which the postmodern writer focuses the cultural work of fiction. Unlike parody and metafiction in at least this regard, however, satire is a particularly aggressive means for interrogating and subverting those semiotic structures. Satiric activity urges some of our most strongly aporetic, cynical figurations of that "incredulity toward metanarratives" so central to postmodernity.

For a number of compelling reasons, this chapter singles out fictions by West, O'Connor, and Hawkes. First, their novels made such a radical break from conventional practice. There was simply no precedent in the narrative satire of a Sinclair Lewis, whose *Main Street* (1926) targeted the narrow-minded ethos of middle America, and did so by operating dead-center in the tradition of realist fictions. Indeed, the persistence of that conventionally realistic mode of narrative satire can be traced well into the postwar decades, in the work of J. P. Marquand and Mary McCarthy, even Terry Southern's *The Magic Christian* (1959), sometimes hailed as an early Black Humor classic. Yet that is the tradition from which West, O'Connor, and Hawkes made a clean and self-conscious break. West, for example, saw himself operating far outside its conventional norms. In a jacket blurb he wrote for the 1931 release of his first novel, *The Dream Life of Balso Snell,* he seemed to entirely reject the American tradition of humor, claiming that it "is difficult to compare N. W. West with other comic writers, as he is vicious, mean, ugly, obscene and insane. In his use of the violently dissociated, the dehumanized marvelous, the deliberately criminal and imbecilic, he is much like . . . certain of the *surréalistes*."[2] For O'Connor and Hawkes as well, an awareness of that break produced a record of self-commentary, reappraisal, and speculation invaluable to literary scholarship. To date, however, we have used that record only piecemeal, though it shows a clear line of development into the sixties.

Secondly, the novels of West, O'Connor, and Hawkes not only demonstrate that break from the generative satires of earlier ages, they also exemplify an experimentation with the regressive form, grotesque style, and carnivalesque *topos* that are all so distinctive to postmodern satire. These features are much more than thematic nebulae. They are indices of a narrative poetics every bit as disruptive as West claimed in 1931. In that poetics literary scholarship can identify the premises for sound criticism and reappraisal. Especially, one recognizes a steady movement away from the conventions of realism and toward a narrative poetics founded not on the serio-comic orderings of older satires but on the possibilities for structural repetition, doubling, inversion, embedding, and the like. (In fact, this "antirealist" tendency accounts for a seeming anachrony in the ordering of this chapter: Hawkes's *The Cannibal* was published three years before O'Connor's *Wise Blood* but merits treatment after, because it more radically subverts realist conventions.) Still, there is much in West, O'Connor, and Hawkes that harkens back to modernist aesthetics. For example, especially in O'Connor but also in West we recognize a strong drive to maintain the modernist dream of an ordering, transcendental signified. And all three writers work from the idea of a decisive split between art and mass culture; for West in particular mass culture seemed the bottomless wellspring of a modern, hysterical terror. See these three novelists, then, as transitional. Had two of them (West and O'Connor) not died young, their continued work would surely have made the argument of this chapter much more obvious, much sooner.

## The Art of Regression: Nathanael West

William Carlos Williams once asked him, "How did you get that name?" Nathanael West, son of a wealthy Manhattan builder named Weinstein and a grandchild of the European Diaspora, replied that "Horace Greely said, 'Go west young man!,' so I did."[3] Here are ironies deeper than anything that the satirist in Nathanael West might have foreseen. For as westward the course of empire had taken its way, so his course took him to California and the crossroads of a fatal automobile crash. One year before his 1940 death, *The Day of the Locust* had even translated that westward progress into a fictional satire on the type of easterner who migrates "to California to die." This book should have marked the close of an apprenticeship and the start of truly innovative work in the novel. Instead it closed the career of America's most remarkable, influential satirist of the prewar era. To read *The Day of the Locust* now is still to be stunned by the contemporaneity of West's vision and the poetics used to put it across.

In a 1932 essay, West argued the proposition that "In America, violence is idiomatic."[4] He meant it literally: American idioms conduce to violence; language itself is shaped by, even serves as a "cover" for, deeply ingrained patterns of aggression; thus, when language breaks down, violence breaks out. In the mottos and myths of American culture West recognized the tickets of a massive scam, the counterfeit bills passed back and forth in frenzied attempts at a promised redemption. "The Cheated" was the working title he affixed to draft manuscripts of his last novel, *The Day of the Locust,* and it reinvoked a principal idea of West's satirical practice: the tickets are irredeemable. Attempts to arm the self against pain and loss by galvanizing it with fables out of popular, artistic, or spiritualistic discourse lead only to more, and more self-corroding, fictions. The expense of symbols is, simply, a waste. All of culture, West foresaw, might be consumed as the disposable icons of an accelerated mechanical communication that knows no stops, except in the impotence, catatonia, and atavistic rioting of its gulled victims. Still more disturbing, this process revolves around no goddess of Dullness, and West's satirical fictions target no identifiable source of Evil, unless it is fiction making itself.

One very influential picture of Nathanael West would have us see him as a displaced person, American by birth but really European in his avant-garde genius. Other readers who caution against "the too-easy parallelism" between West and, for example, the Dadaists and Surrealists, are probably right.[5] Still, there is an appreciable comparison on one count. The Dadaists in particular had emphasized the accelerated iconography of mechanical culture. Unlike the Futurists, who rejoiced in that acceleration because it furthered their dreams of a "hygenic" catharsis in fascist warfare, the Dadaists employed an art of ironic incongruencies to reveal in such dreams the nightmare of a designifying chaos, where we are startled to see the human become indistinguishable from broken machines, trash, and excrements. We could read West by the light of this highly valorized European modernism. To do only this, however, would be to neglect his anticipations of a contemporary American writing that radically shifts the forms and functions of narrative satire. West's novels foretaste the rotting dreams, the macerated and mass-consumed wastes of a by now recognizable line of successors. Beyond his "Chamber of American Horrors, Animate and Inanimate Hideosities" (*A Cool Million*) and his "dream dump" of Hollywood (*The Day of the Locust*) lie the cloacal wasteland in Hawkes's *The Cannibal*, the shrunken Arab mummy that is taken for a wonder-working savior in *Wise Blood*, the cheap counterfeits in Gaddis's *The Recognitions*, Barthelme's inventors who strive to be at "the leading edge of this trash phenomenon" (*Snow White*), an Orphean underworld quest down a toilet (*Gravity's Rainbow*), as well as numerous other symbols for the deceptions and dissimulated aggressions and atavistic regressions of modern consumer society. Anticipating this terror of the ridiculous, West stays on home ground. His four novels subject the American fables of betterment and progress to unremitting anatomy. The first three undertake that project from the uninfected standpoint of an omniscient irony, while *The Day of the Locust* shows the contagion spreading into all corners of the artist's satirical workshop. It is that problematic self-referentiality that best foreshadows the coming of an American postmodern satire.

West claimed that he wrote his first novel, *The Dream Life of Balso Snell* (1931), as "a protest against writing books."[6] It is, more precisely, a satirical protest against the decadent conventions that accompany and confine acts of writing in a modern economy. West is already moving toward a satire of the jaded motives governing both the production and reception of art, developed most fully in *Locust*. Here, his principal concern is with the "dream" of origins, the writer's search for inspiration by returning to traditional "sources" whose overuse makes them always and already into materialistic clichés. In his dream the poet Balso Snell remembers "Homer's ancient song" and finds himself amid weeds, gazing up at the Trojan Horse. He enters via its anus ("O Fountain!," he exclaims), begins a "journey" up the alimentary canal, and soon realizes that its other occupants are all, like himself, "writers in search of an audience."[7]

The subsequent narrative fragments into six encounters allegorizing different aesthetic motives. Balso meets a series of vaguely drawn figures whose only function is either to stun him, or to bore him, into realizations that writing is just (1) a plagiary of quotations pretending to be learned, (2) a means of venerating the ridiculously grotesque in a counterfeit of holiness, (3) a dissimulated sexual conquest, (4) an historical chain of self-interested "influences," (5) a dream of violence deflected by means of infinite regress, and (6) an adolescent wet dream. This last emerges as West's dominant metaphor.

A few instances will have to do. In his fourth encounter Balso meets a young woman, Miss McGeeney, who is writing a book into which she hopes "to put the whimsical humor, the kindly satire of a mellow life" (32). It is a biography of Samuel Perkins, the biographer of E. F. Fitzgerald, the biographer of Hobson, the biographer of Boswell, himself the biographer of Samuel Johnson. She dithers on about Perkins's "genius for smell," but her real motive for writing is a self-centered one. By making her own work "another link in a brilliant literary chain" it is inevitable "that someone must surely take the hint and write the life of Miss McGeeney"; thus they "will all go rattling down the halls of time, each one in his or her turn a tin can on the tail of Doctor Johnson" (33). Balso's reaction, which the reader can take as a rejection of her "kindly satire" and its merely comical fictions of inheritance, is to deal her "a terrific blow in the gut" and move on (36). In the fifth episode, he dreams an encounter with a grotesquely crippled girl who resists his sexual advances with the demand that he first of all murder another suitor, Beagle Hamlet Darwin. She produces his letters to her. In them, Darwin imagines what she will feel when he abruptly ends their romance; by means of indirect discourse he even fantasizes Janey's decision to take her own life, a *Liebestod* that will canonize him as a Romantic lover-writer. The only engaging thing about these otherwise boring fantasies is that they are revealed as if from a Chinese box: the girl's inner speech appears in Darwin's letters, which is introduced in her narration to Balso, which is part of Balso's dream, itself embedded in the dream-quest which is the novel. Yet nothing comes of the entire proairetic sequence. The promised violence of sexual conquest, or suicide, deflects (potentially) infinitely deeper into the embedded discourses. The only stop comes when Balso awakens (from his dream within *The Dream*), just as at the novel's end he will awaken from the dream of seducing Miss McGeeney and feel "relieved" (62). His quest for origins, and for an audience, culminates in that wet dream.

The Dream Life of Balso Snell thus locates modern writing along an infinite regress of epigonal losers, each more distant from an imagined "source." Or, it sees writing as a Chinese box of surface disguises ultimately hiding nothing at all. Its satire looks across infinite expanses of banality and cliché that stretch between the artist and his audience, expanses that the artist crosses at the risk of death. In locating that danger West's first novel sets the theme for all of his best writing. Yet there were other triumphs. Among the novel's grotesque similes are intimations of West's later stylistic brilliance. There are hints, too, of his play with nuances of narrative structuration. For example, in Miss McGeeney's sixfold regression that ends in self-aggrandizement there is a recognition of the novel's sixfold episodic structure, which ends with

Balso using discourse only for seduction, itself an ironic commentary on the storied "origins" of the Trojan War in Paris's seduction of Helen. For all of this, however, the book seems too sophomoric in its excremental humor, too labored in its attempts at surrealistic excesses, and too diffuse. Its idea — art as aggressive wet dreams played for a jaded audience eager to watch because it "sits in a cloaca to the eyes" (9) — seems mainly to express West's self-doubt at the onset of his career. Still worse, its audience wasn't watching: only three hundred copies of West's first novel were printed for American distribution, and one reader has reported finding a shelf full of unsold copies as late as the mid-forties.[8]

If *The Dream Life of Balso Snell* was too diffuse in its satire, West's third novel, *A Cool Million; or, The Dismantling of Lemuel Pitkin,* fails because it tries to locate the national malaise of the thirties in a single source. The idea was to satirize the racist, fascist system of values encoded by, but of course never acknowledged within, the Horatio Alger narratives of success. By itself, the parody of Alger is sufficient retaliation against any reader who might have believed those myths of advancement. All of Alger's straining devices are there: the earnest epithets that lay their arm on the reader's shoulder ("our worthy lad"), the cheap cliff-hangers, the narrator's paternalistic sermonizing, even those moments when the narration forgets its own semantic code (a dog that viciously chases Tom Baxter through one scene turns out, a page later, to be "Tom Baxter's dog").

Structurally inverted, a composite Alger plot serves as base-text for West's satire. In Alger, for example, the young hero always ascends on a combination of good luck and naive directness when meeting kindly paternal figures, who reach down with aid and lessons of industry and self-reliance. West's protagonist takes the bathetic plunge, summed up at novel's end as a "progress" of "Jail . . . Poverty . . . Violence . . . Death" (178). Lem's first encounter is with a gentlemanly "idler," an inheritor of "a cool million" who picks the young man's pockets. Subsequent adventures in "the Golden West" bring him into contact with every stereotyped con man, drunken Indian, snake-oil dealer, "inscrutable oriental," blustering "ring-tail roarer," lynching Southerner, and Jacksonian man of action in what the narrative will finally actualize as the "Chamber of American Horrors" (160). Chief among them is Shagpoke Whipple, former U. S. president jailed for bank fraud, an antisemite, spokesman for American cracker-barrel values, and leader of a homegrown American fascist party called "The Leather Shirts." Earlier frauds had almost used Lem up, until the only employment he can find is as a scalped, one-legged, thumbless, one-eyed, toothless human punching bag between two tent-show comics. Whipple's con, however, is (in retrospect) the century's grandest. Proclaiming a fascist dictatorship, his "Leather Shirts" take Lem into their patriarchal clan only to enable his easy assassination, then they apotheosize the boy's "story" in an obvious parody of the Nazis' "Horst Wessel Lied." Lem thus becomes "the American Boy," foremost icon in a popular ritual of national salvation and family values. West's satire compels the reader to turn that formula around: in a horror show of nationalist xenophobia, the American Adam is our common gull.

The question is whether or not Alger's metanarrative can bear that weight. Already crushed under West's ludicrous parody, now charged with perpetrating a deadly fraud, Alger seems too much the stock "target," and West too uncertain of his distance from it. The problem, one suspects, is that West tried to generalize *from* his own self-disdain as an artist struggling for recognition *to* a cool anatomy of the national malaise. For Alger remained, at the time, one of America's most popular writers, whereas West's novels sold dismally until their reissue, six years after he was in the grave.[9] In brief, West was full of envy, but he also recognized its result. At one point he even jeers at the image of his own publishing flop, introducing Sylvanus Snodgrasse, keeper of the Chamber of American Horrors, as a writer who "blamed his literary failure on the American public" and turned his desire for recognition into "a desire for revenge. Furthermore, having lost faith in himself he thought it was his duty to undermine the nation's faith in itself" (162). But in targeting only Alger, West diminished the depth and breadth of that loss.

By contrast, one of the most remarkable moments in this book is the violent exhortation of a displaced Indian who charges that European invaders "rotted this land in the name of progress," filling it with "toilet paper, painted boxes to keep pins in," as well as "syphilis and radio, tuberculosis and the cinema." "We accepted this civilization," he goes on, "because he [the white man] believed in it. But now that he has begun to doubt, why should we continue to accept? His final gift to us is doubt, a soul-corroding doubt" (156). This moment has nothing specifically to do with Alger, and its rhetoric is never fleshed out as a narrative action. Nonetheless, West's discovery of that Luddite mood, that need for violence against something nameable only as "progress," stands as the singular achievement of an otherwise labored satire.

Without question, then, *Miss Lonelyhearts* (1933) is West's breakthrough fiction. Its subject: the perverse triumph of secular intercession. West called this brief book a "moral satire," and it turns his lens on a modern culture no longer trusting its traditional intercessors, its priests and poets, and seeking relief instead from mass media that thrive on the titillations of violence and loss.[10] Searching the newspaper for any source of compassion to transfigure their own suffering, West's weary customers find only a machine for the generation of more "stories," more icons of a banal, unremitted suffering. Eventually, some recognize the pandemic nature of that condition. Even the roles of "victim" and "intercessor" are parts of a general fictionality; one's daily newspaper, the synecdoche for a greater lie. Desperate for any "sincere" role, West's characters dizzily turn in their uncertainty, its only resolve coming to them in dumbshows of aggression.

The plot is hardly diminished by synopsis, and Miss Lonelyhearts himself provides one:

> Let's start from the beginning. A man is hired to give advice to the readers of a newspaper. The job is a circulation stunt and the whole staff considers it a joke. He welcomes the job, for it might lead to a gossip column, and anyway he's tired of being a leg man. He too considers the job a joke, but after several months at it, the joke begins to escape him. He sees that the majority of the letters are profoundly humble pleas for moral and spiritual advice, that they are inarticulate expressions of genuine suffering. He also discovers that his correspondents take him seriously. For the first time in his life he is forced to examine the values by which he lives. This examination shows him that he is the victim of the joke and not its perpetrator.[11]

Concise as this may be in its ironies, the satire reveals it as just one "script" among many, and a naive one to boot. Miss Lonelyhearts initially perceives his role as that of a traditional intercessor, refiguring his correspondents' "inarticulate expressions" of pain by employing "a thick glove of words" (33). At first he also assumes his own objective distance and privileged difference: "He too considers the job a joke." But these assumptions, which in retrospect are narratological, only "accelerated his sickness" (33) by teasing him with the hope of finding an authoritative, genuine "story." "Everyone has a life story," shouts Miss Lonelyhearts as he tries to beat one out of an old man found cowering in a public restroom (17). Yet the stories he provokes, like those ground out by the media, are all self-serving and inauthentic. Newspaper ads traffic in a lucrative "business of dreams" (22); Mary Shrike shields her teasing sexuality behind a "tale" concocted from the "poetic" clichés of frustrated genius (23); Peter Doyle, a barren cripple, covers his wife's desperate adultery by concocting bits of make-believe about "our child" (30). All fifteen episodes of Miss Lonelyhearts are occasions for such shallow but exemplary fabling. In fact, though neglected by West's critics, the dominant action of this narrative is the characters' making or receiving narratives, in the form of "letters," "stories," "dreams," "tales," even a mock "gospel." Among them, the "Miss Lonelyhearts" role dissolves in the general lie. No different from "the escape to the soil," or Art, Hedonism, Suicide, and Drugs — other possibilities that Shrike enumerates — that role is simply another scenario one might "do" (32). West's satire thus brings the very "business" of plots under attack. It blasts the frenzied exchange of "life stories" as a ritual in which one person begs another for pathetic acceptance, and the mob concentrates its fictions of suffering on one victim.

The arch-fiction, then, is religious myth, with Jesus Christ as "the Miss Lonelyhearts of Miss Lonelyhearts" (6). That structure is essential West. In it a potentially endless regression, an unstoppable mediation of discourses, undercuts authority in all directions. Shrike puts the case in his last mocking harangue: "There's a game we want to play," he tells Miss Lonelyhearts before an assembled party. The game is " 'Everyman his own Miss Lonelyhearts.' I invented it, and we can't play without you" (51). But if every man can play "his own Miss Lonelyhearts," then is not the dream of secular intercession in Protestantism, as well as the sanctification of individual achievement under capitalism, perversely fulfilled, and has not the stature of any mediating authority been radically subverted? The roles of intercessor and victim become empty, exchangeable forms.[12] Or, their boundaries melt in a fever of nondifferentiation that West compares to "hysteria" (9) and approaches stylistically by way of Shrike's stunning play with grotesque similes. At stake here are "values" by which Miss Lonelyhearts "lives" (and dies) but which he never examines. This is why, when he last seeks to articulate "the Christ business," he turns "hysterical" (49) and falls into "the rhetoric of Shrike" (50). Desperate to stop this designifying regression by once more asserting the old forms, Miss Lonelyhearts imagines himself as the static "rock" of the Church. His murder, a mute travesty of Christ's, can only be read as a "miracle" (57) of self-indulgence.[13]

In *A Cool Million* the satire strains because West takes aim at a single target, Alger's metanarrative of ascent that serves as parodic base-text. *Miss Lonelyhearts* gathers strength by opening the narrative structure. Not one but at least four intertexts appear to have shaped the novella. Biographical and textual evidence is clear on the influence of two: a set of actual letters written to an advice columnist West knew, letters that inspired the book and served as models for his own fictional missives, and West's idea of writing an episodic "Novel in the Form of a Comic Strip," which he later claimed to have abandonded, while keeping the serial format.[14] Two other base-texts were more appropriate to his stated intention of satirizing "a priest of our time who has a religious experience."[15] Miss Lonelyhearts' indiscriminate loving travesties the lesson of Father Zossima in *The Brothers Karamazov*, whose injunction to "love everything" West quotes in episode 3 (8). But a more powerful shaping force was certainly his idea of parodying the Roman Catholic ritual of the *Via Crucis*, or Stations of the Cross. During High Mass, the celebrant re-enacts Christ's progress toward Calvary by proceeding clockwise around the church, stopping at each of fourteen iconic "stations" that represent moments of that progress, and finally mounting the altar steps beneath the crucifix to celebrate Christ's death and resurrection. In fifteen episodic chapters West follows that model, parodically inverting the fourteen "stations" until, at last, his "priest of our time" stands at the top of a stairwell, "with his arms spread wide for the miracle" of communion that comes, instead, as mindless violence (57).[16]

These intertexts power the episodic development of West's plot, generate a pattern of inversions to guide the reading of its ironies, and establish a narrative structure for its aggressive dialogism. Clearly, one need was to balance two contraries: the pull of Shrike's grotesque similes toward what the text defines as "disorder, entropy" (31), as against the interpretive counterpull toward symmetry characterized in Miss Lonelyhearts' "tropism for order" (31). The *Via Crucis* parody settles that score even as it reopens the question of what is West's moral in this "moral satire," for in numerous ways he has turned satire against the concealments of *all* discourse. The cynical tones of hard-boiled street slang are shown thinly masking sexual violence (14), and religious ritual may just as easily dissimulate the self-destructive violence of modern solipsism. In this light Shrike seems a premonition of the postmodern satirist. His functions, as mimic, are to assail the presumption that any speech is inherently innocent or privileged and to mock the reader's desire for the too easily naturalized story. Such, in his second novel, is West's radical understanding of the satirist's role, which he then proceeded to squander in *A Cool Million*. His last novel would recoup that earlier gain and spell out in more detail the possibilities for a nontraditional satire.

*The Day of the Locust* portrays a young artist, Tod Hackett, at the turning point of his maturation. It narrates his progress toward the artistic mastery that enables him to paint an important satirical picture, "The Burning of Los Angeles." But here is the paradox: Tod can only progress by simultaneously regressing in time and space. Imaginatively, he must work backwards through art history, and from the American West back to Europe.

Structurally, this regression is figured by Tod's systematic studies of earlier and earlier American and European artists, with the purpose, not of recreating their vision, but of wrenching free his own form of satire. It is also figured by Tod's plunge into the atavistic depths of modern popular and folk culture. There he picks up the very germs of disease and dementia infecting those people he wishes to represent. Implied, again, is that without this regression Tod would also be unable to paint his great canvas. In short, *The Day of the Locust* is an "apprenticeship plot." Its principal subject is artistic process, specifically, the artist's struggle to define his own work against a dynastic past and a diseased present, yet the most important result comes with the satire's inability to claim any stable, higher ground. At the last its self-reflexivity flees from the idea of a normative satire, and this is exactly what makes the novel so central to its time. *The Day of the Locust* can be read as a narrative satire *about* the troubled emergence of a radical, degenerative mode of satire.

West's theme is still regression: the disintegrations of the person, of art, and of national myth in which he locates parts of a general loss. Also, like *Miss Lonelyhearts, The Day of the Locust* interrogates that loss by deploying aspects of it in paired characters. Shrike's function in *Miss Lonelyhearts* is to load up West's zeal for parody and fire it at Miss Lonelyhearts' naive belief that the suffering of his correspondents is genuine and not mediated by the empty discourses from which they suffer. In this sense he is a quite traditional satirist, for Shrike still plays out the same assumptions of distance and difference that plague his "target." Moreover, Shrike and Miss Lonelyhearts respectively satisfy Frye's requirements for the *eiron* (or deprecator) and *alazon* (imposter) of traditional "low norm satire."[17] But there are subtle changes in West's last novel, as he moves to drop these conventional features of satire from his narrative. In *The Day of the Locust,* Tod Hackett craves the stimulation of empty forms as much as any of the characters he will eventually satirize. His only difference from Homer Simpson is an intellectual awareness of that craving: Homer sleeps through the disintegration, Tod cannot. Unlike Shrike in yet another way, Tod has no extemporaneous capacity for deprecation. His satire is wholly ex post facto and in fact exists only outside the narrative frame. By thus relinquishing the power of a character to voice authorial scorn in dialogue, West was compelled to do the satirical work by other diegetic means, for example, in description, free indirect discourse, recurrent images and proairetic sequences, and allusions to anterior "texts."

The narrative opens with Tod Hackett gazing out his window at a ridiculous conflation of "chronotopes" — Depression Hollywood, Frontier America, and Napoleonic France — all within the locus of a movie lot.[18] The narrative then proceeds by means of a double action. On the one hand, it *regresses* toward an atavistic howl, as West ends with Tod riding in an ambulance and listening to its scream with hysterical interest until, in the novel's last sentence, he begins to "imitate the siren as loud as he could" (185). Simultaneously, we know that, on the other hand, Tod *progresses* toward a satirical painting that by novel's end is completed, at least in his mind (only the brushwork remains). From the novel's opening paragraphs we also know that the picture, "which he was soon to paint, definitely proved he had talent" (60). The specific purpose of these framing devices is to fix the reader's attention on events leading up to that artwork. In addition, they give a particular rationale for Tod's association with the half-cocked people he meets in Hollywood: "he could only be galvanized into sensibility" (141), and he needs their atavistic energy in order to paint.

Tod Hackett's regression unfolds through a series of references that, from the first chapter, guide the reader's reconstruction of plot. Immediately following the statement about his proof of "talent," the narrator makes another important opening gesture by describing Tod as "a very complicated young man with a whole set of personalities, one inside the other, like a nest of Chinese boxes" (60). A motif carried over from each of West's prior fictions, this mechanical image of the *regressio ad absurdum* reappears throughout *Locust*. Here it is linked to Tod's sexual frustration. Its first transformation occurs in a similar context, during the screening of a pornographic film at Audrey Jennings's bordello. In "Le predicament de Marie," a family of four tiptoes one by one into the bedroom of a servant. Marie hides each one in turn until no more family members are left, whence comes a last, mysterious rap on her door; but the film snaps at the moment when this Chinese box situation must reveal itself. The motif soon reappears when Tod asks Claude Estee to ask Mrs. Jennings to ask Mary Dove, who works at the bordello, to inquire of her friend Faye about purchasing her sexual favors. Faye feigns outrage and refuses, yet later she tries essentially the same ploy on Tod. Having stored in her memory "some swell ideas for pictures" (105), she proposes to unfold them before Tod, who can script them for his bosses at the movie studio, who can rework the scripts into successful films, leaving them all wealthy. Faye even arranges her dreams mechanically, like a pack of cards in a kinescope, an image that anticipates Harry Greener's last days when, like a broken windup toy, he replays for Tod the poses of a bathetic career. These regressive motions in *Locust* all conclude in somnolence, frustrated desire, incompleteness, or death. At their heart is always a cash motive or — what is the same thing in West — the desire to exchange trumped-up stories for acceptance among one's cheated fellows. Like Tod, Harry Greener "seemed to enjoy suffering"; and like the other characters Harry has made suffering into the definitive scam, "a second-act curtain groan, so phony that Tod had to hide a smile" (119).

This regressive sequence is fully expressed in Homer Simpson, whose retreat into womblike serenity adds psychological coordinates to its meaning. Early on, West characterizes Homer's emotional life as an "enormous wave" building until it seems to "carry everything before it. But the crash never came" (86–87). As the narrative reveals more about Homer's past, however, we come to understand that his progress into adulthood is not simply suspended, it is a growth betrayed by successively degrading backsteps toward infancy. As with most of the lesser examples, there are four stages in his regression. First he retreats from the anxieties of sexual maturity (Romola Martin, of Waynesville). Second, in Los Angeles he assumes a vegetable, cactuslike awareness, neither happy nor sad, "just as a plant is neither" (89). Third, Homer degenerates to a set of elaborate psychomotor tics, absurdly noticeable in the "here's the church and here's the steeple" routine that his hands fly through in the novel's final chapters. Then, in a fourth stage, he becomes the merest baby, and seeing him coiled up on a sofa Tod thinks of Homer in relation to a photo, captioned "Uterine Flight" (171), that he once saw in a psychology textbook. By then Homer has made a regression that has all but consumed him in the poses of self-pity. His mock-sacrifice by the mob only completes a motion prefigured in the prior regressive sequences. At the same time, Tod's involvement with Homer and his own siren-scream in the ambulance compose a brilliant analogue to Homer's regression, and signify once more the importance of his immersion in the surrounding dementia. What *appears* to save him, then, is the regression Tod makes through the history of art.

Jay Martin has made an important observation about the typescripts of *Locust:* into his last draft of the novel West carefully worked *all* the references to the Old Masters that Tod studies.[19] Yet the effect of his emendations is still more telling. These allusions trace a careful, idiosyncratic inheritance, a line of influences running back to Europe and backwards in history. Recovering this inheritance, Tod recognizes older precursors until he learns enough to paint. And like Homer's infantilistic regression, Tod's retrograde studies also unfold in four main stages.

The first, like Homer's, occurred outside the frame of the novel and before Tod arrived in California. In the novel's opening paragraph we learn that he began his career under the influence of artists suited to a New England upbringing and a Yale training; that is, he used to study the landscapes of Winslow Homer and Albert Pinkham Ryder. But after seeing the people of Los Angeles Tod rejected that world of the "sturdy Nantucket fisherman" and "turned to Goya and Daumier" (60). In doing so he leaves behind two painters known for their reclusiveness; he then finds inspiration in a farther chronotope, that of mid-nineteenth-century Europe, and in the satirical view of two painters who targeted the sociopolitical evils of their epoch. Then, midway through the narrative, Tod once more changes masters. Contemplating the studio movie lot as a shrine to the American desire for surfaces and wastes, he reconsiders the virtual backdrop his Californians move against: "He had begun to think not only of Goya and Daumier, but also of certain Italian artists of the seventeenth and eighteenth centuries, of Salvator Rosa, Francesco Guardi, and Monsu Desiderio, the painters of Decay and Mystery" (131). Here is Tod at his most idiosyncratic. In fact, because West cannot rely on the reader's knowledge of these painters, he not only places them in historical time but also supplies several paragraphs describing their work. A close reading will show that Tod has returned to landscapes, as in his first stage, but now with a key difference. His new interest is in the sinister, almost surrealistic backdrop of crumbling architecture against which the paintings show men enacting wild forms of sacrifice. At the same time, Tod begins acknowledging a need for types of ritual catharsis. There is plentiful evidence for that need in the spectacles of sexual violence: the fight over Faye at Miguel's "camp," the subsequent cockfight, and the dancing that turns into a fistfight at Homer's house. Yet it is not until his fourth stage that Tod connects those secular examples with the types of far-out spiritual striving in Hollywood. Sketching worshippers in bizarre tabernacles and temples, he begins to consider the work of Alessandro Magnasco and how that seventeenth-century artist "would dramatize the contrast between their drained-out feeble bodies and their wild, disordered minds" (142). With this new interest Tod returns once more to human figures, as with Goya and Daumier, but with the certainty that he must incorporate the larger ironies of Magnasco: "He would not satirize them as Hogarth or Daumier might, nor would he pity them. He would paint their fury with respect, appreciating its awful anarchic power and aware that they had it in them to destroy civilization" (142).

In this passage West defines a radical satire that develops, not from the logic of "objects" or "targets" that shapes his earlier satires, but from narratives of violence and degeneration — in short, from ultimate conditions. The monstrous, with its "awful anarchic power," simply *is*. Instead of deceiving himself that it can be corrected, the satirist can only draw its atavism "with respect." So West summarizes Tod's new intentions. However, while Tod may intend for his satire to leave such curative fantasies behind, West also makes it clear that Tod still desires the shamanistic power of conventional satire. Even in his second stage, Tod had realized that as an artist his "work would not be judged by the accuracy with which it foretold a future event but by its merit as painting." However, in the next sentence West adds this important qualifier: "Nevertheless, he refused to give up the role of Jeremiah" (118). Indeed, there is nothing in the remainder of the novel to suggest Tod ever gives up that role. Quite simply, then, he continues to base his work on dreams of correction and, still more interesting, of closure. Tod paints his grotesque subjects rioting amid apocalyptic flames because that image seems conclusive, a terminal violence in the form of a satirical jeremiad. "The Burning of Los Angeles" can thus be read as Tod's attempt to impose a stop on a cultural regression that can really have no end, except in another fable. It is also an attempt to make that cultural regression follow the logic of his personal regression in art history, which he ends at the work of Magnasco. One way of phrasing this difference is to note that despite his own degenerative recognitions Tod needs to be engaged in a hopeful, corrective work, a generative satire like that in the old Puritan jeremiads. West, in contrast, is engaged on a darker, degenerative satire that, as Sacvan Bercovitch has noted, can only be called an "antijeremiad." We will encounter the form again, amid the political satires treated in chapter 4.

Here it is worth noting the structural brilliance of West's plotting. Tod Hackett's artistically fulfilled regression stands as the counterpart to that sheer emptiness revealed in Homer Simpson's eyes just before the riot. In its four stages, Tod's regression also recalls the four episodes in "Le predicament de Marie" or the four steps of Tod's request (passed along the line) for Faye's sex. It also stands in dialogue with Faye's plan for transforming her "swell ideas" into motion pictures and with Harry Greener's replaying his squalid memories on the day before his death. Furthermore, West's allusions to Tod's Old Masters involve an elegant choreography. The landscapes of "Decay and Mystery" in Tod's third stage counter the naive, New England pastoralism of Ryder and Homer; then in Tod's fourth stage Magnasco's figures of apocalyptic satire stand against the low comedy caricatures of Goya and Daumier in his second. Tod's calculated backsteps in the history of painting oppose the confusion of places and times marked everywhere in West's far West, from the counterfeit furniture in his multiform California houses to the polyglot stage props of Tod's employer, "National Films."

As West himself might put it, the artistic references in *The Day of the Locust* compose "a painter's clue, that is, a clue in the form of a symbol" (76). Though inconspicuously situated in the work, they guide the reconstruction of plot and finally compel the reader's interpretation of its ending. On that score, the conventionality of West's readers is remarkable. Most see Tod's study of Old Masters as the counterpart of Homer's regressive infantilism and thus interpret his great canvas as redeeming the anarchism and counterfeit poses of those who "come to California to die." Typical is Edmund Wilson's opinion (in *Classics and Commercials*) that Tod Hackett, "as an educated and healthy human being, is supposed to provide a normal point of view from which the deformities of Hollywood may be criticized."[20] There is much that is seductive in this reading. It seems supported by the structural counterpointing detailed above, it valorizes art over the discontinuities of life, and it naturalizes Tod's hysteria by making it a prerequisite to the artist's work. There are problems nonetheless. For one, in *The Day of the Locust* virtually all regressions conclude in frustration, somnolence, or death. Tod's may appear different — after all his regression ends in the great canvas — yet in a further, potentially unstoppable extension of the novel's satire West may just as well be inviting readers not to contrast his canvas with those regressions but to read it as a close analogue: Tod's "The Burning of Los Angeles" as still another frustration, another sleep of reason.

Few readers have commented on Tod's placing himself among the grotesque figures of his painting. In the foreground, he runs madly with his friends before the crusading mob:

> Among them were Faye, Harry, Homer, Claude and himself. Faye ran proudly, throwing her knees high. Harry stumbled along behind her, holding on to his beloved derby hat with both hands. Homer seemed to be falling out of the canvas, his face half-asleep, his big hands clawing the air in anguished pantomime. Claude turned his head as he ran to thumb his nose at his pursuers. Tod himself picked up a small stone to throw before continuing his flight. (184–85)

Behind them, led by "A super Dr. Know-All Pierce-All," the "united front of screwballs" rushes hell-bent "to purify the land" (184). The sudden switch here is striking. West's narrator has continually insisted that through their frustration Homer, Faye, and the others are benighted participants in, and virtual exemplars of, a potential for mob violence. But now all of them, including Tod, are depicted as embattled *victims* of that potential. One unavoidable inference is that by translating a perceived malaise into apocalyptic forms Tod has succeeded in creating just another fable, another self-indulgent tale like Miss Lonelyhearts' "miracle" of self-sacrifice. He has pursued an authoritative, genuine "story" and caught it, he believes, in a satirical jeremiad underwritten by the practices of "Old Masters." Yet another inference follows: Tod's work on the painting is nothing more than the "small stone" his depicted self prepares to throw against an implacable anarchy. In fact, the subsequent narration derogates Tod's (mental) "work" on the canvas as an "escape" from "his predicament" amid the grinding mob (185). This is West's final word on the painting, as the remaining three paragraphs relate Tod's evacuation from the scene. Thus, if the character Tod Hackett is "like a nest of Chinese boxes" (60), so, more significantly, is its representation. The self-depicted Tod, ready to throw "a small stone" (185), appears within "The Burning of Los Angeles," which yet exists only in Tod's imagination, itself the product of a regressive search for artistic inheritance, framed by the text's proleptic promise — "a picture *he was soon to paint*" (60) — and all contained within West's narrative satire.

These embedded figures, like the embedded fantasies of Beagle Hamlet Darwin or Shrike's version of Jesus Christ as "the Miss Lonelyhearts of Miss Lonelyhearts," compose a potentially endless regression, an accelerating mediation of discourses and forms. They cross-examine one another until, their cover finally blown, the action dissolves in unspeakable violence and Tod's schizoid mimicry of the siren's howl. One can well interpret that wailing as the ironic outcome of the law and order he has desired all along, a desire figured in his painting. Tod's studies in art history have been driven by his need to transmit and conserve form; but the dialogism of West's satire, its flux of discourses undermining each other, subverts that need for a reasoned inheritance and finally reveals it as a self-deception. Such subversions are the singular gift of West's finest writing.

Michael Seidel has argued that in narrative art, inheritance is the rationalized, naturalized insistence on laws, especially laws of descent and difference, property and propriety. Inheritance, he writes, is the "victory" that "civilization celebrates over regressive potential." Nothing could more aptly define Tod's idea of his work, vis-á-vis the Hollywood mob. In its most radical forms, however, at its best, narrative *satire* represents the pandemic spread of that potential for regression. The satirist, in Seidel's view, "penetrates to origins that are potentially compromising to his subjects, to himself, and to society at large." This is because, in penetrating to what is often monstrous in "origins," in uncovering the violence by which that monstrousness was ordered, the satirist "compromises society's renewing and 'cleansing' dispensation."[21] In this light, the work of Magnasco in *The Day of the Locust* must be seen as a counterfeit ticket on the course of Tod's search for satirical forms. In comparison, although he scarcely knows it and certainly cannot will it to happen, Tod's deepest penetration into satirical stuff occurs during the riot. In that mob he struggles amid something too monstrous, too regressively violent and culturally degenerate, to be rendered with the tools of a conventionally representational "moral satire."

One last analogy, then. As Tod places a version of himself in his satirical painting, so does West, in *The Day of the Locust*. For it is tempting to read Tod Hackett as West's version of an earlier self: that artist who, despite the bent of his material, clung to a corrective, normative understanding of the satiric action. His last novel abandoned those limiting conventions. Moreover, although saying so may run into the teeth of what his best satire teaches, that flight from realism was the heritable legacy of a career too soon cut short.

For Flannery O'Connor and John Hawkes, West's legacy was an idea of satire as a narrative mode that undercuts assumptions about narratives. Stylistically, West's grotesques seemed to unleash an atavistic violence in the order of signs. Not only psychological, as with Miss Lonelyhearts' fevered "hysteria," that violence is also deeply inscribed, but thinly veiled, in a mass culture that West both feared and desired. So dangerous is this condition that whenever West's "cheated" convene for the purpose of venerating stories of success and glittering redemption, a mindless violence threatens to rear its monstrous head. Given this incredulity toward the functions of storytelling in a machine age, it was inevitable that West would begin to distort the conventions of narrative art. In particular, he experimented with narrative orders that proceed by means of a relentless regression: sequences that are mechanically and seemingly endlessly embedded, sequences operating as parodies of narrative "progress," with characters and events that are doubled and redoubled in the text. It was a remarkable achievement. For O'Connor, West's fictions composed the one source of inspiration she would consistently point out in American letters. To Hawkes, writing just one year before O'Connor's death in 1963, West's fictions were a singular example of innovative work against which his own achievements, and those of O'Connor, might be critically gauged.

## New Grotesques: The Example of Flannery O'Connor

Few novels have been more painstakingly composed than *Wise Blood*. Two years in, but still three more away from completing the book, Flannery

O'Connor explained the slow progress in a 1948 letter to her agent, Elizabeth McKee: "I must tell you how I work. I don't have my novel outlined and I have to write to discover what I am doing. Like the old lady, I don't know so well what I think until I see what I say; then I have to say it over again."[22] O'Connor's singular devotion to the strange proclivity of her book led to a break with one publisher, whose editor wanted her to map it out be done, and to lengthy delays with her next editor, Robert Giroux.[23] Finally, in late 1951 she could announce to friends that the "Opus Nauseous No. 1" had at last gone off to Farrar, Straus. In the next breath she rang up what *Wise Blood* had cost: five years' writing on a novel just 45,000 words long; "fiendish care" over its every sentence; and an unqualified trust in satire as the mode by which she would "discover" the "odd direction" her novel had to follow.[24]

O'Connor never backed away from that trust, although the period of *Wise Blood*'s public reception, like that of its composition, must also have tested her patience. Early reviews glibly dismissed the book as yet another picture of the squalid South. Still worse, the book's first generation of scholarly readers charged that it presented "a classic set of unsolved novelistic problems." Ever since 1952 they have complained that its episodes are too self-contained, its narrative line is too disjointed, its subplot involving Enoch Emery is too tangential to the main plot, and that its main figure, Hazel Motes, has no human depth of character.[25] O'Connor saw clearly that these "problems" were by-products of a collision between the *mode* of satire and the *genre* of the novel, although here again there are problems, for O'Connor may also be read as clinging to a modernist aesthetic and a traditionally corrective idea of satiric writing.

Yet *Wise Blood* must be read as a key instance of that new sensibility whose precursor was Nathanael West. Moreover, along with the text itself we have a wealth of information pertinent to its writing: letters O'Connor wrote during and afterwards, evidence showing its evolution from short stories to novel, a tally of her readings from the period, and O'Connor's subsequent comments in reviews, addresses, and essays. In addition we have a full range of reviews, essays, and scholarly studies attesting to *Wise Blood*'s reception. Taken together, this record shows that O'Connor's struggles with the satirical novel are typical of a generation that followed West. Hawkes, for example, has gone so far as to identify plot, character, and the like as "enemies" he once sought to banish. In their own terms, such different writers as Vonnegut and Coover advanced similar claims. Curiously, however, it was not until the appearance of *Gravity's Rainbow* — by a writer known almost exclusively through the text — that such "novelistic problems" were received as the marks of satire.

As for O'Connor, the grotesque style was always one key to her intentions. When critic Irving Malin included her work in a hotchpot of "Southern Gothic" fictions, she complained about it in a letter to John Hawkes: "The word *gothic* means nothing to me. I always use the word grotesque." She saw grotesque satire as an art of distortion whose end was revelation. Shortly after *Wise Blood* was published, she wrote, "I am interested in making a good case for distortion because I am coming to think of it as the only way to make people see." And when John Hawkes once described her grotesque tropes as "perverse," like mere material pranks, O'Connor countered that "only the bourgeoise mind" would think so, reminding him, "Thomas Mann has said that the grotesque is the true anti-bourgeoise style."[26] As she intended it, then, the grotesque defied any conventional or proper relatedness; its function was to displace vision from any middling categories.

In practice this meant writing at what seemed like cross-purposes. The tropes of *Wise Blood* emerged not from common southern idiom, as critics too easily supposed, but from the practices of satire itself. "I make them up as the need arises," she wrote to one scholar who had marveled at her similes. Yet there was a double logic to this technique. For even as the figurative content of her work enacted a kind of aleatory magic and stretched toward "the fantastic," in turn its "visual content" needed to be "more precise" and to reconsecrate some normative ground.[27] To put it another way, by seeming to discover themselves during the process of writing, her grotesque similes were meant to disrupt the categorical system of language itself; at the same time, O'Connor strove for a "precise" structure of visual images, an anatomy of being whose aim was to put across allegories of orthodox Catholic belief. These normative aims were central to O'Connor's practice. In fact, she is almost unique among American postwar satirists because of that orthodoxy. Yet good intentions could not corral renegade energies, and in what is still the most perceptive essay on her satire, "Flannery O'Connor's Devil" (1962), John Hawkes would find paradoxes in *Wise Blood* that seemed to radically subvert her orthodox intent.

The letters O'Connor wrote during the years of *Wise Blood*'s composition show that she labored hardest over those portions of the novel where the writing had to be "precise," especially those final chapters treating Haze's death. In comparison, the middle chapters treating Enoch Emery, with their conventionally "low-norm" style of the bestial grotesque, came early to her and with apparent ease. The textual evidence shows that they were the original short stories out of which the novel grew, and that their uninhibited, grotesque energy was what O'Connor sought — quite literally — to frame.[28]

Through these revisions O'Connor insisted on going her own way and declined John Selby's offer to take the manuscript and, in her words, "train it" into a "house pet." She warned him off: "I am not writing a conventional novel, and I think that the quality of the novel I write will derive precisely from the peculiarity or aloneness, if you will, of the experience I write from." In 1949, however, the American novel confided few models for her "experience." With remarkable tenacity, O'Connor stuck by her sense of *Wise Blood* as a satire written after the manner of Nathanael West.[29]

Writing *Wise Blood,* O'Connor loosed all the satiric power — and then some — of Ben Jonson's character Carlo Buffone, who "more swift than Circe with absurd similes will transform any person into a deformity." Similes are the most insistent feature of the novel's style. Unlike the conventional grotesque trope, however, O'Connor's do more than deform human characters. It *is* true that beastlike characters abound in the novel: there is a "cat-faced baby"; Asa Hawkes's scarred face resembles that of "a grinning mandrill"; another child's face is "fox-shaped"; while background figures resemble game hens, frogs, and crows, even "a skinned animal writhing in a box." The most startling of these beastly deformations suggest monstrous insects, as with the museum guard who looks "like a dried-up spider," or Haze's grandfather, a "waspish" circuit-preacher who rode "over three counties with Jesus hidden in his head like a stinger."[30] Yet only a fraction (about one-fourth) of O'Connor's similes involve bestial deformation. Still more extend the declension of human features downwards into the inanimate: other characters resemble dried fruits or gnarled trees, and several, like the zoo attendant with "a jutting shale-textured face" (79), assume a downright geological presence in the text.

Slightly more than half of the similes in *Wise Blood* figure a declension of the human to lower existential orders. As for the rest, in them the vehicle operates on the tenor in such a way as to give it an upwards boost.[31] The wiper blades of Haze's Essex automobile "clatter like two idiots clapping in church" (74), and a chair in Enoch's "mummified" house mimics "a man in the act of squatting" (131). These similes confer on dead matter an aspect of lively, instinctual being. The headlights of Haze's car probe the dark like an insect's "stiff antennae" (202), and after Haze has run that car over Solace Layfield it stands like an animal "pleased to guard what it had finally brought down" (204). O'Connor's grotesque tropes thus insinuate a far more complete deformation of being, as if the text were furnished wall to wall with monstrous simulacra.

Initially, the most striking feature of O'Connor's tropes is their singular outrageousness. The most exaggerated of them defy any readerly anticipation. When the horn of Haze's car blares "like a goat's laugh cut off with a buzz-saw" (160), or when Enoch's heart reels vertiginously, "like one of those motorcycles at fairs that the fellow drives around the wall of a pit" (83), O'Connor extends the possibilities of *discordia concors* to an outer limit of feasible resemblance. Yet the vast portion of her tropes are also done in swift, sure strokes. She has, for example, an eccentric genius for hair styles: one woman shouts at Haze from beneath a coiffure "stacked in sausages around her head" (105), while Enoch describes a "welfare woman" whose hair "was so thin it looked like ham gravy trickling over her skull" (47). O'Connor's are just not the type of Faulknerian comparative that begins with "seems" or "as if." Hers are pure simile: the direct, instantaneous linkage of vehicle and tenor leaves the reader no hinge into doubt. Her similes *do* recall those punctuating the pages of West's *Miss Lonelyhearts,* but even West does not reach so far, nor does he reach so often, to find a likeness.[32] Moreover, while Nathanael West's similes almost always imply a human world running amok in mechanical forms, O'Connor's take in a full taxonomic range of being. Unlike West's in yet another regard, hers also occur wholly under the aegis of narrative viewpoint. In *Miss Lonelyhearts,* the grotesque enters the text principally through dialogue, and always in connection with Shrike. Of *Wise Blood*'s grotesques, the only one to issue from a character's mouth is Enoch's description of the welfare woman's gravylike hair. Indeed, O'Connor's letters demonstrate that she took great pains to achieve just that separation of her character's southern idiom from the grotesque idiosyncracies of her narrator.[33] This was consistent with her intentions for a normative satire: that voice of moral authority, the omniscient narrator, must (she believed) dissociate itself from the bedeviled world it circumscribes.

In turn, most readings of *Wise Blood* interpret its grotesque tropes as figures of a morally degraded culture, where erring mankind discovers itself as hopelessly displaced. Enoch Emery seems to typify that degradation, as though he were proof positive of Dr. Johnson's maxim: "He who makes a beast of himself gets rid of the pain of being a man." Such a way of putting the "moral" of O'Connor's satire assumes that the grotesque is a conscious, rhetorical means of signifying a theme for one who writes or reads the text. In concord with the conventions of realist narrative, it also assumes that the literary trope simply makes present an abstract theme or moral, while it "does not trouble the representational function of language."[34] Nevertheless, O'Connor's own comments about the similes of *Wise Blood* ("I make them up as the need arises") tend to underscore the need for alternate readings. Poststructuralist theories hold that through the system of its own linguistic resources a text constantly *outstrips* any intentional design. The writing's self-awareness, its potential for subverting authorial intent through (for example) reiterated types of signs, may thus be (and O'Connor sensed it) self-revelatory, even to the extent of embracing an atavistic violence.[35]

In *Wise Blood*, O'Connor's grotesque similes do not merely signify a degraded culture; they set down a virtual chaos. They deeply "trouble" the representational foundations of her narrative. This occurs partly because, as Mikhail Bakhtin observes in his study of Rabelais, the vehicle of a grotesque simile violates the tenor, disrupting any material surface, if not through a monstrous hybridization then directly, through bodily orifices.[36] Similarly, O'Connor's grotesque style deranges the boundaries between "character" and "scene"; its function is to erase difference.[37] This erasure has a purpose. Bakhtin has argued that while "the artistic logic of the grotesque image ignores the closed, smooth, impenetrable surfaces of the body and . . . in its extreme aspect, it never presents an individual body," nevertheless it "is a point of transition" in a world that is always disrupted.[38] In general, the purpose of such disruptions is to background the reassertion of a differential code whose force now seems redoubled, owing to its apparent emergence from primordial chaos. This, as we shall see, appears to have also been O'Connor's aim. Yet the grotesque satire of a text like *Wise Blood* obliges one to press Bakhtin's arguments still further. O'Connor's insinuation of the grotesque certainly actualizes an external, molecular state tantamount to entropy; still more, it concretizes an internal, psychic state comparable to *dementia praecox* or schizophrenia, a flux of signifiers threatening to engulf all.

There is a sound basis for using just that psychological comparison. Early in *Miss Lonelyhearts,* the protagonist ponders "something secret and enormously powerful" he has known since adolescence, when, like Hazel Motes, he was raised by a Baptist preacher. That "secret" has to do with "the Christ business" and it involves Miss Lonelyhearts' certainty that making a grotesque parody out of orthodox religious ritual would open for him a wonderfully destructive yet corrective power. He defines this process as the embodiment of "hysteria, a snake whose scales are tiny mirrors in which the dead world takes on a semblance of life. And how dead the world is," he considers further, thinking of his society as "a world of doorknobs. He wondered if hysteria were really too steep a price to pay for bringing it back to life" (8–9). This extended conceit makes a profoundly concise statement of how the grotesque is supposed to function in traditional satire. Its style plunges one into a nightmare of degenerate forms, figuring a world of marvelous absurd resemblances, strange "tiny mirrors," or similes, wherein lively being seems dead and inanimate stuff leaps with purposeful action. Miss Lonelyhearts believes, however, that its hysteria is only a beginning step, a "price" paid out in his self-sacrificing effort *to renew* "the world" (the satirist's "wage," according to Harry Levin). Such is his generative supposition. But West's satire points toward its dismantling and unmasks such a desire as yet another egocentric "dream" about the existence of a supreme fiction.

In its degenerative mode grotesque satire erases the categorical system of everyday signs. It is the true enemy of conventionality, presenting both writer and reader with a world beyond reason, *ratio*. It asserts "all those forces whose dominance over men increases or seems to increase in proportion to man's attempt to master them." This is René Girard's definition of the sacred, and while the context of his discussion is the ritual significance of the double, he treats it in terms of "non-differentiation" and the monstrous.[39] To Girard, the monstrous, like *Wise Blood*'s mummy (Haze's double), always and in spite of itself gives access to that which is unique in terms of categories, therefore exterior to culture and threatening, an embodiment of absolute violence. As shapes out of hysterical consciousness, the monstrous and the grotesque thus seem to rebuke the very idea of category. No doubt this is the structural logic behind Enoch's removal of the mummy from its carefully labeled "home" in a glass museum-case: if it is sacred, as his "blood" tells him, then it must be exterior to any boundaries. Yet his every attempt to "master" the monstrous ends by rebuking him. In a precursor of his final humiliation in the gorilla suit, Enoch places the stolen mummy in a new container, a gilded cabinet that emblematizes his regression to banal materialism. He believes it will make him into "an entirely new man, with an even better personality" (175); its only effect, however, is to bring on a violent sneeze that cracks his head on the cabinet.

The reader's interpretation of *Wise Blood* will begin to turn on how she compares Enoch's action to the progress of Hazel Motes. Haze's self-chosen role in *Wise Blood,* like that of Miss Lonelyhearts, is to be the scapegoat in a ritual of (supposed) renewal. He presents himself from the start as an outcast of "Eastrod," a fallen man who wanders into a type of Babel, Taulkinham ("talkin-ham"), where his search for a mortal home is always vagrant, in part because discourse is in chaos. To transform this degenerate condition, Haze takes it upon himself to embody the human need for exteriorized violence. As an archetypal (sacrificial) victim, Haze would transform violence into something literally monstrous and vagrant, something physically outside this earth, because sacrificially murdered. One irony is that none of the characters in *Wise Blood* recognizes the sacred difference Haze tries to embody. In a travesty of Paul's blinding on the road to Damascus, Haze announces to Mrs. Flood his intention of blinding himself. She responds by expressing the same condition of hysterical non-difference that prevails earlier in the narrative: "She was not a woman who felt more violence in one word or another; she took every word at its face value but all the faces were the same" (210). When he soon begins scourging himself in the manner of the medieval saints, she will stupidly insist to his disfigured face that "people have quit doing it" (224). In a hopelessly deranged world, she clearly has no sense of herself as witness to acts performed as if they were sacred. This, with all the greedy ordinariness by which the narration marks her, seems to have made Mrs. Flood an obvious butt of O'Connor's satire. Nevertheless, the reader may find it hard to disagree with her thought that in a deranged world Haze Motes is himself "a mad man" (220). And it is easy "to laugh" with her at Haze's self-annointed Paulist mission, in which she envisions "him going backwards to Bethlehem" (219).

Amid the hysteria of *Wise Blood*'s tropes, reading the implied uniqueness of Hazel Motes means depending, still, on some kind of differential system, so the reader turns to that "visual content" over which O'Connor labored as a structure for her beliefs. Like her grotesque tropes, it is there from the novel's beginning. And when Haze responds to Mrs. Flood's complaint that "people have quit" mortifying their flesh like saints, saying "They ain't quit doing it as long as I'm doing it" (224), he argues a concept of boundary and difference that has been building in the text for some time. From the beginning, the chapters open her anatomy of being by focusing on the taxonomy of incarnate matter and finally work through the differential system of language, signified in the text by images of containment.

*Wise Blood*'s readers have already noted several images that "frame" its narration. There is a *memento mori* in the novel's last paragraph — "The outline of a skull was plain under his [Haze's] skin" (231) — that carefully echoes an observation in its fourth paragraph: "The outline of a skull under his skin was plain and insistent" (10). References to Haze's "going home" at the novel's beginning and end, each linked to the matronly attentions of women, Mrs. Wally Bee Hitchcock and Mrs. Flood, have a similar framing effect, but there is still another frame within the narrative, one that contains Enoch's story. He first arrives in chapter 3, among a throng gathered around a street vendor whose cheap kitchen appliance works like this: "The machine was a square tin box with a red handle, and as he [the demonstrator] turned the handle, the potato went into the box and then in a second, backed out the other side, white" (38). The inverse of this event unfolds at Enoch's exit, architecturally placed in chapter 12 (of 14). There, Enoch himself steps into a new dark skin and leaves his old white one behind: "In the uncertain light, one of his lean white legs could be seen to disappear and then the other, one arm and then the other: a black shaggier figure replaced his" (197). Taken together, these two moments comprise a ludicrous emblem of just that process described above, the grotesque dismantling of being prior to its containment within a new, proper home.

There are other and more literal frames within the narrative. Enoch, for example, has three pictures hanging on the walls of his room. One, from a business calendar, shows a young woman "wearing a rubber tire"; another, advertising a funeral home, shows a young boy praying in his "blue Doctor Denton sleepers" (133). Third is a picture of a moose, and Enoch ascribes to it a strange, totemistic power. He pours streams of silent vituperation at the animal because he feels some immanent thing is in store for that space, and Enoch does not "want to have the feeling that the moose was running it." This fear inspires one of Enoch's more eccentric intuitions: "taking the frame off him would be equal to taking the clothes off him (although he didn't have any) and he was right because when he had done it, the animal looked so reduced that Enoch could only snicker" (133). A remarkable attention to clothes and frames, to the significance of surfaces and boundaries, runs throughout these paragraphs. Their argument is that removing a boundary, confounding space, constitutes an aggressive, satirical action, because frames, like clothes, shield the naked body from ridicule. In place, they confer a formal justness on an otherwise grotesque corpus. Frames and clothes also provide a makeshift covert — in hunting jargon, a "blind" — behind which the ridiculing, aggressive eye attempts to hide. Thus Haze examines himself in a "white-framed mirror" and quickly reaches for his dead mother's glasses as a self-protection against the "dishonest look" he detects in "his naked eyes" (187). An ape suit used in a string of "Gonga" movies provides its occupant with a redoubt from which to launch invectives. After becoming one of its victims, Enoch wants the suit.

Still, for it to confer shelter against the predations of a violent world, the frame or clothing must be proper. Solace Layfield's "glare blue suit," the double of Haze's, cannot mask either his imitation or his con game. As such Haze sees Layfield as a direct threat to his own position, and when a bystander asks if Motes and his double are "twins," Haze cryptically replies that "if you don't hunt it down and kill it, it'll hunt you down and kill you" (168), thus expressing a motif of reciprocal violence that haunts the book. Indeed, before running Layfield down like a real prey, Haze orders the man to "Take off that suit" (204). But these are differential signs of which Enoch Emery remains unaware. When he buries his old clothes before climbing into the gorilla skin, it is "not a symbol to him of burying his former self" (196). That negation concisely states the case: if not "to him," certainly to the omniscient narrator the action is symbolic of a blindness afflicting other characters.

Frames, clothes, and skins are only three types among a score of related container images — of automobiles, boxes, buckets, cabinets, cages, cells, chests, closets, coffins, drawers, holes, houses, and trunks — whose deployment throughout Wise Blood is remarkably consistent. For example, Enoch seems to marvel at the "tin" potato peeler because, when he was a child, his father returned "from the penitentiary" with a similar "tin box." When Enoch opened it, "a coiled piece of steel had sprung out at him and broken off the ends of his two front teeth" (178). Haze Motes recalls the funerals of his relatives and how he feared the corpses would spring or "shoot out" of the coffins (20). To him, all such boxes seem typologically involved with the sexual guilt he had felt after sneaking into a carnival sideshow to watch a naked woman writhing like "a skinned animal" in a casket. Afterward Haze hid himself in the cab of his father's truck, where he listened to "the tin roar outside" (62). The day after recalling these events Haze deserts Mrs. Leora Watts, whose name he found scribbled in the "narrow box" of a "tin" bathroom stall, and he purchases an Essex automobile, "mostly to be a house for me," as he tells the dealer, for he "ain't got any place to be" (73). From it he will soon spring out like an avenging demon over his double, Solace Layfield.

An aggressive redoubt as well as the locus of sexual and mortal guilt, such a space may also grant temporary safety and well-being, yet Wise Blood's characters vainly search for any true "home." Condemned to wander east of Eastrod, as it were, their fate in O'Connor's world is to remain displaced and vagrant in spite of their need to quell the reciprocal aggression all around them. Haze, for example, makes a desperate attempt at inheritance and stable proprietorship when he finds his mother's chiffarobe in the empty house where he was raised. He ties the bulky thing to the floorboards and leaves a scribbled white curse ready to spring out of every drawer: "THIS SHIFFER ROBE BELONGS TO HAZE MOTES. DO NOT STEAL IT OR YOU WILL BE HUNTED DOWN AND KILLED" (26). Similarly, Enoch makes elaborate preparations to house "the New Jesus" in his own "gilted cabinet." But once he places the mummy inside, nothing happens beyond the sneeze that bangs his head backward out of the cabinet. So he cannot understand "why he had to let himself risk his skin for a dead shriveled-up part-nigger dwarf" because, as far as he can tell, "one jesus was as bad as another" (176). In these moments, O'Connor's narrator belittles her characters for confounding the difference between "proper" places and the more banal idea of "proprietary" rights. For much of the narrative Haze is as blind to that difference as Enoch. A few days after settling in Taulkinham, he preaches that "everything is all one" (122), and from the standpoint of O'Connor's grotesque similes he certainly preaches a truth. Yet Haze's cure for this condition is to reject *all* incarnate being, as when he preaches to a theater crowd that "nothing outside you can give you any place" (165). The narrative marks that moment as the beginning of his apparent redemption.

In *The Poetics of Space,* Bachelard comments on the function of such everyday containers as one finds throughout O'Connor's novel. They are, he writes, signs of "intimate space," and only an "indigent soul" neglects their power. Within them exists "a center of order that protects . . . against uncurbed disorder." Yet at the same time intimate space constitutes a virtual invitation to forced entry; it even seems to beg for violation.[40] In *Wise Blood,* any full, marvelous container, any repository of a character's desire for order, is liable to be emptied into its chaotic, grotesque surroundings. The characters' desire for the fullness of being is always frustrated in the emptiness of O'Connor's fictional world. The plenum of sacred being has no place on earth, O'Connor suggests, and thus she ridicules her characters for seeking their peace within the bounds of corporeal existence.

What then of language? In fact, virtually the same full/empty dichotomy obtains within the frame of discourse. Enoch's mind seems a house divided against itself, one side empty of significances and the other full: "The part in communication with his blood did the figuring but it never said anything in words. The other part was stocked with all kinds of words and phrases" (87). Still, when Enoch stands most in need of aggressive words, face to face with Gonga (his double), the best insults fail him and Enoch's "brain, both parts, was completely empty" (181). Inversely, when speech finally pours forth (in the form of a personal narration), Gonga turns the tables and curses Enoch: "You go to hell" (182).

Tied as they are to material being, itself emptied of significant content, words are cut adrift and differences blur. Haze preaches to Sabbath Hawks that "there is no such thing as a bastard in the Church without Christ," because "things are all one" (122). Onnie Jay Holy demands that Haze introduce him to "the New Jesus." Instead Haze rebukes the man: "That ain't anything

but a new way to say something" (158). Elsewhere he charges that "Fornication" and "Blasphemy" are "nothing but words" (33). "Preaching," as full
speech, literally hasn't a prayer in *Wise Blood* because whenever any tin-
pot "prophet" begins to speak and one is implored to "Listen to his words!"
(167), meaning dissolves amid the doubled, counterfeited signs that epito-
mize O'Connor's material world. Echoed in the harangues of Hoover Shoats
(alias Onnie Jay Holy) and echoed yet again in the "preaching" of Solace Layfield, Haze's words degenerate to the merest "motes" of potential meaning.

Only in the final chapters does O'Connor represent Haze acting on these
recognitions. First, after murdering Layfield, Haze restates yet again his em-
piricist doctrine: "He said it was not right to believe anything you couldn't
see or hold in your hands or test with your teeth" (206). Then the ensuing
sequence of actions confronts him with an exercise in that doctrine: a patrolman detains Haze for driving without a license, orders him to park the "rat-
colored" Essex atop a high embankment, then pushes the car over, explaining, "Them that don't have a car, don't need a license" (209). How does this
enigmatic action mean? In brief, if words ("a license") and material property
("a car") have been inextricably linked until this moment, then O'Connor
would have this action figure Haze's release. Cut loose from the automobile,
symbol both of his mortal guilt and his ability to run from that guilt in the
emptiness of material and verbal being, Haze now speaks in fragments, if at
all. Singular in his purpose, he takes the final steps to which all of O'Connor's
container images have propelled him: he fetches "a *tin* bucket" (210) for mix-
ing quicklime, then uses it to blind himself because, as he will soon riddle
Mrs. Flood, "If there's no bottom to your eyes *they hold more*" (222, my emphasis). To Mrs. Flood, the world will always be a platitudinously "empty"
place. Yet Haze, presently well on his way toward becoming nothing, a mere
"pin point of light" (232), has evidently found access to a fullness, a sacred
plenum.

O'Connor's spatial imagery generates this unnameable, paradoxical resolution in the manner of a Platonic dialectic. The novel's ceaseless pairing and
redoubling of objects and characters, as well as its repetition and isomeric inversion of proairetic sequences, all occur under the aegis of one aim, to make
the grotesque chaos, and all the reciprocal violence of its doubled forms,
yield to an ordered anatomy of being, thus to bring the sacred into (distant)
view by means of a meditation on material existence. Her writing classifies
the frame of being according to categories of the bestial and the human, corporeal and incorporeal states, empty and full, dark and light, profane and
sacred. In the final chapters, and at the upper right of the diagram below (see

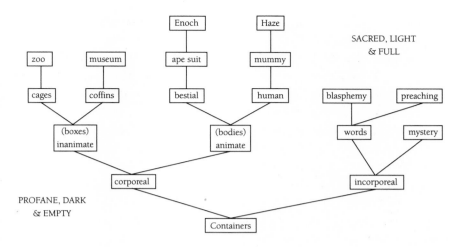

FIGURE 1

fig. 1), that meditation wants to skyrocket, like Platonic argument, into the mysterium that is materially represented after Haze loses his car and gazes over the horizon, his face seeming "to reflect the entire distance" (209), and is iconically available to the reader only in the novel's last sentence, with its image of pure light.

In a lecture written after *Wise Blood,* O'Connor related her fictional techniques to orthodox Catholicism. "The Manicheans," she noted, erred when they "separated spirit and matter. To them all material things were evil. They sought pure spirit and tried to approach the infinite directly without any mediation of matter. This is also pretty much the modern spirit, and for the sensibility infected with it, fiction is hard if not impossible to write because fiction is very much an incarnational art."[41] In her subsequent discussion she singled out Haze's "rat-colored automobile" as an example of the "symbolic" power she sought in such images, telling her audience, "The fact that these meanings are there makes the book significant. The reader may not see them but they have their effect on him nonetheless. This is the way the modern novelist sinks, or hides, his theme."[42] The stated purpose of O'Connor's satirical anatomy was, by these means that are so conventionally "hidden" from the reader-hermeneut, to reveal Haze as, in the words of her 1962 preface, "a Christian *malgré lui.*"

In thus reading herself O'Connor assumes, again, that the "meanings" of her tropes and images make present a "hidden" moral, and that (as Culler puts it) those figures do not "trouble" its representation. But any such reading must rest on a "metaphysics of presence" just as squarely as her design for *Wise Blood* rests on the tenets of orthodox Christianity. It longs for a unitary truth behind every sign, a plenitude in which form and meaning are no longer displaceable and one cannot speak of sliding signifiers. This is also the "standard" reading of O'Connor prevalent in the major criticism, though it is by no means the only approach.

A contrary reading appears in "Flannery O'Connor's Devil," John Hawkes's 1962 essay, which grew from a lengthy correspondence and several meetings with O'Connor. His argument, which O'Connor emphatically contested, is that while her work intends to be "vigorously moral," the writing nevertheless "seems to depend on immoral impulse." Channeled through "the 'demolishing' syntax of the devil," that impulse commits the writer, as if against her will, to eccentric, aggressive strategies.[43] Her grotesques thus "demolish" the very moral that inspired them. Hawkes argues that her similes put a wildly distorted, monstrous territory into severe balance against everyday, familiar reality, then her writing laughs away the distance between the two, becoming a self-justifying authority bent on destroying any moral content.

One should be prepared to go still further than Hawkes in developing the implications of this reading. Indeed, *Wise Blood*'s similes are but one resource for its aggressive mockeries. Among others, certainly, are the "syntax" of its proairetic sequences and its characterizations, as well as the "precision" of its imagery. For example, in every one of the novel's sequences where an object, corpse, or person springs from its confinement in a box, coffin, or skin, the result is an injury *and* an affront meted out to a witness. Can it be any different at narrative's end for Haze Motes, who mortifies his flesh in order to spring free of its earthly confines? He says, paradoxically, that he wants to "empty" his body so that it can "hold more" (222). The diabolical, degeneratively satirical side of this novel argues, instead, that these are "nothing but words" (53), and moreover that his self-mortification is significant only to himself, mocking no one or nothing save the ideology of a Supreme Being proposed by its imaginative double, the omniscient narrator. This reading is further encouraged by the relentless doubling of *Wise Blood*'s characters. Enoch Emery's search for "the New Jesus" is a parodic inversion of Haze's attempt to run from redemption, while Solace Layfield, coached and managed by Hoover Shoats, stands as a mockery, a counterfeit of Haze. Yet Haze himself is clearly also a type, even a counterfeit, of St. Paul. There may be no reason why the parodic semiosis should stop, why its satire should not finally include Haze, even the narrative of St. Paul, or finally even O'Connor, who sets these signifiers against each other.

Wise Blood's readers have often commented on the difficult task of seeing Haze as "a Christian *malgré lui*," when he manifests none of the *caritas* that Christian doctrine holds as essential to the redemptive life.[44] Some readers go out of their way to see Haze's discarded money, found by Mrs. Flood, as evidence of charity. But one may just as easily note that the narration, especially in its last chapters, shapes an image of earthly life as unyielding victimization, by one's own self and by others (Mrs. Flood cozies up to Haze in order to cadge his government stipend). It is also a world indifferent to violence: Haze murders Layfield simply because he "ain't true" (204), as if anything in O'Connor's world of counterfeits could lay claim to truth, and Mrs. Flood responds to Haze's self-destructive claims "with no more change of expression than the cat" asleep in her lap (211). Attempts to read these conditions as an earthly chaos from which Haze is redeemed are attempts to contain the aggressive semiosis of Wise Blood's technique, to naturalize its violence by aligning it with scriptural metatexts. Such efforts are guided by the interpretive conventions of realist fiction.

The contrary reading takes its warrant from the way O'Connor's satire "demolishes" those possibilities. At his most diabolical, Haze preaches that "there's only one truth and that is that there's no truth" (165). He argues that claim of absence until the end, and the actualization of that claim through-out other aspects of the narrative discourse subverts O'Connor's most deeply held designs for the story. The real "problems" of Wise Blood thus had less to do with any novelistic shortcomings than with the reach of its satiri-cal powers. Its structural features — clusters of monstrous tropes jointed to the dialectic of its spatial imagery, proairetic sequences that are inverted or isomerically reflected — were meant to stand in place of any conventional "novelistic" plotting. Similarly, her "characters" seem virtually subordinate to the needs of her anatomy. Like any other "container," they stand as subcate-gories in her dialectic and have no significance except as parts of a binary relational system, itself threatened with destruction because of O'Connor's own poetics. Wise Blood seems to foreswear any middle ground on the two intersecting planes of discourse that semiology defines. On the "associative" plane (Jakobson's "metaphoric"; the plane of "indices" in Barthes), O'Con-nor's similes stretch to an outer limit of representational possibility. They ap-proach madness, an irruption of unconscious, atavistic, regressive potential. On the "syntagmatic" plane (Jakobson's "metonynmic"; the plane of "func-tions" in Barthes), her spatial images seek to inscribe a relentlessly logical anatomy of being. They want to set down a reasoned, orderly, progressive drive toward redemption.

"The middle road," wrote composer Arnold Schoenberg in his foreword to *Three Satires for Mixed Chorus,* "is the only one which does not lead to Rome." For O'Connor, who could not throw off the modernist desire for a totalizing fiction, the discovery of satire's fierce contrasts became a key problematic in her writing. The ferocity of her satire threatened to demolish *all* roads to Rome. Unique among her contemporaries, she sought to resolve the struggle in favor of a theodicean metaphysics. To bring that settlement off, everything depended on her achieving an unqualified unity of perspectives. This is precisely what the art of satire, in its contemporary, degenerative mode, makes difficult. O'Connor never fully worked through these cruxes, and for that reason she seems to straddle the modernist and postmodernist epochs, like Nathanael West. By contrast, John Hawkes worked through them to a truly postmodern satirical novel.

## Carnival of Terror: John Hawkes

In the mature aesthetic of John Hawkes, satire is not just one mode for the novel among others. It is the paradoxical essence of novel writing. Polylogical and aggressive, satire to Hawkes is "design and debris" riding in the vehicle of a genre. By 1962, thirteen years after his first novel was published, a concept of satire had come to generalize Hawkes's view of his art. In "Notes on the Wild Goose Chase," one of two key essays published late in that year, he wrote, "If the true purpose of the novel is to assume a significant shape and to objectify the terrifying similarity between the unconscious desires of the solitary man and the disruptive needs of the visible world, then the satiric writer, running maliciously at the head of the mob and creating the shape of his meaningful psychic paradox as he goes, will best serve the novel's purpose." As in its companion essay, "Flannery O'Connor's Devil," or in subsequent interviews, Hawkes's examples in this piece were always Nathanael West and Flannery O'Connor. Their "hard, ruthless, comic" practice seemed to fit any broad definition of satire, because they delighted in revealing both "wit and blackness in the pit."[45] Yet Hawkes was significantly immune to the corrective-normative bent of prevailing definitions. If he had read any of the formalists, there is not a hint of it in the critical essays or interviews from the period. His concept of satire developed from his own practice, seen in the light of what others had been accomplishing.

In America, John Hawkes is thus the first novelist to write satire from an idea of its contemporary exemplars and its possibilities as a postmodern art. During the sixties and the early seventies he veered into more distinctly comic forms, for example with *Second Skin* (1964) and *The Blood Oranges* (1970). Still, the mode of his most powerful work remains degeneratively satirical. Those risks Hawkes identified in reading West and O'Connor, risks of the devil's "'demolishing' syntax," have shaped *The Cannibal* (1949), *The Lime Twig* (1961), *Travesty* (1976), and *The Passion Artist* (1978). He remains self-reflective about the trajectory of this growth and even allegorized it in *Travesty,* a novel he has described as "a comment on *The Cannibal*" and a book that "reflects back on my entire writing life."[46]

I close this chapter by deferring consideration of Hawkes's later work until chapter 3 and focusing on *The Cannibal* because, in retrospect, no novel of the forties or early fifties more forcefully set the agenda. Turning aside the main conventions of realist fiction, *The Cannibal* defied those readerly demands for a naturalized, totalized narrative unfolding in apparently seamless space and time. Instead, it locates modern violence in a fanatic hysteria, a third-rate fascist mentality that exists in jagged shards. The novel's controlling image is the carnival, a feast not only of fools but of actual madmen. Its fascist mentality exists, moreover, in forms that have nothing to do with the ideology of history's winners and losers. This novel's image of the American as conqueror, brilliantly minimized as a lone private (named Leevey) patrolling his "Zone" of devastated Germany on a motorcycle, eventually yields to an image of the Quiet American as unwitting vehicle of a resurgence of terror. These tendencies of the book, themselves the direct result of its sometimes difficult technique, limited Hawkes's early readership. Still, in a 1962 "Addendum" to his original introduction, Albert J. Guerard could report that having been "reprinted and read," *The Cannibal* no longer seemed "as willful or eccentric as it did in 1949, nor as difficult to read," partly because by that time Hawkes had contributed to "the taste that will eventually applaud him." The novel also seemed to stand with others (Guerard mentions works by West, O'Connor, Nabokov, and Donleavy) as one sign of "a public awakening to new types of fictional pleasure and suasion."[47]

Just how that suasion operates is still an open question. As with many later satires, scholarly readers have overanalyzed *The Cannibal* for its symbols and "themes" while leaving its poetics unexamined, yet all of Hawkes's comments indicate that he has regarded satire as a narrative practice whose function is to defy the uses of theme, plot, and character as found in fictional realism. The similar achievements of writers like Barthelme, Gaddis, and Pynchon underscore the accuracy of his view. The aim of my discussion, then, is to trace basic narrative structures in *The Cannibal,* especially those involving deformations of conventional novelistic story and discourse, keeping in mind both Hawkes's later works and other satires of the American postmodern age.

In its barest outline the story is a joined structure. Two proairetic sequences run parallel and merge at an apparently sacred moment: the "salvation," "resurrection," and "birth of the Nation" (195) in Germany, during April of 1945. One sequence follows a pompous, bungling duke as he hunts down, sacrifices, and offers up for cannibalistic consumption (with wine) the body of a boy, identified only as "Jutta's child" and variously described as girlish, a "fairy," and a "fox." The other sequence, paired to its counterpart by a narration that alternates with it, pits the narrator, Zizendorf, and his two foolish cohorts against the American military overseer, Leevey. They wait in ambush, murder him, seize the symbols of his power (the motorcycle and his pistol), then disseminate tracts proclaiming a reborn Germany. Now, these two sequences are carefully structured opposites (see Fig. 2). Zizendorf's recuperation of time, his reorganization of spatial boundaries and community, and his reconsolidation of language in "the new voice" (175), all follow from the intersection of those sequences in the story's end.

In this "significant shape" we read one of the constituting tropes in all Hawkes's work. Whether it appears as inversion, simile, paradox, oxymoron, or antiphrase, its function in *The Cannibal* is to plot exactly that unification of semantic opposites or contraries — the activity of pursuit and the passivity of ambush, sacrifice versus murder, cannibalistic intake against the outflow of discourse — that Hawkes generalized as "the terrifying similarity between the unconscious desires of the solitary man [the Duke] and the disruptive needs of the visible world [Zizendorf's fascism]." As in a grotesque simile, the effect of such a story is to collapse two essences, the monstrous and the too familiar, into one identity. A horror, but also a banal absurdity, its trajectory is therefore downwards, and bathos is its emotional aspect.

Embedded in that joined structure is another joined structure, separated from its frame as the second of three parts and related to them by analepsis, to June 18, 1914, and after. Just as the Duke's story runs counter to Zizendorf's, here Jutta's briefly told story runs in ironic juxtaposition to the larger focus of part 2, Stella's emergence as a perverse Valkyrie who "survived and hunted now with the pack" (101). Joined at the start, their stories diverge from the deaths of Stella's parents, "Mother" and "the General," ancient figures presiding over a household that epitomizes bourgeois *Gemütlichkeit*. Stella, freed from living as a nursemaid in her dying father's bedroom, marries Ernst.

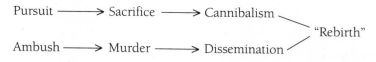

**FIGURE 2**

They honeymoon in the mountains, and in that "superior . . . upper world" (85) she emerges as the better "soldier" at sex, whereupon Ernst launches into an extravagant spiritual passion. Returning then to "Das Grab" (literally, "the grave," one of the novel's apparent settings), a pregnant Stella nurses Ernst's influenza until he dies. Hers is a story of loss, for she also loses her son to Ernst's father, impotent "old Snow," who evidently raises the child. At the same time Jutta, sick and abandoned after her father's death, is packed off at age thirteen to a nunnery. In its "lower world" she worsens, and to the "Mother Superior" she rejects any offers of aid through confession and absolution. Subsequently she nurses herself through the crisis by what appears to be a sheer, "cold" act of will. Though she emerges alone and "unloved," Hawkes writes that Jutta "assumed more of life" after her recovery (122). Now, these two sequences are also paired opposites (Fig. 3). And the degradation of family and all filial ties, which the two plots entail, is (in retrospect) a beginning condition of "Part One — 1945." Parts 1 and 3, composing the frame narrative, thus bring the story line full circle: a patriotic "rebirth" answers the deaths of the parents in "1914"; the national family reconstitutes itself, but only by consuming its own. Structurally, the "1945" story is the stereoisomer of its "1914" counterpart.

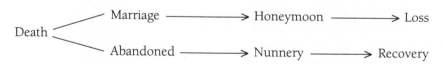

**FIGURE 3**

Other structuring features elaborate this pattern. André Le Vot aptly describes the movement of Zizendorf's narrative as the transit *from* a semiotic shambles *to* a renewed semantic corpus, itself the ironic counterpoint to the dismemberment of Jutta's boy.[48] One might well add that precisely the opposite transition shapes part 2, beginning with the brief, displaced statements of Stella's aged father and ending at Herr Snow's wordless impotency with his nurse Gerta (a blockade of all forms of exchange), and at the oneiric chaos around Ernst's deathbed. There is, furthermore, the widely noted juxtaposition of winter, cold, and darkness in Zizendorf's frame narrative, and the summer, warmth, and light pervading, in particular, the early chapters of part 2 entitled "Love" and "Stella." In addition there are several images and references framing the whole narrative. The "butcher shop" that appears in the beginning (7), with all its premonitory horror for Jutta's boy, reappears at the end as a metaphor for the site of his slaughter (191). Zizendorf also claims at the beginning that Jutta is pregnant, "bearing child again" (8) at age forty-four, an affirmation of his virile powers over the human body that is extended, at novel's end, to include his power over the corpus of a tired language. Readying his "Indictment of the Allied Antagonists," Zizendorf is "the compositor" who "put the characters, the words of the new voice, into the stick," the metaphoric phallus used to inseminate each printing plate with signs (175–76). Finally, in a key reference, there is the opening image of Death, the Teutonic god "Tod" (27), who is a banished presence as Zizendorf closes, "when Spring's men are beating their fingers on the cold earth and bringing the news, Death travels away" (194). Thus Zizendorf's disseminating "the news" is at once both the copy *and* the contrary of his inseminating Jutta.

These signs of formal closure underscore two key aspects of Zizendorf's story. It is retrospective, his epigraph before part 1 being written from the vantage point of three years and some distance beyond Spitzen-on-the-Dein. And it is reflexive, employing myriad strategies for the isomeric inversion, contradiction, obversion, and repetition of events occurring across time. All events thus collapse into a closed, crystalline abstraction of History. Indeed, embedded within "Part Two — 1914" is a brief recollection, focalized through Stella's father, concerning the seige of Paris during the Franco-Prussian War of 1870 (67). Yet "1914" is contained in "1945" (and Zizendorf's virile successes there), itself framed by the analeptic glance of Zizendorf's epigraph, all finally shaped within the satirist's fictional projection. By such regressive means *The Cannibal* shatters the temporal succession and causality of conventional narrative, deflecting them inwards like jagged fragments whose dynamic is one of repetition and violence.

Not that the novel has been wholly stripped of conventional plotting. The dynamics of "pursuit" and "ambush" launch the story from its opening condition of unchained lunacy. As *The Cannibal* begins, the mental institution on the edge of Spitzen-on-the-Dein has spilled its inmates into the town, where they remain unaccounted: "[its] feeble brothers were gradually absorbed, whole corps at a time, into the yawning walls, mysteriously into the empty streets and outlying dark shuttered farms, were reluctantly taken off the streets" (3). Zizendorf's narrative continually strives for the reassertion of boundary and difference which the asylum once signified to him. At one point, his fellow townsmen convene at the asylum for a grim, silent carnival of dancing, "a clockwork of custom, a way of moving that was almost forgotten" (30). To Zizendorf, the asylum is therefore a locus of ritualized discipline to which its former inmates will return at story's end, in "long lines" of souls "revived already with the public spirit" (195). In terms of narrative structure, the galvanizing moment in their return is the cannibalistic feast, a ritual violence around which the whole carnival of horrors circulates but which is never named and only implied by Hawkes's title.

To a great extent, Zizendorf's "story" is the orderly march toward that almost unnameable violence, but it can never wholly shake a certain banal, lunatic absurdity. After all, this is a story in which the protagonist-narrator bludgeons one of his hometown political "opponents" to death with a tuba; in which the principal women characters, Stella and Jutta, are the offspring of two doddering, babbling parents well into their seventies at the time of conception; in which Ernst's "heroic" chase after Stella's carriage (explicitly likened to Gavrilo Princip's June 18, 1914, assassination of the Archduke Ferdinand) halts while, fearful of his mother's eyes, he urinates behind a bush; in which a mute escapee from a lunatic asylum is called "the Kaiser" and the novel's eponymous cannibal the "Chancellor" of a resurrected State; in which Zizendorf's newspaper, "The Crooked Zeitung," trumpet of that grand restoration, is composed in a bird-limed garage; in which the corpse of one character, the Merchant, lies impossibly dead in two different locations at the same time; and finally, a story in which the unspeakable horror of cannibalism takes place as if it were the most inanely bourgeois of everyday customs. Residue from a tradition of gaily farcical and carnivalesque satires, these details plunge Zizendorf's heroics satirically downwards. Into his desire for an abstracted, crystalline History they insinuate the terror of the ridiculous.

Like his techniques of correspondence and recurrence, such details are certainly part of what Hawkes meant in his often quoted remarks of 1964, that his novels are "not highly plotted" but are "elaborately structured."[49] It is a formal obsession Hawkes shares with other contemporaries. The elaborate structural patternings of West and the obsessive doublings of O'Connor come easily to mind. Still other postmodern satires, not only *The Cannibal* and *Travesty* but also Nabokov's *Lolita* or Pynchon's *Gravity's Rainbow,* uncover the desire for structured, abstracted time as a consumptive, self-destroying need. The very need for story, for history, what the narrator in *Travesty* calls a "room of glass" (28) and "our glassy web" (84), consumes characters in a chamber of their own terrors. Storytelling is at once their Grand Guignol and their death-row cell.

Metafictional in some of its aspects, what we are defining is decidedly not "metafiction" per se. The principal function of that postwar mode, according to its principal theorists, has been to enable the reader to discover, through the laying bare of diegetic codes, a new freedom.[50] But against the openness of that metafictional paradigm, generative in its irony, we may stand the practices of postmodern satire, degenerative in its irony and, above all, a fictional mode which repeatedly thematizes humanity's self-imprisonment.[51] A development, perhaps, of that old practice of the satirist satirized, this negation of storytelling through the very devices of story is a primary trait of Hawkes's best work, and it is also the cause of some misreadings. For instance, a number of critics have derogated Hawkes's 1976 novel, *Travesty,* for strong-arming the reader into the "suicide seat" of its speeding automobile.[52] Yet one could just as well read the aggressive tactics of the narrator's discourse as being precisely to the point of Hawkes's satire. Understanding his novels *as satires* also renders moot the host of problems that persist if one reads according to conventions applied to realistic novels: Kermode's sense of the "open ending," for example, or any other means of naturalizing story elements like plot, settings, and character.

In fact, "settings" and "characters" in *The Cannibal* further illustrate its range of degenerative satirical practices. This narrative opens in a chaos of signifiers. We read not so much a syntagmatic chain of described scenes and chronicled events as a set of associatively arranged catalogues. Successive paragraphs take shape around lists: of absent nourishments (8–9), bodily parts (10), colors (10), and fragments of proverbial wisdom (14). Instead of proper names many characters are designated only through bureaucratic titles or filial slots ("the Census taker," "Jutta's boy") whose signified possibilities are absent or meaningless. In descriptions of character and scene, deictic pronouns that seem exophorous at first glance turn out to be either hopelessly ambiguous or lacking any reference. Place names like "Das Grab" or "Spitzen-on-the-Dein" seem loosely interchangeable, and excepting the orderly arrangement at Stella's house and the hotel of part 2, this narrative lacks any relational prepositions that would focus a maplike visual image of its shell-shocked landscape. In a virtual sense, this fragmentation, this undecideability, *is* the setting; these empty, exchangeable names *are* the characters.

Reading Hawkes one could easily collect remarks by characters and narrators testifying to that seductive power of the surrounding fragmentation, that motive force of signifiers loosened from signifieds. In *The Cannibal* Zizendorf claims that after months of bombardment "the people had stopped talking, except for fragments of a sentence" (14). Similarly, there is Papa's "debris" (in *Travesty*) and Konrad's "joyful indecency of wreckage" (in *The Passion Artist*). This fragmentation of signs is one half of the antinomy that rests dead-center in his satirical practice. Its opposing half, that tendency to "design" and order, always emerges from the chaos of signifiers as a primitive, highly formalized violence. In *The Cannibal* this tendency is traceable not only in aspects of plot but in compulsive patterns of setting and character. The juxtapositions of winter/summer, cold/hot are obvious enough, but there are more. André Le Vot has described the formal symmetry of Stella's house, ordered by "deux grandes zones affectives dont chacune des soeurs constitue le pôle d'attraction" (490). In the lower floors Stella holds sway over the elementary consciousness and its primitive drives (cannibalism), while from her uppermost, fifth-floor vantage Jutta rules the symbolizing consciousness and its attempts to speak and justify, through substitution, those primitive drives. This juxtaposition, high/low, extends throughout the narrative.

It is overtly displayed in part 2, which begins in the German low country. By chapter 3, "Ernst," the setting abruptly shifts. The hotel where Ernst and Stella honeymoon not only perches in "the upper world," said to be "superior" (85), it also occupies "the final peak," and Ernst in turn stalks its "highest porch" (86). There he feels "nearer God" (84), and his sense of privileged omniscience builds when an aged crucifix carver points out into the abyss and seems "to laugh" (87). Similarly rejecting the valley and its warring multitudes below, Ernst soon plunges into contradictions and paradoxes for which the grotesque crucifixes he buys are an attempt at symbolic resolution: "both small and large, rough and delicate . . . more human than holy, more pained than miraculous" (87), these icons unite all opposites. Under their aegis, "the whole family" (or Holy Family?) seems to reconstitute itself in Ernst and Stella's rooms (89), as though reversing the dispersal of actual families and transcendental signifiers that is now well under way. Interestingly, however, the failure of this particular signifier follows immediately upon two narrative turns. First, Stella's victories on the battlefield of sex drive Ernst down: she presses him (like a horse) "against the fence, *under* the thicket, forcing him *down*" (91, my emphasis). Second, a character named Cromwell arrives and speaks "with ease about the lower world" and the war (92), further infecting Ernst with the influenza of a beastly life he thought to have symbolically left below. Thereafter, "the mountain slid lower" (94) for him. When a draft horse arrives from below and dies, Ernst's inverse course back to "the lower world" and death seems certain. In short, the transit of settings in part 2 (low-high-low) underscores the failure of a higher, symbolizing consciousness. That failure is driven home as the embedded narrative ends, with Ernst nearing death and the "demonic" Christ of the carvings transformed now into the "demon" face (116) of his father, impotent Old Snow, who reproves his son's weakness.

Next, one notes how part 2 stands, once again, as the stereoisomer of its frame narrative. For the novel begins in the elevation of Jutta's fifth-floor rooms, then progresses down into the ruins before returning to her vantage in the last paragraphs. While less obvious, this transit (high-low-high) inverts that of part 2 in still other ways. Where Ernst failed on the sexual battlefield, Zizendorf depicts himself as its master tactician, and where Ernst's transcendental signifier ironically turns against him, Zizendorf's (is it his "Indictment" or the narrated cannibalism, or both?) is represented to us as the master trope. In fact the high/low antinomy is so fully encoded within the narrative that it appears, as well, in the momentary recollections of Stella's father, in which one recognizes the deepest level of embedding: there the idea of encircling Paris is "*pride on the heights*" (67).

It is the only moment when this novel makes possible a conventionally satiric, moral assessment of characters. Not only Ernst, but also by association Zizendorf stand guilty of pride. Standing "on the heights," both have overreached the horizons of their knowledge and experience. Of course they are in many ways different. Ernst's extravagance mounts up in spiritual forms, Zizendorf's through the codes of a petty fascism. Ernst at his death is the recipient of fatherly discipline; Zizendorf at story's end doles it out to the young woman named Selvaggia. Yet such strategies for marking difference, represented as Zizendorf's story, can just as well be read as techniques for *deferring* the question of the narrator's identity with other characters. Zizendorf the prideful Fool, like Ernst or the Duke: for him to acknowledge the likenesses would be to deny his own greatest claim on difference: "I, the Leader."

This obsessive stipulation of difference, through opposition and contradiction, shapes characterizations throughout *The Cannibal*. A primary opposition is that between a fervor of romantic, high heroic desire, the (German) *Lust* that Ernst feels when pursuing Stella, and its absence felt as an aversion or at worst a castration, "the original *Unlust*" (59) Ernst feels when he falls defeated in swordplay. That *Unlust* is always predicated on paternal order and discipline, on being "under his father's thumb" (51), with the obvious implication that *Lust* flourishes in the Father's absence. It certainly does for Stella after the General's 1914 death, as it will in Spitzen-on-the-Dein until Zizendorf's paternal leadership returns the city's festive "madmen" to their cells in the asylum. So the reader in *The Cannibal* is continually aware of two warring semes: the *Lust* of heroic desire and the *Unlust* that comes with the imposition of paternal authority. At this very elemental level, the story of *The Cannibal* is Zizendorf's reassumption of that fatherly force that was lost in 1914 and which will empower him to rule over a joyless, castrating state.

Zizendorf's narrative develops the other characters through a wholesale pattern of commutation and exchange across the boundaries of these opposites. Ernst moves from *Lust* to *Unlust,* Zizendorf in the opposite direction. The Stella of "1914," driven by sensual desire, becomes the coldhearted cannibal of "1945," while the frigid Jutta of "1914," whose religious rituals celebrate a symbolic cannibalism, takes on Stella's sensual powers in "1945." Balamir's "demented brothers" (3), having escaped, are swallowed up once more by the asylum, symbol of an orderly *Unlust,* and the Duke's social grace recodifies the cannibalistic feast, normally interdicted by taboo, such that it seems a lusty middle-class meal, with "full courses and wine" (193). Jutta's boy, the victim, is in a sense nowhere, merely a counter for these exchanges, while Zizendorf is everywhere, the psyche containing and animating these aspects, the surrogate Father in Stella Snow's household, "Leader" in the reborn Nation.

Zizendorf subsumes all characters, and he is the novel's greatest cannibal. Taking Jutta (in 1945), Zizendorf in effect takes Stella (circa 1914); he symbolically counters Ernst's failure in the nuptial bed and virtually supplants Jutta's husband, missing on the Russian front. His orders to Selvaggia at the novel's close reassert paternal authority, supplanting the Duke's merely titular powers. Interestingly this occurs only after the feminine is revealed as either too unaware to succor its offspring (Jutta) or, worse, in dire complicity with an unspeakable violence (Stella). In sum, first Zizendorf reveals himself in contrast with an abreacted horror, the devouring woman, then as petty, paternal dictator he brings the boot down.

To the protagonist-narrators of Hawkes's satires, woman is a degrading, dangerous power when she keeps to covertly using and trading her sex. Zizendorf's idea about Leevey's prostitute in *The Cannibal,* her vagina perhaps "packed with deadly poison" (144), is an early example. One will notice it again in *Travesty,* with its disciplining prostitutes. However, woman is still more incisively abject when socialized as wife and mother. Then her covert domination of the family economy erupts in crises of degradation, and she is the locus of an original horror. Tormenting and devouring, she is the baleful symbol of victimization. Such is Stella, the first in a series of Hawkes's characters who keep a narrator-protagonist "faithful to the landscape of his mother's punishment."[53] Recent American narrative satires afford other examples of this type: Katje Borgesius as *Domina Nocturna* to Brigadier Pudding, Ethel Rosenberg humiliating Richard Nixon in *The Public Burning*. To such men, Woman is the mother of pain and loss in a landscape where ancient violence erupts and where only tin-pot family dictators propose to maintain sanity and order. But the satire, in all its techniques of paradox and inversion, also reveals through the storytelling of such characters the true castration of modernist power, the fascistic father, ultimate token of a civilization utterly lacking in pleasure and capable of ordering being only through a ridiculous terror, or, what may be taken as the same thing, by telling themselves stories of Oedipal violence.[54]

To read a narrative such as this, with one's laughter so tempered by horror, is to submit oneself to a series of displacements which Jean Starobinski has aptly called "le discours maniaque." First one seeks to grasp the sense of the text by being detached, refusing to assume the cynical (and, here, the misogynistic and antisemitic) humor of its narrator. But the difficulties mount. The conventional markers of a stable viewpoint are absent; chief among these in *The Cannibal* are the customary distinctions between an omniscient third-person and a limited, first-person narrator. Worse still, customary ways of attention and tone are subverted. The great events and atrocities of history disappear in ellipses or, if they appear at all, do so by means of antiphrasis, and in a cynical or sarcastic tone. Yet the narrator's smashed everyday world, its actual grotesque debris, comes under microscopic attention and is given to us in a coolly objective, toneless discourse. Then, in a narrative so stripped of *ratio,* the final blow comes with a travesty of objective detachment itself, for one can discover no other way of reading the Duke's dismemberment of Jutta's boy, with his "infernal humanness" (181).

How then does a reader get above this hive of contradiction, paradox, and antiphrase? It becomes a matter of discovering how the narrative interrogates itself. First is the way of narrative comment on discourse, both its own and discourse in general. On this aspect of *The Cannibal* readers have been quite active, almost from the start. In his introduction, Albert J. Guerard was the first to describe how the novel's "nervous beauty of language" plays against the impulses of story "to imprison us." Criticism subsequently showed, through analyses of symbol and theme, how Zizendorf's desire for absolute control dissolves in the disorder of his own discourse, but Thomas Armstrong was the first to notice that comments *about* speech are important throughout *The Cannibal*.[55] This is so from the moment (in chapter 1) when Zizendorf first states how, in a city where "The Signalman" has "nothing to say" (8) and no longer transmits, the people nevertheless take *everything* as a sign. They too have "stopped talking, except for fragments of a sentence" they all repeat, a sentence in which Stella Snow is said to have commanded their death (14). All have had this "same experience," and all struggle to repress its cannibalistic terror. That repression is precisely what makes a sign of every microscopic detail of Spitzen-on-the-Dein; therefore, to speak the topic of their repression at all would be to risk electrifying the whole network of signs. Indeed, when even fragmentary speech comes forth people are "unable to believe their own words, expecting some agent to rise out of the middle of the table and condemn or laugh" (14). In short, they take any dissociated part of language as a reflection of the entire speech act, that process of production and reception which threatens to make them, once again, a victim. Yet this remarkable passage also implies that the same reflection will exist for Zizendorf in relation to his narratees. His putative readers are meant to share with the citizens a primal, inarticulate horror at Stella Snow: "Of Nordic stock, they were silent, the tribal cry long dead from their rolling tongues" (14). Zizendorf, "leader" of their tribal catharsis, will rearticulate that ancient "cry."

Or so he proposes. As narrator he does indeed command the shared discourse of terror, so much so that his meanings are thematized in everything from the most deeply embedded past to the present. Likewise, the theme of inadequate speech recurs, from Ernst Snow's religious babblings (88) to the Duke's inability to butcher Jutta's boy in the way it "should have been done," according to "a manual" (182). It is a disturbingly banal metaphor of a collective need, shared equally by Zizendorf's fellow citizens and his narratees, the need for an authoritative code, some believable metanarrative (in this case, Oedipal). But the Duke's cannibalism galvanizes all such needs on one object, Jutta's boy, an embodiment of non-difference. Seemingly male and yet also feminine, human and yet also animallike, he is the one character who never speaks. He runs quite literally at the frontiers of discourse in this novel, and so the ultimate need of the Duke and his fellow citizens is to "incorporate" him, to bring him virtually *inside*. Zizendorf's putative narratees might share that need, but the slaughter of Jutta's boy completes an absolute separation of actual readers from the fictional narratees. That separation, traditionally stated as the difference between "real" and "implied" readers, is a primary way any narrative satire goes about interrogating itself.[56]

A second way involves the power of other, prior discourses to interrogate the satire within its intertextual space. Perhaps overcome by its mimetic horrors, readers have been uncommonly disinterested in this aspect of *The Cannibal*. Most simply acknowledge that Zizendorf "reenacts the myth of his Teutonic heritage," or that Hawkes's "blackly comic" references to the Teutonic traditions of mythic narrative are used to satirize a romantic ontology in which myth becomes history and vice versa. Others also point out an obvious but crucial connection, that the Duke's cannibalistic meal, with its "full courses and wine" (193), travesties the Christian eucharistic feast.[57] Still, the main questions remain unexplored: What are the narrative intertexts, and how do they shape both story and discourse in *The Cannibal*? Where do the Teutonic and Christian narratives meet, and with what results to our reading of the satire?

Hawkes's comments, generally useful on his other novels, are of little help here. Beyond his mention of having consulted introductory textbooks on European history, his recollection of source texts is unclear. A widely quoted statement, in which Hawkes claimed to have found the seed for this novel in a *Time* magazine article referring to actual cannibalism in occupied Germany, does not check out.[58] One had better consult the text itself. In particular there are the framing references to the Teutonic god of Death, Tod (27), banished from Spitzen-on-the-Dein at novel's end: "In Winter Death steals through the doorway searching for both young and old and plays for them in his court of law. But when Spring's men are beating their fingers on the cold earth and bringing the news, Death travels away" (194). These references are correlated with the discourse of fertility and rebirth that suffuses *The Cannibal*, and they also correlate with a number of other details in the narrative discourse: the frequent references to fools and madmen (like Stumpfegel and Fegelein, "Spring's men"), the driving out of foreigners, the idea of a "resurrected" state hinging on the cannibalistic sacrifice, and certainly Stella, a representative of ancient Germanic traditions who even sits with "crossed barbaric swords" over her head (13). These references to Teutonic myth and custom lie all about; before inquiring as to their source, one cannot help but note their diegetic importance in key episodes of the story.

A good example occurs in chapter 2. With the near presence of Tod on the "chilly wind" (27), Zizendorf rousts Jutta from her "cold" bed to attend the evening's carnival at the asylum. Its buildings, "combed of reality," appear in the narrative discourse as a sacred space: "a lonely sanctum," "awesome and yet holy" (29), and a "place of congregation" (30). Inside, Zizendorf says, he and Jutta "bowed [their] heads" and watched as Europe's insane, infirm survivors stepped "in a clock-work of custom, a way of moving that was almost forgotten" (30). The dancers, their tongues "curled back to the roots of forgotten words" (31), have in fact completed a regression in history that has recuperated their insanity, making it significant. For they are "masqueraders" now (35), participants in a carnival ascribing to foolishness a generative power. Interestingly, it is mostly "not the Germans" (31) who come together in this way. And with a sarcasm characteristic of his whole discourse, Zizendorf mocks those of his countrymen who must learn Teutonic custom from "the rest of Europe — bedridden with idleness, dumb" (32). Because *he* is one of the "few true Germans" (32) and "different from them all" (33), Zizendorf claims to recognize the mythic power of what is otherwise a pathetically banal event, and so he turns from his participation in the dance, now "a distasteful ritual" (36). Two remarkable narrative turns then close this chapter. First, with no transition from that "distasteful ritual," Zizendorf imagines the desperate flight of Jutta's son through cold night (36). Second, Zizendorf recalls arriving at the ambush laid for Leevey, the "He" now identified (through a telling grammatical error) with "*der Tod*" (37), soon to be banished. With the premonitory references to the god Death framing it and with snippets of the two main plots (of pursuit and ambush) intersecting at its end, the narrative discourse of this chapter encodes, in miniature, the structure of the novel. It unmasks Zisendorf's entire narrative as the banal dissimulation of a brutally sacrificial rite.

What are the intertexts of that discourse? Clearly the most important are those pertaining to ancient Spring fertility rites, especially the "driving out" of Winter/Death common to European carnival plays. For the young Hawkes, Eliot's *The Waste Land* would have been a key example, though he clearly supplemented it with detail from other texts. The important elements are the following: In ancient Germanic rites Winter/Death was exiled or ritually killed each Spring, and with him went all the evils of pestilence and war. Munch's *Norse Mythology*, a standard resource for decades after its appearance in 1926, indicates that these prehistoric rites, held always in April, undoubtedly included blood sacrifices, perhaps human, and were specifically meant to bring "victory." The representative of Winter/Death was beheaded, dismembered, and either eaten or scattered. In medieval centuries these rites became associated with Easter and Pentecostal celebrations, and slowly took shape as pagan versions of the passion drama.[59] In these performances the old vegetation spirit, or "King," played by a mummer or carnival fool, was executed to make way for the young (and sane) spirit of Spring. During the "Sword Dance," mummers performed a highly stylized and sexually charged pantomime of these fertility rites. There were variants on the pattern. In one of the carnival plays, titled *Jutta,* the maiden character of the title is imprisoned in Hell. There she watches the lascivious dance of Lilith with various foolish old devils, until finally the Virgin Mary intercedes on Jutta's behalf, redeeming her from the underworld and, aided by the Sword Dancers who enact the ritual murder, driving out old Winter from the upper world.[60]

Correlations to *The Cannibal* are obvious, and telling. The narrative is set in the "Pentecostal chill" (36) of April 1945, for reasons both historical as well as mythical.[61] It is populated everywhere by fools and the infirm, and their city is represented as a dark, cloacal pit of Hellish degeneration. These are the elements that Zizendorf describes as "unresurrected," literally a grave (*Das Grab*). In their regeneration he constructs a "history" out of borrowed discourses from folk custom, myth, the violence of sacrificial rites. The humor and horror are however incomprehensible until they intersect everyday events. Then the Duke's "cane" (10), later a "sword cane," transforms at last into a "sword" (180) beneath whose strokes the filleted victim of sacrifice loses, ironically, any "value" (181). Worse still, he is not old Winter at all but an innocent young victim. His mother, Jutta, caught up in these "old repeating dreams and murmured words" of custom and myth, steps hollowly through "a play she well knew" (21), yet without ever grasping its topsy-turvy power over her. The other players? All can well be read as parodic inversions of their mythic counterparts. Jutta's boy most of all: served up as "full courses and wine" (193) he travesties Christ in the passion drama, Eliot's key locus of regenerative hope.

*The Cannibal* thus stands the whole *Waste Land* episteme on its head and uncovers through Eliot's "mythic method" the sinews of a fascist power. In potentially endless regression, each war described in this novel (World War Two, The Great War, The Franco-Prussian War) seems to replay a monstrous violence, some unspeakably "distasteful ritual" for which storytelling nevertheless tries to find generative words. This search is brilliantly fixed in Zizendorf's grotesque image of the dead "Merchant," shot on his first day of warfare in 1914: "In his open mouth there rested a large cocoon, protruding and white, which moved sometimes as if it were alive" (94). Again and again, *The Cannibal* undercuts that desire for generative form, for the safe "cocoon" of popular myth that readers might wish to mouth, as yet another dissimulation of violence. The satire insinuates that there is no chrysalis, no transforming sign or sacrificial host, no transcendental signifier that can put a stop to the violence or end the chaos of signification. In this doubt, and through its inversion of the *Waste Land* episteme, *The Cannibal* severs the main ties with American modernism.

In American writing, late-modernist satires found laughter in the depths of regressive psychoses and grotesque ecstasies, where power and logic break down. *The Day of the Locust* and *Wise Blood* are key early examples. Later, the postmodernist satires of Coover and Pynchon would further exhaust meanings beneath a weight of aggressivity and banality until one laughed at understanding that "ultimate" meanings are ungraspable, without any axis; meanings are as arbitrary as any linguistic sign. *The Cannibal* stands as key instance because it decisively pointed the way toward that laughter, which finds its freest stylistic play in texts like Vladimir Nabokov's *Lolita* and Donald Barthelme's *Snow White,* its most public absurdity in the satire on Richard Nixon in *The Public Burning,* its most nightmarish logic in the apocalypse of *Gravity's Rainbow.*

Following the example of Nathanael West, these postwar satirists recognize in storytelling itself the resources of our worst terrors. The "targets" of their disdain are no longer conceivable as standing external to the narrative representation but are identified within the very semiotics of narration. The enemy is symbolization itself: the whole domain of sign production and consumption. This is why contemporary satirists have seemed so willfully averse to the strategies of presenting character, scene, and action in realist fictions. The contemporary narrative satire approaches these "elements of fiction" as linguistic constructs. Characters become mere subcategories in a logical anatomy of things; action and scene are doubled, inverted, isomerically opposed. In these ways narrative satire becomes a postmodern art whose cultural function is to subversively assail the dissimulations of signifying activity, its pretense of making present universal Truth, its instrumentalities of mastery and control, its masked violence. Postmodern satire thus evolved into a form for gazing at that "eclipse of reason" that Horkheimer (for example) had already acknowledged, in 1946, as a defining phenomenon of the new age.

# 3

# What Was Black Humor?

Not many years ago the Black Humorists were rogue talents trampling the conventions of narrative art, snorting at the degradations of Eisenhower's big sleep and Kennedy's New Frontier, and trumpeting nothing less than "a new sense of reality." Then, in a trice, they had broken through to respectability. Hailed in May of 1964 as "the one genuinely new postwar development in American literature," Black Humor seemed to enter the literary mainstream after a remarkably brief and rancor-free period of critical polemics. By early 1965 even the conservative pundits at *Time* had reported their approval, and the endorsement of academia came in 1967 with Robert Scholes's extensive treatment of Black Humor in *The Fabulators*. But acceptance had scarcely come before its promoters were attacked from other quarters. Older, liberal intellectuals, writing in *Dissent, Partisan*

*Review*, and *Atlantic*, saw Black Humor working in complicity with the very middle-class discourses it denounced, advertising in particular and the mass media in general. Still worse, they argued, the Black Humorists had retreated into aesthetic cleverness and traduced their world instead of passing moral judgment on it.[1]

Nothing was more central to these developments than the assertion that Black Humor had moved "beyond satire." Chapter 1 argued that such claims typically depended on formalist theories of satire and expressed a sense that sociopolitical events, indeed the very conditions of knowledge, had surpassed the reach of traditional narrative satire. Thus Black Humor was granted a vanguard status at a time when the validity of many causes, such as racial equality, free speech, and opposition to the Vietnam War, could only be urged by actual political vanguards then taking to the streets. The pacifism and "countercultural" bent of many Black Humorists appeared to reinforce that connection. To old-guard liberals, however, Black Humor was *not satirical enough*. They charged that its practitioners had erred in neglecting the normative and corrective elements supposedly essential to satire and that Black Humorists had finally dissipated the force of their assault through "verbal immersions in dreck," that is, through banal secretions of the mass culture they had (evidently) set out to ridicule.

Today, the political tracery of these moves and countermoves has largely faded, but the theory of satire that informed them still persists. The idea of "Black Humor" also hangs on, as a marketing label on paperback novels and in academia as a focus for scholarly articles, dissertations, and books.[2] It is time to reevaluate these developments. During the sixties, promoters of Black Humor fiction were quick to imagine it occupying a territory "beyond satire," doubtless because traditional theories of satire accentuated its punitive action, while Black Humor flogged nothing except perhaps a malevolent cosmos. At the same time, its detractors were just as eager to deport Black Humor to some far territory. Using formalist ideas of satire's curative and normative functions, they charged that Black Humor violated every precept of a "moral fiction." In a sense, these two factions were speaking different idiolects of the same language, since both argued their case from a formalist standpoint on Neoclassical satire and Romantic irony. Subsequent readings of Black Humor novels have done little to interrogate the points of difference. Black Humor has therefore remained an enigmatically vague concept in American literary studies, when it might well have been understood as a central development of postmodernism in this country.

## Beyond Satire?

What was Black Humor? For too long, no one "has been able to define [its] exact qualities to the satisfaction of anyone else." Critics have not agreed on even the most basic terminologies. To some it was "a school," to others "a movement," while to skeptics it was "less a school than a sensibility," or "a convenient handle for referring to a divergent body of literature," or "a mere fashionable label for elevating all kinds of shoddy work to artistic status." These last assessments are seconded by one of its central figures, Kurt Vonnegut, Jr., who said in a 1973 interview that "critics picked up on the term because it was a handy form of short-hand" for naming a diverse group.[3] This seems the only reasonable view. The most frequently mentioned writers were a baker's dozen of unaffiliated talents: John Barth, Donald Barthelme, William Burroughs, J. P. Donleavy, Bruce Jay Friedman, William Gaddis, John Hawkes, Joseph Heller, Vladimir Nabokov, James Purdy, Thomas Pynchon, Terry Southern, and Vonnegut. None of them came to professional maturity together, nor did any ever issue a collaborative project, much less even agree on the aptness of the term "Black Humor."[4]

There were more fundamental problems of typology. To some critics, "Black Humor" was the term used to designate a full-fledged "genre"; to others, a "mode" or "a technique, not a form"; while to more cautious observers it only designated "a sensibility" or "tone." Scholes, perhaps desiring to cover all bets, refers to it in the space of two pages as "one of the literary kinds," "a mode," "genre," and "form."[5] Such omnibus cataloguings of Black Humor point to the deeper failing of its early enthusiasts. Most tried to define its innovations in the context of what Hassan called "the birth of a new sense of reality, a new knowledge of error and incongruity."[6] Black Humor, they argued, was a response to new conditions for representation itself, and some commented on the antirealist tendencies of its alleged practitioners. None inquired further, for example to probe the relations of Black Humor to that antipathy to mimetic conventions that has always been a modal feature of narrative satire or, more generally, to inquire how that antipathy was related to an emerging sense of literary postmodernism in this country.

The figure of Jack Ruby — assassin of the presidential assassin — loomed (oddly) large in all of this. He first appears in the one truly seminal piece on Black Humor, Conrad Knickerbocker's September 1964 essay for the *New York Times Book Review*, "Humor with a Mortal Sting." Repeating a comment from his May review of *Candy* (newly issued in America after six years of underground notoriety), he welcomed Black Humor as "a new — perhaps the only new — development in American fiction since the war." Knickerbocker then went on to describe its innovations as a response to changed sociopolitical conditions, arguing that "traditional forms cannot accommodate a reality which now includes Jack Ruby. . . . Events have become too mysterious."[7] Six months later, Bruce Jay Friedman echoed that connection, arguing that the "new mutative style" responded to the "near-hysterical new beat in the air" as well as to the "new, Jack Rubyesque chord of absurdity" that seemed to run through it all. Ruby, and the mind-boggling series of political assassinations in the sixties, were often used as benchmarks.[8] Raymond Olderman, like many others, would later generalize from these references to "a world made mystery by the extraordinary nature of fact."[9] These are large claims, and worth pausing over.

In saying events demanded a "new mutative style" the Black Humorists were not repeating the belief, then widely held, that the post-Holocaust, post-Hiroshima West was facing an all-out "exhaustion of verbal resources in modern civilization" (in George Steiner's words), nor were they making any claims about an associated phenomenon, the expected "death of the novel."[10] Instead, their focus was on the seemingly plotted or *performative* nature of events and, more particularly, on the possibilities for being an (usually paranoid) audience to them. In fact, Friedman and other promoters of Black Humor referred to contemporary political events *only* in the changing context of their representation in electronic and print media. The "Jack Rubyesque chord of absurdity" was a way to symbolize a revised conception of what it meant to be an audience, a "reader." Confronting the multiform programming of electronic media (news, comedy, narrative fictions, documentary, and so on) one was obliged to recognize not only the melding of usually discrete forms but also the viewer's hand on the dial and thus a deep, disturbing potential for cross-examination between "texts" and different media. Given these "mutative" tendencies, and with the extreme violence of events, there is indeed a bothering reflexivity, a troubling doubling of forms, especially of documentary journalism and fabulative narration, history and fiction. Many early enthusiasts for Black Humor echoed Bruce Jay Friedman's explanation: "What has happened is that the satirist has had his ground usurped. . . . The journalist is certainly today's satirist. The novelist-satirist, with no real territory of his own to roam, has had to discover new land, invent a new currency, a new set of filters, has had to sail into darker waters somewhere out beyond satire and I think this is what is meant by black humor."[11] Such statements rested squarely on a belief that the mimetic, didactic, and curative powers of documentary forms had "usurped" the very powers that formalist critics then defined as essential to satire (a problem I take up again in chapter 4). Here it is important to note that no one questioned the assumptions underlying claims that Black Humor was "beyond satire," nor did anyone carry the idea of "a new set of filters" any further. Yet Friedman was describing a conceptual shift that obliges one to ponder a radical displacement of forms, of conventional value hierarchies, and perhaps *any* fixed reference-points supposedly contained in those forms.

Described in this context, "Black Humor" seems very much the early, literary expression of an emerging postmodernism. Lyotard characterizes postmodernist writing by its departure from an idea of the work as a linear or spatial abstraction to an idea of the reader's "intertextual" transaction with it, and furthermore by a relativization or "delegitimation" of the text's foundations (for instance, the foundation of determinist plots) in rationalist science or conventional mythic structures. David Harvey argues that the collapse, in postmodernity, of "Fordist" models of production, with their determinist assumptions and a full baggage of assumptions about linear, totalizing systems and hierarchized global cartels, further spells out the sociocultural consequences of this shift. There are Charles Newman's characterization of a postwar, inflationary culture that devalues all "currencies" and relativizes any transaction, and Brian McHale's of the decisive shift from the epistemological dominant in modernist writing, to the ontological in postmodernism; and Alan Wilde's, about the "suspensive" ironies of postmodernity. The persuasive themes, in such diverse fields as drama, music, painting, and fiction, are a minimalist arena of survival, the incorporation of commercial or "pop" media, and the staging of a wholesale deconstruction in the domain of signs. Through it all runs a postexistentialist suspicion of *any* received structures.

Black Humor gave voice to this new, postmodern condition. Its exemplary works manifested "the writer's and putative reader's assumptions about man's nature and situation," and this is furthermore to say that Black Humor should be interpreted as a literary *mode,* a "power of action" we assume about events.[12] Still, throughout the sixties and seventies there were attempts to claim a certain generic legitimacy, and stability, for it. Significantly, however, all such attempts were predicated on assertions that it had departed from a historical line of satires, for example by Swift, Céline, and Waugh.[13] But the critics, for reasons considered below, then decided not to examine whether, and in what ways, the Black Humorists had been revising the modal conventions of traditional satire. They were doubtless encouraged not to do so by the sense, from 1965 on, that the really important examples of Black Humor were novels, new forms, that is, of a traditional *genre.* They doubtless also felt the necessity of making a formal, generic contrast between Black Humor fiction and absurdist drama.[14]

These typological confusions — Was Black Humor a genre, mode, technique, temperament, or tone? — were symptomatic of still more central problems. For example, the topic of Black Humor's pedigree was bound to come up, and whenever it did the critics pointed to fairly recent and usually American ancestors. In 1964 Ihab Hassan singled out the grotesques of Sherwood Anderson, West's "torture-house parody" of Alger, and the more contemporary satires of Hawkes and O'Connor; Knickerbocker and Friedman both pointed to Céline and West. In the earliest American use of the term that I know of, Albert J. Guerard praised the "fine black humor" in Hawkes's *The Cannibal* and went on to make comparisons with the satires of West and O'Connor.[15] His own fix on the term also owed much to André Breton's surrealist, and sometimes traditionally satirical, *Anthologie de l'humour noir* (1939), but the French connection is one that later critics all but ignored. Most also slighted the possible links to kinds of degenerative satire by premodern fictionists. *Time,* the rare exception, claimed that Black Humor was the same kind of bitter laughter "to which other ages moved Juvenal, Rabelais, and Swift"; in short that Black Humor was, as the *Time* essayist put it, "a vigorous *new growth of satiric talent.*"[16] In comparison, most used Swift, for example, as a benchmark for finding only what Black Humor *was not,* insisting that the new writers had moved way "beyond satire." In an important sense they were right: the best Black Humor fictions *did* challenge the broadly accepted conventions for generative satire. Yet the critics' equally insistent mentions of recent American satirists, in particular their references to West, O'Connor, and Hawkes, undercut any avant-garde proclamations of a total break with the past. The popular press, in identifying Black Humor as an important change in the satirical mode, was therefore seeing more clearly through the commercial hype than a score of solid scholars.

The *Time* essayist went on to say that "satire has always been an aggressively complex response to the world. As employed by the black humorists, it is a response to a world grown mechanized and impersonal." A generality, this nevertheless has the virtue of keeping an open eye for satire's changing forms and ethos, while in contrast the scholarly critics were hindered by the blind spot of conventional theory. For instance, Hassan's important early essay, "Laughter in the Dark" (1964), established narrow boundaries that none would later question. Mindful of Frye's formalist proscription that a satirist could "not speak for the twentieth century" because the mode itself had "gone stale and mouldy," Hassan argues that contemporary circumstances are "inhospitable" to satire. The horrors around us, he claims, are "irremediable" and "unrelieved." The "new" laughter therefore derives from something closer to Romantic irony: "The ironic attitude," explains Hassan, "lies close to the satiric. In the latter [however] the object of attention is not the monstrous, which is irremediable, but rather the follies and vices of man, things merely reprehensible."[17] This rested squarely on earlier formulae for a generative satire, that it should be close-targeted, corrective, and normative. Clearly, however, the Black Humorists had stepped "beyond" this formalist demarcation into "darker waters." Knickerbocker and Friedman were even glib about it, Friedman especially in his explanations that "the journalist" had "usurped" the satirist's ground. Subsequent critics did little more than dress that idea up in scholarly language, arguing that Black Humor surpasses satire because it gives up the element "of didactic social criticism that the great satirists of the English Enlightenment cherished"; that criticism is necessary to "the task of social rehabilitation" and "the service to man" which (supposedly) define the satiric process. Summarizing her predecessors, Barnes (writing in 1978) reaffirms that distinction: "Whereas satire, being moralistic, aims to correct by holding within brackets a vision of what should be, Black Humor does not tell us how to live; its concern is rather with perception [that is, with] forging through surface reality to present life as it is."[18]

Those promoting Black Humor were almost habitually hemmed in by the reigning theory, its constraints often triggering some of their most central contradictions. Whenever critics sought to differentiate Black Humor from satire, the old shibboleths were repeated and the badges of satire's old-time authority were flashed: *satire,* they reminded readers, was rhetorical and undertook a sanative project, yet *black humor* was (and did) not. At the same time, however, their definitions of Black Humor were often shot through with the language of formalist satirical theory. Thus a critic might note that satire's "didactic social criticism" is a key "operative element" in differentiating it from (a nondidactic) Black Humor, while two pages earlier the "heavily didactic" nature of much Black Humor had been its defining quality.[19]

A more incisive instance occurs in Max Schulz's 1973 study, *Black Humor Fiction of the Sixties.* After an opening chapter that attempts to spell out Black Humor's differences from satire along just those lines traced above, Schulz comments on the moral aims of writers committed to treating the inherent "multiplicity" of their culture: "If he [the Black Humorist] cannot be numbered among those moral activists who change the visible face of things, he is, nevertheless, in his passionate concentration on the hallucinations of reality, as Knickerbocker insists, one of the 'keepers of conscience' "; and his goal is to "instruct us anew in ways of perceiving reality."[20] In this remark, satirists ("moral activists") are writers committed to the rhetorical, didactic force of their practice, are committed, that is, to changing "the visible face of things" on the basis of some moral norms. But then, if one looks closely, so too are Black Humorists: like satirists, they are morally normative ("keepers of conscience") and equally as committed to, even "passionate" about the didactic, corrective force of *their* practice, with its power to "instruct us anew" in ways of perceiving reality. The one nominal difference lies in Schulz's allegation that the satirist operates on "the visible face of things" while the Black Humorist turns his scalpel within. In fact, however, this also stemmed from Knickerbocker's important early essay, which argued that the Black Humorist aimed at few of the satirist's external targets; instead, "within there are worms. The new humor is self-directed. Underneath lie spasms of self-loathing."[21] There are similar versions of this idea scattered throughout the criticism in comments that Black Humor targets no extrinsic "culprit," just "anxieties and neuroses," our erring constructions of reality that need to be set right.[22]

These attempts at differentiating Black Humor only inherited the problems of the exclusively generative theory of satire. For example, by asserting that Black Humorists force their scalpel "within" whereas satirists operate on the "visible face of things," the critics were simply repeating the doctrine of satire's extramural "targets." I have argued that narrative discourse can only actualize a "target" by reconstructing it out of *other* representations, therefore the "target" is, if anything, a composite of erring constructions from "within," or at least, *within representation,* precisely those "hallucinations of reality" that Schulz described. Similar problems arose when critics tried to differentiate Black Humor by its lack of the corrective purpose of satire's "moral activists," although virtually any act of semiosis can challenge a reader to reformulate his understandings, and there is no reason to privilege this aspect of satire. Some satires embark on a moral jihad and clearly identify familiar targets; some do not.

Because they never surmounted this narrow view, what the critics called "Black Humor" often sounded very much *like satire*. That uncertainty about such key points of difference was bound to let in the wolves, whose withering attacks came within only a few years. It was only fitting, too, after such contradictory attempts to place their writing "beyond satire," that the Black Humorists were criticized for not being satirical enough. This was the charge, in 1968, of old-guard liberals like John Aldridge, Burton Feldman, and Philip Rahv. Aldridge, whose 1968 essay for *Atlantic* was the most detailed, justly praised Black Humor for revitalizing the novel at a time when many were predicting its death, but his prognosis called for yet another exhaustion, because the "high claims of its [Black Humor's] initial publicity have not been fulfilled." Having seen through the early, inconsistent polemics, Aldridge identifies Black Humor as an attempt at *new* satire. Paradoxically, however, he too falls back on the time-honored conventions: "The prime requirement of successful satire was never fulfilled by Black Humorist writers," he claims, because "the living reality of the object or condition being satirized was too obliquely suggested in their work or was altogether missing from it." Black Humor had thus "cut itself off from the vital source of effective satire — the close observation of the social and political world."[23] Like other critics, Aldridge wanted identifiable "targets." The reply to his critique should have been phrased something like this: Black Humor *was* innovative in bringing new energies to the novel; further, the most important of the writers associated with Black Humor, Barthelme and Pynchon for example, had come to understand how one might satirically interrogate the "social and political world" by cross-examining, not extramural targets per se, but forms of social and political discourse used to construct ideas about that world.

In fact Aldridge came within a hair's breadth of that position. "It has often been argued in defense of Black Humor," he continued, "that fiction in our time has lost the possibility of making this social connection because the events of the social world have become themselves fictitious."[24] Aldridge here recalls the statement, by Friedman and others, that journalism had "usurped" the satirist's ground. As Aldridge himself later suggests, this is a frivolous claim, but behind it always lay an aesthetically enabling idea: if ordinary human events seemed extraordinarily *plotted,* then one very well ought to treat them as cultural constructs, discourses that the novel could assimilate for purposes of exposing the degenerative violence they mask. The point, again, was the Black Humorist's concern for the *performative* nature of verbal "reality." In his 1967 novel, *Snow White,* Barthelme even thematized that idea as the various "universes of discourse" with which the characters indiscriminately play. Fully investigated, as Jerome Klinkowitz suggests in a 1974 review of Schulz's study, this theme should have led one to see how these fictions had abandoned the aim of providing a "reordered presentation of reality" in order to question the very ways that we shape reality, and even, one must add, how the fictions worry that our most horrifying hallucinations tend to become actual events. The work of Hawkes, Nabokov, Coover, and Pynchon is testament to at least that much. There is indeed an outraged "moral" content or "social connection" if readers insist on having one.

Critics like Aldridge and Feldman, however, took the negative view. Concerned liberal humanists, they were alarmed that Black Humor had destroyed "any moral or sympathetic bond between itself and the reader," or that it failed to demonstrate how "events might be interpreted meaningfully in relation to the self."[25] They demanded the kind of morally certain, easily decoded satire that Anglo-American formalism defined. This was exactly what the Black Humorists, at their best, had foresworn.

## Beyond Formalism

If the benchmarks of conventional satire were of little use, then what *was* Black Humor? To sum up, it appeared in the sixties as (1) an expression of the postmodern sensibility; (2) a satirical writing, for so it was received, covertly by those promoting and overtly by those attacking it; and (3) a challenge to then-accepted modal conventions for satire, specifically to the formalist idea of satire as a didactic, targeted, corrective, and normative literature. Moreover, as a set of constraints deeply influencing its reception, those modal conventions in (3) have been a source of the most telling confusions and contradictions about Black Humor fiction ever since its promoters began touting the new work in 1964. If anything, the Black Humorists had ventured, not "beyond satire," but beyond the generative view of satire promoted by formalist critics. And once we put aside those theoretical confusions, there *are* other structural features that identify Black Humor, features much more apparent in actual fictions than from the critical record. Indeed, from the first it was set apart as a writing that had bestowed narrative breadth to the "sick joke," reoriented the functions of irony, and opened fictional discourse to the corrosive "languages" of pop culture. Some of Black Humor's most dubious as well as its most telling achievements stemmed from these innovations, and they define a postmodern satire that still shapes the contemporary American novel.

Critics frequently mentioned that Black Humor treated life as a joke. By 1969, indeed, Philip Roth's character Portnoy could complain to his analyst, Dr. Spielvogel:

Doctor, *please,* I can't live in a world given its meaning and dimension by some vulgar nightclub clown. By some — some *black humorist!* Because that's who the black humorists are — of course! — the Henny Youngmans and Milton Berles breaking them up down there in the Fountainbleu, and with what? Stories of murder and mutilation! . . . Doctor, get these people off my ass, will you please? The macabre is very funny on the stage — but not to live it, thank you![26]

This complaint was doubtless prompted by a number of observations from Black Humor's salad days. Early critics claimed these fictions developed from an ethos that also produced comedians like Lenny Bruce, Woody Allen, and Dick Gregory, and satirical cabaret groups like Chicago's Second City.[27] Scholes, who wanted to bring such claims under the interpretive roof of "fabulation," argued that "the joke is one key to the fabulative impulse, especially the impulse behind Black Humor," the concern of which was not with "what to do about life but with how to take it." Obviously, one reason the analogy with jokes seemed so suggestive is that joking requires none of the corrective and normative impulses which the formalist critics had ascribed to satire. Scholes's comments in *The Fabulators* implied as much. Yet because this connection was never developed in any detail, it later became still another cause to dismiss Black Humor. Some charged, for instance, that even "at its best it always verged perilously on the sick joke, the nightclub wisecrack," or that Black Humor never "rose above its own sick jokes."[28]

One certain debt of the Black Humorists was to the European tradition of gallows humor. Hassan acknowledged that link in "Laughter in the Dark" when he noted that "[e]verywhere, the spirit of gallows humor dances crazily on the wind"; and Vance Bourjaily, who mistakenly tried to differentiate gallows humor from Black Humor by saying that the European tradition was more "kind hearted," saw it as Vonnegut's definitive trait.[29] Vonnegut himself, in a 1973 *Playboy* interview, looked back on the rise of Black Humor and noted that if anything it was a resurgence of the gallows humor that "Freud had already written about." He went on:

> It's people laughing in the middle of political helplessness. Gallows humor had to do with people in the Austro-Hungarian Empire. There were Jews, Serbs, Croats — all these small groups jammed together in a very unlikely sort of empire. And dreadful things happened to them. They were powerless, helpless people, and so they made jokes. It was all they could do in the face of frustration. The gallows humor Freud identifies is what we regard as Jewish humor here: It's humor about weak, intelligent people in hopeless situations.[30]

A chatty generalization, there is nevertheless something to this claim. Gallows humor comes down to us as a tradition of self-conscious joking wherein the categories of subject (the joker) and object (the joked about) collapse into one. This occurs, not through an operation of reason, but through a free and contingent intelligence, wit.

Freud's example of the form, in *Jokes and Their Relation to the Unconscious,* illustrates what he felt was "the crudest case": a "rogue who was being led out to execution on a Monday remarked, 'Well, this week's beginning nicely.' " Freud next spells out the admiration one feels in the presence of such a wit. It arises from a feeling of "something like magnanimity in this 'blague,' in the man's tenacious hold upon his customary self and his disregard of what might overthrow that self and drive it to despair." Freud had earlier linked that victory to two features. The first "arises from an economy in the expenditure of affect," that is, from the humorist submitting his overwhelming emotions to the rigid structural demands of the joke itself. Doing so, he refuses to submit his intelligence to antagonistic realities. In the second place what the humorist does is to play out the petty customs of everyday reality in order to triumph over the (now) hostile monolith of which they are just emblematic parts. Thus, as Freud notes, another rogue on his way to the gallows stops and requests a scarf to cover his bare throat against the chilly winds. In this way the jokester uses "customary" concern to assert the pleasure principle — whose outward sign is laughter — at precisely that moment when its normative master, the reality principle, would seem in total command.[31]

These qualities were certainly common to the nightclub comics that *Time* and others hailed in connection with Black Humor and to Vonnegut's "Jewish humor." Yet the Black Humorists went further, employing the *schtick* (the brief, narrative joke with a stable viewpoint and thematic links to adjacent jokes) as a structuring force on narrative. In Vonnegut's most widely acclaimed work of the sixties, for example, the joke becomes a principal form of episodic development across chapters. A typical instance occurs in chapter 73 of *Cat's Cradle,* entitled "Black Death." Philip Castle, a "mosaicist and hotel-keeper" known throughout the Caribbean isle of San Lorenzo as the son of altruistic doctor Julian Castle, recalls the time he was fifteen and an epidemic of bubonic plague swept through the population: "We had stacks of dead so deep and wide that a bulldozer actually stalled trying to shove them toward a common grave. Father worked without sleep for days, worked not only without sleep but without saving many lives, either." When the plague had nearly run its course and there were scarcely any patients left to treat, Julian Castle began to laugh and took his son "out into the night with his flashlight." Playing his beam of light over the stacked bodies, Castle laid a hand on Philip's head and solemnly vowed, "Son, someday this will all be yours."[32] This theme, of everyday routines continuing in the face of virtually empty hope, carries over to the following chapter, "Cat's Cradle," with its central image of busy hands weaving patterns in the empty air, and even into the next, when the narrator finally meets a still-cynical Julian Castle, who runs down the life's work of Albert Schweitzer. Finally these short, joking chapters can well be read as synonyms for the novel's global meaning. A loose analogy, then: *schtick* is to monologue, as chapter is to novel.

This structuring potential of jokes is something Vonnegut began to develop in writing *The Sirens of Titan* (1959). Chapters of his next novel, *Mother Night* (1961), compose a joking, confessional lead-in to the finale of gallows humor that ends the monologue-novel: the American/Nazi double agent Howard W. Campbell preparing to hang himself for "crimes against himself" and hoping, as he bids "Goodbye, cruel world," that the otherworldly music he is about to hear will not be Bing Crosby's "White Christmas."[33] Then, from *Cat's Cradle* through *Breakfast of Champions* (1973), with its visual puns and scatological drawings, the joke is increasingly to Vonnegut the minimalist form for a narration in which the sum is identical to its parts. In his *Playboy* interview Vonnegut even described his novels as humorous piece work: "I'm in the business of making jokes; it's a minor art form," he says, "like building a mousetrap. You build the trap, you cock it, you trip, and then bang! My books are essentially made up of a whole bunch of little tiny chips; and each chip is a joke" (258). This suggests again the analogy between a comic monologue and a Black Humor fiction, so that narrative elements like character and suspense unfold across the continuum of episodic jokes. Here indeed, as Vonnegut himself concedes, were "minor" possibilities for innovation. Jokes could spin the narration off center and scatter, or at least ironize, the desire for a totalizing, culminating insight at the work's close. Bokonon's "final sentence" in *Cat's Cradle,* for example, with its image of the holy man "thumbing [his] nose at You Know Who" (191), reformulates the tag-end on countless of the novel's 126 prior chapters.

During the heyday of Black Humor this predilection for the joke defined Vonnegut's work and was also its most diminishing trait. Jokes became the principal structuring feature of his work but eventually proved too limiting. In *The Sirens of Titan* (1959), he spun the novel's plot out of a single cosmic joke: the idea that history as we know it was preplanned by an extraterrestrial intelligence, with the aim of producing, for some future space traveler, the spare part his spacecraft will require to prevent the poor fellow's becoming stranded in an otherwise useless backwater of the galaxy, namely, Earth. Finally, this served as little more than the hinge into a loose, enjoyably pointless parody of a Pop form, science fiction. Similarly, at the end of *Cat's Cradle,* with his wisecracking Jeremiah delivering the brutal punch line to a world wholly locked up in ice, the idea is to joke back the pain, to do like Bokonon and go out thumbing one's nose at the divine fictionist. Yet the reader still bears in mind the novel's opening gesture, its warning that "nothing in this book is true." That disclaimer certainly draws attention to the text's status as a fictional performance. However, little else in the novel presses us to question further, to ask, for example, what kinds of fictive illusions become deadly? The putative author, after all, had begun by wanting to write a book about Hiroshima, entitled, "The Day the World Ended." What connects that desire to his condition at novel's end? Why did fiction become fact? One hasn't a clue. As Michael Wood noted in a 1973 essay, the mythologies Vonnegut offers up are always, as jokes, held too distant from human violence and misery to form a meaningful dialectic with them.[34] In *Cat's Cradle,* the hip gospel of Bokononism, based on the notion that fictions are useful to distract anxiety from intransigent political and natural evils, simply suggests it is pointless to ask "serious" questions about fiction making. Compare this treatment to West's. In *Miss Lonelyhearts,* the narration opens with the protagonist's realizing that what was initially meant as a sick joke (his job) becomes something much more corrosive and disruptive. The remainder of the narrative explores that degenerative potential and the inability of storytelling to quell it. Vonnegut, like the West of *Balso Snell,* never gets beyond the joke itself.

Excepting *Slaughterhouse-Five* (1969), a novel the next chapter treats in detail, Vonnegut continued this slide well beyond the sixties. By *Breakfast of Champions* (1973), life has diminished to something even worse than inane jokes. A rental truck, for example, lives an agonized life of pain because of the brand name, "Hertz," emblazoned on its side. The narrator, one who has come "unstuck in time" like many of Vonnegut's protagonists, addresses Americans with a smug awareness of what the future will unfold. Vietnam, he instructs us, was a country whose inhabitants were being saved from Communism by Americans who dropped exploding gizmos on their heads. Fucking was how babies were made. Throughout, Vonnegut's drawings of flags, anuses, and tombstones press home the idea of a purely referential, minimalist (and men's room) language. A ridiculous hieroglyphics, language is thus a machine that anticipates the narrator's conclusive "joke," itself finally beneath humor: human beings may really be amoral machines and vice versa. This merely pessimistic fancy seems to derive its idea of an object-language from part 3 of Swift's *Gulliver's Travels* and its mechanical conception of humanity from Swift's mock essay, "The Mechanical Operation of the Spirit." Yet those concepts gain no decisive hold over the epigonal doom dominating the novel.

Indeed, the failure of *Breakfast of Champions* suggests that Vonnegut was less a Black Humorist than, as his least amusing fictions demonstrate, a popular novelist who sought the mantle of higher "seriousness" by working slight revisions on traditional satire. A few critics would even try to rescue him from the drifting jollyboat of Black Humor by arguing that his corrective, normative satire, concerned with "the follies and vices of men" who are enslaved by their own "unexamined traditional viewpoints," is exactly what set him apart from contemporary American fictionists.[35] This was an inflated claim at best. Vonnegut has written nothing to change Leslie Fiedler's 1970 assessment of him as "a transitional figure in a time of transition." Arguing from Vonnegut's "uncertain hold" on the materials of his fiction, Fiedler sees both the shortcomings of his work and his eventual reception as a minor figure. Simply put, the bleakness of his social vision was too often shortchanged by simpleminded jokes.[36] A minimalist form, even the extended humor of the *schtick,* has little tolerance for narrative traffic, the byways for temporal ordering, focalization, and speech representation that have characterized the twentieth-century novel. The alternatives are either overtaxing the joke or limiting one's narrative, and Vonnegut's joking has alternately worked both sides of that auditorium.

For most of the Black Humorists, the joke was a minor feature of their writing. In Joseph Heller's *Catch-22* (1961), jokes reiterate a theme of circular, tautological entrapment, and they tend alternately into verbal slapstick or into horror, as with the "soldier in white," a mummified casualty whose emptied bag of liquid nourishment is switched with his bag of excrements after a catheter fills it up. There are similar moments scattered throughout the novels of Thomas Pynchon. In his first, *V.* (1963), "Esther's Nose Job" (chapter 4) develops an extended grotesque pun on sexual violation, with the doctor's assistant, Trench, injecting anesthetics and chanting, "Stick it in . . . pull it out." At its end, the scene breaks out in a kind of Marx Brothers insanity, with the doctor singing: "Have I told you fella, / She's got the sweetest calumella / And a septum that's swept'em all on their ass."[37] In *Gravity's Rainbow* (1973) there is, similarly, the well-engineered joke on Brigadier Pudding, whose coprophagia with *Domina Nocturna* unfolds as an extended pun on spiritual transcendence. These narrative episodes, with their relentless displacement of horror into humor, are always only subordinate to the satirical project of cross-examining and overthrowing structures of domination and control. This was the joking of Black Humorists at its best, a familiar, even popular form for the radical dialogism of narrative satire. But at its worst the joking deflected laughter into a dead end. Two cases in point: J. P. Donleavy's *The Ginger Man* (1958) and Terry Southern's second novel, *The Magic Christian* (1959).

Donleavy's first book earned him a great notoriety here and abroad; he was compared with James Joyce and Henry Miller, and a number of enthusiasts lauded *The Ginger Man,* with Nabokov's *Lolita,* as one of the earliest Black Humor fictions. In retrospect it seems a book that confuses the age-old link between humor and malevolence. The plot, a modern picaresque, unfolds as an extended, ill-tempered joke. A boozing, sexually unprincipled, financially irresponsible figure, Sebastian Dangerfield, stumbles through a sequence of scrapes with bourgeois authority. The novel begins in "a rare sun of spring" and ends on Christmas Day, some nine months later. That movement, Spring to Winter, from ribald comedy to more mortal ironies, sets the protagonist up as a desperate man running, amorally, from the consuming jowls of Death. Donleavy makes that sprint his justifying theme. Living off the GI Bill while he studies law in Dublin and patiently waits for his stateside father to die and bestow a fortune, Dangerfield is married to a genteel English woman, Marion. His favorite joke is to badger her, mock her conventional pieties, sometimes to beat her and threaten to smother their child for crying. The rest of it is a simple pattern running through successive chapters: "Danger," as his classmates call him, meets a vulnerable working girl in a pub; he awes her with his college aspirations, and wins her sympathies by playing the genius frustrated in a leaden marriage; he then seduces her, abandons her with empty promises, and moves on to the next woman. To pay for this sexist sport, he filches the baby's milk money (she gets rickets), cons the butcher and landlord, and pawns furnishings from their rented houses. The cycle finally ends when Danger meets his ideal match, Mary, who is simply more insatiable — and bigger breasted — than any of his prior women. Mary talks sex as vulgarly as Sebastian himself, drinks him into a stupor, and is the perfect blend of virgin and whore. By comparison, his wife Marion is just what her name implies — the diminutive version of omnivorous Mary, represented in the novel as Death's proper antagonist.

Problems abound. There is Marion's unexplained disappearance from the narrative. Another is the resurrection (almost literally, from an evident suicide) of a classmate, Percy Clocklan, who shows up with enough cash to bail Dangerfield out of all his financial woes, a coincidence too cheaply bought to close the story. In particular these are problems if readers hew to realist conventions, as *Time* did in its 1965 essay on Black Humor. They nevertheless still praised the novel for the way Donleavy first of all stands our "moral universe on its head" and then makes us "love Dangerfield for his killer instinct" that, "ironically," keeps him alive in a "fierce, two-handed grab for every precious second of life." Yet such a reading ignores the way that Dangerfield's "grab" is structured, chapter by chapter, around his misogynistic jokes, his malevolent disgust at children, whom he sees as the beshitted by-products of lust, and his obscene ravings and drunken hysteria. In satire, as Bakhtin and Kristeva have shown, these tendencies often depend on a carnivalesque ethos that subverts an overpowering everyday wisdom. The disruptions of *The Ginger Man* only serve an aggressive, hegemonic patriarchy. The novel's one innovative strength, its blending of limited first- and omniscient third-person forms, is engaging. Still, this blend is never used to examine the relations between misogyny and money, and it was trifling alongside what Hawkes, for example, can do with a similar blending in *The Cannibal*. Otherwise *The Ginger Man* was a cul-de-sac for the novel. Its antibourgeoise rebellion (a kind of fashionable anomie) was phrased out as a joking prodigality and sexual licentiousness that only titillates the bourgeois sensibility that underwrote the novel. The culture would come to know the dead-end of it during the sixties, which similarly played at danger.

Like many Black Humor fictions, *The Ginger Man* only deflected laughter back toward conventionally stable ironies. Its joking subversion of cultural forms was set to work on the most simpleminded of middle-class norms, those regulating ordinary, bodily pleasures. In the same way, *The Magic Christian* turns on a solid axis of antibourgeois jokes. First we are quickly introduced to the fabulously wealthy protagonist, Guy Grand, a fat little man with a "balding bullet head," and to the aunts Agnes and Esther with whom he shares a mansion on Manhattan's East River Drive.[38] Then each of the remaining fourteen chapters (out of seventeen total) begins with the three Grands in banal and usually bungled conversation, some comment of which triggers a brief analepsis illustrating how Guy Grand "made it hot for them," that is, how he joked various pretentious, bigoted, greedy, and nouveau-riche exemplars of those American boom-times after the Second World War. The end of each anecdotal chapter comes with the remark that Grand's elaborate practical jokes brought on legal problems, always narrowly escaped by bribing the authorities: "Investigations were demanded. . . . It cost him two million to keep clear" (35). This device, especially in its transitions between chapters, soon becomes formulaic and tiresome.

The striking thing is the way these chapters attempt to reveal Guy Grand as the consummate satirist. His practical jokes — millions of dollars given free to anyone willing to plunge within a sewage-filled swimming pool, or a "Black Devil Rocket" automobile so huge it cannot turn corners on city streets — all snap shut on Grand's dunces with an obvious, morally satirical purpose. At the moment each trap closes, Grand has engineered both a recognition of their folly and a belittling reversal, when they recognize themselves transformed from profitmonger or petty hotshot into the butt of another's joke. This much is standard, generative satire. What's disturbing, though, is the way Southern represents the satirist as a privileged gentleman, implying that only a prince among the wealthy, one used to sitting on the thrones of power, could be authorized to attack the vanities and excesses of monetary culture. Equally disturbing, he implies that a satirist keeps his privileged distance, away from the contamination he vilifies, by rarely, and then only prodigally, manipulating the very germ of that contamination: his money. In fact one is never allowed to forget that Guy Grand can afford to *pay* for the practice of his art. Hence (again) the close of each chapter reminds us that "it did cost him a good bit to keep his own name clear" (46). At the most abstract level of story, these inferences of authority and distance are inextricably tied to the narrative logic of Southern's satire. It rephrases a popular American myth about the wealthy but cynical gentleman bohemian who uses his privilege to ridicule the very culture that endows him, as if only the princely can be authorized to assail the terms of their mastery.

Finally, the most problematic thing about *The Magic Christian* is Southern's failure to question that myth. There is one point, midway through the text, when he comes close. Having taken over a firm called Vanity Cosmetics, Grand lectures the board members in streams of cliché. This ends when he addresses the twin needs their new advertising campaign must meet. "One, the insatiate craving of the public for an *absolute;* and two, the modern failure of monotheism, that is to say, the *failure* of the notion that *any absolute* can be presented as a separate thing" (67). Momentarily, Grand verges toward what this novel aspires to be, a satire of a society in which any material product, including texts, can be marketed as the substitute for that "absolute," or transcendental signifier, demanded by an "insatiate" population of gulled consumers. Yet just as quickly Southern veers away from that theme, no doubt because Guy Grand, as both profiteer and satirist of that hungry public, was simply too self-contradictory. Fat "little" Grand was clearly meant to exemplify that feisty pugilist in Southern's epigraph, from the Texas Rangers: "Little man whip a big man every time if the little man's in the right and keeps a'comin." But it's never certain who, or what, that "big man" must be, unless it is also Guy Grand, himself the wealthiest aboard that actual ship of fools, Grand's most elaborate practical joke, that gives the novel its title.

Despite Southern's failure to resolve these contradictions, *The Magic Christian* was widely received, in the decade after its publication, as a "profoundly satiric and wildly comic account of our life and times," and later as a seminal work of Black Humor.[39] Davis, whose 1967 anthology included the novel's first chapter, even praised its contradictoriness as "the ultimate cool in Black Humor," because Southern neither "approves nor disapproves the behavior of his hero."[40] The idea was to applaud the book for a renegade amorality that seemed, like Donleavy's, "beyond satire." Still, this neglected the really conventional nature of Southern's humor: a "practical joke," by its very essence, contrives everyday custom into a "plot" constructed to embarrass and shame the victim. In sum, it adheres to the didactic, punitive, corrective, and normative elements of traditional satire; it is a generative aggression. Moreover, such practical joking maintains that subject/object dichotomy, or "ironic distance," defining traditional ridicule. It develops none of the ambiguity that Hassan and others, recalling Freud, had identified in the new "humor." This is *The Magic Christian*'s greatest shortcoming, something pointed out by a few reviewers but never addressed by the promoters of Black Humor. Indeed, even until 1980 the book was still referred to as "the movement's major text," in whose unfortunate "castration" by American editors one might have foretold the decline of Black Humor. Probably overstated, this claim nonetheless indicates the quality of argument that has surrounded Black Humor for too long.[41]

In Freud, humor is significant as an overthrowing of what drives the self to despair. Humor surmounts the subject/object dichotomy, erases the conventional ironic distance, upsets the legitimacy of rationalist conventions, and breaks up in its explosive laughter the causalities of ordinary narrative. The Black Humorists aptly discovered a renewed source of antirealist power in such modes of joking humor. Too often, however, that tendency produced a writing that, as Charles Newman has said, functioned chiefly as a wisecracking, hard-boiled parody and thus as a "counterweight to apocalyptic existentialism, as if someone had put sunglasses and jogging shoes on Camus' Sisyphus."[42]

Fictions like *The Magic Christian* gave credence to the charge that many Black Humorists had retreated into aesthetic cleverness. In Southern's writing, as in the fiction of Donleavy, Friedman, and much of Vonnegut, the predilection for jokes, especially for types of practical joking, was evidence of an adroitly fractured but finally old-fashioned, generative satiric practice. However discontinuous, such novels still voiced a single-minded rhetoric, clearly targeted and normative. They performed the work of hegemonic consensus-building. This is why a good deal of Black Humor never lived up to its billing.

More deeply at issue were problematic concepts of irony that the Black Humorists and their critics never fully untangled. The ironies of a novel like *The Magic Christian* — indeed, the ironies of most garden variety Black Humor — are easily decoded, what nineteenth-century theory called "specific." In Wayne Booth's terminology, such ironies are "stable," because the reconstruction of meanings is always "local, limited," and it does not further "mock our efforts by making general claims about the ironic universe, or the universe of human discourse." In Alan Wilde's alternative terminology the ironies of such a text are "mediate," expressing a familiar "world lapsed from a recoverable (and in the twentieth century, generally a primitivist) norm."[43] Yet from its first proclamations Black Humor was differentiated as a writing that hinged on "general" and not "specific" ironies. Black Humor, said its promoters, locates symbols of "a metaphysical void" and thus ironizes "questions of ultimate significance." This was its putative difference from centuries of satire: insofar as they focus on "the chaos" of "a vast, indifferent universe," the fictions "of authentic black humor are predicated on an overwhelming vision of despair" that lies "beyond satire." The critics were also well aware of the intellectual heritage authorizing such distinctions, many noting that, as one put it, "[t]he technique of Romantic Irony therefore reappears in the Black Humorists' fondness for the put-on, the joke."[44]

In Booth's rhetorical categorization, general or romantic irony situations are "unstable," so-called because "the truth asserted or implied is that no stable reconstruction can be made out of the ruins revealed through the irony" (240). Wilde's historical approach identifies two subcategories of that ironic instability: first, the modernists' use of a "disjunctive irony" that accepts fragmented being as a kind of oxymoronic, paradoxical wholeness, and second, in the postmodern decades, a "suspensive irony" that moves to actually "embrace" multiplicity, randomness, and disorder (10). I mention these two recent studies because they rest on two centuries of theory that limits satire to ironies classed as specific, "stable," or "mediate." Indeed, so content is Wilde with this historical schema that he refers to his "disjunctive" and "suspensive" ironies as "postsatiric" (29).

This is not the place for a full-scale study of irony, and one need only make several observations before moving on. The first is that students of modern irony invariably begin their surveys by defining it *against* a model of generative satire. When Wilde, for example, claims that "satire is, relatively speaking, a minor form in modern times, its notion of correctable error or folly superseded" by types of general irony (28), he is setting the stage for a diachronic theory that nevertheless always recalls, like a dream of origins, this synchronic idea of satirical irony — again, that "ridiculing of human vices and follies in order to correct them" — repeated in countless textbooks and handbooks.[45] But there is simply no warrant for assuming the stability of satire, when satire is seen as a function of modal conventions that are, by definition, always responsive to cultural change. My second observation, then, is that theories of irony have been so crucial in our narratives about the Romantic, modern, and (now) the postmodern "breakthroughs" — indeed, irony itself is so central in our critical and pedagogical lexicons since the New Criticism — that theories about it are (ironically) quite resistant to change. Anyway, it is doubtful that a more diachronic approach to satiric practices will pose any serious problems for prevailing concepts of irony. The concern, here, is with literary reception. For while concepts of irony have had increasingly less to say about satirical practice, those concepts nonetheless continue to skew the promotion and discussion of new writing. Black Humor is a case in point, one that reminds us how theories are not passive descriptive constructions.

Now, if Black Humor mattered, it was as a satirical practice of potentially endless subversion, something genealogically related to the writings of West, O'Connor, and Hawkes. Had they wanted, the Black Humorists could also have located a powerful precedent for this shift in André Breton's definition of *humour noir*. In his preface and in the various introductory comments about writers included in the *Anthologie de l'humour noir* (1939), Breton defines such writing as a "mécanisme de subversion intellectuelle."[46] Intelligence can use it to "set aside" or even surmount the utilitarian, normative limits to which reason insists that we submit. This is possible because "intelligence" comprehends both the total freedom ("toute licence") and the precision ("rigueur") essential to *humour noir,* and as such intelligence has no *necessary* links to the didactic, moralistic purposes that reason conventionally attaches to "L'intention satirique" (17). Equally interesting, Breton also describes this process with reference to Freud's discussion in *Jokes and their Relation to the Unconscious.* To a point, his is a rather standard deployment of Freudian concepts. Breton sees *humour noir* as a confrontation of the pleasure principle with the apparent limits of the "real" world, as reason (the reality principle) would delineate them (19–21). Like the joking of Freud's gallows humorist, then, *humour noir* is to Breton a free and subversive displacement, into pleasurable laughter, of affective energies such as anxiety or disgust. In comparison, traditional satire intends those emotions for cathexis (on the satiric "object" or "target") in order that they might be inhibited, recontextualized in some morally normative order.

A revision of the rules for satire, Breton's *humour noir* gave up the stability of norms for a potentially unceasing disruption — surely its most remarkable move. His black humor registers the anxiety and even the abjection one feels amid the myriad of mass-produced artifacts in late-industrial society, but it neither represses nor sublimates that emotion according to some other ideal. Instead, it displaces the emotion into a laughter that verges right back into the centerless midst of things. It is an art of surfaces where, taken at face value, ordinary mass-cultural artifacts seem to carry on their own (humorous) discourses. At an extreme the writer risks even that vaunted detachment of the conventional satirist, risks succumbing to what, in prefacing a selection from Swift, Breton calls an "atroce lucidité" about our everyday surroundings (26). Its laughter does not stop and is "l'ennemi mortel" of utilitarian reason, which finds no way to put it to work (21).

This summary suggests some important parallels with American Black Humor, with the kind of "suspensive" ironies often linked to it, and with the mode of satiric action previously seen in the fictions of West, O'Connor, and Hawkes. The concern for both precision ("rigueur") and freedom ("toute licence") is highly suggestive of, for example, O'Connor's technique in *Wise Blood,* and the proneness to hysterical lucidity characterizes the writing of West and Hawkes. Unlike their cousins, the "suspensive" ironists, these writers are not willing to "embrace" the chaos of surface-realities about them. They *are* willing to displace laughter into its midst and thus disrupt that environment by turning the culture's fables of order and repression against itself. There are fundamental differences here. In all its forms, *irony* sustains a fixed reference point, a continuous ego to embrace the surrounding disorder. By contrast, Black Humor illustrates what happens in the postmodern novel when that fixed point can no longer be trusted, when the "subject" begins to dissolve and *humor* reveals it as yet another surface, or masking fiction, of a dissimulating humanity.

To illustrate this shift from an "ironic" to a "humorous" satire in American postmodernism, it is instructive to compare two related but greatly different novels of the late fifties, Nabokov's *Lolita* and Southern and Hoffenberg's *Candy.* Because of censorship problems in this country, both texts were first published in Paris by Maurice Girodias's Olympia Press, *Lolita* in 1955 and *Candy* in 1958 (under the pseudonym of "Maxwell Kenton"). Both books were eventually released at home (by Putnam's, *Lolita* in 1958 and *Candy* in 1964); both became best-sellers, then films, and were hailed as early Black Humor classics. There, however, the similarities end.

*Candy* is a satire based on traditionally "stable" ironies.[47] Resilient in the tradition of a Gulliver or Candide, Candy's coed naiveté is overthrown at every turn by her antagonists' voracious appetites for sexual usury, a mechanistic lust to which she always yields, as her chance "to help" others. At novel's end these excesses are literally unmasked, the illicitness of both their mastery and her naive altruism driven home in Candy's final refrain, a squeal of delighted (incestuous) apprehension — "Good grief, it's Daddy!" — when she finds herself in the arms of her resurrected, mud-smeared father, Mr. Christian. The authors' simile for this usurious economy is brain damage, figured in the accidental lobotomy that Candy's hispanic lover inflicts (with a trowel) on her father. As for Candy, the satire plainly identifies the etiology of her own damaged psyche in the surrounding culture, whose "appearances" (a recurring word) are overthrown, in chapter after joking chapter, through specific ironies that disclose practices of white slavery behind every polite, genteel mask — medical, educational, political, spiritual — of the repressive consumer culture in which American girls are raised to be faithful, yielding spouses.

*Lolita* can be read as an unraveling of the limits to that traditional satire. It takes off from a similar formula, paternal lust for the (apparently) naive schoolgirl, and Nabokov situates that obsessive desire within the same material culture, in the forging of which he appears to have known the delights of Daedalus, for he described it in his afterword as "the task of inventing America."[48] The difference, and it becomes a very great one, is that Nabokov comprehends America as a "language" (288). This opens possibilities for satiric disruption that run well beyond the gamut of typecast targets and anticipated unmaskings in *Candy*. Indeed, the reader's progress through the text of *Lolita* is like a journey through the forms of traditional satire and irony considered here toward the subversive satire of postmodernism.

*Lolita* opens with a ruse. Its "Foreword," subscribed by "John Ray, Jr., Ph.D.," introduces the narrative as the confessional autobiography of a convicted murderer and self-described nympholept. Excepting the names, many of its details are, as Ray goes out of his way to suggest, verifiable for "old-fashioned readers" (6). More important, he next proposes a reading of Humbert Humbert's "memoir." See it, he urges, as the *document* of a monstrous passion; Humbert's craving for adolescent girls "is horrible, he is abject, he is a shining example of moral leprosy." Nonetheless his affliction would have been curable in the hands of "a competent psycho-pathologist" (7). Not only an indictment, then, the putative memoir should also be read as a "lesson. . . . 'Lolita' should make all of us — parents, social workers, educators — apply ourselves with still greater vigilance and vision to the task of bringing up a better generation in a better world" (7). The "Foreword," in sum, proposes the same corrective-normative potential of documentary forms which, as the Black Humorists complained, had lately seemed to crowd satire. And for a time Humbert's own comments tend to support such a reading. He "tried hard to be good" (21) and even wistfully strove, in marriage, for "the eventual flowering of certain moral values" (22). Moreover, Humbert suggests his abjection has an identifiable origin in the unconsummated passion for little Annabel Leigh in their "Kingdom by the Sea." Thus he infers that the memoir, if it hews to the conventions of narrative order (origin, action, and dénouement) and of documentary realism ("I am only a very conscientious recorder") will finally trigger (in readers, at least) the catharsis that John Ray, Jr., had expected at the hands of "a competent psycho-pathologist."

Humbert himself razes the structure of this reading. Recalling "a bout with insanity" just preceding his arrival in Lolita's household, he describes finding a method of "self-cure":

> I discovered there was an endless source of robust enjoyment in trifling with psychiatrists: cunningly leading them on, never letting them see that you know all the tricks of the trade; inventing for them elaborate dreams, pure classics of style (which make them, the dream-extortionists, dream and wake up shrieking), teasing them with fake "primal scenes"; and never allowing them the slightest glimpse of one's real sexual predicament. . . . The sport was so excellent, its results — in my case — so ruddy that I stayed on for a whole month after I was quite well. (34)

A remarkable passage, this can well be taken as a description of Humbert's entire "memoir." If so, it discounts, as mere "sport" or play, every quality of the text as a documentary narration: its plot, its well-managed enigmas, its otiose "style," even the supposed origin or "primal scenes" of Humbert's obsession, still fresh in the reader's mind. It travesties any curative prospects for a truthful narration, and even delights in the power of hyped-up storytelling as a form of counterterrorism against interpreters, such as ourselves, who "extort" performances from tortured psyches (for stories about normal folks would be as compelling as eight hours of Andy Warhol's film, *Sleep*).

Humbert proposes the next reading. He is not, he pleads, "abnormal" at all. His only difference from other "big males" is in the pursuit of a romantic rapture. In fact, this reading develops the potential of an earlier comment: "the sensations I derived from natural fornication were much the same as those known to normal big males consorting with their normal big mates in that routine rhythm which shakes the world. The trouble was that those gentlemen had not, and I had, caught glimpses of an incomparably more poignant bliss" (20). Chapters 10 through 33, the remainder of part 1 after he takes up lodging in the Haze household, amplify this possibility. Humbert regards himself as a poet; during these chapters he frequently sets himself apart as a member of that fraternal order, "we poets," and his endeavors for Lolita he therefore portrays as the search for a transrational, poetic "rapture." However, what he realizes all along, and what the banal details of that pursuit make clear, is that this "romantic soul" (51) strives to possess, not Dolores Haze, but his "own creation, another fanciful Lolita — perhaps, more real than Lolita; overlapping, encasing her; floating between me and her, and having no will, no consciousness — indeed, no life of her own" (59). Humbert's is the will of a romantic, the rage for intimations of an unalterable "bliss" that imagination creates beyond the ravages of time. So when he first sees Lolita, Humbert exclaims that the "twenty-five years I had lived since then [Annabel Leigh], tapered to a palpitating point, and vanished" (39). And when, astonishingly, contingent events seem actually to conspire with his gargantuan will, by killing off Charlotte Haze, Humbert sees "the beginning of the ineffable life which, ably assisted by fate, I had finally willed into being" (104). Yet his retrospective narration is equally well aware of the Romantic ironies. A wearying mediocrity, and mortality itself, conspire against him. Thus Humbert, on the verge of possessing his ideal: "I should have understood that Lolita had already proved to be something quite different from innocent Annabel [and that] nothing but pain and horror would result from the expected rapture" (115). The reader further recalls that Humbert was, amid other pursuits, the author of a paper on Keats, and therefore the reading he puts before us would make Lolita into his Lamia, Keats's symbol of a rapturous, unobtainable beauty always ironized by the monstrous. Indeed, as Humbert's great seduction scene draws nigh he laments, "The beastly and the beautiful merged at one point, and it is that borderline I would like to fix, and I feel I fail to do so utterly. Why?" (124).

Why indeed? First, because that seduction tends toward a drugged imprisonment (he has slipped little "Lo" a depressant), itself a reflection no doubt on the nature of Humbert's romantic obsession. Also, (ironically) because experienced Lolita *initiates* their copulation. She is not the Lamia at all, just a somewhat precocious, sometimes vulnerable adolescent already well on her way toward Humbert's last image of her, married and pregnant at seventeen, "with her ruined looks and her adult, rope-veined narrow hands and her gooseflesh white arms, and her shallow ears, and her unkempt armpits" (253). Finally, because the rapture had "plunged into nightmare," a condition Humbert defines as nothing more or less than a return to everyday morality and its "pangs of guilt" (129). His quest for romantic "rapture" has turned into a cacoethean lust. The attempt to "explain" his life as grand romantic irony has collapsed into everyday banalities.

In part 2, that residue of banal, mortal guilt turns into venomous satire. Suddenly Lo seems "a most exasperating brat" and "a disgustingly conventional little girl" (136). This surely comes as no surprise to readers, who have already noticed the marks of her callow vulgarity in prior scenes. But in fact Lolita is *not* the target of Humbert's scorn, the worst of it falling instead on the culture that shaped her. He snarls, "She it was to whom ads were dedicated, the subject and object of every foul poster" (136). In one sense this is literally true: her first attaction to Clare Quilty, Humbert's nemesis and grotesque double, was through that popular playwright's endorsement in a Drômes cigarette ad. Yet in a broader sense Humbert has defined Lo's truly central, monstrous role, as both signifier and signified, product and consumer, aggressor and victim in a popularly marketed travesty of husband-wife and father-daughter love. So Humbert's method, throughout these chapters, is to let the surrounding dolts convict themselves. The most obvious example unfolds when Miss Pratt, headmistress at Lolita's new school, speaks of "groping," like "a gynecologist feeling a tumor," toward a "relevant" pedagogy that will bestow "the knowledges and the skills, and the attitudes they will need in managing their lives and — as the cynic might add — the lives of their husbands." She concludes this homily with a paean to practicality: "We live not only in a world of thoughts, but also in a world of things. Words without experience are meaningless. What on earth can Dorothy Hummerson care for Greece and the Orient with their harems and slaves?" (162). For all her preaching about the meaninglessness of words "without experience," Miss Pratt's connection of words to their referents is loose at best, as the name "Humbert" slides into "Hummerson." A further point of this passage is that none of the novel's other characters treats adolescence any differently than she does. Despite their practical wisdom, childhood is simply a time to "normalize" sex roles within useful economies, the "harems" of which Humbert's is an exemplary microcosm. Toward the same end Charlotte used to consult what Humbert calls "a fool's book" on "Your Child's Development" (76), but he himself gropes for hints in the newspaper's "Column for Teens" (169).

So one irony is that part 2 reveals Lolita as learning *to use* what she always had been: "a modern child, an avid reader of movie magazines, an expert in dream-slow close-ups" (47). Taken into the world of "experience," when Lo cajoles Humbert into a second round of touring, the "knowledges and the skills" of that media-informed upbringing make possible her successful "management" of a mock-husband and even finally an escape with the object of her own romantic fancy, Quilty. The double irony is that this commodified mythology provides Humbert his only (ephemeral) satisfactions.

The penultimate target in these satirical chapters would seem to be Clare Quilty, the playwright-nympholept-sodomist who passes himself off as Humbert's "brother" (225) in order to spirit Lolita away. With his collection of erotica, his popular plays, his "Aztec-Red Convertible," his Drôme cigarettes, "slaves" and other hangers-on, Clare Quilty is just what his name implies: the glitzy, patchwork travesty of every lofty romantic passion Humbert attributes to himself. So overwhelming is this travesty by narrative's end, that after shooting Quilty a "burden even weightier" (277) falls on Humbert, for he is literally as well as figuratively "all covered with Quilty" (278). The man who was his alter-ego, "this semi-animated, sub-human trickster" (269), is Humbert himself, only stripped of high aesthetic pretense and re-covered with a thick blanket of popular culture. The surface trivia of that culture runs throughout these chapters, in lists of geographical detail from Lo and Humbert's travels ("On N. Broadway, Burns, Oregon, corner of W. Washington, facing Safeway, a grocery"), American pop history (several log cabins "simulating the past log cabin where Lincoln was born"), magazine and newspaper back pages (a column called "Let's Explore Your Mind" wonders "Would sex crimes be reduced if children obeyed a few don'ts?"), and popular entertainments like Quilty's own play, "The Enchanted Hunters." If Humbert sojourns in this landscape like an existentially displaced person, Quilty is its grandest manipulator, perhaps (therefore) Humbert's hero. The final blow is that, as the older, pregnant Lolita tells Humbert, this man who starred in the Drômes ad was the only one she ever loved, "and he threw her out" (252). In addition, unlike Humbert (who could be said to cuddle Mnemosyne herself), Quilty can scarcely remember Dolores Haze, except as another disposable object in the commercial exchange that is his life. This is not, as in *Candy*, a mere matter of overthrowing polite, genteel "appearances" to reveal the wormy putrefaction underneath. In *Lolita* appearances are exactly all there is, with nothing beneath the surface.

The novel's ironies, the generatively satirical and the romantic, end there. Lolita is gone and the satirist, in an old device of satiric art, examines a monstrous version of himself. What follows next in *Lolita* is something subtly but crucially different. Humbert announces the shift at the beginning of chapter 25 in part 2. "This book," he says, "is about Lolita; and now that I have reached the part which might be called *Dolorès Disparue*, there would be little sense in analyzing the three empty years that followed" (231). Having earlier given up the prospect of a "cure" through documentary realism, having seen his precious romantic ironies smash into ordinary junk and his modernist satirical fabling come up short against the sheer breadth of American mass culture, Humbert now gives in to the degenerative drift. He gives up the demand for factual veracity, leaving behind representation for language play, mimesis for diegesis.

This means, in sum, leaving behind the morally normative aims of a traditional satire for a "humorous" (postmodernist) satire. Humbert does this by plainly acknowledging his guilt, then moving on:

> Alas, I was unable to transcend the simple human fact that whatever spiritual solace I might find, whatever lithophanic eternities might be provided for me, nothing could make my Lolita forget the foul lust I had inflicted upon her. Unless it can be proven to me — to me as I am now, today, with my heart and my beard, and my putrefaction — that in the infinite run it does not matter a jot that a North American girl-child named Dolores Haze had been deprived of her childhood by a maniac, unless this can be proven (and if it can, then life is a joke), I see nothing for the treatment of my misery but the melancholy and very local palliative of articulate art. (258)

In terms of the novel's temporal ordering, this nearly catches one up to the same imprisoned, backwards-glancing Humbert who lamented to Lolita, at the beginning: "I have only words to play with!" (32). One symptom of this playfulness in the final chapters is Humbert's long lists that now approach a chaos, the key moment of which is his insanely lucid, poetic death sentence (a redundant parody of T. S. Eliot's "Ash Wednesday") recited to Quilty before he calmly spatters the man over his papered walls. Yet that grotesquely playful aggressiveness — in "articulate art" — has been there all along, in the puns, pastiches, and parodies strewn from one end of the novel to the other.

Formerly the reader had been allowed the luxury of seeing them as petty indulgences and aimless coincidences, in all, a concupiscent verbal sport, but in the closing chapters one sees them, no matter how contingent their origin, as parts of a pattern. For if Humbert's relations with his legal stepdaughter have been read as the travesty of a conventional morality governing paternal love and the passion of lovers, then his language play has also disclosed how that conventional morality is encoded in language. Thus Humbert's "memoir" has become, at this stage of the reading, a colossally humorous labor of subversion, its "target" that ordinary language which had all along been conspiring with but also *against* him. This is as true of the American advertising idiom, with its punning invitations — "Children welcome, pets allowed" (134); "Children Under 14 Free" (135) — as it is of self-help books like *Know Your Daughter,* with its "unintentionally biblical title" (159), or even of laws such as the Mann Act, "a dreadful pun, the revenge that the Gods of semantics take against the tight-zippered Philistines" (138).

*Lolita*'s first generation of critics, no doubt bearing in mind the "mythic method" of canonical modernism, have tended to focus their remarks on Nabokov's broader parodies: his uses of Poe, of romantic myth and the myth of Lilith, his parody (sometimes quite overt) of the detective fiction genre. The reading argued here, and toward which Humbert himself takes clear steps, would see the novel's parodies as larger structures for that disruptive consciousness strewn, in miniature, throughout the text. Humbert says, at the start, that he has "only words to play with." At the end he has demonstrated not only that the narration was forged out of words and not documentary facts, but that words have played with him, forging that atrocious lucidity which is his madness. After killing Quilty, he acknowledges it: "This, I said to myself, was the end of the ingenious play staged for me by Quilty" (278). He recognizes how ordinary language, itself an arbitrary system of signs, has victimized him. But even this is not all. Nabokov's postscript, framing the text with John Ray's foreword, speaks of how the narration was ordered by "secret points, the subliminal coordinates by means of which the book is plotted" (287). Those "secret points" are nothing else than the countless puns and bits of surface trivia, like the mentions of Quilty in gossip or the popular press, about which Humbert reminds us at key moments of disclosure. More than just a seconding of Humbert's recognition that ordinary discourse has sported with him, Nabokov's postscript thus drives home the crucial uncertainty for readers: one can move from the everyday language of America to the language of narrative plot and then back, seeing how both compelled the other. In the midst of such a back-and-forth shuttling (for that is what it means to reread such a text) *Lolita* refuses to settle on any totalizing "theme" or "moral." There is nothing to "explain" it, except as an enormous act of manipulation, by and against the several voices and idioms performing the text that we read.

In this sense, *Lolita* does make what Wayne Booth and others call "general claims about the ironic universe, or the universe of human discourse."

And doubtless this is why the novel was widely acclaimed as an early Black Humor classic: it actually did push "beyond" traditional ironic-satiric modes into a disruptively playful, morally uncertain ethos that Nabokov himself had trouble identifying with satire.[49] Still, like many other fictional protagonists from the period, Humbert Humbert is all surface, another construction of dissimulating human language. Like Zizendorf in Hawkes's *The Cannibal* or the fictional "Richard Nixon" in Coover's *The Public Burning,* he travesties the stable narrating subject: look at it very long and the one figure dissolves, as if in a print by Escher, into another figure composed from the objective trivia of American discourse. Humbert's only constancy is in acts of counterterrorism against the storytelling machine of which we, as "dream-extortionists," are always potential cogs. In its relation to American popular culture, this is *Lolita*'s unsettling legacy and is what makes it a classic of American postmodern satire. With its joking antipathy to the mimetic conventions of realist narrative, its blurring of the old subject/object split, the book self-consciously records the emergence of a destabilizing "humor." In addition the novel locates that humor against each of the modes of documentary realism, Romantic irony, and traditional satire that successively prove inadequate to the subversiveness of its vision.

The example of *Lolita* shows how, at its best, Black Humor could stand as a counterweight to the forms of existentialist irony prevalent in the American postwar decades. Too often in recent American fiction, irony has operated like the "non-denial denial" of contemporary politicians. Irony confers seriousness; it reaffirms the historical place of an authoritative Self, who coolly tips the hand of Secret Knowledge, promising but never disclosing the whole, and at worst it becomes static, referring principally to itself. Black Humor was capable of satirizing that game, of turning its disruptive spasms against the languages with which the game has been played.

Humbert's narration is, as he implies, covered with a thick "quilt" of pop-cultural stuff. Elements of what Jonathan Culler terms "a descriptive residue" from realist narrative, references to American material culture belabor the text in lengthy catalogues, themselves disconnected from any symbolic or thematic codes. Their only conventional function, "that of denoting a concrete reality" outside the book, is troubled by sheer excess and by the obvious pleasure Humbert takes in their ephemerally verbal surfaces.[50] The nouns refer back to themselves and, even further, back to a shadowy magical power, for in a further travesty of their function in realist novels, such references even seem to *become* the narrative force. It would be quite effective to say that the plot of *Lolita* is determined, not by some distant memory of Eros, but by a magazine ad for "Drômes" cigarettes, itself the commercial displacement of erotic desire.[51] No longer just parts of the mimetic illusion, pop culture thus seems to mock characters' efforts to structure meanings. And whereas the modernist avant-gardes regarded it as the sign of intelligence suspended, pop-culture now reveals itself, as Roland Barthes has shown in *Mythologies,* as the displaced shape of thought.

That shape increasingly became the *topos* of new satirical work. As the figure made by a welter of competing discourses, it is both subject and object, vehicle and "target" of the satiric aggression. *Lolita,* a novel that charts the progress toward that *topos,* brilliantly anticipated the Black Humorists' concern with American pop culture and its expression in everyday speech. Indeed, by the time of Donald Barthelme's 1967 novel *Snow White,* the satire is no longer "about" any denoted "reality," but about signification itself. As one character remarks, in a loose parody of linguistic discourse, "You know, Klipschorn was right I think when he spoke of the 'blanketing' effect of ordinary language, referring, as I recall, to the part that sort of, you know, 'fills in' between the other parts. That part, the 'filling' you might say, of which the expression 'you might say' is a good example, is to me the most interesting part."[52] Pop culture is what "fills in" the contemporary world, and an interest in it holds throughout Barthelme's novel and others from the sixties, where signs that were in between, or simply backgrounded, are made central and shoved into the foreground. Black Humor turned on such playful disruptions of field. Critics saw such techniques as evidence of how, for the Black Humorist, "all versions of reality are mental constructs," whose use in the text demonstrates that no one construct "verbally or morally preempts all others."[53]

Yet the concern of these new satirists was not merely (nor even primarily) with this apparently relativistic, morally neutral ethos, what became known as the "metaphysics of multiplicity," a phrase that Schulz coined and a number of critics quickly seconded.[54] Instead, the Black Humorists' concern was with the conflict between "the real," as a Babel of signs, and "the self," as both manipulator and victim of those signs. Language, and especially storytelling, was taken as the best index to that conflict, a locus for the frictions, losses, disorders, combustions, and aggressions that result when signs are turned loose in seemingly aimless dialogue or passive description. As such there is nothing morally neutral about Black Humor fiction. In *Snow White,* for instance, Barthelme's self-conscious play with languages generally regarded as verbal wastes, as "dreck" or a "trash phenomenon," was one aspect of a mode in which all signs, as Susan Sontag once remarked about the "Camp" sensibility, are bracketed within scare quotes.[55] Beneath either logo, Black Humor or Satire, these fictions thrived on a mode of exposure, of humorous, often outraged dismantling.

Clichés, scraps of conversational idiom, brand names, familiar quotes, commercial images, and popular anecdotes are, after all, only deceptively inertial. Whenever used, they threaten to rub against one another, then perhaps take off, releasing vapors of desire and aggression that normality would successfully absorb or displace. This abnormal, subversive action was thematized, probably better than in any other Black Humor novel of the sixties, in *Snow White,* where all significations, especially the different versions of "Snow White" itself, are displaced either into forms that frustrate desire (for connection, completion, comprehension) or, what is nearly the same thing, into forms of aggression. A number of proleptic references suggest that Paul, the novel's frog/prince, will be eaten. And language itself becomes cannibalistic, as Jane threatens in a letter to a total stranger, Mr. Quistgaard, picked at random from her telephone book. "The moment I inject discourse from my u. of d. [universe of discourse] into your u. of d., the yourness of yours is diluted. The more I inject, the more you dilute. Soon you will be presiding over an empty plenum, or rather, since that is a contradiction in terms, over a former plenum, in terms of yourness. You are, essentially, in my power. I suggest an unlisted number" (46). In brief, here is a portrait of satire as postmodern, semiotic terrorism.

As such, Black Humor was a close sibling of Pop Art. Like Black Humor, Pop traced its beginnings to the mid-fifties, when mass-produced images began appearing within the picture space, and by the early sixties it was also fully recognized as an innovative mode.[56] In its purest forms, Pop mediated *all* representation through preexisting, mechanically forged signs. Susan Sontag rightly saw it as a violence against formal conventions and therefore as a true "anti-art": Pop resisted "interpretation" in any accepted sense. Pop rejected depth for surfaces (Warhol's Brillo boxes), it confused the individual subject with machine-made objects (images of Marilyn Monroe arrayed like huge postage stamps), and it abandoned the search for transcendental signifiers in favor of banal fancies (as in Johns's "Alley Oop"). Yet in carrying out these subversions, the best examples of Pop always *seemed* morally neutral, like Black Humor. As one critic put it, Pop Art wore a very deceptive "mask of subversive acquiescence."[57] Its initial signs, bits of an "information society," were "white," so incessantly iterated as to seem void of meaning.

As a consequence, many chastised Pop for being willfully amoral and for refusing to affirm or negate anything except the accepted ways of representation and interpretation. One way out of this apparent dilemma, as Lawrence Alloway notes, was to view the Pop artist as a traditional satirist, "whose low images in high style magnify the absurdity of popular culture and, by extension, the shallowness of those who use it."[58] There is an analogy here with the reception of Black Humor fiction, which was similarly misconstrued. If anything, however, this only illustrates how formalist definitions of satire have also muddled the discussion of nonliterary art, and the contrast of Pop with Black Humor further suggests that a revised theory of satire should account for a range of postmodernist phenomena. But one reply to these problems, neatly summarized by Iser (following Sontag), was that Pop reacted not against mass culture but against the interpretive conventions that had kept high culture separate from it.[59] In particular, Pop was a blatant challenge to the norm of "hidden meanings" whose "representation through art" could be disclosed by well-trained hermeneuts. As such, Pop also rejected the forms of traditional irony for a new "humor." By remaining faithful to surfaces alone, Pop "resists translation into referential meaning" and makes "an exhibit out of the representational intention."[60] Thus Pop directed attention to the processes of semiotic production and reception, and its exaggerated use of mimetic conventions served to undermine them. In all these respects Pop was quite comparable to the postmodernist satirical novel, with its assaults on storytelling. Still more important, Pop focused on the *dialogical* aspect of any representation. It depended on a "play of signs of different kinds within the picture space" and exposed even with "mere copies" further and deeper layers of derivative signification.[61]

A superb and very influential early example is Lichtenstein's 1962 painting *Takka Takka*.[62] Dominating the lower plane, above green palm fronds, a machine gun spews red flame; suspended above it, in mid-trajectory, are a number of shell casings and a grenade; still higher, overlaid on a highly stylized explosion, is the onomatopoeic phrase, "TAKKA TAKKA," which gives the painting its title; finally, in the upper plane, is a comic book story panel: "The exhausted soldiers, sleepless for five and six days at a time, always hungry for decent chow, suffering from the tropical fungus infections, kept fighting!" A number of Pop's early critics took this and similar examples as quotations of the comic-book originals, but the case, as it happens, is far more complex. Lichtenstein's reworking of the initial image (from a comic about the World War II battle at Guadalcanal) shows a high degree of stylization. He eliminated the horizon line along with any other marks of depth, such as foreshortening; and eliminated furthermore all signs (a hand, an easily identifiable helmet, the Japanese "Rising Sun" insignia) corresponding to the human subjects mentioned in the story panel. One result is a tension between the verbal and visual elements: those "exhausted soldiers" are nowhere to be seen among the machines. Yet this internal, dialogical tension also extends beyond the picture space. *Takka Takka* parodies the "realist" conventions of a comic-book panel, but the panel was itself an abstraction, from countless photographic and cinematic images, of modern warfare, and those images are always ideologically loaded. *Takka Takka* is therefore "about" pop culture, a subversion of its interpretive conventions, but more important it interrogates a shared idea about war, that war's sublime violence heroizes.

Pop Art worked with images belonging to an acquisitive, aggressive culture. Its paintings confront the ordering of that world and the ways of discourse in it and call attention to the dialogical aspect of *any* representation, the way it is composed of anterior images, images "owned" and "exchanged," quite often, by the most venal and violent of souls and institutions. In this sense Pop Art, the "Camp" aesthetic, and Black Humor fiction, all phenomena of the sixties, express the same postmodern satirical temperament. An expression, also, of what many have noticed in the decade's political turmoil, Pop aimed "to undermine the distinction between high culture and popular culture," and to destroy "the illusion of [high] culture as a separate and autonomous development uninfluenced by the distribution of wealth and power."[63] Pop Art was a self-conscious mode of aggressive exposure, and its "targets" were not extramural but other modes of representation and their codes of violence, heroism, and mastery.

Black Humor's early promoters made similar connections. Many echoed Knickerbocker's comment that the new fictions worked "with a kind of glossolalia of imagery" testifying "to a world filled with discontinuities too huge for normal expression." The Black Humorists, he went on, "distrust every vested social interest that claims the right to articulate the national identity," namely "the press, the movies, television, advertising, the universities, business, the government, the military, medicine." This accurately described the *mode* of Black Humor, especially its incredulous outlook on contemporary "universes of discourse." Yet what were the means of putting that outlook to work within a *genre*? The critics never opened that question. Schulz, for example, remarks on the Black Humorists' tendency to mix literary genres such as the detective novel, confessional, and science fiction, but like the other critics he does not go beyond this "farrago of literary syntaxes" to probe the clash of other, more specific, and sometimes nonliterary "syntaxes" within the novels.[64]

Had critics opened that line of inquiry, *Snow White* might have been recognized as a major Black Humor text. Instead, such different writers as Gerald Graff and Christopher Lasch have censured the novel for not providing a morally certain critique of American mass culture, and censured it in language that could not conceal their desire to uphold the authority of "high" culture.[65] They therefore try, erroneously, to read *Snow White* as the discourse of a stable, omniscient narrator, when the text goes out of its way to shatter the dream of a monological narration. Its one hundred and seven episodes employ at least eight separate narrative types. The most prevalent of them, a troubling kind of "dispersed," first-person plural who could alternately be any or all seven of the dwarves, speaks in one-fourth of those episodes, and because each dwarf is associated with a decadent commercialism, this voice is deeply implicated in that dissolution which the narrative records. The other episodes, encompassing a broad hodgepodge of techniques (omniscient third, inner speech, catalogues, monologues, dialogues, quotations, and letters), also implicate the history of narrative in that decline.

Barthelme strengthens that implication by summoning earlier versions of the Snow White tale. In its oral renditions, such as Grimm records, it is a story of deep pathos. A quite vulnerable girl, gifted with physical beauty but unprotected by family, is forced into exile by the monstrous jealousy of a more powerful woman. In a wild forest Snow White nonetheless chances into a dwarfed society, whose equanimity reflects negatively on the violent authority of that larger world she has fled. This inversion makes understandable her attainment of the good, symbolized in the kind Prince she was always fated to have. Yet her achieving that goodness is delayed, first by the need for her to earn it in lowly labor (keeping house), and second by way of a threefold trial (the attempted poisonings) that ends with the wicked Queen meeting a violent end and the Prince accepting Snow White as what she always was, a pure gift, beyond bargaining. As Roger Sale and others have pointed out, these oral versions were unabashedly violent. The Disney film, however, represses that violence while accentuating the theme of glad commitment to one's workaday lot. Disney's is an unabashedly capitalist, Protestant revision: one earns the good by cheery faithfulness to one's "personal calling" in socially useful work, summed up in the "Heigh-ho" song that Barthelme mocks. His dwarves sing it as they skip off to the shower for intercourse with Snow White.

Barthelme's revision of Disney, in its turn, is self-consciously performed as the fantasy of a hip culture in open revolt against the Protestant work ethic. Barthelme's dwarves are humorously diminished versions of an American archetype. Each of them was born in a different National Park, and just as the parks are a nation's reminder of its origins in Edenic wilderness, so the dwarves recollect a dream of the American Adam, that self-made man who mastered the open spaces. But these garden-variety bohemians are only the epigonal versions of that Edenic myth; they are depicted as little fat-cat businessmen amassing a fortune in the manufacture of baby foods. Representatives of privilege and wealth, they move in that pop-cultural world of brand names (like "Chix"), clichés (like a "papered over" crisis), and quotations ("Murder and create!") that Snow White bemoans as a worn-out language (6). Snow White's investment in their workaday world is, as the satire makes abundantly clear, a matter of options strictly limited by anterior discourses (curricula, questionnaires, laws, catalogues, and the like, all predicated on exchange values) just as the film and folktale versions of "Snow White" represent limited economies and have themselves been "marketed" with their ideological messages. By thus containing these anterior versions as intertexts, Barthelme's novel implies that the apparent sexual "revolt" of sixties hipsters against the Protestant work ethic is little more than a dissimulated version of an old, usurious economy. Moreover, with its veiled cannibalism and a botched murder Barthelme's story returns "Snow White" to that violence which Disney had repressed, reminding one that the doctrines of labor and wealthy privilege are often only displaced sides of the same violently acquisitive desire.

To say this much is to spell out implications one would have thought obvious to the novel's main critics. The first is that "Snow White" always contained a "critique," namely, of the high culture from which the young girl is exiled. The second is that like many satires Barthelme's Snow White inverts its "source text." These dwarves departed their wilderness birthplaces long ago; the story begins with Snow White comfortably at home in the main society she will finally leave; and it ends, not with her accession into some "higher" level of being to which she was always entitled, but with the death of its princely representative and her departure into uncertainty. Moreover, it ends with the execution of one dwarf, Bill, for "failure" (180), the primal transgression in a culture whose mania for commercial exchange is rooted in a capitalist ideology of progress and whose most prized artifacts (like stories) are often tools for promoting the doctrine of success. This, at least, is what the intertextuality of Barthelme's Snow White, including its parodies of art criticism and other discourses of hip and *haute culture*, would have readers confront. To speak of this novel in terms of a "gap" between high and mass culture is thus to neglect its main implications.

*Snow White* well represents the "new mutative style" that Friedman detected in Black Humor. Using the dialogical power of various pop-cultural forms to interrogate each other, Barthelme created a satirical fiction whose topic is the concealed violence in seemingly all forms of cultural exchange, including that of storytelling itself. But if that critique of cultural violence were fully accepted, then what should writers *do*? The arch reply to this question produced one of the most malignant of Black Humor texts, James Purdy's 1964 novel, *Cabot Wright Begins*. Denouncing a wholesale degradation that affects all strata of American society, this book ends with one of its many artists declaring, "I won't be a writer in a place and time like the present." Purdy's answer is to impose an offensive silence, itself the flip side or other limit to the condition of satirical hysteria or "glossolalia."

The primary narrative of *Cabot Wright* is straightforward enough for a brief synopsis. Bernie Gladhart, an unpublished novelist whose prior stories have all been about himself, is sent by his wife to "get the story" on Cabot, recently paroled from the penitentiary after his conviction for over 350 rapes committed during a two-year rampage through Brooklyn and Manhattan. For Bernie, Cabot Wright is the perfect subject to bring him successfully "outside" his own troubles. As a former convict, Bernie himself was "corrected" by replaying the "movie" of his crimes "thousands of times with the prison psychiatrist."[66] The job of similarly correcting the life of this mechanical rapist, Cabot, by composing "the truth like fiction," may at last make Bernie "a real writer" (4). Nevertheless, except for locating Cabot Wright through the most improbable of coincidences, Bernie discovers nothing beyond what was already available in journalistic accounts. Bernie therefore slips into a grand alcoholic muddle, the last depot for failed modernists. The further composition of Cabot Wright's life then falls to Bernie's acquaintance, Zoe Bickle, wife of another failed novelist, and herself a failed writer now editing encyclopedia entries. In collaboration with Cabot, and with her own efforts ghost-edited by promoter Princeton Keith, she finishes the manuscript only to have it rejected by Al Gugglehaupt, "the Goethe of publishers," who sees the book as unmarketable, both "dirty *and* hard, and, worse yet, two years out of date" (201–2). Excepting Cabot Wright, who exits laughing, all return home to failed careers and marriages, their bitterness summed up in Zoe's renunciation of even trying to write in contemporary America.

This is the frame narrative. *Its* subject, the "supposititious" young man named Cabot Wright, unfolds in the middle chapters as a composite drawing, both Bernie's and Zoe's. Moreover, that collaborative narration is a virtual hodgepodge of "endless corrections and addenda as it reeled and retraced itself, was interrupted, continued, ran on over lapses of memory, lies, vague echoes, police tapes, gossip-columns and eye-witness stories" (97). This patchwork quality is further complicated by Cabot's lack of *any* stable identity beyond what the media have given him. To Zoe Bickle, he "looked like the mythical clean-cut American youth out of Coca-Cola ads, church socials" (69). He seems a true all-American success story: a boy who overcame a questionable birth, got a Yale education, a beautiful fashion designer for a wife, and employment in a well-known Wall Street brokerage house. But this "mythical" front dissolves into the "composite" which is the young man's language: "Each sentence he spoke seemed to be from a different geographical section of the country" (71). When actually raping, Cabot appeared to his victims as everything from "a Black Muslim" to "a noted Jewish nightclub comic" (176). He has no identity except in performing these media-induced roles, themselves implicated in his pathological yet putatively curative violence against previously frigid middle-class women. Still worse, his recall of those crimes has evaporated into the general haze of stories about himself in the mass media: "In newspapers, magazines, foreign and domestic," he tells Zoe, "I read so many versions of what I did, I can safely affirm that I couldn't remember what I did and what I didn't" (93). In such circumstances, any attempt to discursively "explain" Cabot's violent lapse, to create a totalizing narrative about it, fails at the outset. Cabot's "true" life, which might unlock the origins of his criminality, therefore exists like "beads all strung along" but without "the necklace" (93). It exists as discrete memories, themselves hopelessly corrupted by errors and lies in the popular accounts, which became the basis for Bernie's narrative, itself revised and expanded by Cabot and Zoe, edited by Princeton Keith, and finally abstracted in the reports of three in-house reviewers who recommend against publishing it — among them, a "Talcum Downley" (Malcolm Cowley) who valorized "the Flat-Foot School of Writers" (201). In this sixfold regression Cabot Wright's identity disappears; the beginning signified in Purdy's title is never disclosed.

The problem is not that Cabot Wright is unsuited to the Algeresque myth of success, but that he is impervious to the omniscient, hegemonic perspective such a metanarrative demands. Every attempt at omniscience is struck down by the novel's relentless dialogism, the centrifugal pull of its "versions" away from any stable understanding. At first, for instance, Princeton Keith explains that Cabot's degeneration originates from his being an adopted or "supposititious child" with an apparently "rotten heredity" (39). Later, in Bernie's narrative, Cabot Senior claims his son was "technically not an adopted son," but supposititious only in the sense of being "illegitimate"

(76). Then, whatever significance these putative origins might contain is further nullified by contradictory evidence as to when the young man learned he *was* "supposititious": Cabot says he never heard the charge until a magazine used it *after* his parole (93). Yet even with the genetic explanation thus undercut there remain possibilities for psychosocial explanation. Cabot, for example, seems to remember one day feeling overtired and consulting a quack psychoanalyst, who promptly diagnoses a mysterious, chronic "American exhaustion," then preposterously hangs Cabot like "a side of beef" over a huge padded hook (81). Soon after, he began his "career" as a rapist. But even this version derives wholly from Bernie's suspect manuscript, and nothing Cabot subsequently tells Zoe will lend it any credibility. Instead Cabot's malaise later appears as "America's," a general manic-depressiveness originating from "Hurry-tension" (146). Or, the malaise is laid at the foot of marriage, "the only human destiny, where alone riches lie, Cradle of Commerce! sole reality!" (156).

Between these contradictory reasons, the novel cannot locate Cabot Wright's criminal "beginning" because it never was "inside" him waiting for someone like Bernie or Zoe to "milk it out" (95). His aggression is not psychological but cultural, a condition so general as to symbolize the system of commerce itself. Cabot's wife Cynthia regards intercourse as "sexual commerce" (111), a metaphor whose accuracy is revealed when she embargoes herself against Cabot's sexual advances just prior to his beginning the new "career" as rapist. In Purdy's satire, marriage is the rudimentary economy of that commercial system; Big Business its displaced, monolithic expression; and speed its principal value. About such matters as adultery, for example, "News travels fast," as Zoe tells Bernie (53). And on actual commercial markets, accelerated exchange is the way to increased riches, as well as boredom. Cabot therefore tells one of the court-appointed psychiatrists, "I knew only boredom was possible then, because there was no time for pleasure today, you can just allow yourself that second-and-a-half to hear the message, which is an ad" (139). This general explanation, that Cabot performed his speedy rapes "through boredom," something indigenous to capitalism, provides his only credible motive, however monstrously absurd. *Cabot Wright Begins* thus unfolds as the satire of a relentless fury of commodities exchange encompassing everything — products, bodies, words, stories. "Rape" is Purdy's metaphor for this condition, with its repeated violations of one's private life by public necessities, such as the need to "get the message across" in imaginative work, business, and marriage alike. To be sexually violated is to be one with the cash nexus, and vice versa. For how else can one explain the weirdly curative aftershocks of Cabot's assaults? Like many of his "victims," one woman appreciatively describes how the rape shook her out of an ill-tempered "conformist" life and made her "dynamically integrated," with a husband, hobbies, a thriving "frankfurter stand" on the corner, and an eternal gratefulness "to one Cabot Wright" (181). At his peak — two assaults per day — Cabot regarded himself as a one-man philanthropic fraternity.

If extended, as Frederick Karl notes, this metaphor threatens to spread satire through the entire culture.[67] But it is instructive to trace what happens instead, for the resolution is typical of many Black Humor fictions. As Purdy concludes *Cabot Wright Begins,* he deflects the degenerate satire in two directions. First, into invective satire, which mobilizes the common sense of a speaking subject against single targets. Invective reinforces the processes of values-identification, thus of normative judgment, and as Purdy seems well aware, like Cabot's "rapes" it has the socially curative result of maintaining an aggressive discourse within lanes of commercial traffic. In the embedded narrative, this curative potential is signified by the "Sermons" of Cabot's former boss, "Warby" Warburton, whose writings are a "mausoleum of wrath, indignation, hatred, loathing, distaste" directed against every "stinking level of American life" (170). Cabot reads the sermons in prison and claims "they had such a marked influence" on him as to help — along with police truncheons — in effecting "a cure" (169). Invective is therefore, like rape or prison "discipline," a means of swinging disruptive affects back into economically "useful channels." And Warby's authorship clearly indicates their connection with a supposedly privileged, official wisdom.

Second, however, the novel deflects satire into simple laughter, a "humor" that moves to wipe out common sense. Laughter resists values-identification, is associated not with a judging consciousness but with an instinctual drive for pleasure that is anterior to consciousness, and is opposed to forms of officially sanctioned or absolute knowledge. The same "dark laughter" of which Ihab Hassan had spoken in the very month Purdy's novel was published, such laughter exposes the illegitimacy of any privileged, authoritative discourse. In the embedded narrative, it is well represented by Cabot, who breaks into uncontrollable storms of laughter with Warby's wife Gilda, after raping her and pondering with her the various ways "Life is terrible!" (129).

To fully entrust the novel to such laughter would have also meant trusting the destabilizing effects of its dialogical structures. Yet Purdy was apparently unwilling to do that, insofar as he regarded the cacophony of contemporary mass culture as the culprit, hence the target of his own wrath. In a 1964 letter to Webster Schott, he describes America as "a culture based on money and competition." He went on: "I believe the human being under capitalism is a stilted, depressed, sick creature . . . and that our national life is a nightmare of noise, ugliness, filth, and confusion. I don't believe America has any future."[68] This sounds quite like Warburton's "Sermons," and it suggests that Purdy himself could not (as Nathanael West said of his protagonist, Tod Hackett) "give up the role of Jeremiah." In fact, the connection is confirmed at the novel's close, as Purdy moves from the embedded narrative to its frame. With Warburton now absent from the narrative, an omniscient voice clearly identifiable with the author continues to rage, like Warburton, against the "spiritual emptiness and bodily numbness" of America (208). But now, in the same passages, this rage is also linked with Cabot Wright's laughter, similarly narrated by what can only be a traditionally omniscient, authorial voice, because the events described here unfold after Cabot has deserted his Brooklyn flat and any of his prior "narrators." In a muddy Brooklyn gutter, we are told, "Cabot relieved himself in laughter," and through internal focalization, we are told that his laughter brought "the only relief from the pain of being human, mortal, ugly, limited, in agony, watching Death cornhole you beginning with the first emergence from the winking slit above the mother's fundament, pulled into existence between piss and shit, sorrow and meaninglessness, drudgery and illusion" (213). This grotesque monologue of cosmic gallows humor continues for some time. So powerful is its apparent union of laughter and omniscient invective that Cabot gets the first erection since his imprisonment began, feels "one prolonged orgasm" of delight, then curls up "like a new-born babe" (213). This is our penultimate image of him. Cabot's parting shot comes in a letter to Zoe Bickle in which he describes the absurd deaths of Gilda Warburton, Princeton Keith, and others and claims to have given away all his property, stopped watching television, and developed a total disinterest in the "story" of his life. All of this, he claims, has been preparatory to "running out on America" (228). It inspires Zoe's renunciation of art at narrative's end: "I won't be a writer in a place and time like the present" (228).

As the sixties wore on, Purdy's critique was so overwhelmed by the clichés of antibourgeois, countercultural politics that one must pause for a moment to reconsider how conventional this satire really was. Its degenerative laughter is so tied to the privileged omniscience of his narrator, so much at the service of what the text itself identifies as an aggressive, normative, and curative satire, that its apparent newness could easily deceive. Its conclusion attempted to meld traditional invective, functioning as a generative satire of targets and cures, with the new "humorous" satire, operating as a degenerative aggression (tending to schizoid laughter), that Purdy was unwilling to wholly trust. The result was a satire that tries to have it both ways, and comes up short. The novel's truly radical powers — a merging of the grotesque with subversive laughter and a relentless intertextuality that is very much the *condition* of mass culture — were finally compromised by traditional forms of satire. Yet this was true of many Black Humor fictions: *The Ginger Man*, all of Southern's novels, *Catch-22*, much of Vonnegut and Friedman. In retrospect, a number of popular Black Humor novels were not "beyond satire" at all, but case studies in the principal elements of generative satire as formalist critics had spelled them out.

## Two Exemplary Fictions

The annals of Black Humor thus present a scrambled portrait of the American postwar decades. Many of Black Humor's apparently central figures like Friedman, Southern, and Vonnegut were largely painted in with contemporary techniques of mass promotion, then they either drifted out of the forefront and into other media (Friedman and Southern have been writing filmscripts) or (in Vonnegut's case) produced a kind of novel whose easy adaptability to the screen attests to its conventionally mimetic character. Other figures — Coover, Gaddis, Purdy, and Pynchon — have so assiduously dropped out of the public eye that we scarcely see them, their wariness and cynicism about American mass culture being matched only by their use of it to subvert conventional mimetic forms. In between stands a polyglot group — Barthelme, Donleavy, Hawkes, Heller, and Nabokov — difficult to categorize on formal grounds. Surrounding them all are critical camps whose differences seem to recapitulate lines of sociopolitical debate in the sixties: the formalists (old-guard liberals) who complain that the Black Humorists would accomplish more practical good if they worked within the system of traditional satire and who square off against a seemingly amoral cadre of younger, insurrectionist critics who see the old rules as almost useless in a contemporary information society.

To select representative novels from this canvas is difficult yet necessary. Two novels, by Thomas Pynchon and John Hawkes, do however exemplify key tendencies of all Black Humor fiction. In particular, their fictions are conscious of pressing beyond the formalist conventions for satire. By inviting opposed, even paradoxical readings of their text, both works encode the norms of traditional satire only to cancel them out. By doing so they shift the focus away from "targets" in the actual world — whatever that might mean in the semiotics of fiction — and toward structures of language, taken (at best) as synecdoches for that extramural world. Also, they tend to collapse the boundaries between subject and object, a general tendency of the new humor as distinct from irony, and finally invite one to read their fictional events as a monumental joke. In addition both novels, Pynchon's *The Crying of Lot 49* and Hawkes's *Travesty,* illustrate the tendency of Black Humor to work best in short, novella-length performances that move toward their endings by means of an episodic narration. A word about those endings: a good deal of Black Humor is overtly apocalyptic and approaches that visionary end by means of plots that are almost classic in adhering to traditional "unities." Just so, Pynchon's novel has often been praised for the "structural purity" of its quest-narrative that ends seemingly on the verge of a Pentecostal revelation.[69] Hawkes is also utterly faithful to the Aristotelian unities of space and time in a narrative performance that its narrator refers to as a "private apocalypse." However, like most Black Humor fictions these two novels only achieve such a unity by means of a loose parody, or travesty, of realist forms.

Finally, *The Crying of Lot 49* well represents one tendency of the new satires, their incorporation of pop-cultural discourse, while *Travesty* exemplifies another, the move away from irony and toward the more decentering forms of humor. Hawkes's 1976 novel is also important because, if critics are to find a lasting significance in Black Humor, it must be in new modal qualities of satire that persist long after the promotional hype and theoretical disorder of its reception in the sixties.

### The Crying of Lot 49 (1966)

This was Thomas Pynchon's second book, a "story," he recalls, "which was marketed as a 'novel,' and in which I seem to have forgotten most of what I thought I'd learned up till then."[70] In contrast to that self-deprecating squib, most readers quickly and consistently recognized the book as a major new satire. The paperback edition (1967) certainly hyped that sensibility, its every blurb calling attention to Pynchon's "grim" and "satirical" vision of contemporary America. Comparisons with the work of Nathanael West were also frequent, though never well developed.[71] The novel was generally received as, in Tony Tanner's words, "one of the most deceptive — as well as one of the most brilliant — short novels to have appeared since the last war."[72] This "deceptive magic," he concludes, relates to the quality of its "paradoxes." Similarly to *Cabot Wright Begins,* Pynchon's narrative ends without a conclusive result, which would be a hypothetical beginning for the novel's protagonist, and it does so because the more we learn the less we know.

The problem is to define these qualities in light of that new satirical modality associated in the sixties with Black Humor. It is the traditional satire that foregrounds an inclination to deceit, a doubling of forms resolvable on normative grounds, whereas the postmodern satire embraces paradox, an irresolvable, suspensive doubling that is apparently "beyond" norms. Moreover, *The Crying of Lot 49* is specifically about an inheritance, a central theme in the repertoire of traditional satire. As Michael Seidel shows, satire's degenerative fictions subvert the claims that dynastic descent makes upon continuity and inheritance, and the traditional satirist reveals how man's stubbornness in the face of natural decay is the spur to his greatest deceptions. But like many of his contemporaries Pynchon has further radicalized this idea by locating that decay not only in nature but in culture, and more specifically in the resources of language and interpretation.

The plot of *Lot 49* develops from the complexities of a testamentary inheritance. Oedipa Maas, similar to her tragic namesake, succeeds to a "will" that both determines and betrays her. Her propulsion into that future comes lightning fast, like classical "Fate." Oedipa is jolted from the ordinariness of a fondue-dipping Tupperware party and marriage to a rock-and-roll disk jockey named Mucho Maas by the news that she has been named the "supposed executrix" of a megalosauric estate amassed by her one-time lover, Pierce Inverarity, a California real estate mogul and military-industrial tycoon. Inverarity's sprawling city, San Narciso, seems a virtual microcosm of Cold War America, a masterwork of managerial control. His "interests" have run supply lines into practically everything, from the charcoal in cigarette filters to the "Yoyodyne" engines powering intercontinental rockets. Oedipa inherits nothing less than this America, a contemporary information society so rationally organized as to eclipse reason. Yet San Narciso also is, as the name suggests and Oedipa soon discovers, a dissimulation, a glimmering surface of counterfeit objects, former waste products shipped in from around the globe and raised as props in Inverarity's "synthetic" town. This town, indeed the whole estate, is "really no different from any other town, any other estate."[73] It is the "unsuspected world" of an eccentric power elite, an America Oedipa had never known existed, but only because she had never looked.

Still more unsuspected is the underground economy Oedipa believes she has discovered within this America. Named for its founder, a Spanish nobleman called Hernando Joaquín de Tristero y Calavera, the "Tristero System" has supposedly operated as an alternative postal service since the Holy Roman Empire shattered into a host of Protestant nation-states during the sixteenth century. With its signs apparently all around her in California and derelict persons everywhere using its receptacles — garbage cans labeled "W.A.S.T.E." ("We Await Silent Tristero's Empire") — an Oedipa Maas newly "sensitized" to this system begins haphazardly encountering evidence of its reach. This evidence includes some of the novel's most brilliant satires: the texts, both written and performed, of a mock-Jacobean revenge play entitled "The Courier's Tragedy," an unspoken theme of which appears to be Tristero's struggle; a paranoid group of anticommunist extremists called the "Peter Pinguid Society"; a paradoxical society of "isolates," attempted suicides who call themselves the "Inamorati Anonymous"; the landscape grid of San Narciso itself, bits of which seem to encode moments of the Tristero's past, including a violent rebellion that implicates the whole of American westwarding expansion, including the Pony Express system which first brought mail by overland routes to California; and she encounters it in a batch of eight stamps forged, evidently, by Tristero operatives. This group of stamps both initiates and concludes her quest, when it is designated as "Lot 49" to be "cried" in a philatelic auction at, or really *after,* the novel's end. Its significance is simple. The bidding, as an objective valuation, would disclose how extensive is the secret subversion of those "choosing not to communicate by U.S. Mail," and thus existing "in calculated withdrawal from the life of the Republic, from its machinery" (92). If she is right about the Tristero, or rather, if the "tabernacle" of historical texts dedicated to the Tristero is to be believed, then this system has grown continuously since its founder was "disinherited" from the established postal monopoly in 1578 and compelled to further his rebellion by setting up "his own system" (120).

These two discoveries, equally unsuspected yet insistent, soon begin to shape Oedipa's interpretive choices. They are, Pynchon writes, like an "act of metaphor," being both "a thrust at truth and a lie, depending where you were: inside, safe, or outside, lost" (95). To a large extent Oedipa's dilemma is to decide where *she* is, for claiming her inheritance may necessitate recognizing how disinherited she always already *was.* On the one hand, Oedipa discovers that the dream of managerial control signified by San Narciso, like the "tenor" of a metaphor, has been forged out of base cultural stuff, the literal "wastes" that are its "vehicle." On the other hand she learns this same "W.A.S.T.E." can be raised yet again, as vehicle of a second tenor, the Tristero, which apparently thrives as mortal enemy of the first, in four centuries of bloody rebellions against, and unsuccessful attempts to reclaim an allegedly stolen birthright from, a patrician elite.

This brief summary can hardly do justice to the complexity of detail and digression in what is, after all, just a novella-length fiction. Yet it does serve to introduce the central paradoxes of Pynchon's book. As the protagonist/detective, Oedipa's penultimate induction is that "every access route to the Tristero could be traced also back to the Inverarity estate" (127). Moreover, the entire sequence of events may have been laid out for her like "some grandiose practical joke" Inverarity had "cooked up, all for her embarrassment, or terrorizing, or moral improvement" (128). This realization then triggers what is certainly the novel's key passage, as Oedipa considers the logical alternatives:

> Either you have stumbled, indeed, without the aid of LSD or other indole alkaloids, onto a secret richness and concealed density of dream; onto a network by which X number of Americans are truly communicating whilst reserving their lies, recitations of routine, arid betrayals of spiritual poverty, for the official government delivery system; maybe even onto a real alternative to the exitlessness, to the absence of surprise to life, that harrows the head of everybody American you know, and you too sweetie. Or you are hallucinating it. Or a plot has been mounted against you, so expensive and elaborate, involving items like the forging of stamps and ancient books, constant surveillance of your movements, planting of post horn images all over San Francisco, bribing of librarians, hiring of professional actors and Pierce Inverarity only knows what-all besides. . . . Or you are fantasying some such plot, in which case you are a nut, Oedipa, out of your skull. (128; my ellipsis)

Whichever alternative it reveals, the anticipated "crying of lot 49" must therefore inaugurate the apocalyptic overthrow of Oedipa's former world. The first pair of alternatives would point either to a wholly revised, redemptive image of America or to the deceptive fantasy of such an image, and the second, either to an immense practical joke or to the fantasy of such a joke and, hence, madness.

Another way of conceptualizing these alternatives is to see them as boundary states for narrative representation. According to the first alternative, the utter pathos of society's preterite, every lost, suicidal, derelict soul Oedipa encountered during her search, is recontextualized by some transcendent signifier, an actual or fantasized Mystery-of-Redemption beyond the power of a narrative fiction. According to the second, there is no worldly order at all, no redemptive signifier, just a terrible persecution, an actual or fantasized Madness that, again, lies outside the reach of a narrative fiction. As Molly Hite phrases it, "Pynchon has projected twin 'resolutions' to this second novel that cannot be realized within the novel."[74]

We should press still further and ask how *The Crying of Lot 49* associates these boundary states with two possible readings, both quite conventional, which the text invites readers to formulate. In the first reading, Oedipa Maas appears as a relatively stable subject, a kind of semiotic investigator sifting through troubling but apparently systematic signifiers, mainly the congeries of pop-cultural stuff, and attempting to match their pattern with a single meaning. That meaning will, she suspects, disclose yet another mode of meaning beneath or beyond what is visible on the surface, one that will redeem the American Leviathan and the human wastes to whose production it seems wholly dedicated. As a number of Pynchon's critics have argued, this reading focuses a plot of detection, itself a form of the quest narrative, and its desire for hermeneutic closure is well figured in the novel's final image of Oedipa locked into the auction hall.[75] In a second reading Oedipa would appear as an extremely unstable verbal construct or object, the sacrificial goat in a vast, obsessively detailed hoax, a simple signified that has spun itself out in a welter of signifiers intended to embarrass, terrorize, or instruct her and which finally goad her into fantasies of persecution that mock the desire to connect particulars. In this plot a seemingly obvious meaning — "It's just a joke!" — covers all: *there is no meaning.* So this second reading is equally closed. It interprets the plot, as many of Pynchon's critics have also done, as a form of the anti-quest, in particular as a conventionally parodic inversion of the detective genre.[76] Here, Oedipa is traced through a quotidian, banal world into a madness where every sign of that familiar reality points to her objectification by ghostly hegemonic figures of power and bureaucracy.

So far, these readings are shaped only by the generic constraints associated with novels, yet one might additionally interpret the text, according to prevailing modal conventions, as one or another type of *satire,* again quite conventional. In the first case one would read the text as a social satire whose polemical intent is the correction of an institutional vice; in the second, as the satire of Oedipa as the type of particular folly.[77] The commentary on this short novel is rife with examples of critics who emphasize one reading and diminish the other. However, in associating these satirical conventions with states that the novel (as a form) cannot contain, *The Crying of Lot 49* invites a further inference: with this particular novel, the conventions themselves are invalid. To read by the light of such constraints is to be endlessly caught in a cross fire of interpretations. Eventually, this terrible symmetry will "break down [and] go skew" against the unmanageable possibilities lying in between. As Pynchon writes of Oedipa, "She had heard all about excluded middles; they were bad shit, to be avoided; and how had it happened here, with the chances once so good for diversity?" (136).

What is that "excluded middle," that "diversity" which Oedipa and her conventional reader both neglect? It dins all around her in episodes whose only "point" seems to be the great inconclusiveness, the lack of finality, in that heteroglossia defining her everyday life. Significantly, Pierce Inverarity is its initial representative, a master impersonator whose last phone call to Oedipa had modulated from the "heavy Slavic tones" of someone "at the Transylvanian consulate," into "comic-negro," into "hostile Pachuco dialect," a "Gestapo officer," and then his best Lamont Cranston, voice of radio's "The Shadow," before an ominous and threatening "silence, positive and thorough, fell" (2–3). The incompletion of this telephone call, and its ludicrous fall, neatly anticipates other narrative digressions, indeed the incompleteness of Lot 49 itself.

The lengthy digression of chapter 2 is perhaps the finest instance of this structure. It is, in sixteen pages, a little masterwork of the shifting intentions and diverse interpretations on which the whole narrative is constructed. With a lawyer named Metzger, her co-executor, Oedipa tries to begin sorting through the Inverarity estate. They meet in an "Echo Courts" motel room in San Narciso, and the dialogue very quickly turns from business. Metzger remarks that he was "one of those child movie stars, performing under the name of Baby Igor," and he ends on a blue note: "I live inside my looks," he says, "and I'm never sure" (16–17). Oedipa, however, quickly sees through the romantic come-on: " 'And how often,' Oedipa inquired, now aware that it was all words, 'has that line of approach worked for you, Baby Igor?' " He momentarily returns to Pierce's will, itself "all words," then pulls up short when he notices that the television, droning in the background, has begun one of his films, Cashiered. She doesn't know how to take the coincidence: "Either he made up the whole thing, Oedipa thought, or he bribed the engineer over at the local station to run this, it's all part of a plot, an elaborate seduction plot" (18). A commercial for one of the Inverarity interests, "Fangoso Lagoons," momentarily deflects them back to the will, but when Cashiered begins rolling again Metzger provides a synopsis of its plot, which, as readers soon learn, seems uncannily analogous to aspects of the Tristero past contained (literally, as human bones) in Fangoso Lagoons. Indeed, this slow dissolve of fact into fiction (or vice versa) is the subject of their next digression, on the generality of "acting": "Me, I'm a former actor who became a lawyer. They've done the pilot film of a TV series, in fact, based loosely on my career, starring my friend Manny DiPresso, a one-time lawyer who quit his firm to become an actor. Who in this pilot plays me, an actor become a lawyer reverting periodically to being an actor" (20). Amid these "endless repetitions" Oedipa tests the credibility of his claim about *Cashiered* by making a wager on the outcome of its plot, but any chance of resolving the bet is forestalled, says Metzger, when the TV station runs the reels out of order.

In countless episodes like this one, *Lot 49* insinuates the absurdity of waiting for completion, which the text elsewhere relates to the fulfillment of a Pentecostal prophecy. Instead the Pentecostal state is already all about, a virtual host of voices babbling over the TV or radio, in background and commercials, as well as in the dialogues, from bored to hysterical, of characters she confronts. Equally as much, narrative episodes keep insisting on the fruitlessness of trying to peel back layers of signification in hopes of finding the one clue to that Pentecostal state. At the close of chapter 2, such efforts are compared to Metzger's sexual game, "Strip Botticelli," against which Oedipa insulates herself in layer after layer of garments, only to awaken later, half-stripped, and aware of having missed the sexual crescendo. Or they are like the epileptic who "knows" his seizure only through its anticipatory signs, the "secular announcement" of what is only "revealed during the attack" (69) yet never recoverable as discursive memory.

In two of the most incisive essays to date on this short but difficult novel, John Johnston and Katherine Hayles explore the ideological ramifications of such details. Johnston has shown how the narrative's six chapters unfold in a series of signs presented for Oedipa's (and our) interpretation. At the same time the chapters unfold in a string of men, beginning with Pierce and concluding with the auctioneer Passerine, who each define a subject position vis-à-vis interpretation (55). All are revealed as aberrant in some fundamental sense. They offer no normative or "official" discourse to counter Oedipa's putatively unauthorized, conspiracy-hunting paranoia. The effect, Johnston shows, is to zero-out any perspective attained by the novel's focalizing of events through Oedipa, thus to erase any semblance of a "history," revisionist or not. Similarly, analyzing the Nefastis machine Katherine Hayles problematizes the idea of metaphor of which it is the chief instance. In its expansive phase, Pynchon treats metaphor as a desire "to drive beyond language, to rip through it to what lies behind." Hayles does not say so, but the novel clearly characterizes this push for transcendence as a male endeavor, and it also recognizes, as Hayles makes clear, that achieving such a view would in any case only reveal the constructed nature of reality. The narrative thus always collapses in upon a "necessary equivocation." It refuses to "resolve whether the endeavor . . . is insane or inspired, divine or demonic."[78] Taken together, Hayles and Johnston help to clarify the political work of *Lot 49*. This satire pulls the rug from beneath vested power by denying it, first, any legitimizing history and, second, any totalizing "word" at its millenial end. Both are exposed as dissimulations always open to rewriting on the middle ground of reading.

In *The Day of the Locust,* Homer Simpson's attempts to act on the strength of his desire are always frustrated by his regression into more infantilistic states. Similarly, through his regression in art history, Tod Hackett attempts to impose closure and finality on a degenerate inheritance that knows no stops, and we may read the novel as West's satire on that modernist doctrine concerning the uses of "tradition" to the "individual talent" (in T. S. Eliot's phrase). In Pynchon's metaphor, history, as discourse, is an active deceiver. It is "layered dense" with "the breakaway gowns, net bras, jeweled garters and G-strings of historical figuration" (36); like Oedipa's ploy in "Strip Botticelli," it is quite literally a *travesty,* a "garment-change" or grotesque adornment of what is already both desirable and ludicrous. Moreover, Pynchon everywhere implies that this travesty has a conventionally "virtuous motive" (29), in the sense that historical "figuration" serves as a "buffering" (10, 95) against something unspeakable. An endlessly regressive layering of factual signs and forgeries, of disclosures and dissimulations, history has the ritual function of "insulating" characters from what Mucho Maas experiences as a "salad of despair" in the trade-ins that cycle through his used car lot.

In its most highly socialized, ritual forms, language aspires to the authority of pure will. Like a testamentary inheritance, language demands of its recipients that terms be executed; it aspires to monological finality, something even transhistorical. Its dream, which in this century just as readily flips into terror, is universal assent to the terms of a "natural" descent. We get a mockery of this ideal in Mucho's imagined "chorus" of voices chanting an advertising pitch — "rich, chocolaty goodness" — in a capitalist "vision of consensus" (106). And Pynchon further satirizes this monological dream in chapter 4, the centerpiece episode of *Lot 49.* In Berkeley, a crackpot inventor named Stanley Koteks shows Oedipa a "machine" based on the principle of Maxwell's Demon, an imaginary being who sits between two hermetically sealed containers and arrests the natural slide toward entropy by "sorting" molecules. Oedipa's failure to operate the "Nefastis Machine" underscores both its absurdity and her own failure as a "sorting demon" among historical particulars. Pynchon's satire reveals this failure as axiomatic: language, a cultural system, is prone to "noise" or misinformation in the same way that any natural system tends toward entropic decay.[79]

Like Maxwell's Demon between two closed cells, *The Crying of Lot 49* invites two conventional interpretations of its satire, then it covers those with yet another, more radical idea of satirical process. What matters, in this more radical sense, is neither the detection of origins and etiologies, nor the revelation of corrective actions, the execution of a will. For the disruptions of history are idiopathic, random gaps like the epileptic's seizure, just as linguistic signs are arbitrary and seemingly autochthonous. Instead it is the frenzied exhange of signs, what the narrator calls "information flow" and "lines of communication," that turns people into victors and victims. These lines often exist sub rosa, are often even subrational, yet they are never without motive, as Metzger's seduction of Oedipa, sometimes intentional, sometimes coincidental, demonstrates. To some extent this confusing "diversity" is media-induced. As senile Mr. Thoth complains to Oedipa about a "Porky Pig" cartoon on television, "It comes into your dreams, you know. Filthy machine" (66). Yet Pynchon, unlike Purdy and other Black Humorists, backs away from identifying that condition as an ethical disease. It is, instead, the polylogical ethos within which we all speak, and Lot 49 is, at most, a cautionary tale, "an incident among our climatic records of dreams and what dreams become in our accumulated daylight" (133). Pynchon's satire neither condemns this condition nor tries to effect a cure.

Always at issue, however, is the legitimacy of monopolistic control over those lines of communication, lines that enable a radical dialogism that constitutes the very "diversity" Oedipa fears she has lost. Amid such a panglossian din, no one is ever wholly powerless to act, even if their only recourse is an "unpublicized, private" withdrawal from the Republic's "machinery" (92). In The Crying of Lot 49, society's lowliest souls conduct their pathetic rebellion along the Trash Mainline. This fact is both a sign of their disinheritance and a definitive practical joke, as much on them as on the monolithic state. Indeed, the essential incompleteness of this joke, its humor without the punch line, is satire's lowest blow. It blasts that dream of a totalizing discursive form which the novel, as a genre, acts out. John Hawkes also explores this possibility for a degenerative travesty in his 1976 satire, but with quite different tools.

### Travesty (1976)

Writing in 1962 about Flannery O'Connor's work, John Hawkes was struck by the way her "vigorously moral" intentions depended on an "immoral impulse," a channeling of the fiction through "the 'demolishing' syntax of the devil."[80] The grotesque, eccentric strategies of her style seemed to "demolish" any orthodox morality the story was designed to frame. Her satire, claimed Hawkes, thus put a violent, monstrous vision into severe balance against a seemingly placid, ordinary reality, then it wiped away any distance between the two.

Hawkes might well have been assessing his own work in *The Cannibal,* or anticipating his return to satire with *Travesty,* the short novel he once described as "probably the purest fiction I've written" and as "a comment on *The Cannibal.*" *Travesty* dramatizes that condition Hawkes so admired in Nathanael West and Flannery O'Connor: "clarity, but not morality. Not even ethics."[81] It also brought to fruition many of the satirical tendencies that critics had once labeled as Black Humor. In its extreme brevity and claustrophobic arena, its image of existence as a cruel, sardonic joke, its subversion of traditional, "Romantic" ironies, and especially its exposure of banal, ordinary surroundings as a cover for the most extraordinarily violent human motives — in all of this *Travesty* in many ways stands among the blackest of novels from the period. Furthermore it well represents the tendency of many so-called Black Humor fictions, such as *Lolita* or *The Crying of Lot 49,* to closely follow the conventions of realist narration, but with the aim of covertly assailing them. As such, to read *Travesty*'s "'demolishing' syntax" is to confront a satirical mode that has been central to a line of American fictions beginning with Nathanael West.

The action in this novel has been reduced to an elegant yet deceptively simple equation: the first-person narrator, a "privileged" man who calls himself "Papa," is "talking as well as driving us to our destination" (97). This destiny happens, however, to be a meter-thick stone wall against which Papa intends to crash his sports coupe at a speed of 150 kilometers per hour. His stated intention is to perfectly fuse the qualities of "design and debris": "What I have in mind is an 'accident' so perfectly contrived that it will be unique, spectacular, instantaneous, a physical counterpart to that vision in which it was in fact conceived. A clear 'accident,' so to speak, in which invention quite defies interpretation" (23). As the narrative begins, he has just announced this plot to his terror-stricken passengers. They include his daughter Chantal, who immediately assumes a fetal position in the rear seat and (except for the sounds of her nausea) is never heard from again, and in the front passenger seat a popular poet named Henri, Chantal's mate and, Papa suspects, once the adulterous lover of his wife, Honorine. Should Henri intervene by reaching for the keys or steering wheel, Papa promises to "pitch us into the toneless world of highway tragedy" even before hitting the wall. Meanwhile all other activity, gesture, and speech, including Henri's pleas and counter-polemics, are represented through Papa's discourse. So his passengers are, like ourselves, made the captive audience for Papa's proleptic imagination of the crash, his anecdotal reveries and coolly "rational" philosophizing, all in the name of explaining his obsessive *plot* — now in both senses of that term. *Travesty* is entirely a monologue, a pure performance. Its narrative even adheres to the Aristotelian unities of place and time, and we are told that its central action was carefully rehearsed. The text thus presents itself initially as the rarefied trace of that final performance.

Outside Papa's car rushes an "undeniable world" of objects and lively signs that are "alluring, prohibitive, personal, a mystery that is in fact quite specific" (28–29). Time and again Papa represents it in long lists of everyday stuff, generally concluding with a condemnation or rejection of its banality, and even disparaging the act of naming as a fruitless exercise in "taking our national inventory" (97). His tally of the debris likely to scatter over their crash site ends with the statement that "it is a commonplace, not worth a thought" (19); he finishes off the inventory of a village through which they will blast, calling it a "wretched place" (78). To him, this objective reality is also suffused with the "dead passion" of sexual connection, and "simply to exist in such a world is to be filled with a pessimism indistinguishable from the most obvious state of sexual excitation" (63). He narrates a condition of epigonal, empty desire.

What validates this nihilism? Papa finally supplies the rationale after an hour of his relentless, jeering monologue. He explains the romanticism of his youth: "If the world did not respond to me totally, immediately, in leaf, street sign, the expression of strangers, then I did not exist — or existed only in the misery of youthful loneliness. But to be recognized in any way was to be given your selfhood on a plate and to be loved, loved, which is what I most demanded. But no more" (85). The logic of this is both simple and familiarly absurd. Recognition by a part ("in leaf, street sign") implies recognition by the whole ("to be loved"); it is to be led to "your selfhood" and to triumph over alienation. Yet Papa's plight is the same as for any romantic: valorize objective reality, but then face its inexhaustible particularity, and therefore (like Whitman) the need to endlessly catalogue its atomized bits, for only when it is completely denominated will outer reality "respond . . . totally" to his "demand" for a transcendent signifier. "But no more," he sighs in an access of romantic loss. In what can only be read as a travesty of that predicament, Papa tries to surmount this overwhelming but only putative *absence*. By cultivating a "dead passion," his frustrated desire for some totalizing fiction will be exposed as a rapture of immobility and domination. Scratch a romantic and find the sadist, as it were.

Inside the car, Papa thinks he finds "the essential signs, the true language"

(33). His automobile is exemplary, but when fear activates Henri's asthma Papa conceives of the young man as "a wheezing machine" (60), while the cowering Chantal is a vomiting machine in the back seat and Papa's mistress, Monique, is recalled for mechanically reciprocating his sadistic violence. Papa himself is a seeing machine. Travestying the romantic poet's lamp, he remarks that "these yellow headlights are the lights of my eyes" (15); and into these cones of illumination rush objects, "like a handful of thrown stones" (78) that flash across the mind's screen. Papa feels the same rapture over photographs of automobile accidents, over his collection of pornographic photographs, over memories of passion held in the stasis of his narrative representation. All refigure the same need to hold fluctuating reality in a freeze-frame, denominate its parts, banish the random and unexpected, then exercise the will to dominate. His demonic romanticism makes victims of everyone, including himself.

Papa's travesty of a visionary discourse relies on numerous transitory devices: alliteration, chiasmus, consonance, oxymoron, puns, even traces of advertising lingo ("Why not leave the seeing as well as the driving to me?" he asks in a parody of the old Greyhound Bus ads [79]). His language, like the world of displaced objects outside his car, is thus what Gilles Deleuze in *Logique du sens* has defined as an "art of surfaces," an art of fragmented and centerless being. Yet Papa constantly denies its centerlessness, through the relentless assault of a conventionally "privileged" irony. Deleuze (especially in chapter 12, "On Humor") argues that *irony* can only be understood according to a romantic theory of the self, where the subject/object opposition is essential, and irony is a structural means of signifying the identity of such contraries. In particular, irony is a means of negating the object in order that the subject might exercise its mastery and hold up the self as a fixed point of reference. In contrast, argues Deleuze, *humour* operates by simply paying those dualities no heed; it is an art of surfaces, and it erases any fixed point.[82] Using Deleuze's helpful perspective, my reading of *Travesty* regards Papa's unrelenting irony, his generative satire of targets and self-centered norms, as a monstrously hegemonic tradition which is stunningly subverted by the novel's humorous, degenerative satire.

Among the most noticeable surface details in *Travesty* are its grotesque similes. They are simply the novel's most insistent stylistic feature, far more prominent than in *The Cannibal* or in anything by West or O'Connor.[83] Papa's narrative reads like a congeries of monstrous hybrids: he imagines a gasoline truck perched dragonlike on the road ahead, with "its great belly brimming with thick liquid fire" (22); his doctor's x-ray machine sounds "like a flock of wounded geese in uncertain flight" (94). Often the intent of such figures is ridicule, as when he recalls Henri reading his fashionable poems to an audience while seated on the stage "like a man on a toilet" (80); or when Papa remembers Chantal and a companion looking "like sniffing rabbits" (116) in the midst of a blatantly sexual initiation rite. At last, however, the effect of these similes is to abjectly blur the boundaries of identity: Papa and Henri, for example, are "like two dancers at arm's length, regurgitation locked together with ingestion in a formal, musical embrace" (28).

This last figure stands as grotesquely near the postmodern sublime as anything Hawkes has written. Papa even nominates himself as theorist of that condition, which so closely dissimulates the "form of ecstasy" (17). Its tendency toward simile he justifies through a "theory of likenesses":

> I am always moving. I am forever transporting myself somewhere else. I am never exactly where I am. Tonight, for instance, we are traveling one road but also many, as if we cannot take a single step without discovering five of our own footprints already ahead of us. According to Honorine this is my other greatest failing or most dangerous quality, this propensity of mine toward total coherence, which leads me to see in one face the configurations of yet another, or to enter rose-scented rooms three at a time, or to live so closely to the edge of likenesses as to be eating the fruit, so to speak, while growing it. . . . For me the familiar and unfamiliar lie everywhere together, like two enormous faces back to back. (75–76)

Rhetorically persuasive as it is, Papa's authority ought to terrorize us. Like Papa himself, the modernist discourse builds structures of meaning out of similes that must be "always moving." Perception should not pause too long over a figure, which must instantaneously (and unrealistically) fix itself and then "transport" readers "somewhere else" — to the next trope as well as to the authoritative allegory under which they all supposedly convene. In this sense, the acceleration of Papa's automobile is the concise analogue to his recitation. He is indeed "talking as well as driving us" to a carefully rehearsed violence, and speech is therefore "dangerous" exactly in relation to its deterministic appearance, its power to generate links of identity chained together by an internal "logic" whose only test is in some transrational field of "likenesses." Taken to an extreme, this is the hysterical power of *discordia concors*. Readers are never allowed to forget that it is the product of Papa's "poised sentences" (46), his "design that underlies all my rambling" (27). Why else would Hawkes so consistently call attention to Papa's tropes, most of which are set off by highly self-conscious markers, phrases like "so to speak," "need I say it," "if you will allow the poetic license," and "that figure of speech"?

Papa constantly reaffirms the belief that his "poetic" reasoning will determine "true" causes. He says, "the greater the incongruity, the greater the truth" (20), and he envisions each of his tropes as "one more unbreakable thread in the web" of his fatal vision (40). Indeed, Papa even extends this condition to the structure of his recitation. Its episodes seem to follow the same "logic" of congruence or simile. Tensed opposite one another like the vehicle and tenor of an extended conceit, episodes in *Travesty* seem to transcribe some essential similarity or "design." The attempted usurpation of Papa's place in the marital bed by his (now) dead son Pascal, and the successful usurpation of Henri, soon to die; Papa's surgically excised lung, and his doctor's amputated leg; Chantal as the rabbitlike "Queen of Carrots" and the rabbits Papa flattens on the roadbed; Honorine as a "natural actress in the theater of sex" and Monique's "parody" of that performance: in each of these correspondences we have the art of simile raised to a still higher pitch, far higher than the traffic of realistic fiction ordinarily allows, in deference to "believability." Surely the most suggestive of these comparisons is Papa's recollection, near the close, of what he previously called "a travesty, involving a car, an old poet, and a little girl" (47). Here it seems, momentarily, as if Papa has driven to the brink of real "clarity," the present action being in some way a recognition of the prior one (and an "explanation" of Hawkes's title). But this extended episode once more ends like all the others. It reveals no origins, objectifies no central and totalizing "truth."

Thus *Travesty* ends by equivocating anything its posited author might say about surmounting the past through "imagined life" (127), or even, for that matter, about how this story "quite defies interpretation" (23). One can read it as a satire on the hyperrational, hysterical violence that is so easily masked by storytelling itself. Against the backdrop of a ceaseless displacement, Papa enacts a terrible need for coherent order, or "design." In his "privileged," upper-middle-class family, he plays out well-scripted episodes of romantic sex and danger, creating a "store" of memories which, as Papa puts it, "defined me, thrilled me, convinced me of the validity of the fiction of living, but which I have now forgotten" (125).

The best Black Humor fictions disclose such losses of our legitimizing fictions as something like the defining crisis of our times. Yet the case of *Travesty* is perhaps the most difficult. A deceptively monological and centripetal narration, *Travesty* seems to reject all the dialogism conventionally associated with satirical fictions. *Gravity's Rainbow* might be taken as a contrasting example. Its vast range of languages and idiolects are all subjected to varying degrees of stylization, parody, and ridicule. Or, in a first-person satire, such as *Lolita,* the narrator embodies a metastasized cancer of language and authority that his own narrative structure ridicules. This movement, made possible by the separation of the posited author from the satirist himself, is enacted (as Mikhail Bakhtin has argued) whenever the narrator filters other languages, such as inner speech and the reported dialogue of other characters, through the refracting lens of his own extremity. Once more, however, *Travesty* pitches this defining feature of narrative satire at a higher level. Like Zizendorf in *The Cannibal,* Papa has been *completely* posited for the other characters. He not only reiterates what Henri has (evidently) said, he expresses what Henri is (probably) thinking, even what he will (likely) say. Papa's containment of all discourse even extends to Henri's poems: "I might have written them myself," he says after quoting one at novel's end (127). This is an elaborately self-contained moment, like one of West's Chinese box regressions or Purdy's embedding of Cabot Wright's biography. The poems are Henri's, but as random scraps of paper are quite literally inside Papa's coat pocket, yet Papa's apocalypse is, at the same time, contained within the satirist's projection of it.

This may seem an insanely ingrown structure, yet it points up the way that any degenerative satire displays language as an enclosed, self-reifying system constantly in need of demolition through laughter from positions further and further outside. While reading such a novel, it is dangerously naive to stay inside at the level of conventional realism with the hysterical narrator and assume, for example, that its details are open to rational debate. That is the tack of at least one early critic, who complains that Henri could easily "pull out the car keys and grab the wheel before the narrator swerves into a tree."[84] This is as unlikely as it is slavishly devoted to realist concerns. For if the reader can be assumed to share anything with Henri and Chantal, it must be the sense that the extremity of Papa's narrative ending, and the coolness with which he approaches it, can only be taken as a colossally sick joke.

In addition, the details of *Travesty*'s structuring invite us to read the novel as an attack on the most powerful weapons in the modernist arsenal of storytelling: techniques like "spatial form," ideas about "ironic distance" and the "objective correlative," and perhaps most of all the transcendent importance attached to everyday secular moments. Hawkes, like the best of the Black Humor fictionists, reminds us of the authoritarian culture behind that mythology. In *Travesty,* he dramatizes the violent claustrophobia of its need for order. We begin to see it as a slick-talking patriarchal dictatorship.

The curious reception of *Travesty,* in particular the insistence that Hawkes is just not "realistic" enough, might be excusable in the case of a novel presented under any other title. Yet the critics' grumblings about Hawkes, in 1976, were only anticipations of more general complaints. As Thomas LeClair aptly puts it, an "open season" on American fiction was begun in 1978 with John Gardner's angry complaints in *On Moral Fiction.* He was quickly joined by Mary McCarthy, Alfred Kazin, and Martin Price, who fired scattershot charges at the American novelist for lacking "ideas" about postindustrial society and for avoiding a moral debate with new forms of commerce and communication. Meantime Robert Alter pined for the political novel, a form for which American writers have proven themselves inadequate, he claims, ever since Robert Penn Warren's *All the King's Men* appeared in 1946.[85]

We cannot ignore the swing toward political conservatism that provided the social context for these grievances. Also, it is hard to forget the charges once leveled against Black Humor novelists in the sixties, that Black Humor wasn't "satirical enough," that it sidestepped moral judgments. If anything, I have argued, the innovative powers of Black Humor fictions were too frequently siphoned off to support the efforts of a generative satire. This was certainly the case in novels by Donleavy, Heller, Purdy, Southern, and Vonnegut. But even in spite of these shortcomings, the best of Black Humor was, as Conrad Knickerbocker wrote in 1964, part of "the one genuinely new postwar development in American literature." This development was the emergence of a degenerative, postmodernist satire, a writing that laid just claims to being "new" because it so obviously challenged the accepted concepts of satire. This is why, in one sense, the best Black Humor novels were *too* satirical: too suspicious of the dissimulated violence, the disenfranchisement and control that is codified in so much of popular commerce and communication. The unrelieved suspicion of these books, and the strategies that suspicion engendered — strategies of humor (as opposed to irony), of antipathy to realist conventions, of pop-cultural intertextuality and the subversion of rationalist knowledge — did in fact move the fictions into a territory "beyond" canonical satire. These shifts were already well anticipated in earlier satirical novels by West, O'Connor, and Hawkes. In the stepwise plotting of *Lolita,* Nabokov also records the release of a renegade humor. Later fictions, by Barthelme, Coover, Gaddis, Hawkes, and Pynchon, fulfilled those early warnings.

Still, the obtuse, acrimonious dismissals still being prompted by the emergence of a degenerative satire are evidence of how intransigent our horizon of expectations can be, of how limited it is by interpretive conventions promulgated in scholarly books and classrooms. At its best Black Humor provides a wealth of social commentary, an abundance of "ideas." Black Humor was satire in a new mode. Its exemplary texts were as politically and socially alert as any American fictions in this century. It is to more of these political satires, by writers like Ishmael Reed, Norman Mailer, and Robert Coover, that I turn in the following chapter.

# 4

# The Sixties and After

## Social and Political Satire

The title of this chapter is certainly redundant. Preceding chapters have mapped the spread of contemporary narrative satire as a form that indicts form, threatening to expose any codified knowledge as a dissimulation of violence and all of us as potential victims. As such, satire is political *by definition*. It is a dissenting discourse of and about modalities of power, ranging from discrete local bases to massively aggressive global hegemonies. Yet the chapter title is redundant in a further sense. I have been specifically concerned with satire in its relations to the novel, but Fredric Jameson argues that narrative fictions are always already the vehicles of a political *pensée sauvage* or "unconscious." Like a force field, this political unconscious both situates and seeks to synthesize those conflicting beliefs and fantasies about its sociopolitical context. Jameson demonstrates its power not only in the popular novel, but in the most revered fictions of "high culture"; they also tend to promulgate a "symbolic reaffirmation of this or that legitimizing strategy" for entrenched ideologies. Jameson's critique compels us to read narrative fictions by the lights of historical forces influencing their production and reception. This is the way to reveal those "substantial incentives" — reified desire, spatiotemporal closure, totalities of knowledge — that fictions offer in exchange for readers' "ideological adherence."[1]

The implications for readings of recent satirical fictions are several. First, such an approach underscores our observation that the satirical novel is, in contrast to the realistic novel, a form for subverting the discursive strategies an ideology would use to legitimize its power. This is also consistent with the argument developed since chapter 1, that satire is an expression of the "incredulity toward metanarratives" or "crisis of legitimation" peculiar to our times. Second, it should be clear once again that this conception is inhospitable to formalist claims about satire as a didactic, targeted, corrective, and normative discourse, traits that would only identify its art with those narratives of tacit political assent that Jameson analyzes. Instead, criticism should try to elaborate those "incentives" specific to the contemporary satirical novel, incentives associated with strategies of dissent and subversion. The key rewards of novels by satirists like West, Hawkes, Nabokov, and Pynchon are not reified desire but frustrated desire and abjection (the grotesque, whose extreme sign is mindless cannibalistic violence), not spatiotemporal closure but the laughable fracturing or deconstruction of boundary and difference (the *topos* of carnival, whose recent avatar was the Black Humor novel), not totalized knowledge but fictions regressing toward atavistic hysteria and chaos.

## Polemics

No doubt about it, these are degenerative pleasures. And no wonder that satire has seemed periodically in need of "defense." This is particularly so in contemporary America, where, as Stephen Vizinczey has observed, novels are seen as entertaining diversions having little to do with ordinary living, especially politics, and where key institutions for receiving new fiction (the book-reviewing and awards-granting establishment) remain averse to politically irreverent, offensive, and disruptive novels.[2] The Pulitzer trustees' last-minute rejection of *Gravity's Rainbow* is one case in point.

Ever since John Gardner launched a counteroffensive in 1978, both old guard and defected liberals have bitterly condemned (what they see as) the *lack* of authentic political content in postwar American novels. For instance, Robert Alter complains that the contemporary American novelist either avoids politics like a dead skunk in the road or else treats it "as sheer farce." Alter presses for a return to the rosier days of fictions with stable characters and continuous plotting, a neorealist "empiricism." This is also Norman Podhoretz's call to arms. Willing to grant the contemporary writer no fabulative quarter whatsoever when it comes to politics, he denounces Robert Coover for reinventing the Rosenberg case and argues that in revising the historical facts (having Nixon visit Ethel Rosenberg on death row) *The Public Burning* is condemnable propaganda. Alter and Podhoretz both think the true political novel went out with *All the King's Men.*[3] Alfred Kazin looks back to still more wistful vistas, the hey-day of Fitzgerald and Hemingway, and concludes that "the full impact of the technological storm" on our sociopolitical lives is simply beyond novelistic treatment. Similarly, Mary McCarthy laments that while looking into the face of that storm American writers have lost faith in the power of "ideas."[4] As for Gardner, the archmoralist, he charges that writers like Robert Coover and Thomas Pynchon tend either to oversimplify or to melodramatize the conflicts of their sociopolitical surrounding. No doubt it would be revealing to trace the shifting political loyalties behind such remarks, especially in the general context of the sharp turn toward conservative Republicanism after 1978. More particularly disturbing, however, is Gardner's stubborn uncertainty about whether or not texts like *The Public Burning* or *Gravity's Rainbow* are really satires. If they were so intended, then how (he wonders) could their authors have composed such (to him) disastrously non-normative, and thus amoral, visions? Gardner's gripes have been widely repeated, and this general uncertainty about writers like Coover and Pynchon can only be attributed to the persistence of formalist models for satire, which the new novels don't fit, therefore they cannot have been meant as satires. Accordingly they are condemned as (in Gardner's phrase) "psychotic non-communication." After all, the formalist critics have been telling us for some time that "the complexities of modern economic and social systems are now too great to be reduced to satiric formulae" and it is therefore "an archaic art."[5] In many ways the old-guard critics have maintained that negative outlook.

This is all the more remarkable because by the early sixties (I have argued) novels were being written from a well-developed sense of lineage, a radical legacy of satires going back to Nathanael West. Only the *reception* of new fictions within this line was spotty and uncertain. The novelists themselves (O'Connor, Hawkes and Ishmael Reed, for example) have spoken quite clearly about their inheritance. Also, the satirical novels within this line are remarkably akin, both in their vision and principal concerns. *The Day of the Locust, The Cannibal, Cabot Wright Begins, The Crying of Lot 49, The Free-Lance Pallbearers, J R, The Public Burning*: all are very much about the mass-cultural bases of power. In these books there are ideas abounding, new technologies in all their "impacts" on semiotic systems, and consciences fully but irreverently engaged with their sociopolitical surrounding. Thus the title of this chapter suggests a too-narrow taxonomy, because all along I have been treating satires that assail structures for reproducing, expanding, and consuming *power*. Here we merely take up those novels whose topics (racism, war) and characters (Richard Nixon) are overtly political.

In addition to the confusion issuing from a stubborn formalist theory of satire, there was the challenge of documentary forms. An increasingly strong mode of social criticism since the thirties, documentary journalism seemed to take over exactly those corrective-normative features regarded as central to traditional satire. As the promoters of Black Humor phrased it, "What has happened is that the satirist has had his ground usurped. . . . The journalist is certainly today's satirist. The novelist-satirist, with no real territory of his own to roam, has had to discover new land, invent a new currency, a new set of filters, has had to sail into darker waters somewhere out beyond satire." Widely repeated in criticism from the period, this claim was never seriously examined, though it cut to the heart of standing definitions of satire.[6]

As William Stott has shown, documentary journalism emerged in the thirties when it threw off two inveterate prejudices, that it had to provide only factual information, and that at all costs it should avoid propagandizing. The new "social documentary" form that arose during the Depression years was unabashedly didactic. At a minimum it was intended to "sensitize our intellect (or educate our emotions) about actual life," but in its stronger forms it was based on the realization that, as filmmaker Pare Lorentz put it, "good art is good propaganda," a positively persuasive, didactic mode.[7] Moreover it was an aggressively targeted and corrective discourse. At its heart was "not form or style or medium, but content" that needed correcting (14), and it focused on "the things that had to be corrected" (21). Always implicit was its normative basis in liberal humanism. Stott sums up this aesthetic very neatly: "Social documentary deals with facts that are alterable. It has an intellectual dimension to make clear what the facts are, why they came about, and how they can be changed for the better. Its more important dimension, however, is usually the emotional: feeling the fact may move the audience to wish to change it" (26). This reads very much like the formalists' definition of the satirist, who "always criticizes" by using "reason," but furthermore encourages "his readers to criticize and condemn . . . by moving them to various emotions ranging from laughter through ridicule, contempt and anger to hate."[8]

Indeed, this affective demand seemed to mount yet another invasion of the satirist's traditional ground. To arouse the corrective spirit, social documentary actively seeks out extremity, even to the point of magnifying the truly grotesque. For in addition to being actual, its subjects need to be "all but unimaginable" (47). As Howard Zinn puts it, great social documentary self-consciously provides "a picture of society given by its victims."[9] Stott has also shown that the most effective documentary *topoi* are scenes of violence, dismemberment, and death, staggering coincidences, and cases of extreme sacrifice. The satirist may share these, though he or she decidedly does *not* share the documentarist's treatment of them. As Stott emphasizes, the nail on which everything hangs in a documentary is "fellow feeling" or "human sympathy" (135); documentary texts are obliged to show qualities of human competence and endurance in the face of otherwise inconceivable loss and degradation. Documentary thus represents the possibility of defeating the extraordinary and returning to a dignified ordinariness (49). Degenerative satire, on the other hand, turns on feelings of antipathy and even, at its extremes, revulsion and abject horror. It levels the ordinary, revealing behind its placid mask the extraordinary, monstrous edge of experiences situated well beyond norms. It may not, even in its classical texts (like *Gulliver's Travels*), locate any paved roads back to normality.

Defined in these terms, there is no question that literary satire is fundamentally different from social documentary. Still, the idea persists that documentary has usurped the functions of both satire and the novel. In one of many "death of the novel" pronouncements from the early sixties, Mary McCarthy argued that nineteenth-century novels "documented" an "actual world," providing "explanations" of the ways that institutions and industries worked, how art was produced and marketed, and political offices won. Fiction, she claimed, was thus "continuous with real life" and performed "many of the functions of a newspaper"; but now documentary journalism has usurped those functions, and the novel is no longer the viable documentary tool that it was, say, for Steinbeck in *Grapes of Wrath*.[10] Subsequent criticism has convincingly shown how such terminal prognoses for the novel stemmed from an erroneous overemphasis on the mimetic aspect of narrative fictions.[11] Similarly misleading, however, are the declarations of satire's banishment by a more aggressive documentary mode. These claims are based on an erroneous identification of narrative satire with the formalist theory developed to account for it. If anything, though, it was only the definition of satire as a didactic, targeted, corrective, and normative literature that had collapsed. Meanwhile the satirical novel was being radically remodeled. Indeed, a number of recent texts parody and satirize documentary forms. For instance, one way of reading Gaddis's *J R,* with the remarkably mimetic quality of its zero-degree descriptions and seemingly tape-recorded dialogue, is to see the book as a document *in extremis* (see chapter 5). Or, at the end of Coover's *The Public Burning,* a drunk, orgiastic audience watches the electrocutions of Julius and Ethel Rosenberg while, in complicity with their political sacrifice, a "documentary" film about their two children plays on a huge screen over the execution site in Times Square. There are similar moments in the fictions of Ishmael Reed and in Pynchon's *Gravity's Rainbow.*

Having finally adjusted our view of satire in its relations to a competing mode like documentary, it is still clear that politics remains a favored subject in satire, and that with rare exceptions (like Dryden's "Absalom and Achitophel") political satires "have tended to be written against the established government."[12] Why is this so? One reason, acknowledged even by formalist critics, is the difficulty of containing satirical aggression. As Kernan has put it, the satirist secures a world dominated by "the inflated, the fragmented, the jumbled," but finally these tendencies spill over, upsetting the "workings" of all of nature and culture until "everything is falling apart."[13] Similarly, in tracing the provenance of satire back to ritual magic, Robert Elliott grants that the power of "socially approved magic," with its sanative and normative aspects, is oftentimes overwhelmed by "magic on its dark and fearsome side," in practices that exert "disturbing and subversive influences." Fully unleashed, Elliott concludes, satire becomes "revolutionary in ways that society cannot possibly approve, and in terms that may not be clear even to the satirist."[14] This conclusion is distinctly at odds with an otherwise standard formalist definition of satire that Elliott uses through the rest of his study, but he does not elaborate the difference.

To date, the best (and only) treatment of satire's radical issue is Michael Seidel's 1979 study, *The Satiric Inheritance.* Focusing on the age from Rabelais to Sterne, Seidel's analysis everywhere challenges the accepted wisdom about satire. As he describes it, satire is "essentially a subversive, deforming mode," not just when it breaks through normative containments but as its definitive modal procedure.[15] The reason, Seidel argues, can be learned from satire's relation to the conventional novel. The novel does more than supply a parodic base-text for satiric plots, though typically that is the ostensible relation. Rather, conventional narrative serves as something like a parasitic host, because its abstracted plot, or metanarrative, is *generative*: the action of a conventional story concerns the lineal transmission of inheritance, in both the natural and institutional sense, and thus it is about the orderly dispensation and legitimation of power (31). Like a parasite, however, satire "takes over the body or 'corporation'" of that generative fiction and threatens to consume it (56). A *degenerative* and disinheriting action, the satiric narrative is everywhere in open revolt "against those symbols of power and generation that dispense" (31). Satire corrupts all those sanative and renewing dispensations by which society maintains order. It deconstructs "history" as a cover-up or sanctification of endless victimization, and it reinterprets the political order as a conspiracy of accommodations to power. In all, writes Seidel, satiric action "is always a double action": it is a regress in the form of a progress, an atavistic violation couched in the mode of a presentation (23). The satirist, by these lights, is always a security risk.

The characteristic signs of his dangerousness are those figures of excremental and sexual defilement, monstrousness, hysteria, and natural chaos common to any strong satire; these figures indicate the corruption or cessation of lineal descent and progress. The satirist manipulates such signs, risking self-contamination, because of the power they confer. That power not only comes from the sanative, reconstructive potentiality of bringing order back out of chaos, though that kind of action well defines the class of normative texts to which Elliott relates the "shamanistic" and "ritual" aspects of satire. Instead, as Seidel concludes, a more radical power stems from the satirist's paradoxical ability to pronounce the text of an otherwise unspeakable violence.

In *Violence and the Sacred,* René Girard defines two kinds of violence. The first is a disintegrative, degenerative violence that grows like a contagion from seeds of vengeance. Its spread collapses all those codified differences composing culture until finally it threatens to become an endlessly reciprocal and thus catastrophic condition. If unappeased, this absolute violence engulfs the entire polity in crisis. The second kind of violence is integrative and generative, and grows out of the need, for the sake of simple survival, to appease the first kind by refocusing it or displacing it entirely. Now absolute violence is diminished by focusing the collective vengeance upon a single target of scorn, a scapegoat or surrogate victim, whose selection itself reestablishes boundary and difference. Thus by a single blow the generative murder "wipes out all memory" of the violent contagion, with its "baleful knowledge" of "man's violent nature," something man glimpses in himself only at the risk of succumbing to it.[16] Indeed, argues Girard, only by dissimulating that violence does man insure the continuance of his line, and this is the function of ritual, a repetition of the generative murder that exists still further removed from the initial crisis. Girard thus posits a sequence of developments one may schematize as in Figure 4.

Sacrificial ————————> Generative ————————> Ritual Sacrifice
Crisis                  Violence              (Symbolization)

**FIGURE 4**

But how does that initial crisis originate? Girard argues that it stems from the most elemental power relation in human culture, that of model to disciple. Girard describes their union as a contradictory web of "mimetic desire": the model's injunction to "Imitate me!" would, if fully realized, bring the disciple into utter competition with the model over any objects of desire, all those trappings of mastery that spurred the mimesis. So in an atavistic conservatism the model's injunction to "Imitate me!" always invokes its opposite command, "Don't imitate me!" Girard further shows that this "contradictory double imperative" initiates that absolute violence he terms the "sacrificial crisis." Mimetic desire is the "catalyst for the sacrificial crisis" (148); its chief symbol is the "monstrous double," signifier of that reciprocally violent competition and loss of difference which would eventually destroy the polity if a surrogate victim were not found to quell the hysteria. Only sacrifice "stems the tide" of vertigo and hysteria, the back-and-forth oscillation of model/disciple, dominating/dominated, and victor/victim loosed during the initial crisis.

This is a good moment to pause and make a general observation about the American postmodernist satire: that its conclusive moments are often sacrificial. We have already noted overtly sacrificial plots in novels like *Miss Lonelyhearts* and *The Day of the Locust, Wise Blood,* and *The Cannibal,* and noted as well the relentless characterological and figural doublings of their plots. Such structures appear in many other fictions, most notably in *The Free-Lance Pallbearers, Gravity's Rainbow,* and *The Public Burning.* Formalist definitions used to hand a powerful, institutionalized warrant to those who would interpret such texts as generative fictions whose purpose is to reconstruct order and sanity out of chaos and hysteria — in sum, as fictions dedicated to a normative moral economy. But in the second chapter I have argued that the satires by West, O'Connor, and Hawkes tend to mock the sacrificial resolution, exposing it as a false stop along a potentially endless continuum of violence. We can now put that argument in a broader context. As defined in these chapters, the postmodernist satire enacts the "return" of a repressed violence, an unappeased and reciprocal aggression symptomatic of the "sacrificial crisis." It penetrates to origins much more horrifying than the sanative processes of ritual and enacts the contagious lapse of all those differences defining a polity against the backdrop of its suppressed, dissimulated violence.

Here Girard's analysis becomes most suggestive. He argues that all symbolizing economies, all the great circuits of exchange that in human culture are based on codified differences, originate in the generative violence that ends the murderous crisis. Language is a "cover" for that prior state of unspeakable aggression. Like all differential codes, language displaces or dissimulates the sacrificial violence. It would seem impossible to go behind this, yet it is this veil that certain kinds of texts do try, paradoxically, to penetrate. The paradox, quite simply, is that any attempt to express "the loss of differences is necessarily betrayed by the differentiated expression of language" (65). No matter how doggedly human discourse tries to catch it, "the reality of the sacrificial crisis invariably slips through its grasp" (64). Language can only approach that crisis, notes Girard, by indirection, using "specific stylistic effects" such as the grotesque simile and endlessly doubled symbol (66) or techniques of "inversion" (160) to trace inadequately the condition of absolute non-differentiation. In fact, Girard specifically mentions these effects in connection with kinds of prophetic-apocalyptic narration and tragedy (66). Clearly, we should add satire to that group, for these techniques are rarely used to compose a "synthesis of elements" along any idealistic or utopian lines, but usually yield "a formless *and grotesque mixture* of things" tending toward "a monstrosity" (160). I emphasize Girard's idea of a "mixture" because that is precisely the way satire has been defined for several millennia: the Latin *satura* means just that, a mixture or hodgepodge. It is also no coincidence that readers have often commented on the necessity of "indirection" in satire.

Surely this is because in trying to pierce the veil over violence satire invariably risks saying at once too little and too much. Techniques of indirection may diminish the satire or deflect it back into normative modes, while too direct a confrontation with the desymbolizing chaos threatens an absolute hysteria. This is why satire often seems to ride like a parasite within its novelistic host: the novelistic order provides a kind of redoubt for satire's atavistic chaos. One must also be cautious with the metaphor of parasitism, however, because it construes the satiric text as a posterior, lapsed, or dependent form, much as Northrop Frye defines satire as posterior to romance (see chapter 1).

Instead, Girard's essay obliges one to take up literary satire as that mode of violence and desymbolizing chaos which rides, paradoxically, in *any* symbolic vehicle. This is so because the symbol was itself (according to Girard) a dissimulation of an originary violence; or, satire is like a renegade, cancerous strand of DNA always already riding in language. If anything its degenerative process was actually anterior to language, preliminary to semiotic activity.

This lengthy synopsis was needed because the concept of satire's atavistic, degenerative procedures can answer a number of theoretical questions. It certainly clarifies what we mean by the (redundant) phrase, "political satire." In particular, while those who want a more "realistic" political fiction may be disturbed, it nevertheless follows from Girard's analyses that in satire, unlike documentary, what matters is not content but style or "technique." Indeed, whenever a contemporary satire seems to be sophomorically tinkering with systems of exchange, disrupting semiotic economies in apparently playful, innocuous ways, it skates on very thin ice because its work threatens the very basis of polity. Usually the narrative style soon breaks through to more chilling, actual violence. In *Lolita,* Nabokov's initially playful style (Humbert's *double entendres,* alliterations, and oxymorons) is the first symptom of an aggressive contagion whose conclusion is Humbert's murder of his mimetic double, Clare Quilty. In *Miss Lonelyhearts* the infectious spread of Shrike's discourse, with its grotesque similes, is also the prologue to murder. The same might also be said about such different novels as *Cabot Wright Begins, Snow White,* and *Travesty.* These are not "political" texts in the narrower sense we mean in this chapter, yet they are very much *about* the dispensations of power and mastery. They forewarn against the danger of dismissing a novel that is overtly concerned with political institutions and activities but seems too stylistically playful for what we generally regard as a serious business.

## Fictions

Perhaps in fear of its degenerative power, novelists will often attempt to contain the spread of satire's contagious violence. Purdy's uncertain return to normative satire near the close of *Cabot Wright Begins* is a telling instance, typical of many satirical novels published during and just after the sixties.

Mary McCarthy's *The Groves of Academe* (1952) provides an early illustration. Her fictional protagonist, Henry Mulcahy, a professor of English and "prophet of modern literature in a series of half-way good colleges," has most recently been hired into a mediocre department at Jocelyn College, whose students have "given in to the forces of conformity and reaction."[17] Jocelyn's president, Maynard Hoar, has lately achieved a liberalist notoriety by publishing a pamphlet, "The Witch-Hunt in Our Universities," championing the rights of faculty against the investigations and "loyalty oaths" used to root out suspected communists. Mulcahy was one victim of that paranoia. Dismissed from his previous appointment for vague associations with "reds," he'd been hired by Hoar (thinks Henry) mainly to demonstrate Jocelyn's resistance to the purges of right-wingers. Yet Hoar has also put Mulcahy on notice from the start: his appointment is short-term, subject to budgetary constraints, and meant only to get Henry back on his feet until a more solid position turns up elsewhere. However, when the dismissal notice arrives Henry takes it as a "blunt, naked wielding of power" (12). He girds himself for war, then puts two lies into the campus rumor mill. First he claims to have been a covert member of the Communist party and insinuates that despite a liberalist reputation Hoar has wilted under outside pressure and fired him out of political expediency. Next Henry puts it out that his wife is threatened with a delicate illness and the strain of his firing could prove fatal, a "fact" which he claims to have told Hoar, thus adding brute callousness to his insinuation that the college president is a feckless hypocrite.

With the political and emotional bases covered, Henry's next tactic is to enlist supporters who are prone to believe "in a conventional moral order and [are] shocked by deviations from it into a sense of helpless guilt" — all in all, McCarthy's omniscient narrator snidely remarks, "good liberals" who can be used (48). Henry's principal enlistee is a young colleague, Domna Rejnev, a typically guilt-ridden, upper-class liberal who makes Henry into a cause célèbre. But their skirmishes with Hoar quickly unmask the faculty as a coven whose members are constantly "backbiting," attending cabalistic meetings, or "emending" their positions (232), and whose hypocrisy, intellectual dishonesty, venery, and sexual usury are not only unpunished but scarcely acknowledged in the first place. They are the "targets" of this conventional satire, yet McCarthy's need to assail them is answered by a wealth of supporting narrative detail (all the novelistic attention to circumstance, characterization, event, and scene) that actually leads to a contrary result. We begin to hedge our judgments and even back away from the narrator's ridicule of these targets.

Hoar is not what his name indicates, but just an average, numbers-crunching administrator willing to compromise for the sake of collegial harmony and his own security. To Jocelyn's conformist student body Mulcahy is not a popular teacher, and to the faculty he is disruptive in meetings and obstructive of everyday bureaucracies, yet both these adverse qualities are, in terms of the satiric inversion, plusses. Even more, unlike his secure but unpublished colleagues Henry is a man with a fistful of articles on James Joyce, in respectable journals like the *Kenyon Review*, and their complaint that Henry's "great learning" only widens the intellectual "hiatus" between him and his ordinary students (105) smacks of professional envy. Finally, with every charge against him thus equivocated, the most damning complaint against Henry is that his mewling children emit a steady reek of urine, a detail the narrator frequently holds up like a dead fish. This (apparent) authorial disdain is disturbingly consistent with Domna's upper-class "liberalism": "One has only to look at Henry to imagine the matrix that framed him — a poor heredity, hagiolotrous parents, a nasty and narrow environment, sweets, eyestrain, dental caries. I detest the social order which sprouts these mildewed souls — all that should be changed, nobody should be permitted to grow up in such a bodily tenement" (171). Yet even having voiced her disdain for the culturally underprivileged, Domna might be expected to put aside her disgust at Henry's tactics, which *did* unfairly manipulate her, and at least recognize his desperate efforts to secure an income sufficient to keep his own family out of an actual "tenement." Instead, McCarthy virtually drops Domna from the narrative, stifling the obvious elements of class struggle — and ending the novel — with Hoar's resignation as president and his judgment on Henry as "a madman" (235).

Is the reckless, petty-deceitful pursuit of a livelihood and family security "madness," and politics nothing but self-interest? This is what McCarthy's *satire* seems bent on revealing, thus implying (in the tradition of liberal humanism and normative satire) that a "just politics" would be altruistic, or at least urged by "enlightened self-interest." However, the text's development as a *novel* continually interferes with these intentions. Increasingly, Henry seems targeted mainly because in these "groves" he advances like an interloper from some genetic proletariat. The reader is blocked from testing that hypothesis by the narrator's obvious sympathy with Domna Rejnev and by an exceedingly close focus on Jocelyn College. The novel's only reference to extramural political struggle comes in a brief summary at the beginning, advising readers that "Dr. Fuchs had confessed; Mr. Hiss had been convicted; Mr. Greenglass and others (including a former Jocelyn physics student) had been tried for atomic spying; Senator McCarthy had appeared" (17). Among those "others" were Julius and Ethel Rosenberg, depicted in Coover's (1977) satire as vaguely ambitious, intellectual, and committed members of that proletariat, and soon to be executed (while liberal humanists stood helplessly by) on the basis of evidence just as ambiguous and self-interested as anything produced to show Mulcahy's "madness."

Yet *The Groves of Academe,* widely acclaimed as a "political satire," is weirdly silent about these contexts, its imagined world strangely insulated from actual events. This insularity prevents our identifying that microcosm with any larger polity, also a trait of McCarthy's later satires (*Birds of America* and *The Group*). For a satire, the book is also uncommonly disinterested in the kinds of discourse and myth that give rise to political power and its conflicts. The discourses of popular media, of law, of extant political parties and factions (such as Senator McCarthy and his ilk), and of a consumer capitalism newly capable of handling politicians and issues as marketable goods — all are absent. Instead McCarthy turns our attention to the many details of dress, manner, deportment, and home decoration which have been hallmarks of rather stable, "specific" fictional ironies since the work of Austen and Thackeray. In all, her satire remains *reasonable* about these details; they are part of an ordinary world McCarthy means to "correct" in order to more fully embrace it. Indeed, if the worst her satire can infer is that politics is self-interest verging on quite familiar forms of "madness," then *Groves* adds nothing to the critique of power in an age of "total war," when the Girardian danger of absolute violence ("Mutual Assured Destruction," in the Pentagon's terminology) clearly theatens. By contrast, through disintegrative means of style and disruptions of novelistic order, McCarthy's satirical contemporaries had already, in 1952, broken through to explore the signs of an extreme, postmodernist hysteria.

McCarthy's fictions illustrate the possibility of hedging the degenerative power of satire by means of a stable and tightly focused novelistic mimesis. Still another way of imposing limits, already noted in several Black Humor novels, is to shape the fiction around one sustained joke. This is the solution of several sixties fictions whose topic is racism; later in this chapter we will observe the same limiting tendency in Philip Roth's satire of Richard Nixon, *Our Gang* (1971).

Chester Himes is probably best known for *If He Hollers Let Him Go* (1945) and *Cotton Comes to Harlem* (1965), novels that once ranked him with Ralph Ellison and James Baldwin as a strong African-American voice for the postwar decades.[18] A writer who, like Baldwin, spent most of his career in self-exile, Himes's readership was restricted by the general unavailability of his books (including a fine set of detective novels) in this country. *Pinktoes*

(1961), a notable little satire, was first released in Paris by Maurice Girodias's Olympia Press, publishers of *Candy* and *Lolita*. When Dell-Putnam released American editions four years later, both firms capitalized on this association. *Pinktoes* was marketed and widely reviewed as a "tanned" and more mature *Candy*, the implied sexual content thus drawing attention away from its political inferences. (A successful ploy: the paperback went through six printings in its first year.)

According to Himes's epigraph, "pinktoes" is a slang term that black men and women apply to their white sexual partners, always with "indulgent affection" and never "adversely." Two parablelike introductory sections then put that bit of terminology in a wider context. The first, "Excursion in Paradox," illustrates a contradictory tendency of the human character to grow "wiser, healthier, and happier" despite those coincidences seeming to conspire for its oppression, so that despite all the deceit and distrust between the races, we go right on "propagating" — often across "the color line." [19] This leads to the second, "A Lesson in History," a more polemical preface in which Himes argues that the tendency of many blacks to have "only a minor fraction of Negro blood" (17) hints at the real reason for segregating them in ghettos. Hence the constituting idea of *Pinktoes*: miscegenation is an act of satirical "faith," a benign subversion of codified difference, a subversion whose best expression is not fear but "laughter" (22). Even more, laughter is "aphrodisiacal" (22) and thus doubles back to that subversive sexuality initiating the process. This is Himes's stated intent. The satire, however, suggests that institutional racism is far too intransigent for strategies of erotic rebellion ever to change it.

The narrative centers on Mamie Mason, a "Hostess with the Mostess" (23) and center of a Harlem demimonde that exists in a swirl of cocktail parties on the margins of *real* New York power. Mamie's self-appointed mission is to "serve the Negro problem" by literally serving it up: her legendary dinner soirées become pretexts for interracial assignations and matchmaking. *Everyone* looks to her for amorous assistance or guidance. Mamie, however, has been married for almost two decades to the same man (a black social worker involved with his white secretary) and does not generally indulge herself outside of marriage. Instead, the contradictions of Mamie's "social work" are displaced into destructive eating habits, binge/purge cycles that always leave her either too bloated or too weak for sexual enjoyment. So debilitating are the demands of her curative work that Mamie progresses from an overweight butterball to a withered hag at novel's end — the toll, one supposes, for a progressive struggle against racism.

Himes's stylistic approach to this "Negro problem" is to treat it mainly through word play, countless puns turning on sexual slang ("come," or "cock," and "white meat") and its links to ordinary discourse. Or he treats it by means of situational ironies, the usual husbands discovered *in flagrante dilecto*, and so on. Much of the treatment could be stood alongside a Neoclassical drama like Wycherly's *The Country Wife*. The purpose, as in Wycherly, is to limn the features of a bilevel discourse whose upper, dignified, and socially authorized layer is in fact shot through with hypocrisy. Mostly, though, this treatment stops short of strong political critique. Ed Schooley, a writer whose book on drug addiction (plagiarized from a W.P.A. pamphlet) has been published to great acclaim, suddenly discovers himself to be unaccountably impotent. What are the links between his drooping member and his recent "submission" to white literary authorities — his editors, publishers, and reviewers? The narrative never takes up the matter. Himes only remarks that it all shows "how far-reaching the Negro problem is in all its ramifications. Schooley swore he was going to knock the white folks' racial preconceptions to hell and gone, limp member or no" (34). But he is a figure of abject comedy from then on, a drunk, sexual braggart and object of ridicule for women both white and black. The white males in this fiction are all simpleminded hangers-on, stupidly applauding whatever an outspoken black might happen to say in his drunkenness. As for the white women, most blunder along, referring to their black paramours as "boys" and scarcely differentiating one from another. The "boys," meanwhile, are too hungry for "white meat" to notice or care, and if they recognize their predicament at all, it is only in displaced forms. Frustrated in his pursuit of a white woman, Panama Paul dreams "he was in a heaven filled with naked white angels," but whenever he tries flying to them he discovers "that his testicles were weighted down with anvils" (91). Or, their predicament is routinized in the media of a consumer culture. When a white husband leaves his long-slaving black wife for a white woman, "race pride" comes "to the rescue" (137) and women's groups bruit slogans ("Be Happy You're Nappy") that are quickly adopted in advertising. Products like "Black Nomore" give way to others, like "Snappy Nappy" and "Burr Maker" (183), and in no time the dominance of white consumer culture takes its toll. Black is suddenly "in"; white women become the chief market for "Snappy Nappy"; and things return to "normal," with hair-straightening products once more popular among Harlem blacks.

To Himes, American "race-conflict" is exactly this great, absurd cycling around the poles of purge and binge, hatred and desire, abjection and affection. In one of the novel's most ridiculously powerful images, Mamie invites over three lusting male "Negrophiles," then chases them through her house, whipping them sadistically about the genitals while the first hollers "I love the Negro," the second, "I hate the Negro," and the third, "Oh, the poor Negro" (209). Between the self-canceling poles of love and hate is only a wasted body of disengaged, guiltily impotent liberalist sympathy. Nothing changes. These sexual economies are merely the synecdoches of a larger, withering intransigence. Himes ends with Mamie entertaining "the cream of interracial society" and, having just emerged from another binge/purge cycle, barely finding the strength to urge her guests toward "More . . . interracial . . . intercourse" (219). So the cycling continues, rolling implacably over exhausted participants like Ed Schooley and Mamie Mason. Himes's sustained joke, the figure of illicit sexual congress, might have spread and assumed the power of great satire to disintegrate *any* socially coded forms of boundary and difference. Instead the text arrests that degenerative potential by relishing miscegenation mostly for the sake of sexual humor. Laughter thus deflects the writing away from long-standing modes of oppression (government, advertising and publishing media, big business) that the satire is clamoring to infect. In sum, Himes may have begun the fiction as a benign little squib tossed at an absurd code of sexual restrictions, but soon it threatened a wider devastation he sought to contain. Another way of reading the satire, however, is to see all of its principal characters as victims or dupes of an intractable racism they habitually underestimate.

Something similar happens in Charles Wright's 1966 novel, *The Wig: A Mirror Image*. The narrator, a "desperate man" named Lester Jefferson, has subscribed to all the Horatio Alger myths of success, so has been willing to "work like a slave" at various menial jobs, but while everyone around him "seemed to jet toward" Lyndon Johnson's "Great Society," he "remained in the outhouse, penniless, without connections."[20] Looking for the wonder cure, Lester purchases a jar of "long-lasting Silky Smooth Hair Relaxer, with the Built-in Sweat-proof Base (trademark registered)" (6), then "conks" his hair. It comes out a fine, straight reddish-brown. With the change Lester feels "reborn, purified, annointed" (9); he expects jobs, money, and gorgeous, sexy women to jump on him as to a magnet. Lester sees his new "wig" as a magic bullet, but his is still the old "Inchin' Along" outlook. Pounding the streets for work, he sings "Onward Christian Soldiers" and tells his dejected Harlem neighbors that "Things are getting better every day" (12), or "My ship is just around the bend" (14). Lester's "wig" is "rooted" in this "something deeper," this desire to "progress" in dignified steps beyond the wretched failures of his illiterate parents (21).

Nonetheless, that desire constantly gives way to slavish dreams of instant success in a white-run economy, and characters' fantasies of wealth and beauty are all media-induced, deriving from stock advertising and film images (*Breakfast at Tiffany's, Sunset Boulevard*). Little Jimmie Wishbone, a lapsed Hollywood star, states the political uses of such dreams: "I worked for the government, man. I kept one hundred million colored people contented for years. And in turn, I made the white people happy. Safe" (32). Still, even this political recognition does not harden them toward the fantasies. Together, Jimmie and Lester dream of a smash career in soul music, and while a white cabby observes that blacks "sure can sing and dance" (70), or a white record producer flips over their bewigged image, the fact is neither one can carry a tune. Jimmie and Lester are tossed from the recording studio, a "disgrace to your colored brethren *and* to this great republic" (83). Lester slides lower: he's turned down for a series of increasingly menial jobs, as "a porter, a busboy, a shoeshine boy" (86); his girlfriend, "Deb," protests that even with his lovely conked hair he has too little money, then she drops him. Lester reflects that "if I had my own natural kinky hair, 'my thorny crown' . . . I'd have made her eat dirt" (113), implying that even while it is a sign of Christlike suffering, his natural hair confers an aggressive virility — precisely what consumer society cons him out of. When Lester finally gets a job, it's as a giant chicken crawling on his knees through the Manhattan streets, calling out "Cock-a-doodle-doo. Cock-a-doodle-do! Eat me. Eat me. All over town. Eat me at the King of Southern Fried Chicken!" (141). A total victory for white consumerism, this break comes on April Fool's Day (155), but Lester believes that it is "progress in *some* direction and that The Wig was my guide" (169). His transition from aspirant to dupe is nearly completed. The novel ends with Lester submitting to a haircut and the cauterization of his genitals.

Wright's subtitle ("A Mirror Image") suggests *The Wig*'s qualities as a distorting surface, neither degeneratively satirical nor even mildly grotesque. Instead the novel is a conventionally mimetic satire, quite clear in its selection of targets: white standards of beauty, racial stereotypes, Uncle Toms and Inchers Along, the emasculation of blacks under institutional racism. These were codes of conduct and morality whose absurdity, in 1966, was already obvious. Indeed, they were assailed with greater force in contemporary nonfictional texts like Malcolm X's *Autobiography* or Eldridge Cleaver's *Soul on Ice*. The problem, as in *Pinktoes*, is that Charles Wright attempted a satirical critique of American racism by means of a single sustained joke. The "wig," Lester's conkalined hair, is the ridiculous signifier of racist values that are wholly reified and offered for sale on the screen or over the counter. The joke is on Lester for naively buying into this consumer society. Eventually, however, that initial signifier becomes so overdetermined that it caves in beneath the weight of racist signifieds. Yet lying undeveloped around it are lodes of satiric possibility. All of Lester's acquaintances in Harlem are victims of the same con: "Miss Sandra Hanover," a black transvestite in need of a shave, masquerades as "a white woman from Georgia" (22) whose image derives entirely from screen stars like Bette Davis; his godfather Tom spends a fortune on newspapers, keeping demographic "charts" on white mortality and anticipating the day, centuries hence, when "they'll be a minority" (97); Deb, a prostitute, fantasizes she is a Junior Leaguer from the society pages; and one of Lester's neighbors, Nonnie Swift, impersonates a high-toned creole woman out of paperback novels. These moments are brief, scarcely even episodic. Yet they suggest how, at its most radical, The Wig strains to satirize the greater range of semiotic slots in contemporary culture, especially its promotion of personalities vulnerable to sexual and racial manipulation. Molding the self to those popular myths means yielding to the terms of a master/slave contract, a form of that mimetic desire which threatens uncontrollable violence if the categories disintegrate and some dupe, some form of the sacrificial victim cannot be found. That was Nathanael West's insight, and Lester Jefferson was potentially cut from the same cloth as Miss Lonelyhearts, Lemuel Pitkin, and Homer Simpson. Lester's sexual cauterization seems vaguely sacrificial, but The Wig is too concerned with its controlling joke, with the humorous correction of manners and morals for which Lester was the negative example. The novel only hints at stalking a larger prey, the semiotic construction of an oppressive polity, though Wright takes the satire of contemporary media much farther than Himes.

Chester Himes and Charles Wright phrased the problem facing any African-American satirist: how to put across a contrary "knowledge," humorously political and radically unauthorized? It can only be written in the language of hegemonic culture, and that language — for it is never one's own but always adoptive — already encodes every quality of oppression the writer might oppose. Still worse, this hegemonic discourse is preprogrammed to absorb any dissident expression by grafting it to massive, securely established structures of power. A more general, stripped-down version of this problem conditions the great range of satirical fictions in postmodernist America. Few writers have faced it with greater imaginative freedom than Ishmael Reed.

The curious thing about Reed's career is this: it began with a book that throws aside every convention of realist narration and traditional satire, then moves toward a more conventional narrative that is the vehicle of a targeted, corrective satirical aggression. There are notable comparisons. John Hawkes began his career with a novel, *The Cannibal,* which remains the most disruptive, antirealist satire he's published. Nathanael West, whose strong influence Reed has acknowledged, also begins with a far-fetched fabulation (*Balso Snell*), but ends by writing a kind of hard-boiled novel (*Locust*) whose realism is fully in the service of his satire. In fact, however, both Hawkes and West move toward a conventional realism only to more fully demolish it with their satire: *Travesty* is perhaps the best example. In Reed's case, the fictions tend to become increasingly embroiled in personal conflicts (for example, the conflict with Alice Walker in *Reckless Eyeballing;* but already in *Yellow Back Radio* there is a satire on Irving Howe). Or, in *The Terrible Twos,* the satire thrashes a single conceit (politics as tyrannous infantile desire) to a ridiculous pulp. So Reed's later satires are diminished by personal vendettas or sheer overkill. During the sixties and early seventies, however, he published several fine novels, and two of them, *The Free-Lance Pallbearers* (1967) and *Mumbo Jumbo* (1972), are among the most remarkable satirical fictions of their era.

An endnote to Reed's first novel, *The Free-Lance Pallbearers,* informs us that it was completed on August 13, 1966, in Hell's Kitchen, New York. This stands as both fact and emblem. The book's immediate context is a second summer of riots that surged over America's inner-city ghettos, in addition to a recent redoubling of troop strength in Vietnam, and — an impossible fantasy in light of these first two developments — a much ballyhooed attempt to fulfill the New Deal agenda in Lyndon Johnson's "Great Society." All of this was glimpsed from Hell's Kitchen, as much actual place as mythical *topos,* a hell-hole that Horatio Alger's match-boys and bootblacks left behind. The novel itself is also the satirical vision of a contemporary Hell, a direct descendent of Nathanael West's "Chamber of American Horrors, Animate and Inanimate Hideosities" (*A Cool Million*). Indeed, an early interview was the occasion for Reed to acknowledge the decisive influence of West's novels on his own work, though even West's writing is scant warning for the extreme disturbances in *Pallbearers.*[21]

Reed's first-person narrator, Bukka Doopeyduk, speaks quite literally from the coffin that is his book. Bukka tries to close the narration with his own grotesque death, after three days of hanging on a meathook in public. Yet this attempt to shape formal English into a narrative leading up to that political execution represents a cul-de-sac for the Afro-American novel. Having reached the moment of death Bukka is suddenly dissatisfied with the narrative, and he doubles back, attempting to find a new plot for his "long story"; he tries several new openings, then gives up "the ghost" as well as his narration: "O, no, that's not the way. What's the use?" (115). At that moment Reed signifies his rejection of the attempt to render in confessional narrative the accession of a naive black boy into the wisdom and mastery supposedly conferred by formal English and its codified ideologies. Early in the novel Bukka tells a "Nazarene" priest, "It behooves me to start at the bottom and work my way up the ladder. Temperance, frugality, thrift — that kind of thing" (8). The death blow to that Algeresque code and all its stuffy-sweet discourse comes when Bukka, a duped duck, finally arrives in the throne-room of white power, a giant commode. There, instead of elegantly formalized mysteries, he finds nothing more than a banally horrifying image of consumption, Moloch-style: Harry Sam, a former used-car salesman with a cannibalistic palate for young men, who hasn't been outside his motel bathroom in thirty years. Bukka, the direct descendent of Lemuel Pitkin (*A Cool Million*) and Lester Jefferson (*The Wig*), moves in this fabulously crude society, which mocks his every naive, optative phrase about Inchin' Along. Still he holds to the code. Bukka's execution thus mocks that Algeresque metanarrative and its Afro-American counterpart, the slave's autobiography describing his progress toward emancipation and knowledge, exemplified in Booker T. Washington's *Up from Slavery*. Ironized in *Native Son* and *Invisible Man* (Ellison includes a parody of Washington's autobiography), in *Pallbearers* that diegetic structure is satirized to bits.

The novel's society is also called "HARRY SAM." It is a literal body politic: he is its dictatorial head, and all political activity occurs "in" him, including a kind of decades-long constipation that has brought *real* historical progress to a standstill while the popular media labor to coat it with the impression of jetlike flux. A grotesque, oneiric version of our own society, Harry Sam's world — or better, Bukka's narrative of that world — collapses American space into the narrow environment around Harry Sam's Island (Manhattan?), where he has taken refuge. Most important, it also amalgamates the age, Roosevelt through Johnson, into a sort of historical bolus. Bukka's story is chock-a-block with dissociated references to contemporary figures like Averill Harriman (Aboreal Hairyman), John Kennedy, and Lyndon Johnson. The Nixons and their famous dog, Checkers, appear in a dream episode (chapter 2); British prime minister Neville Chamberlain appears on television just after his 1937 conciliatory visit with Hitler (57); SAM speaks of napalm as a "beneficent incapacitator" dropped on "them yellow dwarfs" running around the Vietnam jungles in their pajamas (97); and Bukka's death occurs precisely at 3 A.M. on August 6, 1945, the very moment the atomic bomb was dropped on Hiroshima. These references contribute to the shattering of that historical temporality which usually forms the backbone of any political fiction. Instead "history," like a colonic blockage, forms a conglomerate that is, as one reader notes, solidly list-like.[22] It obstructs any sense of organic progression or natural causality, the relations of priority that normally authorize political decisions. *Pallbearers* satirizes such obstructive fictions. In Reed's later novels they will be replaced with an alternate and politically enabling narrative of the Afro-American past.

One way Reed accomplishes this aim in *Pallbearers* is to employ a bi-level discourse. Bukka's speech, an impersonation of that stuffy, formal English he naively takes for the discourse of power, sharply contrasts with an informal, unauthorized speech — slang, non-standard usage, ethnic dialect, obscenity — that we normally associate with political and economic disenfranchisement (at least, until we recall the transcripts of Richard Nixon's Watergate conversations). In what initially seems a classic example of satiric inversion, Reed stands that association on its head. The terms of inversion are clearest when Bukka finally meets Harry Sam and the dictator outlines his "philosophy," the crudest possible statement of a bigoted, xenophobic terrorism: "When they act up and give you some lip, bomb the fuken daylights out of um. . . . That goes for spicks and gooks and all the rest what ain't like us" (98). The reader has been anticipating this from the start. Michel Fabre has shown that these nonstandard kinds of speech are, from the novel's opening paragraphs, as much in the service of political tyranny as standard English.[23] Bukka's friend Elijah Raven, leader of a putatively revolutionary black separatist group, the "Jackal Headed Front," speaks of bringing back "rukus juice and chittlins" and brags that "every freakin', punkish Remus will get it in the neck" (9). He is later found to have been "trickin'" for Sam all along (109) and is really no different from his seeming archenemy, the Reverend Eclair Porkchop, "whose star was rising fast in SAM" (9) and whose standard English sets the tone for Bukka's Algeresque, "Nazarene" fantasies. Indeed, the standard usage of Bukka and Porkchop fiercely parodies what Roland Barthes described as a "white" or zero-degree discourse, unnoticeable like motel wallpaper but nevertheless a powerful ideological vehicle. In Reed's view, though, the same holds true for those channels of discourse that Ralph Ellison calls the "lower frequencies": modes of oral practice, ethnic and folk tradition, or street speech. Thus when Porkchop is no longer successful at "rounding up votes for SAM" and working "to spellbound them colored people" with his preaching, Sam gives Bukka the job of going "down there in Soulsville" to "tell them IT'S GOIN' BE ALL RIGHT, BY AND BY IN THE SKY" (99). This is why the satiric inversion of *Pallbearers* is only an apparent one. There is simply no discourse that escapes condemnation for being the vehicle of an institutional terror.

One reason for this loss is that all kinds of "texts" have been cannibalized by mass culture. Harry Sam's world is a media construct, and within it all "knowledge" is constructed from scraps of signification lifted out of movies, television, newspapers, advertising, and the like. In *Pallbearers,* the "Nazarene faith" is nothing less than this, a mythological black hole, a gargantuan social mechanism for swallowing up prior significations and producing still more images, needs, plots, beliefs, and satisfactions, all in a dissimulation of flux and progress, every "new" signification merely the absurd double of some previous product. A parody of the book of Revelation, the "Nazarene apocalypse" depicts Harry Sam on "the great commode" in the sky, with a businessman, a Nazarene apprentice, and a black slum child on his lap. Next to him stand not the apocalyptic four horsemen but "four washroom attendants. In their hands they had seven brushes, seven combs, seven towels, and seven bars of soap, a lock of Roy Rogers' hair and a Hershey bar. Above the figures float Lawrence Welk champagne bubbles. Below this scene tombstones have been rolled aside and the Nazarene faithful are seen rising from the mist" (45–46). A banal fantasy of servitude and capitalist excess, this is composed by the same means as those apparently subversive acts of semiosis like the "Happening" in which Bukka is the central figure. Organized by artist "Cipher X" of "Entropy Productions," the idea of "Git it On" is to clamp Bukka into a colonial pillory behind which is a tape recorder and a movie screen. The tape spews revolutionary rhetoric ("WHITEY YOU DIE RIGHT AFTER BREAKFAST . . .") while the screen features Leni Reifenstahl's documentary film, *Olympiad,* with its leaping black hurdlers and marching *Hitlerjugend,* and while a robot throws baseballs at a gagged Bukka. Before him, members of the audience rustle their newspapers (the *NY Teeth* and *NY Whine*) and exchange "cogent comments" about the symbolism of Christ on the cross and the scholarship of Jesse Weston (76).

This performance instantly transforms Bukka into the hottest new revolutionist and media darling, but again he's been conned. He's drafted into a "liberation movement" whose chief concerns are with questions like "whether the brothers should part their hair on the side or part it down the middle" (80), and it develops that Cipher X not only receives government payola but also stages private performances for Harry Sam inside his infamous motel (81). One reader has observed that Bukka's work in the "Happening" is analogous to Tod Clifton's degradation in *Invisible Man*.[24] Even more, though, it is a miniature of Bukka's entire story. In its performative, amalgamating construction of "reality" out of mass-cultural signs, in its witless support for ideologies of consumption and oppression, the "Happening" is targeted by Reed's satire just as surely as is Bukka's naive, failed narrative of success and emancipation.

But *Pallbearers* is more than a conventional satire with clearly enunciated "targets" and "norms." Reed's is also the degenerative vision of a world in which popular (ethnic, folk) expression is completely in the service of mechanisms for mass social conditioning. It figures an ontologically *other* but uncannily *familiar* world where power has found the most expeditious means of exerting control and authority in a vast leveling or equalizing of formerly competing signs — in short, in "Entropy Productions." In this world everything can change but it always, deviously, stays the same. After Bukka's death the neon sign over Harry Sam's Motel still flashes the same message — "EATS-SAVE GREEN STAMPS-BINGO WED-EATS" — only now it is "WRITTEN IN CHINESE NO LESS" (116). Harry Sam's cannibalism is only the synecdoche for this larger transformation of all signs into the disposable icons of a mechanical communication. That atavistic, degenerative violence is potentially uncontrollable, so the polity must stage its compensatory sacrificial rites: Bukka standing Christlike in the stocks or hanging three days from a meathook. While these rites are practically *effective* in quelling the danger of real revolutionary uprisings they also are, as René Girard argues, inherently random and thus veritably *meaningless*. This is the great secret of socialized, stylized modes of violence. It explains why Bukka's narrative cannot finally account for his execution.

In *The Free-Lance Pallbearers*, Reed provides no character with whom readers might identify. As such the novel is fundamentally different from Reed's later works, where a Loop Garoo Kid or PaPa LaBas lays out a positive plan of action. In addition, while *Pallbearers* is Reed's most overtly political book in its references to a thirty-year span of American history, the text nevertheless resists making a proper political critique of Harry Sam's world. For how could it? In a blink that world would absorb any radical critique, it would even seem to found its own new knowledge and mythology on the leveled wreckage of the old. These are aspects of "humorous" satire defined in chapter 3. *Pallbearers* disrupts the causal linkages of conventional narrative (the real-world chronology or *fabula*) and furthermore offers no grounds for a rationalist "explanation" (or naturalization) of its disruptiveness. Instead the novel offers up a world of pop-cultural artifacts and behavioral slots, all glimpsed as a moiling, centerless exchange, the postmodern sublime imagined as a too-familiar world of fleeting, grotesque surfaces. Here, the conventions of ironic stability and distance vanish. Such a novel parodically invokes metanarratives (like Alger's) in order to release its withering laughter against them, and this degenerative humor acknowledges no necessary stops, no sanative last rites to close the tale.

Only in his later satires does Reed begin to compose the alternate and enabling narrative so pointedly absent in *Pallbearers*. As such, his later satires are also more didactic and corrective, and Reed begins to imagine himself a Necromancer, a Hoo-Doo conjurer freeing his fellow sufferers from the attacks of evil spirits. Doubtless there is a strong connection between these aims and the kind of corrective-normative satire that Robert Elliott has defined in the light of primitive magic. At the same time, Reed's later satires are more prone to personal invective, the weapon of one aiming at "punishing vice" or at restoring order by piling "scorn" on one "who is also weighed down with guilt" for being linked to that degenerative violence which society must quell.[25] Reed's first novel is therefore also his last full-strength foray into the degenerate, "monstrous territory" Nathanael West identified as a new satirical resource.

Reed's next novel, *Yellow Back Radio Broke Down* (1969), makes its search for a corrective fiction clear at the outset.[26] In the wild west town of Yellow Back Radio the children, stoned on "pearl-shaped pills," have either killed or run off every adult because, as one boy explains, "We were tired of them ordering us around. . . . Made us learn facts by rote. Lies really bent upon making us behave. We decided to create our own fiction."[27] That, in its barest form, is the novel's plot: a revolt against the fictions of patriarchal (and monotheistic) power. A good deal of it was certainly anticipated in Norman Mailer's 1957 essay *The White Negro: Superficial Reflections on the Hipster,* which argued that in the face of The Bomb, Dulles Diplomacy, and Corporate America, a young person of sensitive intelligence had better seek refuge in "hip," self-chosen exile. Such an ideological exodus from repressive America would creatively imitate the Negro's historical alienation, and to Mailer it was very nearly an internecine, countercultural "war," or at least "preparations for war," between the camps of the Hip and the Square. A decade later when Reed was writing, that struggle had actually spilled into the streets, and much of *Yellow Back* reads like a fable about the Berkeley student uprisings of the late sixties. The book's Square essence is embodied in Drag Gibson, an imperialist, Indian-hating marshall bent on grabbing the town of Yellow Back Radio so he can "turn the dial" to his own stations (19). His Hip counterpart, Loop

Garoo, conjuring cowboy and avatar of Satan, begins putting out long, invective spells.[28] "Drag Gibson, whiskey drinker," he disses in one instance, "your Hoo-Doo death will be a collector's item, your head will lie in excrement, the flies will feast upon it" (95). Assisted by an Indian named Chief Showcase, Loop offers up these verbal sacrifices as a "Micro-Hoo-Doo mass to end 2000 years of bad news" (74). The drama concludes with Drag calling in hired guns, from the infamous John Wesley Hardin to Pope Innocent, Loop Garoo being captured and nearly hanged in what he calls a "parody on His passion" (203), then escaping to chase away Drag and the Pope while Yellow Back Radio's children set out for an Eldorado that sounds like a hipster's lubricious pipe dream.

Yellow Back is very much the same temporal salmagundi as Pallbearers (Lewis and Clark trek through as helicopters whirl overhead) and is similarly attentive to the leveling forces that postmodern culture exerts on speech. Yet the novel is a fundamentally different text. Loop Garoo's Neo-Hoo-Dooism is a counterpractice and alternative wisdom that nevertheless speaks with a privileged authority; and too often this leads to tiresomely didactic passages. Especially toward the close, the story frequently dissolves into homilies, and every explanation, every annotative clarification, detracts from the fable and normalizes the satire. Using Loop as his mouthpiece, Reed defines Hoo-Doo as "an unorganized religion without ego-games or death-worship," the purpose of which is to dethrone "all daddies" (198). Yet this attack on patriarchal power is only vaguely developed, and by novel's end any potential of its becoming a political critique has been subsumed in Reed's intention of surveying and defending Hoo-Doo as an aesthetic. It is thus the enabling fiction missing from Pallbearers, and dodgy enough never to be caught and routinized by the likes of Harry Sam or the Pope, who cautions that "Loop seems to be scatting arbitrarily, using forms of this and adding his own. He's blowing like that celebrated musician Charles Yardbird Parker — improvising as he goes along" (184). All too often this defense spills over into preaching or personal argument.

In a review of Pallbearers, Irving Howe had condemned Reed for attempting to write Swiftian satire but achieving merely a "Mad Magazine silliness" and, still worse (according to Howe), being inaccurate about historical details.[29] In Yellow Back, Howe appears as a feared "rustler," Bo Schmo, leader of the vicious "neo-social realist gang" and writer of books in which "every gumdrop machine is in place," instead of being "a blur and a doodle" as in the fictions of Loop/Reed (40). The scene is most of all an occasion for Reed to defend his fictional practice as something carnivalesque ("What if I write circuses? No one says a novel has to be one thing"), improvisational (a way of "scatting"), and aggressively didactic (the dissing and other preachy invectives). Yet that aesthetic debate is never integrated with the novel's political satire, just as the sixties never synthesized "countercultural" practice with political struggle. As a result, *Yellow Back Radio Broke Down* will likely remain a footnote in the literary history of the sixties, evidence of continuing debate between neorealist critics and novelists on the one hand, and on the other those who were changing the rules of both narrative and satirical art.

Mumbo *Jumbo* (1972), Reed's next, is a different matter. Its aesthetics are one with its political aims. Indeed, of all the novels taken up in these chapters it is unique in adhering to the punitive and didactic aims that formalist criticism associated with satire, while also grafting to that tradition the diegetic possibilities of a playfully intertextual postmodernism. Replete with illustrative photographs, quotations, footnotes, and bibliography, *Mumbo Jumbo* is Reed's most studied attempt at parodying a "historical" treatise. The novel is technically similar to the fictions of a Barthelme or a Pynchon. To date, it is also his most far-reaching exploration of a polyphonic, Menippean discourse, the means by which he sought to yoke the traditional with the experimental.

For Reed this was a quite logical move. Julia Kristeva has aptly pointed out that the history of the Menippean novel is, from Rabelais forward, a "history of struggle against Christianity and its representation." Menippean satire subsumes the laughter of carnival, turning it into a discourse that is not only parodic but, Kristeva argues, a fusion of both the tragic and the comic, a "serious" laughter that is neither the temporary disruption of convention and law nor their social reaffirmation. Instead, Menippean satire becomes a discourse of "the other," a radical speech on the margins of Judaeo-Christianity, and a mode prone to monstrous phantasmagoria. Freed from historical and political constraints, it is a "structured ambivalence," a miscellany of discourse types and forms whose montage reveals the sociopolitical backdrop as "a correlative system of signs" and hence freely manipulable by one and all.[30] For Reed, this was the potential he had been seeking to control: from the parody of Judaeo-Christian values and mythologies in the "Nazarene faith" of *Pallbearers,* through Loop Garoo's improvisational, satanic war against Pope Innocent in *Yellow Back.*

As its title already indicates, *Mumbo Jumbo* is a hotchpotch of discourses and genres. Beyond parodying the look and apparatus of a historical textbook on the Harlem Renaissance, it also incorporates at least four other conventional genres. First, it parodies the slangy, hard-boiled detective novel, with Hoo-Doo priest Papa LaBas as an "astro-detective" or "jacklegged detective of the metaphysical," and its plot includes a murder (of Abdul Sufi Hamid), a lost enigmatic object of incalculable worth (Reed's Maltese Falcon is the stolen text of "Jes Grew"), and a mystery unraveled at the end (Abdul burned the manuscript).[31] Secondly, it is the text of a long-suppressed mythology, a narrative of aboriginal backgrounds in Egypt and Africa, of exodus and exilic servitude watched over by helpful spirits, of the secret maintenance of tribal rituals, and the promise, should these beliefs fully emerge from hiding, of emancipation. Thirdly, *Mumbo Jumbo* critiques an age-old political antinomy: rational, Apollonian "Atonists" maintaining their imperial privileges through "secret societies" and technological violence, and the low-down, improvisational, Dionysian practitioners of "Hoo-Doo" who feel that "everybody should have their own head or the head of God which the Atonist's mundane system wouldn't admit." Reed calls this ideal *Homo economicus* (247): man as "manager of his own household," his own "divine plan for worldly government," as the etymology suggests. Fourthly, the novel incorporates a long historical lecture (184–219) by Papa LaBas on the origins and perversions of voodoo practices and metaphysics, from Set's mythical murder of his brother Osiris through the dissimulations of that originary violence in secret societies like the Knights Templar and the Masons. Scattered throughout the novel, finally, are still more forms: mock newspaper reports, telegrams, handbills, a letter (in longhand), boldface quotations from scholarly texts, ads (for the Cotton Club), a graph showing increased "U.S. Bombing Tonnage in Three Wars" (186), and a ludicrous parody of the sort of poem white "Negrophiles" used to write about Harlem during the twenties ("Harlem Tom Toms," 180–82). Finally, *Mumbo Jumbo* is Reed's stylistic tour de force, its jazzy poetics notable from the opening paragraph: "A true Sport, the Mayor of New Orleans, spiffy in his patent-leather brown and white shoes, his plaid suit, the Rudolph Valentino parted-down-the-middle hair style, sits in his office. Sprawled upon his knees is Zuzu, local doo-wack-a-doo and voo-do-dee-odo fizgig. A slatternly floozy, her green, sequined dress quivers."

Taken together these traits breed a fiction that is (like the work of Barthelme, Coover, and Pynchon) omni-generical, multiform in everything from its main diegetic structures to its typography, and heteroglot in its range of speech. It is, in sum, Reed's fullest expression of the "eclectic" and "open-ended" aesthetic he calls "Neo-Hoo-Doo."[32] Its aim, while overtly historical, is also quite clearly political: to reclaim the power of interpreting one's own racial identity, thus to release it from the "lies" that support institutional oppression. In Reed's view, whoever performs this function is immediately condemned as a "sorcerer" or "witch" and then "excorcised" (that is, executed for political crimes). Yet these condemnations are also the African-American artist's strongest evidence that he or she has found the right pressure points, and they drive the artist to embrace that radical practice all the more confidently. For as a Hoo-Doo spirit warns in *Yellow Back*, "When State Magic fails unofficial magicians become stronger" (53).

*Mumbo Jumbo* is specifically about the diminished capacity of "State Magic" during the Harlem Renaissance and, by analogy, once again during the late sixties. Two historical events initiate the narrative: the renaissance of black culture in twenties Harlem, with jazz, dance, and a surging literary production as its main expressions, and Woodrow Wilson's 1920 decision to dispatch the Marine Corps to Haiti and suppress a popular insurrection associated with Voodoo practices. The novel seeks to "explain" these as intertwined events. The cultural renaissance was a modern resurgence of "Jes Grew," a phrase James Weldon Johnson coined to describe any spontaneous cultural expression that belongs to all and that Reed's white authorities regard as a monstrous Voodoo "infestation," a threat to the purity of white civilization that must be eradicated at its source. This accounts for the invasion of Haiti. As such, *Mumbo Jumbo* is subversive, fabulative history, and perhaps the most wildly parodic historical "explanation" written during an epoch that was, as Richard Hofstadter pointed out in *The Paranoid Style in American Politics,* weirdly attentive to "the paranoid style" of popular conspiracy theories. However, Reed's satire argues that Jes Grew went dormant not because of a Marine invasion but because black artists could not find "a speaking" equal to its power. Vanquished for millenia, a "fool" and "vagabond with the rucksack on [its] shoulder — always on the road" (*Yellow Back* 198), Jes Grew is free energy in search of its form or "liturgy."

According to Reed, the mistake of black artists was in forcing this energy into the "privileged," canonical forms of Anglo-European tradition. This was worrisome enough to white arbiters of culture. As the racist Biff Musclewhite explains to a young Negrophile named Thor Wintergreen, "Son, these niggers writing. Profaning our sacred words. Taking them from us and beating them on the anvil of Boogie Woogie, putting their black hands on them so that they shine like burnished amulets. Taking our words, son, these filthy niggers and using them like they were their very god-given pussy" (130). Reed imagines covert agents at work on both sides. Hinkle von Vampton, a caricature of writer-editor-promoter Carl Van Vechten, sponsors a man in blackface, "the Talking Android," whose poem "Harlem Tom Toms" only plays at revolt in order to divert violence into pride over the petty illicitness of Harlem nightlife. An underground cell of Jes Grew devotees, the Mu'tafikah, liberate artifacts held in "Centers of Art Detention" (museums) and return them to their rightful Third World owners. One of Papa LaBas's daughters defects to the "Atonist" way; LaBas himself gives subversive lectures at Atonist universities. *Mumbo Jumbo* is thus the story of a war fought abroad and at home, as later with Vietnam. Its participants are secret agents, fifth columnists, snipers, and faithful grunts, who fight in Haiti with actual weapons but at home mostly with words, artworks, rhythms. The most interesting figure of this war, aside from Papa LaBas, is Abdul Sufi Hamid, the Black Muslim who comes to possess "The Book of Thoth," Jes Grew's sacred "text," but destroys the manuscript out of disgust at the authors' "lewd" imaginings.

Other than LaBas and his followers, Abdul is the sole character exempted from Reed's satiric ridicule. A Black Muslim originally named Johnny James, he grew up in Chicago's South Side ghetto and spent nine years in prison for stabbing a landlord who tried to rape his mother. In prison Abdul realized that his former schoolteachers carelessly "threw the knowledge" at them, because it was little more than "a cabala," and that "stripped of its terms and the private codes, its slang, you could learn [it] in a few weeks." Even more, the system was set up to "remove the rebels and the dissidents," to ensure there will be "people who will serve." So Abdul begins educating himself, proceeding "like a quilt maker, a patch of knowledge here a patch there but lovingly knitted" (41). Like LaBas with his "knockings," Abdul is a character fully alert to the signs and "hieroglyphics" of his culture. His aim, identical to LaBas's, is to build a cross-cultural, improvisational, "eclectic" knowledge (41). Still more, Reed has granted Abdul an accurate historical foresight, a sense of broad trends and even of the specifics of language, validating his approach as a formidable alternative to Jes Grew. He advises LaBas, "A new generation is coming on the scene. They will use terms like 'nitty gritty,' 'for real,' 'where it's at,' and use words like 'basic' and 'really' with telling emphasis. They will extend the letter and the meaning of the word 'bad.' They won't use your knowledge and they will call you 'sick' and 'way out' and that will be a sad day, but we must prepare for it" (43). For all this foresight and his similarities to LaBas, however, Abdul Sufi Hamid is different in ways that disclose a good deal about the structure and purpose of Reed's satire. Most of all he subscribes to a relentlessly monotheistic faith, a Mohammedanism that LaBas discounts as a late spin-off from Judaeo-Christianity. This metaphysic encourages Abdul to pin his hopes for liberation on a new patriarch, a new "strong man." In a letter discovered after his death, he writes LaBas, "One day all of us shall be able to express a variety of opinions, styles, and values . . .

but for now we need a strong man, someone to 'whip these coons into line.' Let the freedom of culture come later! Know this sounds contradictory but I don't have God's mind, yet!" (230). The arrogant confidence of that qualifier, "yet," explains the action he reveals next: the ancient "Book of Thoth" has "gone up in smoke!"; Abdul burned it, having decided for himself that "black people could never have been involved in such a lewd, nasty, decadent thing as is depicted here" (231).

Papa LaBas condemns it as the action of "a Patrolman of the mind handing out tickets to any idea or thought that sped or made U turns" (233). But certainly there is more to be said. Abdul's background so honestly invites empathy and respect, while Reed has gone so far to reveal his practice as both similar to and different from what LaBas espouses and has so exempted him from ridicule while making Abdul a mainspring of the novel's detective plot, that one is compelled to see him as central. He represents a potential threat to the opposition between Atonism and Jes Grew that is driving Reed's satire. To see how this is so we need only sketch out the novel's contraries and their second-order contradictions, yielding the "deep-structure" or semiotic rectangle of Figure 5. This heuristic reveals several traits of Reed's satire. For one, while the first-order contraries are obsessively developed in *Mumbo Jumbo* and are well represented by, on the one hand, Bif Musclewhite and his ilk and on the other, LaBas and his followers, nevertheless those second-order contradictions are all but neglected in the text, save for the faceless hangers-on who associate, for example, with the pleasures of Jes Grew yet are deaf to its metaphysical "knockings." Reed neglects these minor figures because his focus is entirely on that principal antinomy, and thus his fiction differs substantially from texts we will examine later in this chapter and the next. For another, it is clear that the character Abdul embodied a potential synthesis of that primary opposition: the strong-armed monotheism of the Atonists and Musclewhite ("white-muscle") versus the improvisational spontaneity of Jes Grew. In this primary or "ideal" synthesis the narrative would achieve an ideological closure or arrest of the sort that Fredric Jameson identifies with the realist novel. Abdul functions as the potential agent for real social change, with the power of resolving those sociocultural tensions expressed in the fiction.

This begins to clarify, not only why Abdul has to die, but why Reed had to *respectfully* condemn him. Simply put, Reed had staked his fortunes on Jes Grew. Historically, politically, morally, aesthetically, the Neo-Hoo-Doo practices of Jes Grew aspire to be the normative center of his satire. Reed refuses to compromise that aspiration by using a device that realist fictions too often

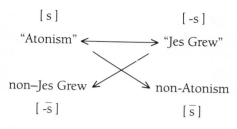

**FIGURE 5**

deploy in covertly defending ideologies of power and mastery. In fact one might well say that this is a hallmark of traditional satire: it must establish a normative center, a complex and bulwarked seme, which the satirist seeks to leave unscathed by the disruptions of his technique. In *Mumbo Jumbo*, this means that the best Reed can offer by way of resolving that antinomy is to have LaBas optimistically claim, "We will make our own future Text. A future generation of young artists will accomplish this. If the Daughters of the Eastern Star can do it, so can they" (233). Yet this sounds too much like Harry Sam's "BY AND BY IN THE SKY," too much like Lester Jefferson's "Inchin' Along." Perhaps this is why Reed included an "Epilogue" set in the late sixties, with its countercultural references that seem to validate LaBas's optimism.

Eventually, students of Reed's work will have to account for the trade-offs he thus achieved. In *Mumbo Jumbo,* he brought his aesthetics into harmony with his political aims by turning to the diegetic potential of a heteroglot, Menippean satire, but that satire is always held in check around its normative center. By comparison, in *Pallbearers* there is no discourse, no "Text," that is fully galvanized against the corrosive doubt of his satire. What's evident is that by 1972 Reed's "Neo-Hoo-Doo" aesthetic was, in his view, so fully articulated that his subsequent fictions of the seventies — *The Last Days of Louisiana Red* (1974) and *Flight to Canada* (1976) — are further applications or specific targetings of its critical and didactic force.

In Norman Mailer's 1967 novel, *Why Are We in Vietnam?* the first-person narrator identifies himself as either one of two opposite types. He may be a spoiled white kid, coddled in the lap of Dallas money, racism, and imperialist fantasies. Or he may be a devious black kid from Harlem, scatting the whole story as a fantastically obscene, aggressive rap about the imperial culture that has him "trapped in a Harlem head" afflicted with insanity, "a Spade gone ape in the mind from outrageous frustrates wasting him and so now living in an imaginary white brain" at a farewell banquet prior to his departure for Southeast Asia.³³ Yet there is also a possibility that it is not a case of either/or at all, but something more paradoxical, a hip teenager *both* sneeringly disaffected with his affluent white parents *and* smoldering with satirical black rage against those who deny him. Taken together in the fictional D. J. but separately in actual white and black teenagers, these aggressive qualities would define the typical infantryman who fought in what Michael Herr referred to as America's "rock 'n' roll war." This realization produces a remarkable narrative critique. Mailer's novel suggests first that America's racial schizophrenia is really a single psychic disease or parasitism, the violent black consciousness riding subversively and satirically in its repressed and guilt-laden white host, and next suggests that the degenerative aggression of this conflict *explains* the nation's intervention in a distant civil war.

The remarkable thing is not just the reach of Mailer's hypothesis, its identification of domestic racism with an imperialist foreign policy, but that the satire was written at all. *Why Are We in Vietnam?* stands alone, *the* major narrative satire written about Vietnam during the American sixties and seventies. Even at that the novel is only offered as a prefatory fiction. The novel's sole mention of Southeast Asia comes in the last sentence, as D.J. (the narrator) prepares to embark: "This is D.J., Disk Jockey to America, turning off. Vietnam, hot damn" (208). Subsequent novels treated the topic according to the tenets of a traditional realism (Stone's *Dog Soldiers,* Caputo's *A Rumor of War*) or of a contemporary magical realism (O'Brien's *Going after Cacciato*). For satire, American novelists turned instead to World War II. The result was two important novels that bracketed the sixties, *Catch-22* (1961) and *Slaughterhouse-Five* (1969), which I will discuss before turning to Mailer. Perhaps the delayed reactions of Heller and Vonnegut indicate that we shall see nothing similar about Vietnam until much later, as if military violence were untouchable in satire until the war itself has been mythicized. Otherwise one is hard pressed to account for the dearth of satiric fictions. In a 1977 foreword to *Why Are We in Vietnam?,* Mailer notes that when his novel was first published it seemed to release aggressions like some malignant "occult force" (4). He fretted over the novel's violent "humor" because it seemed too close to "the pervasive malignity of our electronic air" (5), perhaps even contributing to it. This was an afterthought, however. Whatever may have kept others from writing satire on the subject of Vietnam, one would still think that satire, a discourse of violence, would have something to say on the subject of war.

In late 1961 Joseph Heller's first novel was greeted by reviewers who, as a group, weren't sure what to call it. Half of them read *Catch-22* as "a comic novel about World War II," another half took it as a satiric "repudiation" of our entire military-industrial "civilization." This uncertainty persists. Frederick Karl reads the book as "a comic novel" with "satirical asides" that gather steam toward the close, when Heller depicts war-torn Rome as a grotesque hell out of Hieronymous Bosch. Blurbs on the Dell paperback still tout large helpings of comedy and satire.[34] These are conflicted readings, and there are two good reasons for us to try sorting them out. Doing so should further indicate how political subjects are handled in satire, while also revealing the kinship of postmodernist satire with other modes.

*Catch-22* is a novel with the mimetic potential of satire and the diegetic structure of comedy. Its bureaucratic society stands the familiar world on its head, a standard device of both comedy and satire, but that mimetic treatment increasingly tends toward the satirical. Initially the novel teaches that the worst failures as civilians are paradoxically the most successful soldiers. In civilian life Colonel Cargill "had to start at the top and work his way down" in business, and it "took months of hard work and careful misplanning" for him to become "a self-made man who owed his lack of success to nobody" (28), an effort the government rewarded with monetary aid and, after war broke out, a commission. Similarly, government bureaucracies pay Major Major's father very handsomely to fail at growing alfalfa (85). The only characters with any "principles" are either given impossible missions that kill them off, like Clevinger, or they are demoted like the corporal who "disapproved of Adolph Hitler" (35). In this inverted world it is of course crazy to oppose the unopposable because all-encompassing commands of a bureaucracy whose only principle is absurd conformity. The Air Corps thus becomes Heller's stage for satirizing the rise of what sociologist William Whyte called "organization man." Scheisskopf rockets up in the bureaucracy by "maximizing" the conformity of his underlings; Colonel Cathcart sets the production quota, or mission count, constantly raising it so that no one ever retires; Milo Minderbinder, like William Gaddis's J. R. Vansant, is the consummate middleman whose relentless dealing keeps upper management (Dreedle and Peckem) well supplied with benefits. In this polity the only rule is that of circulation: keeping men and goods in motion is how management is assured of reaching into the flow to surreptitiously grab its "perks." One of Heller's recurrent figures for this condition is "the soldier in white," the bandaged carcass who functions only as a funnel for endless exchange, as workers trade his bottles of excremental wastes with those that feed him. Another is Snowden, whose only "secret" is an abject loss of humanity and whose recurrent plaint, "I'm cold," summarizes the alienated state of organization man.

At first Heller treats this upside-down world with comic bemusement. Its endless circulation of goods, men, and ideas summed up in the tautology of Catch-22, like the relentless pressures for conformity, are subjects for a classically comical treatment. The novel's mimetic focus is on a mechanical humanity that Henri Bergson identified as the essence of the comic. Yet this perspective always also verges into satire. Scheisskopf's plans for better marching, his dream of linking every soldier's arms and legs by means of copper wires attached to "nickle alloy pegs" embedded in their bones and joints (75), is very much the stuff of grotesque satire. A grisly violence waits to explode even amidst the novel's most idyllic moments: a propeller grinds Kid Sampson into hamburger on a warm summer's day at the beach; Snowden's death is dreamily serene until Yossarian opens his flak vest, spilling a chaos of entrails over the airplane floor. To Heller, war is precisely a "world boiling in chaos in which everything was in order" (148), a phrase that neatly summarizes the mimetic potential of satire as opposed to comedy (recall Hawkes's "design and debris" in *Travesty*). For if the end of comedy is in its reaffirmation of orderly social codes, that of satire is to pull off the vest shielding us in convention and conformity, so to reveal the deadly chaos underneath.

In *Catch-22* that satiric purpose slowly overwhelms the comedy until, in chapter 39 ("The Eternal City"), war-torn Rome becomes a classic locus of misanthropic, saturnalian disgust. It has taken this long for Heller's comedy to reveal that "Catch-22 did not exist" (418), to show that it is only the fiction of cruelly self-interested bureaucrats. As such there is "no object or text to ridicule or refute, to accuse, to criticize, attack, amend, hate, revile, spit at, rip to shreds, trample or burn up" (418). In sum, Heller's nominal subject stands beyond the provenance of a targeted, normative satiric aggression. Therefore one function of chapter 39 is to displace satire's conventionally narrow, corrective focus onto the broader symbolic landscape of Rome, represented here as a laughable horror of "grotesque cripples, catatonic mothers and bedraggled children" (421). Rome, during the Christmas of 1944, embodies every prior inversion and ridiculous distortion, every self-interest and lack of empathy that "Catch-22" turns into a positive value. Still worse, to Yossarian "nothing warped seemed bizarre any more in his strange, distorted surroundings" (421), and he realizes that the entire Euro-American polity has dissolved into "Mobs . . . mobs of policemen. . . . Mobs with clubs were in control everywhere" (426). Like West's, or Hawkes's, this is a world teetering on the edge of absolute violence.

As the novel ends we thus recognize one of the classic *topoi* of satire. From *The Satyricon* of Petronius through *The Day of the Locust* and *The Cannibal*, mob violence is the common figure of degenerative culture. Mob violence figures the constructive power of language as a force for mindless, reciprocal violence, or (in the Pentagon's apt phrasing from this time) "mutually assured destruction." Total war, random death, an absence of polity — these are its chief signs. Just so, in chapter 39, Yossarian stumbles across the normally innocent, complacent Aarfy after he's just raped a young girl and then killed her because he "couldn't very well let her go around saying bad things" about him (427). When the military police investigate, Aarfy goes free while Yossarian is arrested "for being in Rome without a pass" (429). Similarly, from this chapter forward Yossarian never knows when Nately's whore's kid sister will try once again to stab him with a bread knife — for simply telling her of Nately's death. Her threat draws attention back to the danger of any one-on-one message.

Modified in organizational bureaucracies, this tendency toward error and random violence erupts everywhere. Yossarian himself mimics it in his hospital bed at the novel's beginning, when he randomly obliterates words from the letters of enlisted men. Finally, however, that disorder is unmasked as a satiric horror. Organizational discourse is not only a cover for the basest, most selfish hypocrisies; it is also a trigger of violence. The disruptions of speech are directly commensurate with the devastation of war. Thus all of Heller's earlier punning, his ridiculously circular dialogues, and well-timed jokes are the verbal preparation for this greater chaos which the satire eventually both registers and insinuates through the system of signs. Catch-22 is therefore quite clearly satirical in fulfilling this intent to mime the degeneration of a human culture absurdly devoted to everything nonhuman, mechanical, dead. The narrative represents a sociopolitical decay so total that the only recourse of its protagonist is desertion.

This is the novel's mimetic conclusion, yet the diegetic structure for Yossarian's desertion stands in sharp contrast to that satiric potential. In its plot, Catch-22 initially seems to bear all the signs of conventional satire. It has the circuitous, episodically disorganized structure, as well as the fractured temporality that Kernan, for example, has identified in satirical fictions. Also, once we reconstruct the temporal sequence of its story from scattered references, it even has the overall trajectory, from Spring to Winter, that Frye would identify as a movement from the mythos of comedy to that of satire.³⁵ This plot would also seem to bolster our sense of the novel's mimetic development, in which the satire seems finally to overwhelm the comedy. Yet how shall we square Yossarian's departure with these aims? Frederick Karl observes that Yossarian must decipher his possibilities for action between "two extremes": an egoistic and mercantilistic avarice represented by Milo Minderbinder and the innocent, self-effacing naiveté embodied most of all by Nately ("newborn") but also by Snowdon.[36] This is well put, but other readings have interestingly stated Yossarian's predicament in terms of another character set: the semblance of an innocent yet very practical complacency in Aarfy that, when possessive desire shatters it, spills over into violence (a rape-murder), and the desolately unsatisfied irritability of Hungry Joe, whose worst nightmares about dying (smothering under a sleeping cat) come true. It is Orr who will decipher *his* way between these contraries: Orr, whose nightmares about flying are well founded (he's shot down on all eighteen of his missions) and whose endlessly patient tinkering with machines (the wood stove) drives Yossarian to raging distraction. In the novel's final chapter, it is Orr (the very name suggests his importance as an alternative) whose "escape" to Sweden in a raft (using an "oar") gives Yossarian "faith."

Milo and Nately, Aarfy and Hungry Joe, together they represent first- and second-order contraries that the novel develops as semantic possibilities for action. If arranged around the corners of a semiotic rectangle, we would see that along its base the potential for a "neutral" synthesis of one narratological conflict (Aarfy/Hungry Joe) is represented by Orr's self-centered escape, while at its top the potential for an "ideal" synthesis of the other conflict (Milo/Nately) is, as several readers have commented, embodied in Yossarian.[37] The principal difference between him and Orr is that Yossarian claims he will be running *to* his "responsibilities," plotting not only his own self-preservation but also trying to save Nately's whore's kid sister. He tells Chaplain Tappman, "There's a young kid in Rome whose life I'd like to save if I can find her. I'll take her to Sweden with me if I can find her, so it isn't all selfish, is it?" (462). *Catch-22* develops this conclusion out of a plot that has, as we have noted, all the trappings of a conventional satire, yet in so doing it reaffirms the principal values of bourgeois society, in particular the value of "responsible" monogamous union (a decisive change for a womanizer like Yossarian) and the ideal of rationalizing one's self-interests along lines that also benefit others (an ideal at least as old as Adam Smith). Even though it is projected outside the space of Heller's narrative, such an idealized resolution is the stuff not of satire but of comedy. Surely this is why different camps have read the novel either as a comedy whose ironies are whetted on its "satiric asides" or as a satire whose vision is blunted by the comedy. In fact it is a little of both. But postmodern satire has little to do with the kind of idealized, ameliorating resolution that Heller wants to discover.

That optimistic ending raises still more political questions. For, in deserting the bureaucratic juggernaut of war, Heller's first generation of readers embraced John Yossarian in the same "countercultural" spirit that they hailed Ken Kesey's hero, Randall Patrick McMurphy, for battling "the combine." Yet how can we compare them? *One Flew Over the Cuckoo's Nest* has been criticized for pinning the hope of resistance to a strong, charismatic leader, a populist *Führer* who stands as the adoptive father to society's chewed-up souls. Even so, *Cuckoo's Nest* at least phrases out the hope of collective action; McMurphy has several chances to run, but elects tribal solidarity. By contrast Heller's fiction leaves one with an image of the survivor in his lifeboat, paddling toward a Sweden that is half-mythical. In retrospect this seems one crucial legacy of the Vietnam era. Instead of seeking political power and a resolution of seemingly hopeless violence, walk away from it all. There is one version of it in *Dog Soldiers,* as a dope-addled Jack Hicks walks into the desert to die, and another in Cacciato's long, fabulous walk to Paris in Tim O'Brien's novel.

At least Joseph Heller could still imagine some possibilities for individual action. In *Slaugherhouse-Five* they seem to have disappeared. The book's protagonist, Billy Pilgrim, voices an abnegated ethics. Whisked away from war-torn Germany to the planet Tralfamadore, where he lives in a zoo exhibit, Billy Pilgrim is granted that great Judaeo-Christian vision, the Pisgah sight of history. Having it, though, does not commit him to the practical ethics of an already-seen yet still individually achieved revelation. Instead he lives in utter resignation before the glacial shiftings of Time's inevitable becoming. Most of all, to him (as, apparently, to Vonnegut) *wars* are like glaciers. And after becoming "spastic in time" Billy's refrain in the face of war's casualties ("So it goes") only punctuates his impotence. This impotency assumes cosmic dimensions when Billy learns how the universe ends because of the mistake of a hot-dogging alien astronaut, like some Tralfamadorian Chuck Yeager—type, a little green being shaped like a toilet plunger, who presses the wrong button in his experimental spacecraft. Seen from the perspective of that end, Time is all a sick joke. The totalizing view therefore commits one to inertia.

The ironies are obvious enough. In narrating history as battle we assume that the "big picture" is what the generals (Rommel, Patton, Montgomery) take into their monumental chess-games with History. In *Slaughterhouse-Five,* a book "about people without power in time of war," the big picture comes to a grunt, a mere chaplain's assistant (also a figure of comedy in *Catch-22*).[38] And what are the fruits of Billy's knowledge? The best he can do is sum it up in platitudes: "Everything is all right, and everybody has to do exactly what he does" (198). Meanwhile the frame narrator breaks in to blame that indolent alienation on the immensity of war: "There are almost no characters in this story," he notes, "because most of the people in it are so sick and so much the listless playthings of enormous forces. One of the main effects of war, after all, is that people are discouraged from being characters" (164). This is exactly the "general" or "cosmic" irony the critics commonly associated with Black Humor, but eventually we must ask just how seriously Vonnegut takes it. For otherwise there are more "specific" and significant ironies in the details of character. In a temporary prisoner-of-war encampment an American high-school teacher reads *The Red Badge of Courage,* an "antiwar" book that generations have nonetheless read as a valorization of battle (99). The man, like Crane's Henry Fleming, has had a harrowing experience behind enemy lines, but he will be ignominiously shot in Dresden for stealing a teapot (214). His story implies that there are neither heroes nor even "characters" in the novel, only pretenders who believe too much in fictions. Roland Weary (a weary Roland), constructs his fantasies of battle from "The Three Musketeers" (42). Billy's favorite writer, Kilgore Trout, thinks of his fictions as the ultimate recordings of observed detail; Billy's mother builds a life around Biblical knick-knacks "found in gift shops" (39); even the Tralfamadorians shape their image of Billy's earthly life from Jacqueline Susann's *Valley of the Dolls* (87). Throughout *Slaughterhouse-Five,* characters turn to fictions in their attempts "to construct a life . . . that made sense" (39), and when these efforts are crushed by the glacial transit of violence over their lives, they turn with ludicrous optimism to the possibility of creating "a lot of wonderful new lies" (101).

That possibility is satirized in the simple ironies of Billy's story. Tralfamadore, his idealized perspective on social history, is the lame ("spastic") embodiment of a Do-Nothing ethos, the chief commandment of which is self-imposed blindness. When Billy asks his Tralfamadorian guide for the secret of peace so that he can take it back home, he is told, "Ignore the awful times and concentrate on the good ones." For Tralfamadore also has wars, "as horrible as any" on Earth, and Tralfamadorians thus differ only in having given up on finding "the secret" that would "save us all" from war (116). Billy's guide advises that "we simply don't look at them [wars]. We ignore them. We spend eternity looking at pleasant moments" (117). Earlier, however, another Tralfamadorian had told Billy that "only on Earth is there any talk of free will" (86). But this obviously neglects their own will to "simply" ignore what is unpleasant. In this quaintly simplified world that Kurt Vonnegut imagines, issues of survival turn neatly on the pivot of a putative free will. Tralfamadore is the narrative projection of an impassive view, a modernist culture that puts too much stock in scientific determinism (to the Tralfamadorian, "every creature and plant in the Universe is a machine"), a warring society whose members live and die by their fictions, or "lies," especially the lie that they had best look away from war. The easily decoded ironies and inconsistencies of Billy's story make all of this very clear. Obviously, Vonnegut intends to put his readers between the poles of a classic antinomy: a despair born out of hopelessness and a set of ridiculously inhuman, inconsistent fictions that are untenable options to that despair, yet sufficiently like our own to make us squirm. Enough of his readers have made this observation that we needn't develop it further, but their way of resolving that antinomy *is* worth pausing over.[39]

The standard reading of *Slaughterhouse-Five* seeks to resolve the split between inertial despair and untenable lies by focusing on the novel's brief illustrations of empathy.[40] Most readers point to Billy's long ride to the POW camp in a cattle car, a ride in which the men pass food in and excrements out, take turns sleeping or standing, and altogether act "quiet and trusting and beautiful. They shared" (70). Well and good. The idea, clearly, is to make empathy the basis for a normative reading of Vonnegut's satire. Yet those men are also captive and frightened and degraded, and one therefore also ought to ask if they carry the simple wisdom of empathy outside the boxcar. They don't: one detainee, Paul Lazzaro, swears he'll murder Billy the first chance he gets (84); as for the rest, their dearly purchased wisdom is already dissolving into acrimony *inside* the boxcar, as they all order Billy to "keep the hell away" because he whimpers in his sleep (79). The one exception appears to be Vonnegut, the frame narrator who intrudes on Billy's story to tell us, "I was there" (67).

This returns us to the novel's frame, Vonnegut's narrative of his struggles to write the book we are holding, thus to counter the pessimism of a movie producer who told him he'd be better off writing an "anti-glacier book" than one against wars (3). Vonnegut certainly *cares*, for this "lousy little book" cost him dearly "in money and anxiety and time" (2). Also, he wants that investment to authorize his didacticism, all the long factual sections detailing what Vonnegut condemns as an unnecessary, inhuman bombing of Dresden. Yet for all his didacticism Vonnegut can only end by making purely factual observations: on the murders of Robert Kennedy and Martin Luther King, on the daily count of bodies "created by military science in Vietnam" (210). About Billy Pilgrim's inertia he says "I am not overjoyed" (211).

That litotes carries like a monkey on its back the great uncertainty of Vonnegut's novel. For Billy's inaction demands some kind of appropriate, active (even subversive) response, while the best Vonnegut can offer is the fact that his father's guns gather rust (210). There is no plan for reform here, no useful purpose to which the communal power of empathy can be put, hence nothing to offer the "sick" people Vonnegut describes as too captivated by their own powerlessness against institutional violence. Vonnegut's message is to exercise free will and put your own guns in the closet, "don't look at them," hope that others do the same, and then like the Tralfamadorian toilet-plunger-men you too can "spend eternity looking at pleasant moments." This absence, this failure to find an enabling "lie," might be turned to other uses in the kind of radical, degenerative satire we find in the novels of a West, Hawkes, or Pynchon. In a conventionally didactic satire like *Slaughterhouse-Five* it is doubly remarkable, and no amount of discussion about the otherwise vague, "cosmic ironies" of its Black Humor can answer this impotence. The entire novel is an expanded litotes. On the one hand, Vonnegut lacks the courage to explore its degenerative, negative satire. On the other, his inability to state a positive, enabling fiction gives the lie to its ostensibly curative, normative satire.

*Catch-22* wavers between the conflicting demands of comedy and satire and *Slaughterhouse-Five* between those of generative and degenerative satire. But *Why Are We In Vietnam?* runs to its vision of hysterical, unappeasable violence with a bravura unmatched in sixties fiction. There are no attempts to shunt its atavistic laughter into joking asides, no desire to blunt its edge on comedy. Here is an experimental satire that worked, a stunning display of obsessive desires that had dogged Mailer's most widely praised novels, *The Naked and the Dead* (1948) and *An American Dream* (1964). In addition it became the fictional capstone to his antiwar activism, described in *Armies of the Night* (1968), and for fifteen years afterward he would publish no more full-length fiction. The book thus remains, arguably, Norman Mailer's best novel, a humorous yet absolutely frightful synthesis of American themes, abject imagery, and hip, poetic stylizing. Looking back, *Why Are We in Vietnam?* is also the most powerful political satire of the sixties.

I have previously noted the apparent dual personality of Mailer's narrator, D.J., who may be "sending from Harlem" or from "the Dallas ass manse." This paradox only opens the novel's uncertainties. When Mailer writes that "there is no security in this consciousness" (134), he means it psychologically as well as narratologically. Using the electronics and broadcasting metaphor that recurs throughout, the narrator remarks that the scenes we are reading could be a means of dissimulating, "putting false material into this tape recorder"; or D.J. could be "making cheerful humorous recs, belly laughter shit pressings when in fact I'm sheer fucked right out of my mind" (26). The point is, there is no single, privileged point of view, the reader has no means of finally naturalizing this novel according to one or another of these possibilities. Representing or dissimulating, laughing or going insane, none has priority, and indeed all might be explainable under the rubric of some unspeakable violence or power that D.J. refuses to name outright. Instead, this narrator rides the leading edge of a hysteria that slashes through every naturalizing convention. From reported dialogue to inner speech and from omniscient narrative to the most self-centered solipsisms, D.J. disrupts and mocks all such indices of difference between narrator and characters, inner fantasy and "actual" event. Whenever one might begin to complacently read according to the poetics of a realist fiction, D.J. breaks in to mock his imagined reader.

Chapter 1 establishes that rhythm. Ostensibly the narrative of a central intelligence "presenting to you the private scene of his [D.J.'s] mother being psychoanalyzed" (and fretting mainly over her son's "recalcitrant," "anti-Semitic, morally anesthetized" and murderous "configurations"), the episode ends with D.J. smirking at its obscenities, while dismissing the text as an "illusion" and its narratee as a "little readster . . . sick in your own drool" (22). Subsequently he addresses the reader as everything from a "grassed-out" and "sedentary send-in-terror auditor" to a "little punster" and "private ear of the Lord." So the novel spreads uncertainty throughout the range of its diegetic structures, in particular through what Genette defines as the categories of "mood" (characterization and focalization) and "voice" (speech representation and narration). There is no "point of view" in such a fiction and thus no reliable center, only a swarming host of aggressive desires, mocking allusions to other "texts" (written or not), and idiot claims to unspeakable "genius." If a satire like this can be said to "target" anything, that target is storytelling itself, as well as its enabling mythologies. Probably this is why the novel's temporal ordering, its elemental structure as a narrative fiction, is relatively unscathed. An extended analepsis transpiring in D.J.'s mind on the eve of his departure for Vietnam, at age eighteen, its plot develops around an Alaskan big game hunt, when he was sixteen. This story loosely parodies Faulkner's "The Bear," though ironic references to Wordsworth (186) and Proust (187) suggest the satirical uses to which it subjects the minutiae of memory; further references to Sade and Burroughs (14) imply that, for D.J., Faulkner's rite-of-passage into adulthood is here imagined as acceptance into a clan based upon victimization and mastery. Indeed, this implication is sharpened on the details of still more distant analepses embedded in the hunting narrative treating events from when D.J. was thirteen and five years old.

"America," says D.J. in his first greeting, "this is your own wandering troubadour brought right up to date, here to sell America its new handbook on how to live" (8). A postmodern "Huck Finn," all "programmed out," the consummate con artist and eventual victim, D.J. scats a "cool" tale that traces the grand tribal metanarrative of heliotropic progress, of reason migrating westward with the sun and claiming dominion over farther territories by dint of its sheer power, its Manifest Destiny. Nathanael West's aging souls were mere epigones to this myth, but at eighteen D.J. lives by it. His father, "Rusty," is one of Horatio Alger's self-made men, "the cream of corporation corporateness" (29) who worked his way to the top. His dues-paying links to various phratries (like the CIA, Masons, and Republican Party) are given in a lengthy Who's Who catalogue. It is Rusty who enlists them all — father and son, some corporate underlings, and D.J.'s best friend, a part-Indian named "Tex" Hyde — in a hunting safari in Alaska, last vestige of American wilderness. For Rusty and his middle-management cohorts, the hunt is simply another expression of their corporate mastery. Animals are herded within shooting range by helicopters ("Hail the Cop Turd," puns D.J.), blasted with state-of-the-art weapons that would stop a semi-tractor, then gutted and dressed out by enlisted personnel while Rusty (General Westmoreland to this undeclared police action) takes the body count. It is Vietnam in all but locale. For D.J., however, the hunt becomes more than a rite-of-passage into that corporate manhood. This hunt plots a regression through myths structuring that manhood and into an absolute violence that myths can only cover or displace.

The safari contract guarantees a clean shot at grizzly bear, or Rusty gets his money back. Still, he wants more than sportsmanlike shooting. Rusty wants the bear *all* to himself, for the trophy stands to reaffirm his entire familial, corporate, and racial mastery. Focalizing through his father, D.J. imagines White America in a twilight phase: its generative skills in fornication have passed to the "niggers" Rusty suspects all white women desire and the result is a crisis both domestic (kids hate their parents) and abroad (the "gooks" hate Americans). Regenerating all of this hinges on getting a prize grizzly, "for if he [Rusty] don't, white men are fucked more and they can take no more" (111). D.J., on the other hand, experiences the hunt not as a rite of passage, the Faulknerian test of a truly virtuous manhood, but as a test of the very terms by which American manhood may be decided. In the first of two quests structuring D.J.'s narrative, he and Rusty break away from the main group to hunt grizzly alone, the only way that either one can meet the different challenges they have set themselves. They sight an immense bear, each gets off a shot that either misses or is ineffective, then D.J. calmly drops to one knee and squeezes off a shot that explodes in blood and turns the charging animal, Hemingway's bull and Faulkner's bear rolled into one, off into the bush. They begin tracking, the hunt now a search-and-destroy mission. When the bear turns up lying in a pool of blood and breathing his last, D.J. advances to pay his respects, eyeballing Death, the victor honoring his victim and hoping for "a message," a certain "forgiveness" or "unspoken cool" that betokens "peace" (146). Rusty steals the moment, slamming home a last cannon shot. Then back at camp he steals authority for the kill, a defeat for D.J. that is total: "Final end of love for one son for one father."

Embedded in this narrative is another, darker recollection. A progress toward new assertions of patriarchal authority, the "chimes of memory" (137) also ring D.J. back, and he regresses toward the vision of an aboriginal aggression. This occurs when D.J. is still tracking the grizzly and feels an attack of vertigo, part fear and part recognition, because "D.J. for the first time in his life is hip to the hole in his center," a mad urge to commit Oedipal murder. He describes it as a "slippery desire to turn his gun and blast a shot into Rusty's fat fuck face, thump in his skull, whawng! and whoong!, with the dead-ass butt of his Remington 721" (136–37). Triggering this desire is a memory of D.J. at five, "shrieking off the fuck of his head, cause the face of his father is a madman ass, a power which wishes to beat him to death" for a transgression he couldn't decipher then and cannot remember now. Saved by his mother, D.J. nevertheless felt in that hysterical moment the "seed of backed-up murder" passing from Rusty into "the seat of D.J.'s brain," where it grew like a "tumor" (137). At once, this disclosure propels the reader backward and forward in D.J.'s narrative. First it recalls an earlier memory of D.J. at thirteen, playing one-on-one football with Rusty and running over him again and again until, feeling "sorry," the boy lets him make a tackle, which "dad" does with "insane" pleasure, afterwards biting D.J "in the ass, right through his pants," to punctuate a lesson in murderous "competition" (40–41). For the bite, D.J. "bopped his daddy over the dead center of his head" with an axe handle (41); for that assault, Rusty sent the boy off to military school. Then we are propelled forward, to a realization of "the inexorable hunt logic" (126). A narratological double of the prior incident, D.J.'s image of the charging bear and its massive jaws brings back every Oedipal terror. Blown up to monstrous size, this grizzly exteriorizes each murderous desire that brute patriarchal power has both germinated and blocked, like a "backed-up seed." Thus the hunt had become an opportunity to expunge that record. Indeed, just moments after disclosing his violent desire D.J. remarks that while tracking the bear, "murder between the two men came to rest, for *murder was outside them now*" (138; my emphasis). A sacrificial victim, magnet for all that is nonhuman and monstrous, therefore outside of human civilization, the grizzly's death is D.J.'s chance to quell his previously unimaginable aggression, to fill the "hole" in his being with symbolic seed and thereby end his Oedipal rages with one act of generative violence. This recuperative possibility is exactly what Rusty's reassertion of power sweeps aside.

The frustrated quest ends one phase of D.J.'s narration and begins another. With Tex, his friend and teenage sex rival, D.J. leaves the main encampment; the two trek deep into the Brooks Range — no Cop Turd or weapons this time, only the basic tools of survival. Now truly "clean and on-edge" (184), with "no other man for fifteen or twenty miles" (200) and only their fire for communal protection, the boys are out there with Natty Bumpo and Chingachgook, Huck and Jim, Ike and Sam Fathers skirting the frontier of things. They hike through a space less actual than mythical, and so unfolds their second quest: for themselves, seemingly, but more accurately for the very terms, the metaphysic, by which they can define a self.

The quest begins with a renunciation of every mechanical aid: knives, guns, compass, tents, and cookware. Simultaneously it opens with a catharsis of language. Alone, D.J. and Tex let fly every obscenity they know, thus to use up "all the foul talk to get rid of it in a hurry . . . and so be ready to enjoy good air and nature" (180). For long stretches they break silence only with simple, declarative utterances ("There's a wolf on the ridge"), and even D.J.'s narrative is remarkably purged of hip sexual slang. The boys' discourse thus approaches the condition of a pure, Emersonian referentiality, in which "words are signs of natural facts."[41] But this petty idealism doesn't last. Before hiking far they turn back for everything in their packs but the weapons, and soon their speech will be as inflected with sexual and murderous aggression as ever. The reason is all around them, in a rage for killing that hangs in the air, its "smell is everywhere," remarks D.J. (184). Its crises are played out endlessly. First, they stare down a more-than-curious wolf, in "two waves of murder, human and animal, [that] meet across the snow" (181); then the scenes pass before them in nightmarish actuality: a fox that swallows a field mouse whole, a grizzly that runs them up a tree, then rolls like a locomotive over a caribou, "like every other fat ass in the world" (188). All around them pumps "the sharp wounded heart of things," in a wilderness ruled by "that Cannibal Emperor of Nature's Psyche" (186). D.J. sums up this visionary confrontation claiming that "everything is altered, not saying how" (192).

Next morning they wake up feeling aged, the "rheumatism of future joints" (199) signifying their accession into adulthood.

D.J. refuses to articulate this mystery ("not saying how"), and the young men lie there awake but "not saying a word," just "breathing hard with all this" electrified aggression on the air (201). Nonetheless, D.J.'s narration does make plain the suppressed terms of his new manhood. Seized by the homo-erotic desire to lay his hand "square on Tex's cock and squeeze," he begins to consider the ramifications of such an act, at last factoring in Tex's "Eenyen blood" and revealing the abject "secret" of his story to be domination, the power to utterly possess and devour another. This battlefield is at once sexual, racial, and genocidal, a home on the range for the murderer and the cannibal. In its western extremity is always played out what historian Richard Drinnon has called the "metaphysics of Indian-hating," that exercise of dominion over "savage" nature which hounds American politics from Merrymount to Vietnam, always moving westward, its repressed cannibalism signified in the practice of taking scalps or ears to verify "kill ratios."[42] One irony, however, is that D.J. and Tex are locked into a Mexican standoff, "all in lust to own the other yet in fear of being killed by the other" (203–4). They compose a classic instance of that monstrous doubling or "mimetic desire" René Girard describes, especially in the symbol of twins. It leaves the two young men in a permanent state of violent crisis: "yeah, now it was there, murder between them under all friendship, for God was a beast, not a man, and God said, 'Go out and kill — fulfill my will, go and kill' " (203). Now D.J. and Tex are "twins . . . killer brothers" (204). Vietnam is just around the corner.

In this narrative progression *Why Are We in Vietnam?* regresses toward states of unappeased, ultimate violence, a permanent condition of the "sacrificial crisis" that Girard describes. The text first assumes the form of a progression toward adulthood, an apprenticeship novel. Initially its meaning is local. The "we" of Mailer's title refers specifically to the "killer brotherhood" of D.J. and Tex: this is why *they* are in Vietnam. Finally, however, one cannot contain the spread of its satire. The novel's intertextuality implicates all of American culture in its plural pronoun: this is why *we* are there. Its two plots, the novelistic and the satirical, come together in one scathing exposure: to achieve American manhood is to inherit a murderous desire that the culture barely represses. The narrative traces the return of that repressed content.

This results from the novel's two-stage quest. D.J.'s first trek is an attempt to quell the Oedipal rage "smoldering" within him, by targeting the bear as an exterior symbol of that monstrous violence which both seduces and repulses him. It is an attempt to maintain the differential system of power relations, and thus of conventional law or morality, by making the victim an ultimate and even repeatable embodiment of difference. Mounted for periodic admiration, the bear would become exactly what Mailer, in his foreword, identifies as a "totem" (5), an index of socialized differentness. For D.J., the bear's killing also promises to be sanative, a reaffirmation of paternal "love." In effect, however, this would also require Rusty to acquiesce before a ritual enactment of his own murder, and his power play at the end thus becomes necessary to destroy any possibility of D. J.'s achieving harmony on those terms. D.J.'s second trek is therefore an attempt to locate, by fraternal effort, signs in nature of a transcendent, mythical power. It begins as just such an optimistic quest to surmount the failures of his first quest, and ever since the book's earliest reviews readers have interpreted D.J.'s aim in light of the American tradition of transcendental Nature, from Cooper through Faulkner. Yet what happens is that the boys instead discover a near-chaos of violent reciprocity whose logic is mimetic desire and whose only balance comes in random, mutual threats of vengeance.

Girard concludes *Violence and the Sacred* by arguing that randomness and monstrous violence are qualities the modern mind refuses to see as attributes of divine will, while the so-called savage mind acknowledged them throughout its whole sociopolitical order. *Why Are We in Vietnam?* is a regression to that savage wisdom. D.J.'s second quest brings him into the presence of a God who is a "beast," who enjoins him, "Fulfill my will, go forth and kill" (204) in a purely random way. This is *why* D.J. is on his way to Vietnam: he cannot control or resist the necrophilic powers driving him there. In tracking his progress to that regressive end, Mailer's novel also graphs the literary history of postmodernist satire, its break from the sanative practices of a moral, generative writing, in order to embrace a degenerative vision of chaotic violence.

Faulkner's novella, "The Bear," is the narration of a ritual in its twilight years. Hunting is still a rite of passage into the duties and powers of adulthood, and it occurs in a forest which, if not totally wild, is at least transcendently rarefied in comparison to the mechanized, corrupt civilization bearing down on it. In fact, eye to eye with Old Ben, the beast of Faulkner's title, sixteen-year-old Ike McCaslin renounces sex, the ownership of land, and his entire inheritance of social power in order to reestablish closer ties with a nonhuman world that is purer, he thinks, because it is not established on principles of mechanization and usury. In many ways, as the critics have noted, Mailer's novel is the parodic inversion of this plot.[43] Wilderness is "where the boys got their power" for waging successful aggression

in the mechanized society around it. By the time Rusty's safari party arrives, the Alaskan wilds have already been overhunted and helicoptered back
to the level of the lower forty-eight; the remaining game, they are advised,
have been in an unpredictably mean humor. This wilderness will give D.J.
and Tex no respite from their fathers, Great White Cocksmen of the board-
rooms and badlands, and everything about it teaches violent use: kill to eat
to keep killing. The message is encoded on D.J.'s entire surroundings, natural
and cultural. His insistent metaphor is the microchip or "crystal" of frozen,
programmable matter scattered all around him, configuring the hip, electrified grooves and airwaves on which he is "Disk Jockey." The ice-laden Arctic
valleys are really just the largest receptors on this "Magnetic-Electro Fiefdom"
or quasi-Emersonian "Universal Mind" on which D.J. believes he is charged
up. He represents himself as the clear channel of a totalizing vision: its message is that of a pure, reciprocal, and (what even the savage mind could not
comprehend) socially authorized murderousness.

Like West, Purdy, and Pynchon before him, the Norman Mailer of *Why Are
We in Vietnam?* is satirically engaged with the mass-cultural bases of power,
but he is different in being essentially disinterested in its actual products, the
detritus scattered throughout a text like *The Crying of Lot 49* in the form of
brand names, references to popular culture, media "personalities," and the
like. Instead Mailer is taken by its structural metaphors both large and small:
the network and the microchip as grids of exchange. Overlaid on these metaphors is a visionary sense of landscape one can only compare with a novel
like Hawkes's *The Cannibal*. This geography is a social and historical palimp-
sest, the stratified mythology of an American dominion that reaches down
through Faulkner and Hemingway, through the Transcendentalists, to the
Puritan doctrine of a wilderness "errand," then further to a prehistorical condition of monstrously violent being that is paradoxically current, our own.
As satire, *Why Are We in Vietnam* is therefore radical in all the best senses
of that word. It reaches into the deepest subsoil, the better to devastate the
fictions of American power.

## The Crises of Richard Nixon

When writers in the sixties and seventies needed an actual target or butt
for their satirical derision, Richard Milhous Nixon was the one. He appears
in chapter 2 of *The Free-Lance Pallbearers* (1967), chasing his infamous dog
Checkers through one of Bukka Doopeyduk's nightmares, and there are references to the Nixon administration scattered through *The Last Days of Louisi-*

*ana Red* (1974). In the final, apocalyptical episode of *Gravity's Rainbow* (1973) he is "Richard M. Zhlubb," Manager of the Orpheus Theater where, in contemporary Los Angeles, Pynchon's readers have been watching while the nightmare of history catches up in a screaming rush. In two satirical novels from the seventies Nixon is also the protagonist, an obsessed caricature of American opportunism, prideful humility, and amoral ruthlessness. Philip Roth's *Our Gang* was published in October, 1971, when resistance to the Vietnam War was peaking. His "Trick E. Dixon" simultaneously defends the massacre of innocent Vietnamese civilians abroad and condemns abortion at home. Robert Coover's *The Public Burning* appeared in August, 1977, three years after Nixon's resignation and, because of legal delays over its allegedly slanderous content, two years after Coover had completed the novel, having intended to release it for the Bicentennial festivities of 1976. To Coover, who unlike Roth focuses on past rather than contemporary political events, Richard Nixon is less the figure of a deplorable hypocrisy and violence, hence the deserving butt of a morally outraged satire, than he is himself duped by American mythologies of success and power. The difference is crucial. A personification of deceit and evil, Roth's "Dixon" has more in common with Dryden's Achitophel or the Colley Cibber of Pope's *Dunciad*; Coover's "Nixon" is more related to Cabot Wright, Bukka Doopeyduk, or Pynchon's Tyrone Slothrop.

Roth spurns the mimetic conventions of realist fiction for a traditionally satiric "distortion." From its too obviously camouflaged names (like ex-Presidents "Lyin' B. Johnson" and "John F. Charisma") through its bathetic plot (an underworld descent with a promised new reign of Darkness), *Our Gang* hews to an essentially Neoclassical idea of satire. For all its exaggeration, the narrative maintains clear allegorical links to actual political events and actors, and this supports a stable point of view. A man who speaks "with great pride" of turning Southeast Asia into "nothing less than Hell on earth," Tricky is quite plainly the spokesman for an inverted, satanic ethic.[44] Roth's is also a vision of evil assuming banally personal, ridiculously ordinary forms. Pope's Dunces collected butterflies; Tricky puts on his "regulation National Football League athletic supporter" while appearing on television to justify the unauthorized invasion of Cambodia (82). Through it all Roth's implicit standards of morality are easily decoded; one reconstructs them from the specific ironies composing the novel's inverted world. Roth's satirical intentions are equally as clear: to expose, criticize, and shame the personification of American hypocrisy and viciousness.

The Trick E. Dixon of *Our Gang* is like a racquetball. Bouncing off the wall of any entrenched doctrine, and bouncing back from any deadening fall or misfortune, he is the ultimate politico, a man with no position except what is likely to sway votes for the next election. He is also a man without desire, other than for "political power" (31), and politics for him thus becomes an endless personal revenge upon those he perceives as detracting from that power. Jane Fonda, the Berrigan brothers, the Black Panthers, even renegade baseball player Curt Flood — in a meeting with his Cabinet all appear on a "list" that uncannily anticipates the subsequent exposure, during the 1973 Watergate hearings, of Nixon's actual "enemies lists." At the same time Tricky still fancies himself the benevolent Quaker spokesman for any demographic faction — even fetuses are regarded as a "bloc of voters" (22) — large enough to warrant bringing it into that amoeboid coalition of interests he calls the "silent majority." Indeed, after Tricky's ludicrous assassination he is eulogized by "Reverend Billy Cupcake" (Billy Graham) as just "the words in which he lived in the hearts of his fellow countrymen" (182). Trick E. Dixon is a way of speaking, a chameleon discourse, nothing more.

The six chapters of *Our Gang* are structured around that central idea. The first begins with a moral crux: on April 3, 1971, Richard Nixon condemned "abortion on demand" and declared his personal belief "in the sanctity of human life," including the "rights" of "the unborn"; at the same time, as commander-in-chief, he had to ultimately answer for the massacre of innocent civilians, including mothers and mothers-to-be, at the Vietnamese village of My Lai. So the opening chapter depicts this contradiction in the form of an interview between Tricky and a "Citizen." He declares the President's conscience "a marvel to us all" (3), then prods Tricky into endless, quasi-legalistic ratiocinations, a form of deceit that Orwell, in "Politics and the English Language," referred to as a "defense of the indefensible."[45] The discussion ends with Tricky proclaiming that if there were any pregnant women at My Lai, they were "obviously" presenting themselves to Lieutenant Calley's troops for "abortion on demand," and were therefore guilty and justly executed. Subsequent chapters take the forms of a press conference, a "skull session" between Tricky and his Cabinet, a televised foreign policy speech, a montage of news flashes reporting Tricky's assassination, and finally his "comeback speech" before the assembled demons of Hell. The consistent thread is political discourse, which in Roth's view of Nixon is never the enunciation of policies founded on morality. Rather he figures politics as an endless appeasement or reactionary process, a ricocheting off the sidewalls of extremism and one-issue "interest groups," all in a trajectory obeying no laws save those of counteraction and vendetta. The novel's plot, such as it is, illustrates that motion. Tricky's championing "the rights of the unborn" leads to criticism from the Boy Scouts, who mount protest marches on the White House lawn to charge that he "favors sexual intercourse"; this prompts a "military response" resulting in the deaths of three Scouts. In the subsequent search for scapegoats Tricky mounts an invasion of Denmark, the "smut capital of the world" and hide-out of Curt Flood, guilty of "impugning the sacred name of baseball" and living with a white woman. Chapter 5, shaped as a sequence of televised newsbreaks, unfolds the details of Tricky's death by drowning, when a "cruel assassin with a macabre sense of humor" stuffs him in a large plastic baggie filled with water, a crime to which thousands confess and which makes Tricky a "martyr to the unborn the world round" (151).

The final chapter, an epilogue to this five-act morality play, is Tricky's speech in Hell, Roth's occasion (a commonplace in traditional satire) to let Dixon/Nixon damn himself. Now running to unseat Satan, Tricky argues that while formerly in power he was "able to maintain and perpetuate all that was evil in American life." He continues, periodically wiping the perspiration from his scales with the back of a claw: "Furthermore I think I can safely say that I was able to lay the groundwork for new oppressions and injustices and to sow seeds of bitterness and hatred between the races, the generations and the social classes that hopefully will plague the American people for years to come. Surely I did nothing whatsoever to decrease the eventuality of a nuclear holocaust, but rather continued to make progress in that direction by maintaining policies of belligerence, aggression and subversion around the globe" (192). He ends with promises of Darkness's eternal reign, a loose parody of Revelation. Such a plot always depends upon the satirist's decision to put his villain into Hell; thus it serves as a strong armature for turning out, by inversion, the work's moral norms. The "sanctity of human life," honesty in political discourse, tolerance for less powerful nations, and the ideal of political ambition as republican service — all of these and more, the whole liberal humanitarian program for social progress, stand behind Roth's satire of a (to him) regressive, degenerative epoch in American politics. As the jacket notes remark, this satire was "plainly conceived in moral indignation."

The book's problems, however, point to key changes in the nature of contemporary narrative satire. For one, the moral norms of Our Gang are so patently obvious and universally acceptable that they overwhelm its plot, which is really little more than a sustained two-stage gag: the exposure of Dixon/Nixon's hypocrisy and the poetic justice of his drowning in a baggie (putting him in Hell seems an afterthought). As such, the text's novelistic elements serve as little more than vehicles for that joke. The point is not that its norms are old-fashioned or inappropriate but that they are, in a sense, too easily purchased. This results because (another problem) Roth's "Trick E. Dixon" is too easily scapegoated, first loaded up with guilt for the degeneracy of sixties America, then packed off to Hell in what can only be described as a ritual of generative violence. As the text itself indicates, it is a "macabre" but cleansing satirical "assassination." Yet this either slights or ignores the central idea of Roth's satire, that Dixon/Nixon is an American way of speaking. He is neither anterior to nor the sole representative of that discourse, and for Roth to sketch its dimensions as a semiotic practice, as mythology or metanarrative, would have required opening the satire to all those *novelistic* potentialities for a greater heterogeneity of voices, for example in disclosing characters and their intertextual culture. Not only would this have lessened the villainy of Dixon/Nixon, equivocating his appropriateness as a satirical "target," it would also have meant acknowledging a much greater infection of that degeneracy for which Nixon is only the sacrificial goat. Indeed this is what Roth's title implies, that Nixon is the leader of *our* gang, although the book's ironies are too specific, too closely targeted, to suggest how. Finally these problems point up the limitations of a traditional satire for the postmodern novelist. On the one hand, *The Groves of Academe* illustrates how the demands of writing a novel tend to undercut the stable, specific aggressions of its satire, a problem McCarthy resolved by narrowly hedging in her fictional world. On the other, Roth binds his fiction around the armature of a single joke in order to solve a contrasting problem, a closely targeted satirical aggression that forecloses any chances of developing the novelistic potential of *Our Gang*.

Overcoming these limits meant discarding the modal demands of a traditional, generative satire. Its stable ironies, close targeting, and normative didacticism proved increasingly unsuited to the heteroglot and multiform possibilities for the contemporary novel, and American postmodernist writers committed to writing narrative satire have therefore had to change the rules. These changes produced a more radical, degenerative mode. With its unrestrained image of a violent being that culture barely fends off and frequently serves, the new satire is marked by a grotesqueness and regression to atavistic disorder that is unique in the history of the novel.

Among those satires expressly concerned with politics, Robert Coover's 1977 novel, *The Public Burning,* is certainly the paragon of vehemence and controversy. The narrative unfolds over three days, Wednesday through Friday, the 17th through the 19th of June, 1953. The Eisenhower administration, barely six months into its first term, is struggling with a range of foreign and domestic crises: the Korean War, unrest in Berlin, a faltering economy, and panic over communist spying in high places. For Coover, the rallying point for all such uncertainties is the "Atom Spy Trial" of Julius and Ethel Rosenberg, convicted for passing atomic secrets to Soviet agents and slated for electrocution on Thursday, their fourteenth wedding anniversary, "thieves of light to be burned by light." The topic itself is not new. Since 1953 the Rosenberg case has been reexamined in dozens of books and articles.[46] E.L. Doctorow's 1971 novel, *The Book of Daniel,* opts for a tense, psychological treatment of the trial's aftermath as seen through one of the surviving Rosenberg sons, called "Daniel Isaacson," the name suggesting a heritage of ritual sacrifice that Doctorow develops only as a minor motif. Coover, however, finds the very heart of the Rosenberg case in the aspects of a ritual murder, the "fierce public exorcism" (4) of two victims loaded down with communal anxiety, then scourged with a fury unmatched since the public burnings of suspected witches. The singular outrageousness of his satire was in approaching these events as secular, political expressions of an all-powerful American myth that comes to us through Richard Nixon, the novel's principal narrator.

Such an approach opened possibilities for being intensely faithful to historical facts while at the same time skewing them in the direction of a grotesque fantasy. Thus Nixon, boning up on the Rosenberg case files in order to gird himself for yet another of his "crises," slides off into autoerotic daydreams featuring a young Ethel, and in the novel's epilogue he narrates his anointing, as future presidential timber, by a fiercely cynical "Uncle Sam," who promptly sodomizes him. Uncle Sam and "The Phantom," an embodiment of every paranoid fear of Communism, are principal actors in this "little morality play for our generation" (119). The executions themselves occur in Times Square, before an assembled multitude enumerated in long parodies of Whitman's exuberant catalogues of democratic "types." (Coover's are, instead, the media-induced heroes of the entertainment and political establishment, demographic "types," one might say.) Still, the satire's most outrageous disturbance of history occurs when the fictional Nixon makes an incognito trip to Sing Sing's death house, where he pursues the romantic fantasy of seducing Ethel and wringing from her a last-moment, life-saving confession. Instead she lipsticks the motto "I AM A SCAMP" on the vice presidential buttocks and spins him through a curtain before the celebrants waiting, in this mythically conflated space, for her "public burning" in Times Square. All this won Coover the furious condemnations of reviewers. Most, like Norman Podhoretz, argued that he had exploited "the novelist's license" until the book had become a "revisionist" distortion of history or a "cowardly lie." With few exceptions, reviewers avoided considering the novel's grotesque fantasy in light of its obvious satirical intent.[47] One result is that *The Public Burning* remains in a kind of exile, out of print and sometimes linked with the encyclopedic satires of Gaddis and Pynchon but otherwise rarely implicated in the literary disturbances of American postmodernism.[48] This is doubly unfortunate. *The Public Burning* is not only a stunning mimicry of Nixon, a relentless aping of his voice that seems the just reward for an ex-president who once noted that "all my humor is situation stuff." The novel also, aside from its topical lampooning, relentlessly exposes the historical myths of the tribe and to some extent historiography itself.[49] For all its excesses *The Public Burning* is thus an American novel to the degree that, like Melville's later novels or an inverted Puritan jeremiad, it rejects both *an idea* and *a discourse* of America. That rejection turns on Coover's sense of the Rosenberg executions as an instance of sacrificial murder.

The novel puts two parallel stories into motion. The first concerns a political-ideological crisis resolved in the Rosenbergs' executions, a conclusion represented as both mob hysteria and a sanative ritual. The second concerns a personal-psychological crisis resolved in Richard Nixon's anointing, a conclusion also represented as both a grotesque victimizing (Uncle Sam sodomizing him) and a covenant promising his future mastery. Uniting both plots is a myth of America, a metanarrative in which "America" is inflated until it becomes a totalizing symbol for the cosmos. America is thus "the hope of the world" (36), and America's history, a unity of both secular and sacred time, *kronos* and *kairos*, is interpreted as divine revelation unfolding in stages, dispensations, each increasingly total and bringing human society that much nearer the Divine Kingdom or "City on a Hill." According to this mythology secular crisis is both a means and an end; the very conditions of crisis reinforce the vision of American society as a progress, an accelerating motion toward fulfillment of the covenant. As Uncle Sam explains it to his disciple, Nixon, "disorder and danger" are the spurs America constantly requires "to keep things from just peterin' out" (95). Furthermore, since "bodies in motion just don't age as fast," then "America, by stayin' off its ass, was stayin' young" and strong for the promised revelation (205). Everywhere in the text Coover identifies this accelerating movement as "the Divine Concursus," literally a "running together" of God's chosen, whose political slogans (Nixon's "Change Trains for the Future!") and campaign vehicles (Ike's "Look Ahead, Neighbor Special") all reiterate the optative aspects of that myth.

Yet its dark side, as Sacvan Bercovitch points out in *The American Jeremiad*, emerges whenever America is perceived as failing that errand, for then the whole world is seen as failing.[50] Suddenly all law, natural and human, seems on a swift, degenerative slide into chaos, and history reveals itself as a failed progress, a joke. Coover's "Phantom" rings the changes on this theme: America is suddenly "the dope of the world," the "rape," the "fake," and "the joke of the world" (36–41). Interchapters between Nixon's first-person narration tally up America's and, by extension, the world's losses. In all, the "Free Nations of the World," as the narrator cautions, are "bracing for the holocaust, are fragmented and exhausted" (25). Capable of swinging both ways, the eschatological hinge of that American myth might as easily resolve itself "toward catastrophe" as into "the Divine concursus" (40). In order to correct that uncertainty Julius and Ethel Rosenberg, Jews whom Coover's Nixon refers to as "spiritual outsiders," are offered up as expiatory victims.

The idea is that their role as scapegoats obviates any question of guilt or innocence. It so happens, though, that Coover, in a 1979 interview, has stated his own belief in their innocence; a number of his readers have also taken the satire as an argument against their guilt.[51] Yet *The Public Burning* submits no brief for either side, because it is more concerned with anterior matters: specifically, whether or not the Rosenbergs were given a fair trial, and more generally, whether or not a fair trial was even possible, given the intense anxieties and sense of impending crisis skewing American politics during the McCarthy Era. The text itself presents a range of views. Ike simply takes the word of Attorney General Herbert Brownell that the Rosenbergs are guilty, then turns to "matters of statecraft." Uncle Sam proposes that their real guilt is signified in transgressions *of style,* in behaviors and even material possessions that are damning "proofs" because they run counter to the American dream of Progress and the Self-made Man. Only Richard Nixon sees Uncle Sam's point and proceeds to further entertain the mere possibility of their innocence. Hence, three quite different views. How does the novel interpret them? It is exactly here that Coover's 1973 review of Louis Nizer's book on the Rosenberg case is a neglected but telling statement. Coming as it did just two years before he completed *The Public Burning,* this assignment from the *New York Times Book Review* afforded Coover an opportunity to synthesize, in several thousand words, his reading of the principal judicial cruxes, political issues, and cultural reverberations of the case, and to do so without the filtering lens, or distorting mirror, of his fictionalized Richard Nixon. Coover's argument, finally, is that the cultural issues, especially the need for some expiatory target, tended to override all else.

Coover opens the essay with a comment on what he defines as the three chief political forces of postmodernist society, the "Communists, Fascists, and Americanists." Americanists, he claims, are "generally disdainful of the 'simplicities' of both Fascism and Communism" and fancy themselves as keepers of the "middle way," a tradition of Anglo-Saxon jurisprudence and American mythologies about God's elect. The Rosenberg case was "a moral lesson" in the virtues of that way, and Americanist historians, Coover notes, have tended to treat it as either a study in the insidious "malignancy of foreign ideologies" or a "touching love story," while the electrocutions tend to both "distress and titillate" them. Nizer, a good Americanist, thus used the case "to extol American justice and fair play," and "to indulge himself in a fantasized melodramatic account of the personal tragedy of Julius and Ethel Rosenberg." Now this, in brief, is also Coover's fictionalized Nixon: a solid "American-ist" who everywhere tries to locate the middle ground between paradoxical opposites, who sees himself as the latest "Incarnation" of American myth, and who loses himself in romanticized daydreams that seem weirdly plagiarized from film fantasies like "Casablanca" (or "white house" — even his daydreams drag around a political ambition). Indeed the problem, argues Coover, is that fictions and myth were constantly imposing themselves on factual "proofs." Nizer, for example, can insinuate his own fantasies into the documentary record, claiming (untruly) that when she was electrocuted Ethel convulsed in the straps and emitted "weird" sounds, "'as if witches were howling in the wind.'"[52] Long after the fact, her death was thus presented as the public burning of a suspected witch; and so even Coover's title seems derivative, a summary of the historians' fantasies spread out before him as he wrote.

Coover's 1973 review points up several important traits of his satire. For *The Public Burning* is as much a fantastic account of the "Atom Spy Trial" as, more important, an outraged account of fictions that cruelly warped one's understanding of the Rosenbergs. In fact, says Coover in concluding the *Times* review, by imposing their fantasies on this case people like Nizer have collectively "produced a satire on Anglo-Saxon jurisprudence" (1973, 5). This remarkable condemnation brings to mind the satirist's age-old "defense": that in times of dullness and decay it is hard *not* to write satire, for the stuff of its dark humors is lying all about. Yet Coover's remark hints at more than his role as satirical compositor. It also points up the key difference between those "satires" (even if unintended) of "Americanists" like Nizer and Coover's satire in *The Public Burning*. Both center on a highly formalized violence, but differ fundamentally in how they present its meaning. The Americanist ver-sion seeks an ameliorating sacrifice, a generative violence intended to restore principles of law and to reaffirm cultural myths. By comparison, Coover ex-poses that generative violence as a long-standing and perhaps the ultimate lie, the wielding of stories, especially those versions available in the *Times* and *Time* (where readers consume "the Spirit of History" [200]), is crucial to the victimizing of persons whose innocence or guilt is never fairly adjudicated, because it isn't the point. Consensus-building, galvanizing a cynical polity through ritualized violence, *is the point,* and Coover's degenerate satire aims to expose its power.

This is why all the principals in *The Public Burning* refer to politics as a blood sport. Early on, Nixon reflects that while he's always wanted to believe that the game is won by "rhetoric and industry" (that is, by well-oiled histories) now he sees that politics flirts "with murder and mayhem, theft and cannibalism" (48). For Uncle Sam it is no mere flirtation. In *The Public Burning* his constant theme is the polity's desire to quell an absolute violence by rushing to embrace forms of sacrifice. Politics thus consists of "ignorin' facts"; it is all "opinion" and "counterattack" functioning amid "flux and a slippery past" (89). Hence his paranoid mottos, quite similar to what lies at the core of *Why Are We in Vietnam?* Screw them before they get you. Some folks will always have to know the axe. In fact, to answer a political calling is an epitome of that ceaseless victimization, for the polity "elects" those who most fully offer themselves up. So "Iron Butt" Nixon prides himself on an unstinting self-denial, a sacrificing of all desires except that for "political power" (295). Like each of his precursors, the future president experiences his "Incarnation" as a grotesque, rip-roaring buggery, a humiliating discipleship which also confers mastery. To him politics is therefore a "visible form of Paradox in the world" (161). An "endless self-exposure" or self-offering (526), successful political agency finally consists in overreaching the "violent disorder" or reciprocal violence epitomized in the Times Square mob. It consists in mastering what Nixon calls the "power in disruption" (363) or in stage-managing what Uncle Sam sees as mere fictions of order: "It ain't easy holdin' a community together, order ain't what comes natural, you know that boy, and a lotta people gotta get killt tryin' to pretend it is, that's how the game is played — but not many of 'em gets a chance to have it done to 'em on-stage in Times Square" (531). According to this formulation, politics is a sort of demoniacal aggressiveness turned, paradoxically, toward the fulfillment of a "nation-breedin'" idealism, the mythic symbolism of a "Puritanism" (531) that Uncle Sam both mocks and employs.

Such satire undercuts every knob of ideological high ground: for example, the Founding Fathers' concept of "enlightened self-interest." As Nixon realizes in one of his blacker moods, this was conceptualized as a tenuous balancing of powers, with self-interest like an age-old root of evil ("like money") thrusting against an Enlightenment ideal of reasoned control ("the rational utopia"). In practice though, Nixon grumbles that the utopian ideal "made men miserable" by first measuring their miserable lack of control, then spurring the "horrors they inflicted on each other through pursuit of the rational — and therefore unattainable — ideal" (230). In pulling down one after another of these ideals Coover's satire regresses toward a vision of mass hysteria and a sense of politics as dissimulated violence. The indices of that regression lie everywhere in the narrative: a Nixon who sees his role as working "backwards, like a lawyer," through each tangled path of the Rosenberg case (132); a backwards diurnal motion, as "night seems to reverse itself and brighten again toward high noon" with the impending executions (398); also, prior to being sodomized, Nixon remembers how his father dragged him off to revival meetings (525). For every hopeful sign of accelerating progress (Change Trains!, Look Ahead!) this novel is equally obsessed with increases in entropy and returns to atavistic violence or primeval chaos. A regress couched in the form of a progress, it degenerates toward "the chaotic violence" at "the terrible center" (195). Moments before the Rosenbergs' executions, Times Square is "imitative of the contained agitation of the universe." Nixon figures it as a "hysterical jangling" or "tribal implosion" brought about in a society which has reached critical mass — too much information, population, and paradox (492). All of Coover's seemingly endless catalogues lead up to this conclusion. Their function is to stand a sheer mass of unassimilable but nonetheless "real" data against the drive for order, for fictions.

In *The Public Burning* fictions compose a "stay" against that violence at "the terrible center" (195), and all the principals are represented as hungering for some explanatory, enabling story. Nixon pores over the Rosenberg case files in search of some totalizing signifier. Julius and Ethel, he thinks, were themselves "seduced by" a "zeal for pattern, for story" (305), and erred only in searching for it outside the Americanist path. This is all the more remarkable, from his standpoint, because everywhere around them are fiction-making enterprises (the *New York Times, Time*) devoted to "the art of subordinating facts to the imagination" (320) and to promulgating the great popular mythologies that Coover, in his 1979 interview, identified as "an unwritten bible" guiding the "day-to-day fiction-making" of Americans. The Rosenbergs' executions are therefore conceived as a corrective, a "little morality play" Nixon thinks of as having been designed to return his "generation" to those apparent verities (119). Still, the fascinating thing about Coover's Richard Nixon is that he almost breaks through that simplistic formulation. In the death-house cell with Ethel he momentarily claims there are "no scripts, no necessary patterns . . . just action" (362). Nonetheless, his every move *does* seem scripted, at times even plagiarized from *Casablanca,* just as his entire narration has been saturated with mass culture: films, pop music, political and historical lore, journalism. The absurdity is that Nixon insistently represents himself as a prophet of the self-made man, an outsider battling "the lie of purpose" (363). In his romantic fantasies with Ethel, rewriting (as he sees it) the "script" of History, he instead plays out the timeworn Americanist myths and clichés. This "Richard Nixon" is thus little more than a congeries of mass-cultural narratives. The point of all his talk about action and, especially, his reminiscences about stage acting, is that he cannot act. Instead he *is acted,* an exemplar of the politico as, paradoxically, an agent without agency.

The technical problem for Coover was to unfold this ridiculous contradiction, or satirical exposure, with the novelist's means. His solution was quite literally to bracket Nixon's narration with other diegetic material. Operating on an extradiegetic level is the narration found in the Prologue and all subsequent even-numbered chapters, in which the subjects are America's world-historical mission and the crises both foreign and domestic. The narrator at this level is like the classic omniscient third-person speaker but focalized, quite often, through Uncle Sam. At the main or diegetic level of story are Nixon's representations, all the odd-numbered chapters plus the Epilogue. Ethel, or rather, one version of Ethel Rosenberg, speaks from a still more embedded position, a hypodiegetic level within Nixon's (also embedded) story. Yet readers would have a more difficult time reading *that* Ethel as the production of Nixon's fantasy were it not for her appearances at the extradiegetic level and, still more important, in the letters that compose the novel's "Intermezzos" and for which Coover served as documentary compositor. Those letters operate on a kind of hyperdiegetic level, overlooking all other fictionalized voices. Ethel's multilevel appearances in the text therefore serve two key functions. First, they underscore a reading of "Ethel" as object, or victim, of various characters' fantasies, Nixon's especially. Then her appearances give the lie to Nixon's fantasized source of power, that middle territory or "place in between" the poles of paradox which he defines as the new "frontier" and "thus the true America. My America" (373). In the text, Nixon quite literally occupies a middle space. But that space is the ground of a lie, a dissimulated violence. As the extradiegetic narrator insists, it contains no totalizing myth, only an "appalling void" (212), a mindless violence as "terrible" as it is age-old (195).

Of the many subtexts in *The Public Burning* one of the more compelling is its satire on "middle America," the Silent (or, later, the Moral) Majority from whom Richard Nixon claimed his mandate. From the Prologue on, the novel focuses on their need for "cleansing," for a "communal pageant" or "fierce public exorcism" of victims sacrificed in acts of generative murder (4). The Rosenbergs, then, emerge as "expiatory victims of the cold war" (42). Most observers acknowledged as much: foreign newspapers like *Le Monde,* which called it a "ritual murder"; the fictional Nixon; Ethel, in one of her letters; even Judge Irving Kaufman, who passed sentence. Indeed, as Coover points out in both the novel's Prologue and in his review of Nizer's book, Julius and Ethel Rosenberg were found guilty of espionage, but sentenced, in words that Eisenhower later echoed, for having "caused" fifty thousand casualties in Korea and, still more absurdly, for *future* deaths: the untold "millions" who *might* die in case of atomic war and who were therefore victims of an "aggression against free men everywhere."[53] In order to fence in that unbridled violence, the Rosenbergs are offered up as sacrificial victims. It would be best, says Nixon, if they would only perceive that role and fulfill it, because during such occasions justice is beside the point; the thing is to just "get the formalities right" (91).

Before his turn in the electric chair, however, Julius refers to his murder as a "ghastly farce" (508). Similarly, the Phantom warns Dick Nixon that these are days of "worn-out rituals" and that he should be wary of "this shit about scapegoats, sacrifices" (273). They are exhausted forms because the violence they were meant to appease has broken uncontrollably loose again. This seems the most telling of subtexts in Coover's title: an atomic "burning" which signifies the return of a repressed, absolute, reciprocal violence, and which is figured everywhere in the narrative as a "hysterical" ingathering, a great "tribal implosion." Its chief symbol: the mushroom cloud rising like a morbid covenant over the crowd in Times Square. Enacting the return of that terrible, "total war," Coover's satire reveals the generative fictions of American politics, that corrective "satire" of "Anglo-Saxon jurisprudence" he refers to in 1973, as the unsuccessful cover for a mindless violence. Even more, his degenerative satire exposes what René Girard has identified as the great secret of sacrificial rites, their essential arbitrariness, for the sacrificial victim can be any outsider, anyone labeled as deviant.

One reading of this novel would therefore see its degenerative satire as surrounding the generative rituals and myths that empower culture, assailing their "lie of purpose," and unmasking a violent being that humanity still has not overcome. *The Public Burning* does this work by means of a polyvocal performance that blurs the history/fiction boundary, skirting closer to libel than any text in recent memory. Experimental as the book is in this technical sense, it is radical in the other sense of transmuting a familiar form. Seen in the line of satirical novels that reaches back from *Gravity's Rainbow* to *The Day of the Locust,* this novel, like others by West, Gaddis, and Pynchon, has the formal qualities of an antijeremiad. Indeed, Coover's novel should certainly take its place alongside the most ambitious narrative satires of American postmodernism. An outraged catalogue of American self-deceits and lies masking themselves as genii of progress, *The Public Burning* is the single most unrestrained condemnation of American civic identity to appear in the postwar decades. Unlike the great Puritan jeremiads, its purpose is not to reaffirm the myths of the tribe but to mock the national enterprise en masse, thus to turn American history against the very symbols in which it was supposed to culminate.

# Encyclopedic Satires

## Gaddis and Pynchon

Alongside *The Public Burning*, three more titles stand as the most daunting satirical fictions of postmodern America. They are William Gaddis's first two books, *The Recognitions* (1955) and *J R* (1975), and (arguably the epoch's master-text) Thomas Pynchon's *Gravity's Rainbow* (1973). Obsessive novels rising out of paradox and contradiction, they envision postwar society as a thousand-plateaued landscape of "plots," detailed in all the exhaustive, erudite minutiae of its own subterranean erosion. This is why critics have often taken them as vital signs of a national culture reckoning its imperial summit as well as the sand beneath, and of a hugely learned narrative type that seems to reappear during such historical watersheds. Midway through the decade, two important essays sought to describe the category into which criticism might fit a gigantic farrago like *Gravity's Rainbow.* Such a book, they claimed, is an "encyclopedic narrative" in the tradition of *Ulysses, Don Quijote,* Dante's *Commedia,* and the *Satyricon* of Petronius.[1] The term quickly took hold. When *The Public Burning* was released in the summer of 1977, *Newsweek* described it as "an encyclopedic narrative of the kind Edward Mendelson has traced." The concept just as quickly entered scholarly discourse on the postmodernist novel.[2]

Encyclopedic narratives have yet to be described in anything more than a précis, and there are lingering problems with the concept itself. Most crucially, a sizable number of encyclopedic narratives are clearly satirical, in whole or part, but what are we to make of the possible contradiction? On the one hand we define the encyclopedia as a generative form, a constellation of objects, events, persons, topics, and frames designed to spur fresh syntheses of those myths (metanarratives) informing it. On the other, I have been defining the postmodern abundance of degenerative satires, with their power for doing violence to such structures of knowledge and their organizing metanarratives. To account for these differences critics should probably distinguish between two opposite kinds of encyclopedic fictions, one whose classical (generative) text might be the *Commedia* and another (the degenerative) represented by the *Satyricon.* Recent essays make no such division. The term "encyclopedic satire" thus remains inadequately determined, and while this is not the place for a detailed treatment of fictional encyclopedism, the present chapter summarizes the critical backgrounds, suggests some possibilities for a sounder theory, then moves on to the novels of Gaddis and Pynchon, capstones of a satirical age.

According to Mendelson, "encyclopedic narratives attempt to render the full range of knowledge and beliefs of a national culture" (62), or as Swigger puts it, their purpose is "to comprehend and articulate a unified and total vision of the world" (352). They also indicate "the ideological perspectives" informing that constellated wisdom, a trait that is crucial to their appearance during imperial epochs. This breadth of vision is also what distinguishes them from Frye's "anatomy" or "Menippean" satire, with its skewed vision of the world "in terms of *a single intellectual pattern,*" such as melancholia.[3] However, the grandiose aims of an encyclopedic fiction are always moderated by practical constraints. Products of dynamic times, when knowledge expands farther "than any one person can encompass," encyclopedic narratives "necessarily make extensive use of synecdoche," says Mendelson (162). They are, then, intimations of a fully reified episteme, testaments of a newly felt national consensus (165). At the same time, Mendelson shows, such narratives originate "at the edge of a culture" (178), as texts of "positive illegality" (174) treating in analytical detail a synthesis that their reading public accepts only afterwards.[4] Aside from these general features warranting the name, encyclopedic narratives all tend to illustrate a more specific range of formal qualities. According to Mendelson, each involves a contemporary or near-contemporary setting and includes accounts of statecraft, socioeconomic structures, and at least one current science or technology, as well as structures of art, language, and literature (for example, styles and plots). This wide-angle focus is achieved at the expense of treating characters' inner lives, and such narratives therefore also neglect romantic love, that staple of conventional novels. In encyclopedic narratives, mythic or epic plotting often appears as a kind of vestigial ordering principal, and in satiric examples of the form, a specific myth or epic usually serves as a parodic subtext. Equally notable in encyclopedic *satires* is the tension between that orderly subtext and the apparently random, indeterminate, even grossly digressive surface. At an extreme, that surface disorder tends toward a kind of narrative monstrousness whose counterparts are the ridiculous monsters (Coover's "Uncle Sam," Pynchon's "Giant Adenoid") within the texts.[5]

This summary makes a distinction between nonsatirical and satirical encyclopedic texts that is missing from the essays of Mendelson and Swigger. No reproach intended: the sweep of their reading and (especially in Mendelson's case) the backlighting it throws on a difficult text like *Gravity's Rainbow* are truly impressive. Rather, I just mean to comment on comparatist as against theoretical approaches to a problem, theory being much needed in this case. Also, Mendelson only inherited the uncertainties of his approach from Frye's treatments in *The Anatomy of Criticism* and from Philip Stevick's 1968 critique of Frye. In Frye, encyclopedic narratives are initially defined as a "thematic mode" involving "a total body of vision" that tends to "incorporate itself in a single encyclopedic form," composed either jointly or individually (55). Amid Frye's extensive catalogue, the Bible, Homeric epic, the *Satyricon,* Dante's *Commedia,* "the expansion of *The Romaunt of the Rose* into an encyclopedic satire by a second author" (56), Erasmus's *Praise of Folly,* and Goethe's *Faust* are all varied examples of encyclopedism in Western literary history. They suggest how, in Frye's schema, the form can swing high or low, but only in a lower phase, the "mythos of winter," does it break into satire. Frye, however, is never clear about that distinction within the thematic mode he calls the fictional encyclopedia. Much later in *The Anatomy of Criticism* he terms the "lower" phase either a Menippean satire, to preserve a sense of its historical origins, or (still better) a satirical anatomy, designated as one of his four hypothetical narrative "genres," along with the novel, romance, and confession.[6] Yet having made this designation Frye never returns to his original formulation, which would now have to specify both nonsatirical and satirical kinds. Instead, throughout he speaks as though encyclopedic fictions and anatomies (or Menippean satires) were loosely coextensive. Like Swigger, Mendelson, and LeClair after him, Frye thus implies that all encyclopedic fictions involve a polyglot, "loose-jointed" narrative, concerned mainly with external (social) realities treated from a single, obsessively detailed theoretical perspective (like rocketry in *Gravity's Rainbow*). Also, he continues, these texts usually succeed in "piling up an enormous mass of erudition . . . or in overwhelming its pedantic targets with an avalanche of their own jargon" (311). In sum, he leaves us with the erroneous impression that they all participate in that normative, targeted aggression that Frye considers essential to satire. To be precise, critics should distinguish between nonsatirical and satirical kinds of encyclopedism and, within the latter, between both generative and degenerative modes of satire.

Later studies of fictional encyclopedism fell heir to the lacunae and inconsistencies in Frye's schema. Clearly, however, we need to specify one kind of book that seeks the center of its parent culture by articulating its main metanarratives (Frye's "total body of vision") and by relating norms of conduct in all walks of social life to those myths. Such are the Bible and the *Commedia,* proper encyclopedic fictions. Then there is another kind of book that, as Stevick and Mendelson too broadly say of them all, seeks the cultural margin, piling up masses of eccentric, often subcultural and downright subversive information in a farrago that resists any totalizing vision, subverts the culture's confidence in its metanarratives, and keeps its own, non-normative (or pre-normative) councils. Frye several times calls them "encyclopedic satires," but doesn't elaborate. At one juncture Mendelson applies the term "mock-encyclopedia" to a kind of text, like *Tristram Shandy,* that only *fails* to meet his criteria because Sterne is too playfully conscious (with his "Tristrapaedia") of the text's ironic posture toward encyclopedic forms (161). Yet one is never sure why this element of metafictional parody, by itself, should exclude Sterne's book. Indeed the term "mock-encyclopedia" well describes the kind of satirical texts under discussion here.

After all, what is an encyclopedia? Today, those hawked along the promenades of American shopping malls are little more than an abecedarian, empirical assemblage of conventional, already outdated information. Yet the encyclopedia was in its golden age a profoundly logo- and theocentric enterprise. In *Dissemination*, Derrida reminds us that for centuries encyclopedias were meant to put across a totalizing metaphysics. Not only an exhaustive taxonomy of the known, a "hologram that would order and classify knowledge," the encyclopedia was designed to achieve nothing less than a "total overlap between nature and the volume, a musical identity of the whole of being with its encyclopedic text."[7] As such the encyclopedia would be nature's double, a true simulacrum. Even more, it would "complete" Nature *through* the Word, as if without the book Nature would lack *order*. One result of this is a paradox: though they are immensely formalized assemblages, most encyclopedias can only be opened by some random device, such as the coincidences of an abecedarian order. This dangerous interplay of chance and law — dangerous because it intimates the artificiality of the whole construct — remains a feature of many encyclopedic texts, fictional or not.

A classical encyclopedic work, like the Bible or any of those produced in the Middle Ages, was thus imagined as issuing from and completing the text of Nature, itself divinely authored. In turn, other books, "literary" volumes, were thought of as issuing from and being authorized by the encyclopedic text, insuring the maintenance of paternal descent even in "lesser" forms. For Derrida, however, this is the crux because, to regard the encyclopedic text as only a simulacrum, but nonetheless *required* to complete Nature, is also to concede "that Nature is somewhere incomplete, that it lacks something needed to be what it is, that it has to be supplemented. Which can be done by Nature alone, since nature is all." Yet it is simply illogical for this to be accomplished by some lesser, "supplemental" form. In Derridean thought, this condition of supplementarity calls up a massive critique of writing, which Western metaphysics long regarded as something less genuine than speech, a less privileged and perhaps even a superfluous form of *logos*. Suffice it to say that once the illusion of this view is exposed, and writing is freed from the overmastering demand that it represent Being, the written text exults in the possibilities for adventurous excess. In Derridean terms, the encyclopedia as a product of "auto-insemination" (a text derived from the divine *logos* in order to be given back, Ouroboros-like, to that source) gives way to an always incomplete encyclopedic fiction seen as the product of "dissemination" (a discourse that subverts the techniques of mastery). Such an unstable text becomes what Derrida earlier described, in *Writing and Difference*, as a zone of play, a possibility for infinite substitutions around the center-less network of a finite ensemble. In *Dissemination*, he exemplifies the breakup of that logocentric dream with the unfinished *Enzyklopädie* that Novalis conceived as "a model both real and ideal — and the germ of all books."[8] With

that breakup it is reasonable to ask if the kind of centrist, traditional encyclopedic narrative described in Frye and Mendelson has not become an
archaeological curiosity.

Finally, then, one may turn from the deconstructionist critique to interpretive concerns. Theories of reading have all in their own way accepted
an idea of the reader's "encyclopedia." In Barthes, it is the "reference code,"
described as little more than an ideological dictionary or catalogue of stereotypes to which the text continually nods. In a much more useful and open-
ended way, Eco posits the "encyclopedia" as a metaphoric way of grasping
that "global semantic construct," the network of semantic correlations, intertextual frames, or metanarratives, and assigned truth values against which
readers continuously verify stages of their own "inferential walk" through a
narrative text. Like that text, the reader's encyclopedic "world of reference"
is itself hypothesized as a "possible world, that is, a cultural construct" different for each reading subject. Obviously, though, there must be a high degree
of conformity among the "encyclopedias" of writers and readers for literary communication to occur.[9] Now, much of this semiotic research remains
at the level of speculation. (In *The Role of the Reader,* Eco breaks off at this
crux, noting how little is known about this encyclopedic construct or how
it functions in reading.) Also, the concept of such a reader's "encyclopedia"
involves theories of "possible worlds" that use modal logics beyond the scope
of this study. Still, these approaches have implications for an understanding of the postmodernist encyclopedic satire. For instance, the encyclopedic
"world of reference" brought to bear on a highly conventional example of fictional realism (a James Bond novel, say) would be so culturally central as to
seem invisible. In fact this is because the text refers to it in so many ways:
sometimes by gestures of mutuality, when the narrator assumes unilateral
agreement about things like superpower relations; sometimes by digressing
into seemingly pointless descriptions of objects (products), digressions that
never are really aimless because they always serve to index the codes of social
classification.

Circumstances in an encyclopedic satire are quite different. It may be defined as a type of narrative fiction that *foregrounds* all those signs of mutual
"knowledge" of the reference world, knowledge as a cultural construct in full
ideological regalia. Moreover, the fiction is anything but subtle or unprob-
lematic about this process. Pushed center-page by strategies of excess (lists)
and eccentric selection (from the arcane, the subcultural), in this kind of
fiction the encyclopedia of knowledge, what Tom LeClair calls the "systext,"
is both mimed and mocked. It emerges from the reading as a patchwork of

biases, incongruencies, and absences, as the works of Gaddis and Pynchon illustrate. In its reading, this kind of fiction thus stands in a quite opposite relation to readers from a work of conventional realism. Rather than implicitly confirming one's own putative "encyclopedia," the narration bluntly impeaches it, adding to the bill of particulars until, its cover blown, the authority of that knowledge may be degraded from myth to simple currency, another exchangeable coinage in the commerce of significations. Gaddis formulates this process in a borrowed phrase: "accelerated depreciation." Pynchon's metaphor is the plummeting of a rocket into disintegration.

At present, the most engaging work on this degenerative potential of some encyclopedic fictions has come from the writings of Mikhail Bakhtin and Julia Kristeva. Swigger's 1975 essay summarizes Bakhtin's definition of the Menippean narrative in *Problems of Dostoevsky's Poetics,* an account with which he (Swigger) is in close harmony. Mendelson refers to Bakhtin's later study, *Rabelais and His World,* discussing the essential "illegality" of Pynchon's sweeping vision. What's striking, however, is that the available criticism never brings Bakhtin's concept of the Menippean text as an illegal, subversive mode into conflict with Frye's generative concept of satire. Perhaps this is because Bakhtin's treatments are as radical as they are (unfortunately) dispersed throughout the body of his critical writings. By comparison, the work of Kristeva concisely defines the kind of nontotalizing, disruptive fiction that Frye and his followers never fully admitted to the class of encyclopedic texts.

The best introduction to Kristeva's argument is "Word, Dialogue and Novel," a 1969 essay conceived as both an homage to and critique of Bakhtin. Throughout, she defines the Menippean narrative in opposition to the "theological" focus of epic forms and the monological (what she terms true-false, or zero-one) insistence of both epic and the realist novel.[10] Instead, the Menippean fiction "transgresses" rules of both linguistic and social codes. If anything, its logic is "poetic," involving a zero-two "logic of the double" or "non-exclusive opposition" (71–72). Already these definitions imply that "logic of the double," so crucial to degenerative violence (see Girard) and to the paralogism (Pynchon's "excluded middles") or schizophrenia characterizing many satires. But there is more. Historically, for instance in Rabelais, Menippean discourse was conceived in opposition to Christianity; it emerges as a counterpractice or antigenre given to the exploration of extremity, a virtual "consecration" of ambivalence, vice, the grotesque, and the monstrous (80). Its essential aims are to be "politically and socially disturbing" and to free ordinary speech "from historical constraints," aims that both "entail a thorough boldness." An omni-generical mode as well, Menippean discourse makes its stand on the fringes of culture, and its most memorable signs are taken from the fantastic, from pathology and dreams, from any subcode that mainstream culture dismisses as scandalous or obscene. It has little interest in lived, individual being, indeed it sweeps aside human individualities as mere slots in the social construct (82–83). So far, some of this is similar to what Frye and his followers also attributed to encyclopedic texts. The significant difference is that Bakhtin and Kristeva both construe these tendencies, not as the staging of a *totalizing knowledge,* but as the staging of an always fluctuating *inadequate language.* Menippean writing is thus "an exploration of language as a correlative system of signs," a system whose absences, double-talk, and stratagems of mastery are always vulnerable to exposure because they are essentially arbitrary and, still worse, incomplete or downright erroneous.

Brief though it is, this summary points up new ways of approaching some of the most compelling fictions of American postmodernism. For if the large-scale novels of Coover, Gaddis, Pynchon, and others often seem to dwell upon signs of incompleteness, entropy, or exhaustion, it is not the symptom of some contemporary anomie. Nor is it necessarily the response to some perceived cul-de-sac of the genre, as John Barth argued in his 1967 essay, "The Literature of Exhaustion." Both of these perceptions (the social and the aesthetic) are influential, and certainly have had a great deal to do with contemporary literary reception. More exactly, however, the (fictional) signs of incompleteness compose a kind of metalanguage, a critique of that finite, totalized "knowledge" whose displacement and deformation are essential to the process of these books. Signs of incompletion and entropy are, in short, conventions of the form. Indeed, just as characters in realist novels often discourse at length about the ways of ambition or desire (that driving wheel of both their and the narrative's plotting), so characters in encyclopedic satires often discourse on incompleteness or entropy. In Gaddis's *J R,* the chief spokesman is Jack Gibbs; in *Gravity's Rainbow,* Roger Mexico.

However massively, the encyclopedic satire moves forward by means of ludicrous excesses and eccentricities, as Tom LeClair has shown in *The Art of Excess.* Its excesses of language were also widely remarked in reviews, but criticism has yet to fully account for the linguistic carnival spread out in these texts. Mendelson remarks on their "polyglot" quality and argues that the functions of linguistic play in *Gravity's Rainbow* are both historical and generative, to show how language stands in a "political" relation to the world and how its use opens the range of actions and responses to conditions

(171). The same very general corrective purpose might also be ascribed to the novels of Coover and Gaddis. Still, criticism has yet to deal with the subversive power of their overdetermined heteroglossia, in particular the ways that the slowly changing "formal" languages (as of the established arts and sciences) are overthrown by a welter of "informal" languages, those pop-cultural and subcultural discourses in constant flux. Obscenities (especially the lingo of excretion and of sex), street slang and ethnic dialects, underworld slang (the black market, counterfeiting), the jargons of esoteric systems and cults (astrology, alchemy) — in the encyclopedic satire these languages are, in unstinting detail, sources of great narrative power. The degenerative stresses they invoke, stresses caused by the withering fire of "informal" and "unauthorized" speech on its "formal" counterpart, are also a great source of laughter. The satires of Coover, Gaddis, and Pynchon all share that trait, though *Gravity's Rainbow* is the most obsessively itemized of them all. Yet these fictions are no less extreme in eccentrically selecting those "disciplines" they deploy as synecdoches of knowledge. Gaddis sets out in detail the processes of art forgery, alchemy, and counterfeiting in *The Recognitions;* in *J R*, the mail-order hustles of his title character stand, with a remarkable accuracy of satiric insight, for the entirety of American commerce, while other references to Wagnerian opera ("Art") and the cosmology of Empedocles and entropy theory ("Science") are equally important to his satiric project. In *Gravity's Rainbow*, Pynchon draws from an astonishingly extreme set of lexical fields: not only rocketry, but such diverse disciplines as the occult, Talmudic and Kabbalistic scholarship, obscure anthropological and linguistic treatises, the papers of I. P. Pavlov, and (much as Coover did with *Time* magazine) the London *Times* of 1944–45, including its most miniscule advertisements and notices.

This heteroglossia is at the same time less and more than a bodying forth of "knowledge" by fields, as in the classical encyclopedia. These deployments attest to an irresolvable strife and incompleteness, an abject and laughable failure of knowledge to constellate itself according to some metanarrative. Further examples of that "humorous" satire defined earlier, these large-scale fictions deflect laughter back into the centerless midst of a whelming, mass-cultural field that lies beyond the conventions of irony. Yet the encyclopedic satire is also *not* the structureless monster it seems at first glance. In fact, one of the most striking features in all four texts by Coover, Gaddis, and Pynchon is their reliance on a vestigial element of the classical encyclopedia, the cyclical order. *The Public Burning* is plotted as a travesty of that wholeness achieved through cycles of ritualized sacrifice. *The Recognitions*, while in many ways a parody of the linear apprenticeship plot, nonetheless finally deposits us, by "another turn of the screw," in the midst of a hysterical decay also present in the fevered hysteria described in its opening chapters and symbolized by the figure of Ouroboros. *J R* is filled with allusions to an eternal, cosmic cycling around the poles of "amity" and "strife," and at its end the title character is poised for another greedy run against the monolith of American commerce. Finally, the elegant shape of *Gravity's Rainbow* — a liturgical calendar whose mandala the text refuses to close — becomes Exhibit A in its satire of man's desire for totalizing systems of thought.

Not only the practical reach of such structures, but their challenges — literary, ideological, epistemological — make these the key fictional satires of our time. In them, the generic conventions of the novel run head-on into the modal demands of satire. The result is something definitively new in American literary history.

## Paper Currencies: The Satires of William Gaddis

Borges tells the *ficción* of Pierre Menard, a modernist writer who poured himself into so much of *Don Quijote,* its lore, and its time that he produced a verbatim duplicate of the Cervantes text. Such a feat of appropriation can be done without Menard's long years of scholarship. One of the minor eccentrics in William Gaddis's first novel, *The Recognitions* (1955), scrawls counterfeit signatures on the frontispieces of books, *Moby Dick* for example, and as he inscribes it amidst the tumult of a party, Mr. Feddle *is* Melville, "sitting in that farmhouse in the Berkshires a century before."[11] Another character, Esme, recreates from her heroin-induced "terror" a perfect duplicate of the Leishman and Spender translation of Rainer Maria Rilke's first *Duino Elegy.*

These achievements are in some sense whole and require at least residual powers of empathy. However, during the twenty years between *The Recognitions* and Gaddis's second novel, *J R* (1975), even those absurdly mechanized powers of empathy have run down. In *J R* we meet Jack Gibbs, a character whose name already betokens the vast entropy afflicting him, and whose habit of mind Gaddis reveals in the symbol of his coat pocket, rarely filled with cash but always with epigraphs taken seemingly at random from an Empedocles, Marx, Wagner, or Hemingway. Most of these quotations have to do with money and the depreciation of all social values, and most are inaccurately transcribed. Entropy and decay, their common subjects, have flawed the transmission itself. It is appropriate that they are all we ever see of Jack's incomplete opus on the "social history of mechanization and the arts, the destructive element."[12]

In both of these immense, obsessively detailed satires the reader deals with written verbal signs as if they were transferable bills, currencies of exchange. Indeed one might well take up the fictional testimony of *The Recognitions* and *J R*, then project Jack's "social history" as a chronicle of paper monies: the epoch, Feddle-to-Gibbs, as a study in accelerated depreciation, the "destructive element" that Jack never wholly comprehends. It is Gaddis's great subject. In his novels all significations are bound over to the authority of a vast market. Money, ordinary speech, artworks, affects, and information in the form of quotes, clichés, data, and sheer drivel — all are traded in a bewildering process of symbolic exhange. Like the novels of Thomas Pynchon or Robert Coover's *The Public Burning* (writers with whom he is often classified), Gaddis's fictions are thus a brilliantly humorous study of what has been called the *société de consommation,* that late-capitalist phase of the cartelized, consumer society. To Guy Debord, this society is a spectacle of images, a vertigo of exchange. In Gaddis's fictions this vertigo is not without patterns.[13] Any currency transaction is open to usurious practices in the form of a "middleman" who lends a fleeting order to the flux even as he takes his "cut." Any currency may be counterfeited, its unlawful double exemplifying the reciprocal violence or chaos always threatening to metastasize from within human society.

Chapter 4 described this potential in terms of a primordial violence, a "desymbolizing" vertigo into which human culture is always in danger of regressing and over which it has built up a virtual Babel of dissimulating fictions. In Gaddis's satires, this condition applies with particular vehemence to language. Like paper currencies, words may be borrowed, stolen, redeemed, and counterfeited. The contructions of language are controlled by writers who, like usurers, evaluate and regulate words through quotation, repetition, and other strategies for "appreciation." In literary modernism, through the work of an Eliot, Mann, or Gide, such literary practices were even raised to the status of a Holy Communion.

Gaddis remains broadly satirical about what this may mean. With the precision of an anatomist, he details the modern obsession with currency, and especially how that obsession disciplines a scarcely recognized continuity of exchanges, sexual, monetary, artistic, and metaphysical. Somewhat like Swift's Houyhnhnms, his fictional characters enact a limited discourse within the closed system of their culture, a system in which they accept the cash nexus as something like Divine Law. The satire, however, discovers in their frenzies of exchange a vast, degenerate fiction. Its topic is the mutual violence (or symbolic collapse) which, as René Girard argues, has always been the signified of divinity, and whose terror it is the business of culture to disguise. Hence one of the controlling ironies in Gaddis's work: his myriad of counterfeiters, plagiarists, and usurers are not eccentrics at all but central figures of their society, itself the debased coinage of a modernist cultural orthodoxy. In revealing their absurdity, Gaddis shares with other postmodern satirists like Coover and Pynchon a mood of analytic, encyclopedic subversion. His shattering and homogenizing of cultural codes is so far-reaching by the time of *J R* that the text becomes purely transactional. Its words are only so many atoms in a Brownian motion of signs that are totally and instantly exchangeable with any others, thus void of all use value save the additional exchanges they prompt, with their transitory indication of new victors and victims.

## The Recognitions (1955)

In *The Recognitions,* Wyatt Gwyon's inheritance from his Puritan forefathers brings a legacy of necessity and guilt. Within the Gwyon line, "each generation was a rehearsal of the one before," and each life is "conceived in guilt and perpetuated in refusal" (18). Each Gwyon seems to counterfeit the previous one, and Gaddis compares them to a line of statues standing against "the vanity of time." Through two centuries only one boy had doubted the family's grand resistance to temporal change, and in despondency he had (in a travesty of Quentin Compson's death in *The Sound and the Fury*) "tied a string around his neck with a brick to the other end" and drowned himself in "two feet of water" (18), demonstrating even in his suicide the Gwyons' tenacious sense of necessity. Now Wyatt does not drown himself, but he does become mortally sick, and through the illness he recovers a sense of dark, unconscious flow, or "recognition." He always identifies this with the half-light of dawn and with his maternal inheritance, especially with his mother's father, the "Town Carpenter," who once tumbled into a well and glimpsed from its darkness, and despite the full daylight above, the constellations of stars. In contradiction to this irrational legacy is Wyatt's Puritan heritage of election, which carries with it the fear of not being gainful, of not heeding Cotton Mather's warning, "That which is not useful is vicious," embodied in Wyatt's paternal Aunt May, with her "Use-Me Society." One ironic result of this doctrine, despite the family's "disapproval" of everything worldly, is a "fortune" that "had grown near immodest proportions" by the time of Wyatt's childhood, though Wyatt sees this wealth as the take of a con game, a "ruse" in which the parishioners look upon their weekly offering of coins as a rendering up to God of that which originally was His (26–27). A second result is Wyatt's inability to complete any of his artworks except those that are copies and profitable, for example the copy of his father's copy of a circular table depicting the seven deadly sins. Wyatt's sale of this piece is his first link to Recktall Brown, the father of his career as a forger, a demonstration that counterfeiting also runs in dynastic lines. The seven generations of Gwyon men copy each other, Sinisterra is the last in a line of forgers, and Wyatt is quoted as having said that "the saints were counterfeits of Christ, and that Christ was a counterfeit of God" (514).[14]

Again, contradicting this nexus of counterfeit monies, men, artworks, and divinity is Wyatt's inheritance from his mother Camilla. She wants to name Wyatt "Stephen," after the first Christian martyr, but with the added significance of a "crown" or "ring" and the implied opposition to the regressive linearity of "Wyatt Gwyon." His legacy from Camilla is also one of incompletion and chance (she dies aboard ship, having unfortunately started labor when the only medical help was Frank Sinisterra, then flimflamming his passage as a ship's surgeon). Under the gun of his father's Puritanism, Wyatt cannot finish the "original" portrait of his mother. His legacy on the maternal side is therefore one of failure or, what is the same thing in the American mythos, preterition. It is, furthermore, a legacy of darkness, the darkness, for example, of Camilla's crypt, at the novel's end, or the darkness of the Town Carpenter's well, at the novel's beginning. It is also a legacy of flux: Camilla dies at sea, recalling the drowned Gwyon boy, and Camilla's father gazes up from his well at a "sea" of stars. Thus Wyatt's maternal inheritance stands opposed to Reverend Gwyon's rational, Apollonian Christianity. The division of his psyche along these lines continues through his marriage, when Esther feels comfortable with him only in darkness; during his career as an art forger, when he works by dim light in order to mimic conditions in the old "Guilds" and thereby foil the light of detectives; and until his journey to Spain brings him full circle at the side of his mother's coffin. In short Wyatt's is not, as Bernard Benstock has claimed, a "quest for the father" in the manner of *Ulysses*. If anything, his is a motion toward the maternal identity. Wyatt's is a search for authenticity in both life and art, an attempt to strike some ground between, or beyond, the irreconcilable demands of his paternal and maternal legacies. This possibility Wyatt thinks he sees in the equipoise of light and dark at dawn (the Latin *oriri*), wherein there seems to be a moment of "origin." And such a moment comes to an artist, Wyatt supposes, "maybe seven times in a life" (102). Gaddis's narrative aside, "Magic number!" implies that this moment of artistic fulfillment weighs against the heritage of counterfeit and decay embodied in the seven generations of Gwyon men and in the forged table of Bosch's *Seven Deadly Sins*.

This dialectic always unfolds *inside*. As Wyatt often remarks, "All art requires a closed space." Gaddis's next novel will further elaborate on this theme in terms of entropy theory, the concept that matter in a closed container will tend toward a degenerative dispersal of energy, a changeless homogeneity that Josiah Willard Gibbs referred to as "heat death." Even in *The Recognitions*, though, Gaddis is well aware that cybernetic theorists had recently discovered a telling homology between the mathematical equation for computing entropy and the equation for calculating the information per message, that is, the message's susceptibility to *semiotic* entropy or "noise." Indeed, some of Gaddis's most sustained satire in his first novel develops from the countless scenes of cocktail party chit-chat, with its non sequiturs, self-canceling declarations of value, and actual noise, the kind of regressive, designifying chaos that I have been identifying with satirical fiction. That condition is present in countless emblems throughout *The Recognitions*. The unnamed "distinguished novelist," for example, mistypes a quotation from Wordsworth — "The world is too muhvh with us, late ans soon, gettijg and spendinf we lay wasre . . ." (946) — and this "noise" is then exemplary of what the reader is told by completing the quote: in the culture of consumer capitalism, we "lay waste our powers." In a so-called "information society," the human being suffers a ridiculously abject loss; even the most basic forms of dominance, patterns of propriety and property encoded in language, erode in the ceaseless flux of signs until, to quote Wordsworth again, "little we see in Nature that is ours." Within the closed order of Gaddis's cocktail parties and counterfeiting "rings," signs inevitably begin to jostle against one another in a furious exchange, a "violence all inclosed in a framework," as Wyatt says of flamenco music (123). Metaphors of disease are prominent. Wyatt argues that for the artist to keep faith with these circumstances is "like saying a man's true to his cancer" (262). In *J R*, Jack Gibbs compares his opus on mechanization and art to a terminally ill patient who never gets out of bed (603). These are exacting bodily metaphors for the state of inflated currencies in which Gaddis deals.

Contrary to the relentless dialectic unfolding *inside*, Gaddis figures an equally relentless, whelming dialogism criss-crossing the social domain *outside*. Both novels reveal signs of monetized exchange flashing even on the darkest corners. In *The Recognitions*, the neon signs of the New York streets add "a note of metaphysical (Bergsonian) hilarity to the air of well-curbed excitement, in tubes of glass cleverly contorted to spell out cacaphonous syllables of words from a coined language, and names spawned in estaminets in Antwerp" (302). Here, even that last (coined) phrase was borrowed from Eliot's "Gerontion," a poem that in turn derived *its* first line — "an old man in a dry month" — from A. C. Benson's book *Edward Fitzgerald* (1905). As Steven Moore has shown, phrases lifted from Eliot, Rilke, the Puritan saints, alchemical treatises, and the Church fathers lie scattered throughout *The Recognitions*.[15] Coinages from Shakespeare are everywhere in Gaddis, here and there are bits of Wordsworth, and in *J R* Edward Bast will run together lines from Wagner's *Ring* cycle and Tennyson's "Locksley Hall" when he performs for his Muse, a half-sister aptly named Stella. In writing his first novel, Gaddis's use of the *tiret* instead of quotation marks was doubtless intended to collapse the proprietary boundaries between coinages, and this tendency will be further accelerated in *J R* by his additional use of ellipses and unmarked changes in scene to further increase the reader's sense of entropy.

Amid this flux of messages one learns never to take the coins at face value, whether they are exchanged inside or out. As simple a quotation as an admirer's comment to the plagiarist, Otto ("'Publish and be damned,' the Duke of Wellington said" [191]) eventually reveals hidden ironies because (1) Wellington's curse may be apocryphal, and (2) even if he *did* write these words, as some of his biographers claim, it was not in the context of a writer suffering indignities at the hands of dull critics, which is how the young man means for Otto to take it; (3) Wellington allegedly wrote the phrase to a publisher threatening to print a former courtesan's lurid half-truths unless Wellington paid them both off.[16] The only steady thing is that Otto's assimilation of the sentence, as with his innumerable borrowings from Wyatt, hinges on finding a self-accruing point of interest: How to turn it for a profit? Exchanges like these are fundamentally usurious. The currencies must pass through the hands of a middleman who takes his cut, as the counterfeiter Frank Sinisterra knows: "Everything's middlemen. Everything's cheap work and middlemen wherever you look. They're the ones who take the profit" (523). This principal both guides and qualifies one's reading, from the slightest quotation to the larger deployments of plot and character. For what are the dealings of a Recktall Brown, marketer of Wyatt's "counterfeit originals," if not those of a satanically masterful "middleman"?

Moreover the satirist brings himself into this great flux. A figure named "Willie" makes several appearances in *The Recognitions*, disclosing to readers the very process of borrowings that are part of the novel's composition. In

*J R,* Gaddis includes a page of bogus titles for pulp fiction coming from the *J R* Family of Companies, each title an anagram of *The Recognitions,* with an accompanying blurb lifted from actual reviews of the book (515–16). One recalls Mr. Feddle, who scissors the titles from book reviews to present them as praise of his own rotten work. In such scenes Gaddis satirizes the commodification of literary and artistic culture, the imposition of mass-cultural economies on the very temple that modernist writers had sought to keep pure. In *The Recognitions,* everything has been transformed into coinage. Or, as the Frankfurt School theorists would phrase it, this is a world beset by "instrumentalization," the wholesale conversion of everything into sheer means, available on a rationally organized, purely transactional market where *all* values (as ends) have been monetized.[17] Indeed, the collapse into one literary-monetary discourse is really symptomatic of a larger collapse, represented in the novel as including all transactions, from the sexual to the metaphysical.

For example, in Frank Sinisterra's underworld cant counterfeit money is called "queer." This bit of slang takes on added significance during a scene when Sinisterra meets the playwright, Otto, the former thinking that Otto is his "drop" or middleman, while Otto mistakenly takes Sinisterra as the long-estranged father with whom he has been trying to set up a reunion. In the ensuing mix-up, Otto receives a packet of forged twenties, "the queer," and thinks of it as a monetary recompense for decades of parental neglect. Meanwhile Otto describes himself as "a writer," a meaningless admission to Sinisterra. He merely takes it as an indication of Otto's homosexual preferences, thus perhaps a come-on, for writers, they say, are "always queer nowadays" (556). Otto is not, but he *is* a counterfeit. And characters who read his play, *The Vanity of Time,* recognize his plagiaries straight away; they cannot pin down the source of his borrowings, but readers can. Our outside perspective tells us that the source of Otto's borrowings, of all his erudite detail, is Wyatt, who even supplies Otto with a title when he recalls his father's sermon on "the vanity of time," derived from William Law. Thus by a comically circuitous route it is Wyatt and his Puritan forebears who "father" Otto's writing. And when, at the end of *The Recognitions,* Otto assumes the identity of his own dramatic character, Gordon, the character being nothing but a concoction of Wyatt's learned ramblings, it is as if Otto continues the Gwyon line, completing what Gaddis terms the inward "turn of the screw" around its endlessly regressive line of generations. In addition, throughout these transactions there runs an especially significant sexual metaphor. Otto frequently holds the text of his play clasped between his legs, and the manuscript has been (fatuously) bound in leather; thus it resembles the wallet Otto frequently checks. Indeed, when Frank Sinisterra passes him "the queer" beneath a table, Otto holds that bundle "clutched against his parts" (554). This conflation of sex, money, and the word reappears throughout *The Recognitions* and again in *J R*, where it looms over Jack Gibbs's unsuccessful first attempt at making love to Amy Joubert, the Muse who is his (temporary) cure for writer's block, financial mismanagement, and sexual dysfunction.

In *The Recognitions,* these three motifs are eventually subsumed within Judaeo-Christian signs of divinity. Using a brilliantly satirical extended simile, Gaddis ranges over the history of procreation, from the time "before men knew of their part in generation," and regarded skirted women as "auto-fructiferous," to the "discovery" of sexual generation and its accompanying displacement of the moon by the phallic sun, then to the "skirted priests" of the early church, when a "new religion which extolled the impotent man and the barren woman triumphed over a stupefied empire." This page-long survey tumbles at last toward a pair of young men exchanging confidences at a party: "So even now, under a potted palm with silver fronds, a youth making a solemn avowal held another youth by that part where early Hebrews placed their hands when taking oaths, for it represented Jahveh" (334). These two young men belong to the same group of avant-gardists among whom the novel's lamb-of-God, literary agent Agnes Deigh (another "middleman"), moves like a demivierge, "collecting members," as she puts it (203). Inside this subculture, to be "queer" is to participate in that vast, entropic "homogeneity" governing every exchange, sexual, monetary, artistic, and metaphysical. This is what is meant by "counterfeiting." In fact, Gaddis's extended simile suggests that the very origins of this condition are to be found in sexual-metaphysical symbolism. To be auto-fructiferous, in terms of his simile, is to be magically generative and therefore different from transactional economies, sexual or otherwise. But the movement from "auto-fructiferous moon" to "phallic sun" subordinates that generative power, and thus symbolically all "production," to degenerative instrumentalities of exchange, over which the phallus or (by association) money, the word, and Jahweh rise as primary symbols in Western culture. Moreover, this analogy invites readers to envision Wyatt Gwyon's movement in *The Recognitions* as being toward some abstracted form of the auto-fructiferous mother. In the face of a monolithic economy his movement is thus, quite literally, a degenerative fiction. The problematics of this plot, so essential to the narrative *as a satire,* are finally crucial to how one reads it.

In modernist writing *Les Faux-monnayeurs* first set forward the idea that sexual, monetary, and literary exchanges form a startling homology. Hence

Gide's complementary idea, that the modernist avant-gardes shape their attack on bourgeois culture by expropriating this same homology, but ironically inverted, in sexual, monetary, and literary outlawry. It is in this spirit that Strouvilhou, exemplar of the literary terrorist, jeers at the wealthy rake Passavant: "I give you fair warning, if I edit a review, it will be in order to prick bladders — in order to demonetize fine feelings, and those promissory notes that go by the name of *words*." Yet Strouvilhou offers the young men to whom he stands as patron (just as Passavant stands as his) no kind of sanctuary once they become outsiders. Cut adrift, the young men soon float back into the safer but literally murderous regime of school. Bernard forgets the issue of his bastardy, returning at the last to his "father" Profitendieu and presumably also to some more actual "profit" than that signified in his name.

Gide's plot may be read as the canonical modernist type of what, in *The Eighteenth Brumaire of Louis Bonaparte,* Marx condemns as our tendency to reject the nightmare of our forebears even while, on second thought, we turn back to borrow their coin. His well-known opening puts it this way:

> The tradition of all the dead generations weighs like a nightmare on the brain of the living. And just when they seem engaged in revolutionizing themselves and things, in creating something that has never yet existed, precisely in such periods of revolutionary crisis they anxiously conjure up the spirits of the past to their service and borrow their names, battle cries and costumes in order to present the new scene of world history in this time-honored disguise and this borrowed language.[18]

In modernist literature, though, the currencies are no longer simply "borrowed." Anterior discourses are either taken in at a wholesale rate, counterfeited, or blithely stolen, by Ezra Pound, for example, of whom Wyndham Lewis wrote, "there is almost nowhere in the Past that he has not visited," or the T. S. Eliot of "Tradition and the Individual Talent," urging his contemporaries to "procure the consciousness of the past" by any means. It was meant to seem heroic. Leaning into a felt collapse, the modernist turns isolated moments of time into those *points d'appui* against which he tries to secure a "purchase." One was to supposed to get an image of the artist as Atlas. The postmodernist fictions of William Gaddis insist that we redefine such feats as profit-mongering, boom-time technologies: not Atlas, then, but Charles Atlas.

Gaddis's satire exposes that modernist doctrine of the isolated moment as a behindhand stroke of market practices or pseudoscience, all intended to counter the invasion that practical reason had mounted on truth-values. Artists sought to forestall devaluations of their currencies through repertoires of rationalistic techniques, of which twelve-tone music, Duchamp's Large Glass, the "constructivism" of *Doktor Faustus*, the preoccupation with the past as a set of energized points, and formalist criticism may all be taken as models. As Gaddis indicates throughout *The Recognitions*, these strategies often aspired to "religious" authenticity and even sought to utterly displace theology. But here is another turn of the screw: in thus displacing religion, *any* substitute practice, whether of art or of science, must also expropriate the forms of sacrificial violence that religious rites maintain. This is exactly René Girard's conclusion about contemporary science and, in particular, about its invention of nuclear terror, an ultimate form of the sacrificial crisis. A jaded public's continuing need for such forms is certainly behind Coover's satire in *The Public Burning* and at the very heart of Pynchon's great novel, *Gravity's Rainbow*.

It is also instructive to stand Gaddis's fictional critique alongside some postwar scholarship. Semiotics in particular has shown how the generation of money, offspring, and texts cooperates under one symbolic hegemony. As early as *Writing Degree Zero* (1953), Barthes argued for the analogy between monetary and linguistic "currencies." In *S/Z* (1970) he develops the association in more detail, arguing for an outright collusion between authorial control and patriarchy, linguistic and legal contracts, and literary and economic exchanges of property, all coalescing under the determinism of a monological, reactionary culture. Against that nexus, he projects the indeterminacy of "multivalent" orders, texts that do not attribute and perhaps even mask quotations, disrespect paternity, origins, property, or propriety. Such works subvert the conventional demand for a "voice" betokening authorial unity. The satire Gaddis makes on the topic of "inheritance" and "origins" in his first novel speaks to this break. Tracing his movement from the fringes of a determinist fiction deep into a realization of the entropy Barthes invokes would be one way of graphing the twenty-year sojourn from *The Recognitions* to *J R*. Yet in many ways Gaddis has carried the anatomy of our monetized culture beyond Barthes. Jameson, for instance, has said that among the *Tel Quel* group only Jean-Joseph Goux ever brought the analysis of currencies to its fullest expression.[19] In "Numismatique: l'or, le phallus, et la langue" (1968), Goux shows the history of money as tightly harmonious with those of the *logos* and of sexuality. These histories are mapped as a progress toward the abstract, then toward the conventional: in each case, from fetish to symbol to the "simple sign" of a currency. During this progress, as Goux demonstrates, the lexicons of spending, intercourse, writing, and divine revelation all become hopelessly cross-referenced. One gets the impression that only Maxwell's demon could ever stand in the middle and sort them.

Gaddis will not sort, but he will supply principles of understanding. He often recalls the degenerative principle of Gresham's Law: bad currency drives out good. And if quotation was a principal mode of high modernism, quotation having been taken up as a program for loosening the word from history, releasing from the quotation unsuspected eloquences ("recognitions") in the here and now, then the logical next step is to wholly conventionalize the coinage. So the progress from fetish to symbol to common currency repeats itself in literature as a century of fiction moves from rituals of *le mot juste,* to venerating the ahistorical symbol a quotation makes, to proliferating currencies for their own sake. Extrapolating from there, one may suppose that, if Gresham was right, the next step would be to erase any difference between the real currency and the counterfeit.

With that erasure, satire seems necessary. Yet consider the problematics of satirical plotting in *The Recognitions.* A kind of apprenticeship narrative, its principal idea is Wyatt's search for authenticity and originality. Throughout, his quest progresses between fierce antinomies: there is Wyatt's paternal inheritance that he cannot reconcile with artwork, just as he cannot reconcile his maternal inheritance to his gift for forgery. Arranging the terms of this struggle on a Greimasian rectangle, each contrary generating its logical contradiction, the ideological nucleus of the novel may be graphed as in Figure 6. These are the main tensions of the novel's plot. For instance, midway through the narrative Wyatt even considers returning to his father and to theological study as a means of ending his "wild conflict." From the notes Gaddis made while writing the novel, we know he initially planned for Wyatt to fulfill his quest through artwork. In turn, many readers have interpreted *The Recognitions* as a narrative that brings Wyatt's quest to a successful conclusion. The representations of Wyatt's final painting and Stanley's "soaring" music, they argue, redeem falsity in both life and art.[20] Behind such a reading stands the modernist ideology of art, the work as last bastion of authenticity and transcendence in a cultural wasteland. Here is the problem: if, as Gaddis claims in a 1981 essay, "Entropy rears as a central preoccupation of our time," then one need is for artwork to surmount the closed system in which the semiotic entropy goes its intractable way.[21]

Does *The Recognitions* depict such an authentically transcendent process? Much depends on how one interprets the concluding chapters. Wyatt returns to Spain and the monastery where his mother is buried; there he also consumes a loaf of bread containing his father's ashes; and he turns his counter-

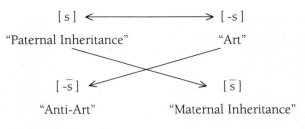

$[s]$ ⟷ $[-s]$

"Paternal Inheritance"          "Art"

$[\overline{\text{-s}}]$          $[\overline{s}]$

"Anti-Art"          "Maternal Inheritance"

**FIGURE 6**

feiting skills on the restoration of old paintings. Everything implies a synthesis of those contraries which have afflicted him. On the trip over he had (to those aboard ship) apparently drowned, and this provides Wyatt an opportunity to be reborn with the name his mother intended, Stephen. In his last scene, "Stephen" also cups in his hands a small bird that has flown into his apartment; he frees it, reversing the moment when as a child he had killed a wren with a stone, in a "recognition" of the saint who supplies the name "Stephen" to Camilla. With this action he is the only character to fully redeem the coin of his "original" name. As for the bird, it flutters in front of several canvasses the monks have employed him to "restore," the bird's error seeming to warrant the *natural* authenticity of their images and suggesting, as well, that the canvasses have broken Wyatt's cycle of mere copying: not mirrors, then, but windows; not more simulacra, but visions. Nevertheless, there are difficulties. For one, in these final chapters the depth of Wyatt/Stephen's madness is never clear. He is consumed by guilt for having murdered a former acquaintance, Han, a homosexual who had made a pass at him. Also, in his derangement Wyatt misses the fact that he has symbolically consumed his father (himself crucified while confined for insanity to a sanitarium). Moreover, Wyatt's involvement with the paintings is purely technical, a matter of scraping away layers of forgery to reveal the "originals" beneath. This painstaking work is his only stay against a completed lapse into the insane violence, the entropy, surrounding him.

In addition, Wyatt/Stephen has been involved with yet another forgery, an absurd attempt with Sinisterra (now using the alias "Mr. Yak") to steal a corpse and use it to construct a counterfeited Egyptian mummy. Only the murder of Sinisterra, in a case of mistaken identity, ends that attempt. Finally there is the death of Stanley, the composer of sacramental music who previously castrated himself. He dies inside and alone, playing the great mass he conceived as a perfected, self-contained design, "every transition and movement in the pattern over and against itself and within itself proof against time" (346). This work becomes so self-important that *it* will literally "come through at the expense of everything" (1020). Indeed, this grand artwork quite literally kills its creator, who was driven to include every feasible voice in the piece, even "the Devil's interval," a low C from the instrument's longest pipe that vibrates at such a rumbling frequency that it brings the entire chapel down on him.[22]

This summary returns us to the semantic "nucleus" sketched in Figure 6 above. The point of introducing it was not simply to propose it as a sign of the conflicts pulling at Wyatt, but to consider it, rather, as a general symptom. The oppositions, Father/Art and Mother/Anti-Art, are not strictly logical as much as they are social antinomies, indices of ideological closure and social strife for which the narrative seeks a generative release. That nucleus is the symptom of a conceptual double life forced on all aspiring artists driven inside by a capitalist mass culture. If the narrative is to positively resolve it, those indices must be occupied by characters, for it is only through their embodiments that the text can take the further step of projecting any possible syntheses of each seme, syntheses also represented by characters, yet now potentially beyond the original antinomies. Thus, if one moves counterclockwise around the rectangle beginning from its left-hand side, then clearly the possibility of synthesizing that Paternal seme (with its rationality, separation, and guilt represented by Reverend Gwyon and Aunt May) and the seme of Anti-art or counterfeiting (with its inauthenticity, disintegrative work, and manifold profits represented by Recktall Brown and Otto Pivner) is embodied by Frank Sinisterra, the guilt-ridden master counterfeiter who takes Wyatt under his fatherly wing in the last chapters.

Moving next to the lower set of contraries, here any possibility of a neutral synthesis must bring together the seme of counterfeiting with that of the Maternal (indicated throughout the text by the irrationality, unity, and redemptive potential in Camilla and the Town Carpenter). This neutral synthesis is well represented by Wyatt, during his most profitable phase as a counterfeiter when, despite his passivity toward the business, opportunities still seek him out. Yet this Wyatt dies a symbolic death by drowning and is replaced, as noted, by "Stephen," a figure of the right-hand synthesis between the Maternal seme and that of Art.

Here, precisely, is the crux. "Stephen" is palpably insane and engaged, not in the creation of original art, but in the restoration of palimpsested Old Masters. Still more, the seme of Art, which the narrative has consistently identified with authenticity, originality, freedom from profit motives, and an

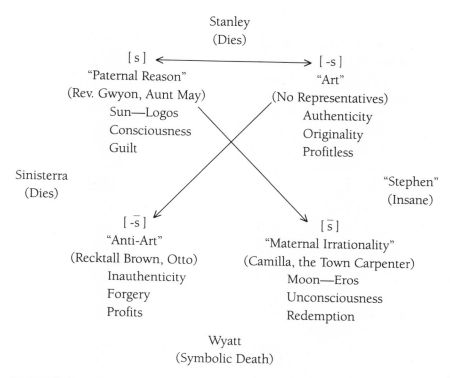

FIGURE 7

integrative process similar to alchemy, *simply has no representatives in the text.*
(One whimsical possibility: "Willie," the figure of Gaddis who makes several
fleeting appearances, once on the telephone to query Wyatt about St. Clem-
ent's "Recognitions.") This absence, the failure of the novel to produce characters embodying its key term, not only underscores the failure of "Stephen,"
it stands as the clear symptom of a radical, non-normative satire whose resolution is bound to tumble regressively back into disorder. This is clear when
we move to the upper quadrant, or what Greimas suggestively refers to as the
"complex" or "ideal" synthesis of the two initial contraries: the union of Art
with the Paternal reason in Stanley. This resolution is represented by some
of the most powerful examples of Black Humor in *The Recognitions.*[23] These
include, at the least, Stanley's fawning devotion to Agnes Deigh, which culminates in his self-castration; an absurdly horrifying sequence of misadven-
tures by which he comes into possession of his mother's amputated leg; his
abject fear of water (marking him as the semantic opposite of Wyatt); and

finally his death under the power of his own artistic practice, in the Fenestrula chapel. Every characterological detail adds to the satirical degradation of this "ideal" resolution.

Thus completed, the semiotic system of *The Recognitions* might be filled in as in Figure 7. This heuristic reconstructs both the network of characters, with its decisive empty slot, and those thematic tensions that it was Gaddis's stated intention to resolve on the side of a modernist ideology, with its religion of Art. The blowup of that intention is therefore triply significant. First, it points to the declining legitimacy of modernist myth during the postwar years. Second, it once again testifies to the subversive power of satirical practice for the generation of novelists after Nathanael West. Third, it suggests one defining characteristic of that practice. Recent studies have shown that a definitive trait of realist fictions is their tendency to seek ideological closure by concluding with that "complex" or "ideal" semantic synthesis. In *The Political Unconscious*, Fredric Jameson has traced the strategems of that desire from Stendahl and Balzac well into the great narratives of Conrad, where it begins to unravel. In comparison, the example of *The Recognitions* teaches that an essential of postmodern, degenerative satire, commonly regarded as an "anti-realist" mode, is its calculated subversion of the realist synthesis. Writing his first novel brought Gaddis to a recognition of those disruptive energies. The consequences of that recognition are widely evident in his next.

### J R (1975)

The principal topic of *J R* is depreciation. In this novel the desire for commercial and transcendental riches once again brings into play the conflated syntaxes of sexual generation, money, and artworks. Yet it is a measure of how Gaddis has accepted the satirical energies of *The Recognitions* that, in this novel, he makes no pretense of shoring up its degenerative drift with ideologies of Art. Now, when money talks, things really fall apart; all discourse accelerates the slide into entropy. Against that dissipation Edward Bast, the novel's artist, struggles to free his work from the institutional usury bleeding his creative vitality. Eventually, however, he acknowledges that usury is itself a natural state, partaking of Nature's vast commerce at all levels: even molecules exchange particles and yield up energy (interest) during the transaction. Thus while Ezra Pound (in Canto 45) could condemn usury as working "against nature" (*contra naturam*) as well as against the abstractions of Art ("with usura the line grows thick"), Gaddis rewrites these age-old dicta according to the viewpoint of a subversive satire he now fully accepts. Recognized now as a metaphor of the degenerative drift in all being, an "accelerated depreciation" that each character tries to manage, usury becomes the central principle of a satirical world.

Everything I've just said implies an orderly structuring of the novel's materials. Its brilliance, however, lies in Gaddis's unfolding such a reading while also making a shambles of conventional narration. The writing in *J R* appears utterly seamless, with practically none of the familiar narrative markers and divisions, such as chapters. The novel's spatiotemporal transitions occur without rank or reason, often in the midst of sentences, as if the role of omniscient narrator had been redefined as a mere mechanical principle of random dial twirling. Indeed, all those aspects that narrative poetics defines under the categories of "order," "duration," and "frequency," all those refinements of temporality that have been resources for narrative experiment through the modernist epoch, have been simplified or effaced.[24] *J R* is, instead, nearly all voices, direct discourse with its speakers and auditors totally unmarked. There is none of the free indirect discourse and internal monologue which have been specialties of the modernist novel. Everywhere, a scattershot of declarations, ejaculations, imperatives, and interrogatives merges in each voice, the voices all merging into one another, then into voices droning over telephones, radios, and televisions, in unceasing, fragmented, but dialogically intelligible noise. Charged as they are with emotive power, these voices stand against the brief descriptive passages (of scene and action) constituting the only intrusions of a conventional narrator. These passages are written wholly in the indicative mood, their power consisting precisely in the absence of emotion. Stylistically, then, *J R* embodies the sharpest of polarities: recorded speech that is fully contaminated by characters' needs and aggressions and the interlaced descriptions operating at a zero degree. There are sharp parallels between this mimetically raw, unmediated narration and the documentary tradition identified in chapter 4. Indeed, one might well read *J R* as a document *in extremis,* and this raises crucial problems of intention.

In its presentation, *J R* marks the extraordinary metastasis of narrative techniques developed, in miniature, in Donald Barthelme's short conversation pieces and in the episodic chapters of *Snow White.* Moreover it seems a more radical vision of chaos than Pynchon's in *Gravity's Rainbow,* for even as Pynchon also traces the interchangeability of codes and their ceaseless expropriation for purposes of terror and mastery, his writing tends to hold back and shape that dissemination through the strategies of a paranoid mythology, his mythic subtext of Judaeo-Christian ritual sacrifice, satirized as the uttermost ruse of political power, its secret "history." The textual counterpart of this myth in *Gravity's Rainbow* is the obsessively detailed four-part, seventy-three-episode structure of its systematic organization.[25] There are no such guideposts in *J R*. In Gaddis's novel all signs — as of sex, cash, consumer products, stocks, artworks, and even of noise — circulate around a center that is just a void, absent any overarching truth, much less the vestiges of an outworn myth. Instead speech only serves as the cover for a massively empty hyperreality; its only point is to spur still more exchanges of speech. Yet even amid this cancer of discourse are minor intricacies of reference and structure. Most important among them are three fields of reference in *J R*: Richard Wagner's *Ring des Nibelungen,* the presocratic cosmology of Empedocles, and entropy theory. Together they synecdochically represent the three branches of human knowledge in art, philosophy, and natural philosophy with which Gaddis develops the satire's degenerative fiction. While nothing like the immense webwork of references in *Gravity's Rainbow,* they fulfill the encyclopedic aim of indexing knowledge in all its dissimulating power.

What Homer's *Odyssey* is to Joyce's *Ulysses*, Richard Wagner's *Der Ring des Nibelungen* is to *J R*. The *Ring* cycle becomes a minor mythological subtext to the fictional plot, and Gaddis introduces the parallels between them early in the book. The initial scene, with Edward Bast's two aunts reminiscing in the presence of a lawyer bent on crucial business, is certainly one of the most ambiguous openings in fiction:

— Money . . .? In a voice that rustled.
— Paper, yes.
— And we'd never seen it. Paper money.
— We never saw paper money till we came east.
— It looked so strange the first time we saw it. Lifeless.
— You couldn't believe it was worth a thing.
— Not after Father jingling his change.
— Those were silver dollars.
— And silver halves, yes and quarters, Julia. The ones from his pupils. I can hear him now . . . (3)[26]

This scene brilliantly introduces the ideas of monetized speech and the degeneration of paternal authority. The lawyer's function here, as a "middleman," is to complete the orderly disposition of "Father's" estate. Before that can occur, however, this scene abruptly shifts to a Brooklyn school where we meet the novel's principal characters. These include Jack Gibbs, seen lecturing on information theory and the Second Law of Thermodynamics to eighth-graders who can't even spell the word "e-n-t-r-o-p-y," and Edward

Bast, working as a composer-in-residence at the school and first seen attempting to direct a class of sixth-graders in Wagner's "The Rhinegold." One of his pupils is J R Vansant, who first appears in a phone booth, "motionless but for fragmenting finger and opposable thumb opening, closing, the worn snap of an old change purse" (31) — a detail that fixes him as the degenerative link to "Father's" power. J R is a runny-nosed, disheveled kid obsessed with the hollow promises of mail-order fortunes, a boy whom the kindly will soon describe as someone hungering for success and the cynical as someone "about as touching as a bull shark" (246). In the school's presentation of Wagner, J R is slated to play Alberich, the grotesque, gnomish creature who renounces love for the power, granted to whomever possesses the Nibelung Ring, of enslaving men. After Wagner, the narrative will provisionally point up Love as the source of beneficent creativity. Thus when J R shouts his lines in rehearsal, "Hark floods! Love I renounce forever!" (36), he signals the genesis of what will become, in the phenomenally short span of just three months, the "J R Family of Companies," an international cartel of cutthroat business interests capable of disrupting every character in the novel. Read as a fable of Business, or as a vast travesty of the Horatio Alger myth, *J R* represents American commerce as a monstrous renunciation of Love — a theme charged with revealing inferences for Gaddis's satire.

Allusions to the *Ring* are scattered throughout the opening scenes of *J R*, and all center on the depletion of love in a twilight age of Nature. Shortly after his renunciation, J R attends Mrs. Joubert's field trip to a Wall Street skyscraper where he confronts the Gods of Finance. For example, in Crawley, a stockbroker who hunts wild pigs "with lances" (88), he meets one of Wotan's spearmen. Yet this is a faltering Valhalla: a stockholder's suit is pending against one subsidiary, Diamond Cable, of which the class buys a share in order to learn high finance, and Dave Davidoff (one of the many characters, like Monty Moncrief, with redundant names) rushes about the offices battling "corporate brush fires" (94). *Götterdämmerung* cannot be far off. Amy Joubert, the daughter of Governor Cates (Wotan in this Valhalla), seems to sense the impending collapse. As Brunnhilde, she represents the gods' estrangement from their own better selves, her very name (Amy = Amity) signifying the power of love as a communal force. Though she seeks to remain dignified, aloof, and sensitive, Amy withstands neither the cynical deals of her crumbling family nor the withering entropy of her culture.

J R moves through this teetering Valhalla and sees it as a fabulous game.[27] Moncrief explains its crass objectives: "I'd just say boys and girls, as long as you're in the game you may as well play to win" (107), and J R will be repeating that maxim until the novel's end. He also learns a pair of simple rules from Amy's father: first, "buy for credit sell for cash," as Cates tells him in the executive toilet; second, "money is credit" for creating more buying-power (108–9). It is a vicious, usurious circle, but precisely the basis of J R's Ring-like power over mankind. His empire begins from responses to mail-order ads. Clipping coupons and operating from the school phone booth, J R works a deal to buy (on credit) four and a half million surplus picnic forks from the U.S. Air Force, sell them to the Army at a wild mark-up, then turn the profits to other ventures. Business quickly booms. J R acquires bank-rupt companies, empty mining claims, an entire New England mill town full of pensioned-off employees, quantities of pork bellies, flawed Chinese sweaters, plastic flowers, an unfinished ship hull as a tax write-off, the Bast family company that manufactures piano rolls and its subsidiary that pro-duces high-grade sheep-gut condoms, and a chain of nursing homes (for the pensioned-off mill-workers), itself useful to feed business into another chain of funeral parlors (which uses the plastic flowers). A growing web of self-reifying, interlocked "interests," the J R Corporation thus grows upon whatever is incomplete, obsolete, empty, fruitless, and dead.

The risible part of it is that J R succeeds because he so concisely mim-ics the gods of Commerce, following their rules to the letter. The irony is that, like Alberich, he becomes a joke. Looking over a class picture taken when Mrs. Joubert's group visited Diamond Cable, Davidoff points to J R and laughs, "Look at this one, down in front here holding up the stock certificate, ever see so much greed confined in one small face?" (461). Yet by novel's end that greed has almost brought down Valhalla itself, a fact J R savors when the *Wall Street Journal* headlines their struggle: "J R Corp. appears threatened by a credit squeeze whose dramatic repercussions could be felt throughout the corporate world" (649–50). The satirical part of it is the degenerative power of this monstrous greed to witlessly bring down the world. Bast's resistance withers under J R's incessant wheedling — "I just thought maybe we can use each other, you know" (135). Within weeks J R employs not only Bast but the same Wall Street brokers who mocked him. A veritable Alberich, J R whips them into action over the telephone, "He does the grunting and we do the work," jokes Dave Davidoff about what becomes a bitter truth (526). Even though Bast eventually denounces J R ("you ruin everything you touch!" [658]) and the IRS and the SEC close down his "interests," J R has plans to rise again, like Alberich's son Hagen. The last we hear, J R excitedly spells out his plans for riding "this big groundswill" of public acclaim into a book contract and lecture tours of college campuses (716).

If J R represents a composite of Wagner's Alberich/Hagen characters, then Bast embodies both Siegmund and Siegfried. In an early scene, Bast and his half-sister (or cousin?), Stella Angel, attempt sexual intercourse in the upstairs room of a tower behind the Bast home. This takes us further into the *Ring* cycle, for countless details (thunder and lightning, the tower) link Bast and Stella to Siegmund and Sieglinda in act 1 of *Die Walküre*. For all these high heroic associations, however, their fractured tryst ends in banal mockeries (and *coitus interruptus*) when Stella's dim-witted husband, Norman, stumbles in. There are deeper ironies. Bast's passions are "romantic" in every sense; he regards their stormy coupling as a true recognition of the *Ring* myth and of romance in general. He even sits down at a piano to begin pounding out "the Ring motif" while singing Sieglinda's lines from Wagner's libretto, then moves into a recitation of Tennyson's paean to romantic marriage, "Locksley Hall" (142). Stella, however, has engineered the scene in order to obtain key legal documents from her half-brother. After this scene, Gaddis's parody of Wagner becomes more generalized, as Bast drifts into the maelstrom of the J R Corporation, becomes its chief agent, even scores a fortune for J R while his own musical scores lie uncompleted among the accumulating products in his 96th Street apartment. Bast's battle with the monolith of business, unlike Siegfried's with the monster, Fafner, is a ludicrous failure, but as with his counterpart in Wagner, that struggle inflames his blood. Siegfried's amazed cry, "Rushing flows my feverish blood!" becomes in Bast an actual affliction brought on by exhaustion and pneumonia. Unconscious on his bed, he burns with a fever just as Siegfried burns on a funeral pyre in *The Twilight of the Gods*. This, coupled with the increasing frequency of Jack Gibbs god-damning everything in the novel's last sections, seems to anticipate a tragic *Götterdämmerung*.

There are still blacker humors at work in Gaddis's tortured fable. Further allusions in *J R* imply that usury and strife are conditions of both nature and the language we use to represent it. In this argument Jack Gibbs plays the central role, a part so large and overwhelmingly cynical that he almost dominates the narrative. As the epitome of that disintegrating center which is the novel's principal topic, Jack's mind, like his coat pockets bulging with the salmagundi of random notecards, bursts with disparate knowledge. Yet while his seems an utterly chaotic intelligence, Jack's frenzied expostulations on Empedocles and entropy add considerably to our sense of the Wagnerian "twilight" age, finally suggesting that the cosmos is running down from sheer use. Empedocles first enters *J R* by way of a bogus Greek inscription over the school entrance (20). Having cooked up the idea as a practical joke, with a friend named Schepperman, Jack supplies it to the blockheads who serve as administrators. They admire its seeming grandeur, and one even considers using it as the epigraph to his "psychometric" volume on learning, if only he can find out what it means. Jack throws out a red herring: "You might try Empedocles . . . I think it's a fragment from the second generation of his Cosmology, maybe even the first . . . when limbs and parts of bodies were wandering around everywhere separately heads without necks, arms without shoulders, unattached eyes looking for foreheads" (45). This bait does come from Empedocles, and Jack does give a fair summary of the "First Generation" in his cosmology, when chaos still reigns and forms have not assumed their proper relations. In fact, however, the inscription itself is a camouflage of Marx's famous dictum "From each according to his ability, to each according to his needs," the English letters having been altered to resemble Greek.[28] This joke comes up repeatedly in the narrative, but more important, Jack keeps making references to the Empedoclean chaos. Whenever he enters the subway crowds, or whenever he wades into the disorder of Bast's 96th Street rooms, Jack remarks that it "looks like the God damn dawn of the world in here necks without heads, arms seeking shoulders, only God damned person live here's Empedocles" (406; but see also 161, 287, 385).

These references neatly dovetail with the "Twilight of the Gods" motif from Wagner and, as one soon realizes, with Jack's ideas on entropy. In the cyclical cosmology of Empedocles, the world-process is shaped by two opposing forces of Love (amity) and Hatred (strife). The process begins, and ends, in a condition of elemental unity, the *Sphairos* or sphere, an apex of homogenous, non-differentiated being in which pure Amity prevails. This represents a starting point of the cosmic cycle, for the workings of Strife in the First Generation begin to differentiate aspects of being into the disconnected parts to which Jack Gibbs refers. In the Second Generation, Amity restores balance and harmony, eliminating the monsters that grew when disparate limbs attached themselves to the wrong bodies. This phase stands for the familiar reality, but it does not last. In the Third, Strife once again reasserts its disordering power, and the cosmos enters a disintegrating, twilight stage until, at last, being once more resolves itself into the *Sphairos*. Jack suggests to the dullards running the school that they should look it up in Empedocles's "second generation . . . maybe even the first," but there are some crucial distinctions. With one hand, Jack is surely playing to their eternal optimism about the business of education, its mission to bring intellectual order and harmony out of chaos, while with his other hand he is surely pointing to the strife-torn

Third Generation. Empedocles describes it as a "joyless place" where "works without result run away like water" and men are ruled by wrath, greed, envy, and sickness. In its ethos, Ugliness has defeated Beauty, Talk has drowned out Silence, and Greed has killed Love. Empedocles calls these adverse qualities "Banes," and nothing could more accurately describe the grim world of *J R*.[29]

In the apartment where Bast tries unsuccessfully to compose music, broken faucets gush water. Characters throughout the novel poison the air with mindless talk, and ugliness abounds. Midway through the novel Gibbs, and later Bast, will be stricken with pneumonia, a disease of the breath (or spirit) that leaves them temporarily, blessedly, speechless. Gibbs signifies this stage of cosmic decay with his every drunken tirade against the usurious chaos around him and his group of artist friends, but the progress of his own life parallels all three phases of Empedocles's Cosmology. It corresponds to the first when, early in the text, he sees around him the strivings of the "dawn of the world." Midway through the novel, he falls passionately in love with Amy (amity), renewing his hope of finishing his monumental "social history of mechanization and the arts, the destructive element" (245). When Amy departs for Europe to settle her divorce, Jack settles into the chaos of the 96th Street rooms, water leaking everywhere in an absurd entropy. There he comes apart under both the distrust of Amy's motives and the impossibility of ever synthesizing his ideas about Commerce and Art. One of the wayfarers passing through the apartment comments that "nothing's holding him together man she's why he hates it [the book]" (613). Having come that far around the cosmic cycle, Jack feels himself an epigone waiting in despair for the inevitable end.

When he is with Bast, Gibbs tries incessantly to explain this sense of futility, his awareness that the depreciation around him connects with a larger degenerate drift they are powerless to stop. Jack believes he may have leukemia, the perfect metaphor of that entropic, usurious, cancerous nature afflicting them all. Still worse, he claims, is the infection of language itself. He incessantly curses the impossibility of holding words "together" in the strife of Bast's rooms. Composing a book in such conditions, he argues, is like nursing a terminally ill patient, "like living with a god damned invalid sixteen years every time you come in sitting there waiting just like you left him wave his stick at you, plump up his pillow cut a paragraph add a sentence hold his God damned hand" (603). Jack's big book will never get up and walk, and in despair he himself seems always on the verge of flinging himself like Empedocles into an Etna of consumptive fire, the *Götterdämmerung* which his curses anticipate. He seems to desire only that non-differentiated state of the *Sphairos* that Empedocles barely describes, Wagner approaches through mythology, and science formulates as entropy.

As his name suggests, Jack is a close student of Josiah Willard Gibbs, whose "On the Equilibrium of Heterogeneous Substances" first set forth the proposition that a closed system, such as the universe, will tend irreversibly toward a virtual state of entropic homogeneity or "heat death." In *J R,* this is Wagner's fiery epilogue and Empedocles's *Sphairos* rolled into one. Moreover, the homology between Josiah Gibbs's equation for entropy, and the equation for noise in information theory, supplies Gaddis a brilliant approach to that vast natural Commerce of which discourse is just one aspect. "Order," Jack explains to his eighth graders, is just "a thin, perilous condition we try to impose on the basic reality of chaos" (20). This description fits countless situations in *J R.* Dave Davidoff incessantly rants about the necessity, in business, of keeping their "communications lines straight" (217). In the 96th Street apartment, Jack looks with amazed cynicism upon Bast's attempts to compose music: "Problem Bast there's too God damned much leakage here, can't compose anything with all this energy spilling you've got entropy going everywhere" (287). The degenerative slide into disorder threatens every cultural institution: big business, marriages, families, language, even the precious isolation that artists seek for their work. One needn't detail the full, encyclopedic reach of the metaphor in *J R,* but only acknowledge its two principal features: its imagery of closure, and the idea that any intrusions of an ordering intelligence will only accelerate the entropic slide.

One might well begin, like Gaddis, with the Bast family. From the chaotic parlor talk of Edward's aunts in the opening scene, it is possible to sketch a genealogy (see fig. 8). This phenomenally closed system of family alliances hangs together by threads of near-incestuous liaisons and by a fundamental split between Commerce and Art. For Edward's grandfather was both a musician and an entrepreneur; he started the family business of making piano rolls while also tutoring children on the piano. In turn he gave their payments (the coins that Julia and Anne remember "jingling" in Father's pockets) to his own children, Thomas and James, for learning *their* lessons well. The split between Commerce and Art widens in the second generation, Thomas becoming head of the General Roll Company (mechanized art) while James becomes a renowned composer.[30]

This split defines Edward's legacy. As the narrative opens, the circumstance of Thomas's dying intestate opens a host of legal and characterological

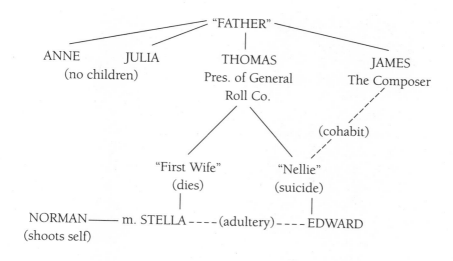

```
                         ⌜ "FATHER" ⌝
                              |
   ANNE      JULIA         THOMAS            JAMES
 (no children)           Pres. of General   The Composer
                            Roll Co.
                                                   (cohabit)

              "First Wife"        "Nellie"
                 (dies)           (suicide)
                    |                |
 NORMAN —— m. STELLA - - - - (adultery) - - - - EDWARD
 (shoots self)
```

**FIGURE 8**

cruxes. Is Edward the son of Thomas, or James's son from the period of his cohabitation with Nellie? Who has controlling interest in the General Roll Company, if Edward has a legal claim to both Thomas's and James's shares? Is Stella his sister or his cousin? As his name suggests, Edward is the "guardian" of this wealth, but is it an artistic or a commercial patent that he shall inherit? For much of the novel, he is caught up in the commercialization of his talent: writing "some nothing music" for television (112), a ballet for a dance troupe that is fired, and the score for a "documentary" (in reality a commercial for big-game hunters) about zebras. When, as the novel closes, he finally turns to writing music he cares about, most of those scores wind up in the trash. At any rate these genealogical struggles make a strikingly apt beginning to the narrative. Gaddis introduces the controlling tension between Commerce and Art, he will soon map Wagner's generations of mythic heroes onto the Bast family tree, and he develops within this genealogy a ludicrous example of the closed entropic system. For when the lawyer, Cohen, intrudes to begin sorting things out ("The law seeks order, Miss Bast. Order!" [8]) the only result of his labors is the promulgation of more misinformation and strife. Yet this rule is basic to both entropy and information theories: any attempt to decrease the entropy or noise of a system must involve an operation of ordering, that is, acquiring more energy or information, which only serves to increase the measure of entropy or noise. As Pynchon shows in *The Crying of Lot 49*, this is why Maxwell's demon never completes his absurd task: simply trying to sort molecules requires an expenditure of energy, in the form of work, that leads to still more disorder. As Jack puts it, chaos results whenever one lets "the God damned outside world in" (116).

But what is J. R. Vansant, if not a type of the sorting demon? His constantly repeated desire is to be "inside" the nerve-center of Commerce. At work, though, trying to "keep communications lines straight," he is only another example of the vicious middleman who arranges transactions and takes his usurious cut. Throughout the novel, this is what it means to be "inside." At the school, Hyde dithers on about how "in-school tv, to be in-school tv, it has to be in-school with lessons piped into school receivers in school class-rooms" (26); what really concerns him are the sales of his own hardware. As for marriages, Stella recalls how her husband tallied up the cost of their dates before proposing (350); married love is depreciated by a nagging self-interest. This is why Jack complains to Dave Davidoff that after "a few years of marriage such a God damned complex of messages going both ways can't get a God damned thing across, so God damned much entropy going on" (403). As for Art, its devotees seek isolation in which to do their work, someplace where, as Edward puts it to Stella, they might find a "balance between de-struction and realization" (69). That idealized solitude always disintegrates when someone steps inside with a purpose in mind. All of Jack's artist friends seek that isolation, and all end their work (or their lives) in abject failure. Jack's friend Schramm, for example, tries to slam the door on a millionaire father who wants him to give up making "useless" artworks, but Schramm winds up leaping out a window to his death. This group is not simply lost, Jack realizes; in his words they are an entire "Turschluss generation."

From the novel's opening line Gaddis collapses both money and language into one transactional system. J R's monstrous success widens that collapse until it draws all semiotic systems into the same depreciating economy, itself finally identified with the entropic slide of all Nature. There is nothing which is not inherently usurious. Against that ruin, all of Edward's romantic notions about Art give way: his desire to be "original," as the romantics understood that term; his sense that "all art depends upon exquisite and delicate sen-sibility" of which "constant turmoil must ultimately be destructive" (289); finally his belief that from Nature he shall learn harmony and the generative power of Love. Early on, Amy Joubert remarks that Edward is "just such a romantic" (245), but it all melts away in the feverish heat of business. The re-maining crux is a quintessentially postmodernist paradox. Here is a novel in which characters are constantly imploring each other, until its last phrase, to

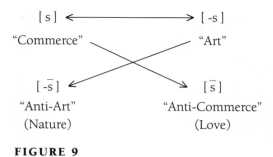

FIGURE 9

"Listen!" yet their only recourse, as George Steiner has observed in a similar connection, may well be a profound silence.

By now it should be clear that, with slight variations, the ideological nucleus of *J R* is much the same as that in *The Recognitions*. Once more the central conflict is between Art and a hostile culture identified, not simply with the Paternal Inheritance, but with the larger system of Commerce represented by "Father" Bast and J R. This revision also meant broadening the focus of those second-order contraries from Gaddis's first novel, the seme of "anti-art" or counterfeiting and the maternal inheritance that pulled at Wyatt. In *J R* these sub-contraries may be defined, first, as the system of Nature itself, which unlike "Art" appears in the novel as a used-up, disordered actuality sliding into entropic chaos, and second as the possibility of Love, which unlike Commerce is a form of nonmonetized desire whose objects are thus capable of infinite "use." (In its barest outline this nucleus may be sketched out as in Fig. 9.) Working from this outline one may see how much further Gaddis has extended the power of his satire. In *The Recognitions,* its degenerative force concentrates especially on the seme of "Art," which has no representatives in the text, and this void disrupts any possibility of the novel's achieving an ideological settlement of its principal social conflicts. In *J R* that void has been considerably broadened.

This becomes clear as one moves around the semiotic rectangle. On the left-hand side, the novel's title character unites the semes of "Commerce" and "Nature," embodying all aspects of a monetized, usurious system of exchange and a trashed, entropic natural surrounding that J R both uses and enlarges. With her romantic view of Nature, Amy scolds J R for never taking in "the evening, the sky, the wind, don't you ever just stop and look?" (474) but the point is that J R does, and sees only discounted commodities. Next, at the point of a lower or "neutral" synthesis, Amy Joubert tries, despite the disorder of her surroundings, to live up to the "amity" signified in her name, but the utter failure of this promise, with Jack, is really symptomatic of a larger failing it will be important to define.

In the right-hand quadrant Jack Bast tries through the first half of the novel to unite the semes of "Art" and "Love." Jack's liaison with Amy Joubert brings him a temporary respite from the disease and dementia he both condemns and represents, and her love returns him to a kind of practical order (laundered clothes, better health) at the same time that she restores his ambition, itself wholly useless, to create a book, an ordered illusion, out of the fragmentary notes and quotations tumbling from his pockets and folders. The possibility of this synthesis will disintegrate under the force of Jack's cynicism. Convinced that there is "a basic lack of symmetry in our part of the univ[erse]" (485), Jack argues to Amy that the "only way to keep something real" is through strife (496). He is, in short, wholly unable to put aside the instrumental, monetary values of Commerce. Indeed, when he says of Amy's nakedness that her "beauty is the promise of function" (504), Jack's surrender to standards of trade (Love as usurious sexual exchange) stands revealed, and soon afterwards Amy departs for Europe. In the remaining pages Jack struggles unsuccessfully to finish his tome on "mechanization and the arts." There, like Edward Bast, he represents that possibility of an "ideal" or complex synthesis of the two initial contraries, "Commerce" and "Art." Bast's failure to straddle that chasm has been the central action all along, and it seems to me that his only change, by novel's end, is in deciding to simplify his artistic practice and go it alone: "I've failed enough at other people's things [ . . . ] now I'm going to fail on my own" (718). We're left with J R's intention to go on the lecture circuit, thus a prospect of the same vicious cycle beginning again.

In its completed form, then, the character system of J R may be shown in Figure 10. What does this reconstruction say about the wholesale failure of Art and Love? In *The Recognitions,* there are simply no representatives of original, authentic Art. In J R, by comparison, there are numerous artists, and evidently some quite good ones, but neither they nor their works withstand the degenerative onslaught of their natural and cultural surroundings. Vilified by his wealthy father and unable to complete any of his writings, Schramm leaps to his death. Dave Davidoff keeps an unfinished novel lying about the house. Tom Eigen *published* an award-winning novel, but the buying public's utter neglect of it condemned him (like Davidoff) to the "long illness" of working with Cates and his group (612). Jack's friend Schepperman is one of the few artists in J R to make a living at his work, but his patroness (Zona

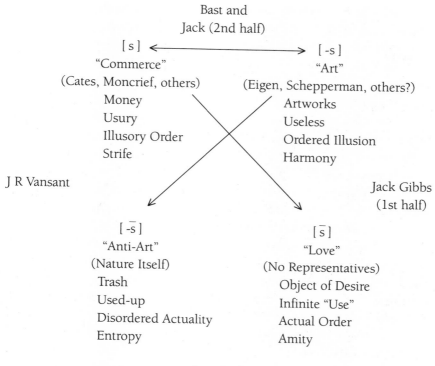

Bast and
Jack (2nd half)

[s] ⟵————————————⟶ [-s]
"Commerce"                                    "Art"
(Cates, Moncrief, others)        (Eigen, Schepperman, others?)
            Money                              Artworks
            Usury                               Useless
            Illusory Order                 Ordered Illusion
            Strife                              Harmony

J R Vansant                                                    Jack Gibbs
                                                                    (1st half)

[-s̄]                                          [s̄]
"Anti-Art"                                    "Love"
(Nature Itself)                      (No Representatives)
            Trash                                Object of Desire
            Used-up                          Infinite "Use"
            Disordered Actuality      Actual Order
            Entropy                            Amity

Amy Joubert

**FIGURE 10**

Cates) stores most of his paintings in a vault while speculators drive up their value. At novel's end, his most "magnificent" canvas has been destroyed by falling plaster. As for Bast, during the course of *J R* his compositions have become increasingly diminutive (in succession, he leaves behind a grand opera, a cantata, and a suite, before finally completing some solo pieces for cello); most of these were consigned to trash cans. As he exits with a few rescued pieces we have only Edward's stated optimism about going it alone, a ludicrous hope in view of the frustrated artists all around him. The point is that they all cling to ideas of originality and isolation for their art. This is why they are listed in the graph with a question mark: none of them lives up to their own idealistic standards.

But there is more. In *J R* we find no strong representatives of that Love which, in a strife-torn society, the characters claim is man's other hope for harmony. Partly this is because Love itself has been monetized. When Marion

Eigen asks her son "How much" he loves her, he wonders if she means "Some money?" (267). Still more significant, the artists of *J R* (to a one, all males) blame their failures on loveless women. Henpecked for money at home (Davidoff), their need for solitude misunderstood (Eigen), these artists feel bereft of their Muse. After his failure with Amy, Jack claims that his problem, like Schramm's, was that he wanted to find "a woman he could trust with everything he had, wanted it so much he knew if he had it and lost it he'd cut his throat" (615). To them, woman is merely an outer semblance of harmony, the dissimulation of an atavistic disorder. Jack, for example, tells Bast that "in spite of its appetizing symmetry woman's body's an absolute God damned chaos" (620). In the same light he represents Stella Angel as a castrating "witch" (407); later, Edward will stupidly tell Stella that she not only ruined his own career but also "destroyed Jack" (716). To my knowledge, none of Gaddis's readers has yet remarked on these signs, which seem to indicate the resurgence of an ancient, well-exercised aspect of satiric literature — its occasional misogyny.[31] Conventional as it was in Greco-Roman satire and again during the Enlightenment, the misogynistic diatribe is rare in American postmodernism. *Cabot Wright Begins* includes tirades against women among Warby's "Sermons," with which Purdy's depictions of character (Zoe Bickle, Carrie Gladhart) and the comments of his omniscient narrator seem in tacit agreement. One would also add the (minor) satires of Donleavy and Southern.

Beginning this discussion, I identified two problems in reading *J R*. First, a problem of intention: how shall we read the depreciative drift of this text in light of its stylistic peculiarities, its value-charged speeches as against its zero-degree narration? Second, a problem of theme: given the parodies of Wagner, how shall we reconstruct the characters' apparent renunciations of Love? Both problems come together in the undercurrent of misogyny. Put simply, this novel gives no warrant for identifying the spoken misogyny of its characters with the satirical intentions of its author or implied reader. Search as one might, there is nothing in the passages of zero-degree narration to spur such an inference. In this way *J R* is fundamentally different from a more elaborately mediated satire like *Cabot Wright Begins*.[32] One *can*, however, draw inferences from structural patterns in the text. For example, the parody of Wagner insinuates that *J R*'s renunciation of Love, like Alberich's, is merely symptomatic of a larger descent from Romantic ideals, yet *J R*'s renunciation is representative. Already caught in the currencies of a monetary culture and a usurious nature, none of Gaddis's characters avoids being entrapped in what the jacket notes aptly describe as a "nightmare marriage of business and the arts." This nightmare captures them like a fate, and their downfall might be tragic were it not for their ridiculous attempts to have it both ways: to play the market at the same time they mouth the clichés of a decadent romanticism.

In satire, misogynistic venom is most often directed against what Michael Seidel defines as the sexual symbol of generative power, such as the woman, in a state of corruption and decay.[33] Eventually the debased woman is symbolic of a larger degeneration, not only sexual but cultural and theological, a total falling-off from the putatively "original" source. Gaddis's artists respond to this decay by attempting to marry the Muse, the common coin in a romantic ideology of "originality," "authority," and "genius" to which they stubbornly cling. When that myth founders, they turn against their women. Their misogyny is a measure of how much further Gaddis has extended the satire in *J R*: the semes of "Art" and "Love" both collapse during the onslaught of commercial and natural decay. The old fables no longer regenerate them, primarily because those conventional narratives have been unmasked as instruments of brute force. In turn, Gaddis's subversive fable assails this cultural horror with its own stuff. This occurs because the very "texts" of characters' works and days are criss-crossed by each others' usurious discourses, discourses that are "traded" in a vast patriarchally managed exchange system that (to them) seems simply inescapable, *because natural*. The encyclopedic dialogism of this novel exposes it, instead, as our own cultural construct.

## The Art of Regression in *Gravity's Rainbow*

In our time the encyclopedic novel hunts, like Ahab, farther and wider than any comparable artistic mode for something (anything) around which to totalize contemporary experience. That hunt falls more massively, significantly short than ever. This delinquency, though, is just what attracts students of contemporary culture to these satirical fables. For in subverting our claims about representation and language, in orchestrating voices in vast libretti bounded by silence, in playing schizophrenia against large-scale crises of meaning that are never resolved, and in parodying the desire for encompassing historical narratives (Lyotard's *grands récits* or metanarratives) — in all its aspects the encyclopedic satire emblematizes the condition of postmodernity. *Gravity's Rainbow* is certainly an exemplary text. From the start, critics received it both as a case study in the new encyclopedism and as a contemporary master-text.[34] It is also the only novel in American literary history to simultaneously make the best-seller lists and book-club catalogues, sweep the major literary awards (except for a unanimous Pulitzer nomination that was so misguidedly overthrown), and win scholarly acclaim as a work ranking in achievement with *Ulysses* and *Moby Dick.*

Since 1973 the major criticism has reaffirmed this praise.[35] In addition *Gravity's Rainbow* has been widely accepted *as a satire,* but many readers also acknowledge the difficulty of squaring Pynchon's work with the formalist conception of satire as a corrective, thus a normative and generative, practice. Some have unquestioningly affiliated the book with the generative program of traditional satire and, following Alfred MacAdam's lead, diminish the importance of any specific corrective element, a move that typically also involves an emphasis on poststructuralist notions of linguistic play.[36] To MacAdam, Pynchon's linguistic uncertainties and subversions are "a game played for its own sake. The ideology of satire, as Pynchon writes it, is not to reform the reader, who would then reform the world, but to reclaim for literature one of the purposes essential to all rhetorical exercises: to delight." There are versions of this reading in still other studies.[37] It has the apparent virtue of keeping intact the idea of satire as a rhetorical, targeted, and normative writing. The only difference is that such a fiction is seen constantly pointing out its "own artificiality . . . as literature." Its metafictional elements mount a humorous assault on "the dictates of literary realism" as ways of explaining the world and propose, instead, an open-ended norm of play or "entertainment." This keeps the idea of satire comfortably within that old ellipse, whereby the purposes of literature are either to instruct or to delight. But on second thought it also reintroduces by a back door the old element of correction: such a fictional entertainment readjusts "the concept that art must mirror life."[38] Even more, to a critic like MacAdam it means that a difficult text like *Gravity's Rainbow* need no longer be dealt with as a novel. Once one has managed to re-frame it by the conventions of a quite traditional satire with which, in his view, the novel has little in common, the problem of its self-reflexivity is shunted aside.

There are several key difficulties with this reading of *Gravity's Rainbow.* Probably the most important is that it ignores the powerful symbiosis between satire and the novel that has shaped the growth of American fiction after Nathanael West. I began the examination of this relationship with an analysis, in chapter 2, of West's art of regression. Now, in bringing these chapters to a close, I want to argue that *Gravity's Rainbow* returns us to the problem of regression in profoundly meaningful ways. This is because the novel thinks about regression as a key, perhaps the absolutely essential element in any narrative construction of reality, itself included. *Gravity's Rain-*

*bow* deploys this sustained critique against the very instruments of hegemonic Western knowledge: its myths, cinematic representations, historiographical efforts, deterministic fables of scientific explanation, and heteroglot lores both elite and popular. The novel locates in all of these the common strategies by which we position ourselves and are positioned, over and over, as masters and sacrificial victims. The novel's sustained subversion of such instruments operates at the level of its narrative sentences, episodes, and overall structuring devices. Its apparently crucial event, the sacrifice of the Nazi youth, Gottfried, in V-2 rocket number 00000, culminates our regressive progress through the book. It also reintroduces the element of sacrificial violence notable in the American satirical novel after Nathanael West.

With respect to style, Frederick Karl comments that Pynchon's technique in *Gravity's Rainbow* can be traced to the practices of Ford and Conrad, specifically their *progression d'effet,* by which the writing accretes characters and detail until, like puzzle pieces, the parts all obtain the ontological massiveness of a world.[39] Employed by the great modernists, this technique was a mode of perception that spurs a reader to *make* the novel's society. In Pynchon's hands, however, what once was employed to construct a world may also be used to demolish it. This happens because, while the *novelistic* construction of a world involves the simulation of temporal continuity, the illusion of homogenous becoming or "history," Pynchon's *satirical* deconstruction focuses precisely on that convention of temporal homogeneity.

Consider an episode that many reviewers condemned as representative of the novel's excesses. In episode 10 of part 1 (60–71) the nominal protagonist, Tyrone Slothrop, receives a hypodermic injection of 10 percent sodium amytal, chemical doorway to a vast scatological fantasy. The narrative quickly progresses through letters, interrogators' questions, then into nightmare visions, Pynchon all along taking the Black Humorists' play with subject-object disruptions to a kind of limit. The subject here is human, but Slothrop also seems the merest instrumentality, a means to an end. His interrogators want to uncover the psychological mechanism enabling Slothrop to "dowse" rockets, to uncannily figure with his sexual erections the *future* site of a V-2 rocket strike. The result of this experiment, Slothrop's fantasy, forms the episode's inner, hypodiegetic narrative. Its object, however, is a systematic environment of wastes. Moving still further beyond the degenerative fantasies about waste products in *The Crying of Lot 49,* Pynchon here imagines a vast network for the signifying and transporting of shit. Under the drug's influence Slothrop remembers — or hallucinates, for the ontological status of such narrative events is never clear — how he once dropped his mouth harp down the toilet in Boston's Roseland Ballroom and reached down, his bare arse exposed, to retrieve it. What follows next is a sustained comical horror show, starting with Slothrop's fantasy that he is about to be gang-raped by Malcolm X and his shoe-shining friends who used to work that washroom. To escape, Slothrop dives into the toilet, swims its pipes, explores the sewer system to which they connect, and notices everywhere the "signs of the toilet world, icky and sticky, cryptic and glyptic" (65). This allegorical satire, with its excremental "world," will return in subsequent episodes.

Read as a metafiction, episode 10 travesties the very idea and potential of the *progression d'effet:* the world signified by these "glyptic" fragments is something spectacularly "real" in historiographical terms (even the Roseland's potted palms were borrowed from *The Autobiography of Malcolm X*); it is "uncannily shit-sensitized" (65), hyperalert to the significance of waste products. Slothrop's sojourn through this labyrinth also becomes a *regression* in history, from thoughts of Harvard classmate Jack Kennedy back through a montage of images featuring Indians and westwarding Americans like Slothrop's own Puritan ancestors. Not only historical and genealogical, his sojourn is also potentially autobiographical, as it returns him to the putatively central mystery of his own past when he was, at age two, the subject of Pavlovian experiments carried out by a Harvard psychologist, a character named Laszlo Jamf. Or was he? The novel later claims that Jamf was all a fiction. But here, stretched out in Pointsman's laboratory, Slothrop scats a tale which, on another reading, degeneratively satirizes Pointsman's desire for narratives. Read as a satire on the temporal conventions of fictional and historiographical texts, the episode's allegory makes viciously humorous sense. It renders the conventions of homogenous temporal flow, for instance, in terms of the subterranean pipes and fluids of a sewer system, and figures the "data" interpreted through such narration as so much human excrement. The originary moment of that "plot," we remember, occurs on the site of a racist hegemony (the Roseland Ballroom) and begins from the abject fear of reciprocal violence, specifically, sodomistic rape. Its dénouement: utterly inconclusive. Slothrop's "harp" remains (for now) a lost ideal, or Faustian *haetera esmeralda,* as the episode ends in the fantasized Southwest dominated by a sadomasochistic "Westwardman."

In returning from that hypodiegetic vision to the framing diegesis, one obvious question involves Slothrop's experimental use to Pointsman and the "White Visitation." Having (allegedly) conditioned him to get an erection in the presence of a soft polymeric plastic, Imipolex G, did Jamf properly "decondition" the subject? Indeed, *could* Jamf have extinguished Slothrop's conditioning "beyond the zero," which has made him so hypersensitive to the V-2 rockets that the young man now perceives the smell of Imipolex G, a component in at least one such rocket, at impact zones the missiles will subsequently strike? The corollary to this biographical enigma is less obvious and has apparently passed unremarked in the wide-ranging interpretations of *Gravity's Rainbow:* Slothrop's function as a *historical* sensor. Somewhere in the pattern of his genealogical conditioning lies a kind of antenna for victimization, for conquest, for the forms of socially authorized violence, as in the myth of Abraham and Isaac. Generations of Slothrops had backslid into abject preterition while trying all along to redeem themselves, and Tyrone Slothrop's own father sold him to Jamf. They struck a deal for the boy's Harvard education, bartered him into servitude for a pot of message. Slothrop's very being has been colonized, and this raises another question. The text hints at other sodium amytal sessions before the one narrated in episode 10; *could* those regressions in family, national, and mythical history have deconditioned him "beyond the zero" of his own victimization at age two, not extinguishing but sensitizing him to every terrified "screaming" that has ever, like Wotan's mad armies in Teutonic myth, arced over western skies?

On the reading I'm proposing here, Slothrop's "progress" not only indexes the regressive forces of Western culture, it is also the central plot in a satire whose practice is designed to subvert the conventional ideologies of narrative-historical understanding. The principal figure for this effort in *Gravity's Rainbow,* widely overlooked thus far, occurs in the numerous instances of *hysteron proteron.* It characteristically appears in passages like the following, inscribing a desire to arrest the reciprocal violence of the war:

> nothing can really stop the Abreaction of the Lord of the Night unless the Blitz stops, rockets dismantle, the entire film runs backward: faired skin back to sheet metal to pits to white incandescence to ore, to Earth. But the reality is not reversible. Each firebloom, followed by a blast then by the sound of arrival, is a mockery (how can it not be deliberate?) of the reversible process: with each one the Lord further legitimizes his State. (139)

As here, further instances of hysteron proteron always play event sequences backward and thus foreground the idea of causality by disrupting it, for even a common locution like "born and bred" seems ridiculous if we pause over it. Most literary handbooks presently omit this rare and almost forgotten trope, or else, following George Puttenham's Renaissance guide, *The Arte of English Poesie,* they degrade it as a literary vice, for "they rather seeme deformities than bewties of language," as Puttenham thought. He classed hysteron proteron among the figures of "the preposterous," and defined it more specifically as "a manner of disordered speach, when ye misplace your words or clauses and set that before which should be behind, & é converso, we call it in English proverbe, the cart before the horse, and if it be not too much used is tollerable inough, and many times scarse perceivable, unlesse the sence be thereby made very absurd."[40] If this is so, then *Gravity's Rainbow* must be a fully "preposterous" and "intollerable" book: by my count, the (de)vice of hysteron proteron occurs some fifty-nine times in the text, an average of once every thirteen pages in the Viking edition.

By any standard of comparison, this perverse figuration has spread so far across Pynchon's narrative discourse that one must eventually reckon with it. For example, in her 1989 essay "Views from Above, Views from Below" Kathryn Hume details a perspectival image complex reticulated through some forty occurrences in *Gravity's Rainbow,* withal disclosing a structure of aerial and earthly views that may, Hume argues, stabilize a set of moral norms in the book.[41] Or consider Kurt Vonnegut's novel *Slaughterhouse-Five,* the only contemporary fiction from which one might recall the hysteron proteron trope. There it crops up but four times and always in relation to a temporal malfunction naturalized by pseudoscientific explanation (Vonnegut's "chrono-synclastic infundibulum"). Its most remarkable occurrence is in chapter 4, when Billy Pilgrim comes "unstuck in time" to watch "the late movie backwards." There follows an otherwise pointless interlude, representing the Allied bombing of Germany in reverse, right down to the guns ("tubes") that extract ("suck") bullets from American airplanes.[42]

Pynchon not only deploys the figure more insistently, he uses it to inscribe a degenerative satire that is radically different from the absurdist fantasy and generative satire of Vonnegut. In the passage quoted above, the backwards-running film reifies a regressive, reactionary desire, as cinematic replay or psychological "abreaction," controlled by the same progressive technologies whose project it is to make a "mockery" of human memory. Their objective is a kind of modernist mastery; in order to manage social processes and norms, they *use* people's nostalgia for a "return." According to Pynchon's narrator, the Rocket-State even "legitimizes" its coup by mocking, in each V-2 blast, the apparent reversal of cause-and-effect process to victims mystified by the speed-of-sound velocities of the Rocket. Thus these signs are exposed as functioning hegemonically. In *Gravity's Rainbow,* hysteron proteron points us to a rationalist culture whose aim is nothing less than the immachination of all being, an apotheosis of the modern. Such tropes may be mere objects of literary play for Vonnegut; for Pynchon they are exposed as the naturalizing strategies of a rationalist enterprise his satire seeks to explode.

In *Gravity's Rainbow* such instances of hysteron proteron trope a western knowledge that employs causal reversal as a primary though often dissimulated logic. The general effect of these figures in Pynchon's writing is to zero in on narratives of reversal that function crucially in modern science and philosophy, for example in Laplacean physics or Cartesian metaphysics. Such disciplines are exposed as regressing to a monadic (or atomic) self (or state) in order to reason progressively and causally forward from it, thus placing deterministic human rationality ahead of (an often indeterminate) earthly being. In effect, then, Western metaphysics and its instruments are shown to have put Descartes before the horse, to make a bad pun on Puttenham. Pynchon's writing keeps insisting by these metanarratives — for that's what hysteron proteron tends to feel like as we read — that Western knowledge has preposterously sought to eliminate the simpler novelties of a "lovable but scatterbrained Mother Nature" (324). So my bad pun begins to suggest why deterministic, Cartesian thought towers in *Gravity's Rainbow* like an insidious enemy: because its ultimate victim is Pynchon's valued "Earthliness," that irreplaceable ground for kinds of horsing-around.

Here, a brief summary of an aspect of current narrative theory will bring this reading into clearer focus. For some time it has been axiomatic that narrativization involves structuring acts that are deeply retrospective. As Gerard Genette puts it, narrative plot (in his terms, "discourse") involves a teleology necessitating that "paradoxical logic of fiction which requires one to define every element, every unit of the story, by its functional qualities, that is to say among other things by its correlation with another unity, and to account for the first (in order of narrative time) by the second, and so on."[43] Put simply, this means that reading the "one, two, . . ." (or *proteron, hysteron, . . .* ) orderings of plot will be always already determined by the backwards-glancing hysteron proteron of narrativization. Indeed, so foundational, so *conventional* is this retrospectivity of narrative in transforming lived experience or knowledge into text (or, story into plot) that Hayden White concludes, "where there is no narrative, there is no history."[44] Still another way of putting this axiom is to note, with Robert Scholes for example, that narrativity always involves a reasoning backward, from effects to causes. Narration depends upon a *post hoc ergo propter hoc* operation that logic defines as fallacious but that narrative accepts as utterly "natural." Interestingly, too, the classic instance of this operation is the deductive crime novel. In it, as Todorov shows, the detective progresses from crime to arrest by *regressing* from clues to causes.[45] Initially this is Tyrone Slothrop's job, just as it becomes the reader's, at least through the first half of *Gravity's Rainbow*. There are numerous other characters (and readers) for whom it will remain, as for E. W. Pointsman, the *only* job, and despite what the second half of Pynchon's novel teaches.

In any event narrativization ties together the strands of mere episodic chronicling. It seems to entail a "progressive *knotting into*" (3), a plotting that seems to more or less "naturally" form a centered structure, a structure whose beginning, middle, and end may be totalized around a thematic origin, itself the *telos*, insofar as it seems to insure the readability of the text by providing a dénouement, or "untying," that once again paradoxically means a tying-up of prior, episodically loose threads. Such closures of narrative are especially crucial in theological texts, as Pynchon's references and parodies throughout *Gravity's Rainbow* tend to suggest. Such (fore)closures also entail, as *Gravity's Rainbow* further suggests, the tying-*down* of any errant, nomadic, or (truly) *novel* potentials in the narrative, their Bondage-and-Discipline to these seemingly absolute demands of determinist thought. One nagging question therefore urged by *Gravity's Rainbow* is whether or not narrativity might escape from that kind of B and D in order to define itself by axioms other than those just summarized. If it could be alternatively defined, what would that mean for the representation of human subjectivity? In *Gravity's Rainbow*, Laplacean science and Cartesian metaphysics have formed a chilling Axis Pact in the form of Pavlovian, Behaviorist, and other "sciences of the mind." Against their deterministic manipulation of human subjectivity, whose aesthetic counterpart is an idea of "character" exemplified in the realist and modernist novel, what alternatives are there? How might these questions bear on the "what-happens-to-Slothrop" problem that continues to dog criticism of Pynchon's novel?

Specific instances of hysteron proteron suggest answers to these questions. The text's constituting uses of hysteron proteron involve Germany's V-2 rocket. "V-2" for *Vergeltungswaffe-zwei* or "revenge-weapon-two": its name signifies not only a technological jump ahead of the V-1's merely subsonic speed, it also points up the logic of its use, to literally *get back* at the Allies for their carpet bombing of cities like Lübeck (see 146, 151), in other words to pay back or retaliate in the legally deterministic sense (the *lex talionis*). Indeed, *Gravity's Rainbow* exposes this signifying economy as a primary ethos of modernity, an ethos of escalating reciprocal violence which is contained only by using scapegoats, typically, adolescent children. This logic of reversal is further explicated by the rocket's seemingly paradoxical behavior. As

Pointsman puts it: "Imagine a missile one hears approaching only *after* it explodes. The reversal! A piece of time neatly snipped out . . . a few feet of film run backwards . . . the blast of the rocket, fallen faster than sound — then growing *out of it* the roar of its own fall, catching up to what's already death and burning" (48). This logic is inscribed in the novel's famous first line, "A screaming comes across the sky," according to which readers are already defined as having been passed over. Readers are specified as operating in a middle ground between that opening sign of survival and the danger of annihilation signaled by the rocket, now gone nuclear, falling over contemporary America on the closing page. In that late-sixties America all are figured as instruments of a politico-military terror, or as Alec McHoul and David Wills would put it, all are overridden by the "material typonyms" (the inanimate written signs) of "texts," manipulated by various interests.[46] Finally, this end authorizes the novel's satirical disruptions, for the novel reinscribes these material typonyms under the modal conventions of satire and specifically under the traditional rubric of satirical "targets." The targets of Pynchon's narrative satire must now be seen as nothing less than the instrumental logics of narrative itself, from the Greeks' *peripeteia* to Greimas's "narrative trajectory."

Most of Pynchon's early uses of hysteron proteron involve these apparent reversals of familiar causality. Most uses also involve the apparently paradoxical behavior of supersonic phenomena. However, in parts 2 and 3 of *Gravity's Rainbow,* as Slothrop's education in rocketry models the reader's own learning, these phenomena are shown to be under the most logical human control. Here are Slothrop's thoughts at the Nordhausen Mittelwerke, in episode 2 of part 3:

> In the guidance, this is what happened: a little pendulum was kept centered by a magnetic field. During launch, pulling Gs, the pendulum would swing aft, off center. It had a coil attached to it. When the coil moved through the magnetic field, electric current flowed into the coil. As the pendulum was pushed off center by the acceleration of launch, current would flow — the more acceleration, the more flow. So the Rocket, on its own side of the flight, sensed acceleration first. Men, tracking it, sensed position or distance first. To get to distance from acceleration, the Rocket had to integrate twice — needed a moving coil, transformers, electrolytic cell, bridge of diodes, one tetrode (an extra grid to screen away capacitive coupling inside the tube), an elaborate dance of design precautions to get what human eyes saw first of all — the distance along the flight path.

There was that backward symmetry again, one that Pointsman missed, but Katje didn't. "A life of its own," she said. (301)

I quote this passage at length because it is just what most readers trained in the humanities have tended to slight or even to skip. Its subject, though, is the very nuts and bolts of immachination, one of Pynchon's dominant themes since *V* and a process structured in *Gravity's Rainbow* around "that backward symmetry" of hysteron proteron. Specifically, the V-2's guidance begins functioning when its pendulum is pulled backwards ("aft") by a forwards "acceleration." Moreover, this release of "current," and its dancelike steps through all the hardware Pynchon names, is a symmetrically backwards motion too, because the Rocket's forward arch retraces a "flight path" (beginning from the desired point of impact) already seen, or mapped, by "human eyes." This is how men "integrate" with the Rocket, which then assumes "a life of its own." The analogy to narrative plotting, as well as to New Critical reading, is quite obvious.

Under the rainbow of Germany's *Vergeltungswaffe-zwei* the characters' fantasies obsessively replay this hysteron proteron trope. Looking over a blasted house, for example, Jessica Swanlake scans "some woman's long-gathered nest, taken back to separate straws." She spots amid the rubble a brassiere, and as it galvanizes her empathy Jessica beats back her tears by fancying that the thing is waiting "for its room to reassemble round it" (43). Later, after screwing Roger in a deserted flat, she will reflect that "she came twice before cock was ever officially put inside cunt, and this is important to both of them though neither has figured out why, exactly" (120). The reason "why, exactly," is that their reversal of cause and effect, of intercourse and orgasm, stimulus and response, corresponds with the same apparently "transmarginal" behaviors of the V-2. Roger and Jessica in this scene appear identical with Slothrop, who "only gets erections when this sequence happens *in reverse*. Explosion first, then the sound of approach: the V-2" (86). Chronologically as well as virtually, then, Roger and Jessica's romantic liaison corresponds with the Rocket Blitz. In addition, their story is represented through some of the most conventionally continuous, realistic discourse in *Gravity's Rainbow,* as many readers have noticed. In all, this suggests why the novel abandons not only Roger and Jessica's romance but the mode of its narration. The critics' nostalgia for its seeming unity might thus be taken as a symptom of many things, not least of which is an unwitting need to be overmastered by texts, including the inanimate "text" of the V-2.

Many of the characters' maddest fantasies replay the hysteron proteron figure. Rollo Groast, for example, wants to link his nervous system back to "some surviving cell-memory" of the primitive, "retrocolonial" central nervous system (147). In the German actor Rudolf Klein-Rogge's starring role as "Dr. Mabuse der Spieler," Franz Pökler thinks he sees "the savage throwback, the charismatic flash" back "toward myth" that might model his own drives (579), certainly a broad parody of the modernist's "mythic method." In their Holland rocket battery, Katje, Gottfried, and Weissman reenact a "formal, rationalized version" of a "Northern and ancient form" of the Hansel and Gretel story (96). As for Weissman's progress, into "Blicero" and on, the novel will define it, too, as a reversion "to some ancestral version of himself . . . back into the pre-Christian earth we fled across" (465). Soon Blicero's progress, like Slothrop's, takes him right out of the narration. As he keeps regressing, "growing toward winter, growing whiter" (666), he ceases to exist in a conventionally realistic sense, becoming instead the originary nexus for emergent Blicero legends.

Slothrop, of course, is the chief example here. The apparently concise homology between his sexual behavior and the Rocket gets Pointsman hunting down causal links in Slothrop's past(s). This hunt takes Pointsman back to Slothrop's apparent conditioning at the hands of Dr. Laszlo Jamf ("apparent," because contradictory statements in the narration tend to trouble our certainty about whether there *was* a Jamf). Moreover, *Gravity's Rainbow* discloses "Slothrop's Progress" through his seven different avatars, themselves suggestive of the seven stages of an initiate's progressive ascent to the Merkabah or Divine Throne in cabalistic Gnosticism, as (once again) a *regress* toward genealogical and cultural origins. So, taking on the mantle of his second avatar, Ian Scuffling, Slothrop goes "back to 1630 when Governor Winthrop came over to America on the *Arbella*." The comment signals one of Pynchon's most fullblown instances of hysteron proteron, as the *Arbella* and its fleet are imaged "sailing backward in formation, the wind sucking them east again, the creatures leaning from the margins of the unknown *sucking in* their cheeks . . . as the old ships zoom out of Boston Harbor, back across an Atlantic whose currents and swells go flowing and heaving in reverse . . . a redemption of every mess cook who ever slipped and fell." The passage finally ends with a "Presto change-o! Tyrone Slothrop's English again!" and ends, too, with a caution: "But it doesn't seem to be redemption exactly that *this* They have in mind" (204). By his fourth avatar, Plechazunga, Slothrop has become the beast-hero out of old Teutonic etymology/mythology. The point is that such reversals are always felt as someone else's *plots,* and extricating oneself from them might therefore mean escaping history, escaping *narrativity.*

When not focalizing through characters, Pynchon's more omniscient narrative voices can be quite clear about what is at stake in this modernist nostalgia for The Return. In episode 16 of part 1, two days before Christmas, 1944, the narrator describes the trajectory of world-historical events as "the Night's Mad Carnival," a progressive/regressive phantasmagoria in which "dynamos whose locations are classified spin faster," so that the clocks, indeed the whole semblance of historical *kronos,* runs "ever faster," its acceleration unnoticed except for the "old faces" who "turn to the clock faces, thinking *plot,* and the numbers go whirling toward Nativity, a violence, a nova of heart that will turn us all, change us forever to the very forgotten roots of who we are" (133–34). Passages like this use hysteron proteron to trope one version of the escape from or end to history, a version enabled by the retrospect of absolute return. The terms of this bargain are always alike: in the lyrically phrased promise of Vaslov Tchitcherine's desired Kirghiz Light ("In a place which is older than darkness . . . this light must change us to children" [358]); in the apparent facts of Slothrop's conditioning at age two; in the occupied Zone which has returned Europeans to "the very earliest days of the mercantile system. We're back to that again . . . the Ur-markt" (336); in the Herero factions of "Erdschweinhöhlers" and "Empty Ones" who desire to move forward back toward what is simultaneously an originary "Eternal Center" and a "Final Zero" ("Names and methods vary, but the movement toward stillness is the same," thinks Enzian [318–19]); and in Blicero's perverse reenacting of childhood *Märchen* like "Hansel and Gretel." In each case the dominant strain involves a nostalgia for early childhood or for primitivism.

*Gravity's Rainbow* treats these as essentially the same, although their similarity is never so straightforwardly phrased as in the novel's last episode. It opens in a burgeoning "Rocket City" defined by the power of "taboo" and its "violence of repression" (735). The narration then focuses on sadomasochism, itself the link between family and state, childhood and the primitive. Here, to thumb back through "the brain's plush album" of memory, says Miklos Thanatz, "is always" to confront the image of "a child begging to be whipped" (736). Yet this picture of Bondage and Discipline is just what the state *must* dissimulate, "because submission and dominance are resources it needs for its very survival. . . . I tell you, if S and M could be established universally, at the family level, the State would wither away" (737). Pynchon follows this argument with a curious (but typical) anecdote about "the kid who hates kreplach." To force it on the boy his mother walks him through the steps of its concoction, though he still collapses in "absolute terror" at the *end* when his meal is recognizable *as kreplach.* Sandwiched between Thanatz's argument and the (symbolically teleological) kreplach story, and separated paratactically and elliptically from them, is another of Pynchon's hysteron proteron tropes: "So the assembly of the 00001 is occurring also in a geographical way, a Diaspora running backwards, seeds of exile flying inward in a modest view of gravitational collapse, of the Messiah gathering in the fallen sparks . . ." (737). By this episode *Gravity's Rainbow* has become disjointed in a number of stylistic and narratological ways. Still, a steady idea links these paragraphs of text: like the concoction of kreplach, the reassembly of a V-2 (with its historical counterpart in actual Allied activities at Cuxhaven in September 1945) precisely replays the story of reciprocal violence and absolute power played out in Mom and Pop's house, as well as in the State-house. Both hinge on the same dissimulation of teleology.

This drama is reenacted, as well, in the constructions of History. Pondering an end to historical process, Blicero claims: "America was a gift from the invisible powers, a way of returning" to primitive structures of dominance. But Europe "refused" that gift, he says; hence the "empire" of "American Death," named on these pages as "Modern Analysis," has vengefully reversed the terms of this bargain and taken Europe (722). This sense of a symmetrical ending, and the sense also that such an end point is logically determined by an originary lapse, stems once again from the hysteron proteron of narrativity. It may be found in *Gravity's Rainbow* at the level of minutest allusion, for example, in a reference to the childhood rhyme about the old woman who accomplishes the goal of getting her pig over the stile by means of an elaborate, ten-stage regression that folklorists have traced back to Gnostic cabalism.[47] Or it may be graphed in the novel's overall plot: in its final episode *Gravity's Rainbow* zooms toward the 1970s only to shift with infinite deftness into reverse and spin Pynchon's (hi)story back to the firing of Rocket 00000, the apparent sacrifice of Gottfried (God's Peace) during Easter/April Fools, 1945. The temptation comes in thinking that one has thereby achieved a readerly measure of dominance over this novel. Yet each of these signs also invites interpretation as a *poisson d'Avril,* an April Fool's joke.

Still, old habits of thought persist. "You will want cause and effect. All right," snipes the narrator at the beginning of episode 5 in part 4. Cause and effect is what "you" think is needed to master *Gravity's Rainbow,* so causalities "you" get. The narrator backtracks to show how Miklos Thanatz was saved after slipping overboard into the Baltic Sea. "He was rescued by a Polish undertaker in a rowboat, out in the storm tonight to see if he can get struck by lightning." Since "reading about Ben Franklin in an American propaganda leaflet," he's been "obsessed" by the idea of lightning-struck people and the "stories *they* could tell!" (663). What stories? Chiefly, of a "discontinuity in the curve of life" that is an apotheosis of hysteron proteron: "do you know what the time rate of change *is* at a cusp? *Infinity,* that's what! A-and right across the point, it's *minus* infinity! How's that for sudden change, eh? Infinite miles per hour changing to the same speed *in reverse.* . . . that's getting hit by lightning" (664). This is the fantasy of reversible Time. The fantasy of instrumental mastery over all temporality, and then over Being itself. Pynchon's obsessed Polish undertaker out in a rowboat during a storm may be read as parodying Melville's monomaniacal Captain Ahab, who once seized his ship's twin lightning rods in his hands, so to zap a charge through his body and leave a scar "branded" like a whiplash or "birth-mark on him from crown to sole."[48]

Pynchon's Polish undertaker also parodies a foundational concept of classical dynamics, the fantasy of reversible systems. As Capek, Prigogine, and others have demonstrated, the "Laplacean Dream" was founded on the ideal of the integrable dynamic system, or "universe," in which separate particles ("corpuscles" or "monads"), finitely dispersed, are totally describable at any particular moment as a "state of the universe."[49] In its fullest realizations this Laplacean universe was understood by means of an absolute hermeneutic determinism: if any moment or state were fully apprehended, then, by an application of causal logic, the system would simultaneously disclose all its past and future manifestations, for just as causes inscribe effects, so conversely may effects be interpreted for their causes.

In such a universe the "preposterous" figure of hysteron proteron has been raised up (*contra* Puttenham) as absolute law. In such a universe, as Laplace put it, "nothing would be uncertain."[50] It is a world that fantasizes, like Ned Pointsman, about "the stone determinacy of everything" (86). Among its "plots" or "trajectories" one may even fantasize an identical acceleration of every point in the system, so that time apparently "speeds up," as in the "Night's Mad Carnival" of *Gravity's Rainbow* (133–34). Or one may fantasize an instantaneous reversal. The Laplacean physicist calculating prior positions of an object in motion simply substitutes a negative sign in the equations, as such reversing time. This happens because, positing the reversal, $V \dashrightarrow -V$, of velocities for *every point* in the system is the same as reversing the direction of time, $T \dashrightarrow -T$, in the system.[51] Capek has also shown how the fantasy of "Eternal Recurrence" — that nostalgic dream of innumerable madcap questers in *Gravity's Rainbow* — was also sustainable in a Laplacean world where the temporal continuum was imagined as topologically homogenous and absolutely symmetrical: in a finite atomistic universe where states can be described by merely changing their sign (or direction), any configuration may recur (124–25). Indeed, this dream was sustainable well into the modern epoch, for example in the writings of Nietzsche and Bergson.[52]

Such theories tend to deconstruct with their own tools. For if the differential or assymetrical aspects of time are eliminated (one moment no longer *other than* its predecessors), then time itself is eliminated as a meaningful concept. Or, in eternal-recurrence fantasies where two moments are seen as identical, "we are dealing with one and the same moment, which is both the beginning and end of the completed temporal cycle"; in other words, the middle has been absolutely excluded, zeroed out, because "the direction of time from the past to the future entirely disappears."[53] Deconstructed by such means, the doctrine of integrable dynamic systems is unmasked as ultimately ideological. The doctrine cannot be separated from the history of western science, especially the *uses* of that science, and Prigogine and Stengers argue that in "this world of automata, both arbitrary and inflexible, to know is in fact to dominate."[54]

Michel Serres points out the economics of this dominance. He cites physicist Leon Brillouin's argument that dynamic descriptions could only *be* determinist if virtually all variables were known, but all the energy in the universe cannot pay back the energic debt for determining every variable. As such, "the law only exists in the interest of someone, someone who wants to take everything and give nothing."[55] In *Gravity's Rainbow* these people are the Gnostic high priests of modern science, usually named "They," as in "Roosevelt, a being They assembled, a being They would dismantle" (374). Their minions are scattered throughout the halls of state-power in this novel: Pavlov, Jamf, Von Braun, Pointsman, Roosevelt, and on the home front parents like Nalline Slothrop or Margherita Erdmann, whose fantasies of dominance presage (in Ensign Morituri's telling) the Nazi invasion of Poland and the onset of World War II. Moreover "They" have minions on "the Other Side": Walter Rathenau for example, whose seance-declamations about the primordial coal tars are thought to illuminate the future. Similarly, in episode 1 of part 4, Slothrop finds a crossroads where he can "sit and listen in to traffic from the Other side, hearing about the future (no serial time over there: events are all there in the same eternal moment . . . )" (624). In short, this "Other Side" functions as just another fiction or instrument of dominance.

What then of the Rocket, and Slothrop? In part 4 of *Gravity's Rainbow* Slothrop thinks wistfully about "a way to get back" to America. The V-2 Rocket also calculates a "return," but one reckoned within a purely deterministic economy that Pynchon identifies in his most daring and arcane analogy with the Torah of cabalistic Gnosticism. The Rocket is "an entire system *won,* away from the feminine darkness, held against the entropies of lovable but scatterbrained Mother Nature" (324). It seems to overcome the irreversibility of natural time with a perfectly integrable, and thus reversible, system. Similarly, cabalists regarded the Torah as the inscribed Name of God, hence the potential for absolute reversibility, for to interpret the Torah rightly means *to end time,* by recuperating the unity of Time's originary moment.

In cabalistic Gnosticism the decisive world-historical crisis occurred during creation, with the "shattering of the vessels" of Being as they received the seeds of divine light. This diaspora henceforth defines all earthly being as lost, exiled, second-rate, post hoc, needing redemption. The most abysmally lost form of being, the Qlippoth or "Shells of the Dead," stalk *Gravity's Rainbow* as war-ravaged souls (see for example 148, 176, 197), while a nostalgia for illumination drives countless other obsessive characters. Many of them, from Lyle Bland to Blicero, also seek methods of transcending "scatterbrained Mother Nature." This feminine Nature appears in Gnostic mythology as the Shekinah, tenth and last of the Sephiroth or levels of being, also known as the messianic bride who wears black and who, in her dark and destructive aspect, makes horrible Qlippoth (shells) of men. In *Gravity's Rainbow* her avatar is Margherita Erdmann. On the eve of war in Europe (August 31, 1939), she calls to a Jewish boy:

> "My home is the form of Light," burlesquing it now, in heavy Yiddish dialect, actressy and false, "I wander all the Diaspora looking for strayed children. I am Israel. I am the Shekinah, queen, daughter, bride, and mother of God. And I will take you back, you fragment of a smashed vessel, even if I must pull you by your nasty little circumcized penis — " (476)

Specifically, Greta burlesques the desire in Gnosticism for the *tikkun,* the gathering-back or return of the exiled sparks of Divine Light to their original home, a return that ends Time with a cosmic hysteron proteron. She thus embodies the Gnostics' revulsion or abjection of all Earthly being, an abjection consistently identified in *Gravity's Rainbow* with modern science, symbolized by the phallic Rocket.

Slothrop's journey is virtually opposed to the Rocket's. He moves *toward* Earthliness, but not out of abjection in the face of it. He also, crucially, moves beyond the orbit of conventionally determined narrativity. This contrast is incisively revealed in Dwight Eddins's study of Pynchon's Gnostic allusions, though he is more optimistic than I am about the stability of satirical norms in *Gravity's Rainbow*. Eddins argues that for Western metaphysics after Plato, primordial Nature is the cave from which human reason must emerge if it is ever to locate the Good.[56] For Pynchon, though, it is Nature alone that ensures any hope of the Good; this is why *Gravity's Rainbow* seems paradoxically to demand a certain artlessness. Its kind of "naturalism" entails the unlearning of cultural conventions devoted to sustaining man's gnostic-scientific dominion over and transcendence of Nature. I would add that this effort also entails giving up narrative technique to the errancies and indeterminacies of that putative Nature; it means unlearning the conventions of causal seriality that have enabled (or "naturalized") fictions and historiography alike. Most of all this effort entails the satirical demolition of narratives about human subjectivity and norms, including those of conventionally generative satires whose project it is to build a consensus around ideas of normative behavior.

Few readers have commented that Slothrop's disappearance from *Gravity's Rainbow* is surrounded by other gaps, seeming narrative errors. Was Laszlo Jamf "only a fiction" needed for etiological explanation (738)? Why did Katje leave Blicero in Holland? ("We are never told why," warns the narrator [107].) What happens to the Hereros and Rocket 00001? Loose threads like these lead, metafictionally, repeatedly, to the far margins of narrative technique. *Gravity's Rainbow* declines to answer such questions by refusing the conventional dénouement that would demand forms of reversal and return.

Contemporary physics has already swept such fantasies of return into the intellectual dustbin. After relativity theory, the two "directions" of time ("backwards" and "forwards") are rendered as meaningless as the spatial coordinates "up" and "down."[57] After thermodynamics, the flow of time is understood to be absolutely irreversible: it drifts without stoppage toward entropy. After the coordination of thermodynamics and information theory, the really significant differentiations are those between thermic order and disorder, between noise and signal, or entropy and negentropy. Serres has noted how the concept of reversibility may still be sustained, somewhat wistfully, as negentropy. Yet even thus, as a principle of system or "knowledge," it is at best a momentary stay, "at most a reversal of drifting, that strange conversion of times, always paid for by additional drift" into "the noise and black depths of the universe."[58] In the view of Prigogine and Stengers, these moments of knowledge must be defined by means *other* than those of causal seriality and its "stale armamentarium" (*Gravity's Rainbow* 632), for causality is but one "style" among others available for describing phenomena. Such moments of knowledge must be defined as well (they argue) by stochastic means, by the "strange" or parallel flows of contemporary physics, by ways of imagining relation instead of mere trajectory, and by using concepts of monadistic behavior in order, paradoxically, to pinpoint the limits of such concepts. They also argue that such means have served, happily, to reintroduce "novelty" in scientific interrogation.[59]

*Gravity's Rainbow* points to this cultural project in Roger Mexico's argument with Pointsman. Roger claims "there's a feeling about that cause-and-effect have been taken as far as it will go"; to which Pointsman stubbornly replies: "there are no 'other angles.' There is only forward — *into it* — or backward" (89). Roger's postmodern scientific project is referenced, too, in Leni Pökler's argument with her husband Franz: "'Not produce,' she tried, 'not cause. It all goes along together. Parallel, not series. Metaphor. Signs and symptoms. Mapping onto different coordinate systems, I don't know'" (159). It is also referenced in Pynchon's uses of Gödel's Theorem, that Murphy's Law of contemporary science which in Pynchon's view underwrites kinds of temporary digression sideways into the moment, the novelty, with potential for saving folks who are "Sold on Suicide" (320).

Certainly it also involves Pynchon's innumerable references to cinematic narration. This topic has been so widely covered in the criticism that we need hardly spend much time on it here. Yet there is one moment when Pynchon's critique of its logic vis-à-vis the satirical potential of the hysteron proteron trope comes into sharp focus. It occurs in a moment of omniscient narration: "The countdown as we know it, 10–9–8 u.s.w., was invented by Fritz Lang in 1929 for the Ufa film *Die Frau im Mond*. He put it in to heighten the suspense. 'It was another of my damned "touches,"' Fritz Lang said" (753). Throughout this chapter one of my intentions has been to reconsider a number of oft-quoted passages from Pynchon's novel using the perspective of other passages. Like this one, above, these less recognized quotes can be read as indexes of satirical energies that subvert the generic conventions governing writing and reading since the Renaissance. Pynchon grabbed the Fritz Lang anecdote from Willy Ley's 1959 book, *Rockets, Missiles, and Space Travel,* but the mock quote from Lang is Pynchon's fictive embellishment, another of those "damned 'touches'" (or material typonyms) registering once more the question of ideological control in narration: What interest is served by the "suspense" of Fritz Lang's countdown? One answer may come in the scholarly sounding passage that Pynchon puts paratactically after the above quote. In a lecturing voice, we are told how cabalistic Gnosticism imagines the *tik-*

*kun* or return to God's throne-chariot occurring as the souls "negotiate each of the Sephiroth, from ten back to one"; indeed, the lecturer warns, the most guarded of instrumental secrets in Gnosticism concern the techniques for managing this passage (753). The issue, again, is modern mastery and its dissimulation.

In *Gravity's Rainbow*, hysteron proteron satirically tropes the exposure of those complex and even self-contradictory stratagems by which Western knowledge — scientific, historical, pop-cultural, theological — has plotted our submission to the demigods of dominance. These stratagems have demanded regressions to a putative Origin; have demanded, too, a causal narrativity capable of inscribing, not the simulacrum of our access to an ultimate reality, but of our ultimate victimization and scapegoating in the system of modern "plots."

Therefore Pynchon's novel itself cracks up as Slothrop disappears from the text in part 4. We might define this process as Pynchon's radical use of modal energies in degenerative satire that operate *in reverse* on the laws of genre. As Michel Beaujour has explained about the poetics of literary genres, it is always a "game" that "may be played in reverse." And the "desire to play a game in reverse usually arises when the straight way of playing has become a bore, or when the usual kind of victory appears self-defeating. The rules of the game which, although arbitrary, had somehow become 'natural' to the players, now seem 'artificial,' tyrannical and dead: the system does not allow for sufficient *play* or freedom within it, and must be discarded."[60] One benefit of analyzing Pynchon's satire in this way is that it restores to *Gravity's Rainbow* that subversive engagement with history and society so vital to the novel's writing, in the 1960s and 1970s.

Satire in its severest mode can be a way of playing in reverse. In preposterously overthrowing conventional strategies for narrative continuity, symmetry, and closure well symbolized by the Gnostic text, *Gravity's Rainbow* refuses a tradition, and an ideology, of storytelling. One basic convention of this tradition is that readers shall come to "know" characters as integral (i.e., "real" or "natural") constructs. Such conventions assume, as well, that characters may be "redeemed" by a plot whose end totalizes their life, right back to its beginning. Against this kind of paranoid fantasy Slothrop's "scattering" into bits of pop and material culture stuff that are (literally) *about* him can be read as composing a schizoid idea of fictional character, an idea of subjectivity emphasizing the indeterminate, "nomadic," unbounded, and intertextual experience of Being described in the writings of Deleuze and

Guattari. In composing an experience of narrativity that unfolds in fitful, paratactic, assymetrical, and acausal episodes, Pynchon has written a kind of Baedeker for an age of post-Laplacean, post-determinist knowledge. As the White Queen says to Alice, in Carroll's *Through the Looking Glass,* "It's a poor sort of memory that only works backwards. . . ."

# Conclusion

## Defining Satire, Reading Postmodernism

In what has itself become the dominant theory of contemporary culture, Fredric Jameson identifies the dominant chord of postmodernist aesthetics with the simulacral and critiques that aesthetics as a site of neutralized values. Late-capitalist society is in this view "a field of stylistic and discursive heterogeneity without a norm," and its central practice is that of the pastiche or blank-parody. Jameson defines this condition as follows:

> In this situation parody finds itself without a vocation; it has lived, and that strange new thing pastiche slowly comes to take its place. Pastiche is, like parody, the imitation of a peculiar, unique, idiosyncratic style, the wearing of a linguistic mask, speech in a dead language. But it is a neutral practice of such mimicry, without any of parody's ulterior motives, amputated of the satiric impulse,

devoid of laughter and of any conviction that alongside the abnormal tongue you have momentarily borrowed, some healthy linguistic normality still exists. Pastiche is thus blank parody, a statue with blind eyeballs: it is to parody what that other interesting and historically original modern thing, the practice of a kind of blank irony, is to what Wayne Booth calls the "stable ironies" of the eighteenth century.[1]

Later in the same chapter Jameson argues that the wholesale expropriation and mimicry of old-fashioned realist forms, together with the loss of critical distance in the new social space of postmodernity, have only compounded the neutralization of values he describes. On the one hand, contemporary works may appear as "peculiar new forms of realism"; in contempoary narrative, we might add, this means reading under the rubrics of "Minimalism" or "Neorealism." On the other hand, postmodern artistic practices can be attacked as "so many attempts to distract and divert us from that reality or to disguise its contradictions and resolve them in the guise of various formal mystifications" (49). In previous chapters I have discussed how conservative opponents of the postmodernist novel (John Gardner, Charles Newman, and Norman Podhoretz, for example) have based their condemnations on exactly those terms.

Such claims need to be read in context with the appalling amorphousness of social conscience during the Reagan decades. Jameson's 1990 book stands as an encyclopedic critique of that condition. Yet these claims should also be read in context with recent demands of academicians that criticism should concretely index art's capacity to play a strong role among the contemporary voices competing for social dominance. In brief, this entails the focus of Jane Tompkins and others on art's "cultural work." To a number of critics, especially those collected in Hal Foster's 1983 anthology, *The Anti-Aesthetic: Essays on Postmodern Culture,* the work of postmodernism consists in an oppositional politics involving the generation and consumption of signs. The problem with Foster's argument, however, is that it repeatedly tropes this potential in terms of aesthetic transgression.

In doing so, as Charles Altieri has forcefully argued, such a reading fails to make a necessary distinction between transgressing and more properly resisting or dissenting practices. There can be no question that mere transgression only serves to recuperate the culture of late capitalism. Disrupting all boundaries or conceptions of the subject and its community, art replicates and thus situates us still more comfortably amid the hyperreality of instant pleasures encouraged by Madison Avenue, Hollywood, and the White House.

As Altieri puts the case, "It is necessary to posit an explicitly oppositional art devoted to resisting dominant social interests. This art would not so much escape limits as make compelling the pain which those limits create and the interests that thrive on such pain, including interests in the myths of taste and sensibility fostered by the ideals of transgression."[2] Yet what *are* the instances of such an oppositional postmodernism, and what would it entail, in practice?

These remain some of the most vexed questions of contemporary theory. I think Jameson is wrong about the lack of an oppositional strain in postmodernism, but also that Foster and others have erred in too easily identifying that oppositional side with transgressive semiotic play, the stale armamentarium of "pla(y)giarism" and so forth. An emerging view of postmodernism promises (I think) to reframe the Jameson/Foster dialogue. Altieri's recent essay, as well as Paul Maltby's *Dissident Postmodernists,* has pointed out a range of telling cases, in the art of Sherrie Levine or Hans Haacke and in the fictions of Thomas Pynchon.[3] My own view, set forward in the preceding chapters, is that contemporary American fiction is rich with telling instances, but that we have been singularly blinded to that effort because of self-imposed limits in theorizing satire. That formalist theories of satire still confound our reading of postmodernism is apparent from Jameson's differentiation (in the passage quoted above) of pastiche from parody and satire, with its wholesale acceptance of the formalist definition.

In proposing a literary history of postmodernist satirical fictions founded on a distinction between generative and degenerative modes, I have sought two ends. First, I have hoped to reopen the discussion of satire itself, by following up on Michael Seidel's argument that the formalist model was limited even when applied to those Enlightenment texts it was initially developed to explain. Second, I have sought to define a tradition of American satirical writings that realizes the subversive potential of the form. From the writings of West through those of Thomas Pynchon, these fictions are keenly attentive to the violence and pain wrought by the structures and conventions for representation in Western culture, the ways that identifiable interests thrive on that suffering, especially in their promotion of violent, transgressive stories whose paradoxical function is to support legitimizing myths of progress and emancipation.

Finally I think it is crucial to use this subversive tradition in making critical distinctions. The seemingly avant-garde but really quite conventional generative practices of a Mary McCarthy, Kurt Vonnegut, or James Purdy need comparison with the subversive postmodernity of writers like John

Hawkes, William Gaddis, Ishmael Reed, Robert Coover, and Thomas Pynchon. In addition, I think this critique needs to be carried beyond the historical boundaries of this study. I have ended it in 1980 for the sake of convenience and a well-rounded (or at least, a numerologically satisfying) historical period. Still, there is no question that the kind of generative satirical fiction critiqued in the preceding pages continues to be written, for example by Tom Wolfe (in his 1987 *Bonfire of the Vanities*) and Gore Vidal (in his 1986 novel, *Duluth*). At the same time, the subversive satirical novel continues to crop up. The publication of Gaddis's *Carpenter's Gothic* in 1985, potentially one of the most corrosive political satires of the Reagan Eighties, as well as the appearance of Thomas Pynchon's *Vineland,* a much underrated novel when it appeared at the tail end of that decade, would (if included with Don DeLillo's *White Noise* and Gaddis's 1994 novel *A Frolic of His Own*) set the agenda for an expansion of the period under examination here.

Moreover, I think this critical examination can and should extend beyond the disciplinary boundary of literature, to include (for instance) the visual art of Barbara Kruger and Cindy Sherman, gallery installations like Hans Haacke's "Oil Painting, Homage to Marcel Broodthaers," and the verbal works (electric readerboards, plaques, and the like) by Jenny Holzer. Indeed, the feminist politics motivating much of this work would provide a strong contrast with the literary history I have sketched, with its notable absence of feminist work. Any theory of satire's degenerative potential should, at any rate, aspire to interdisciplinary utility. Haacke's 1982 installation, for instance, requires two facing walls, on one of which hangs a concisely executed oil painting of Ronald Reagan (derived from a news photo and parodying Broodthaer's canonical canvas), in which the president looks imperially skywards. On the opposing wall Haacke installed various blow-ups of crowd scenes, all drawn from actual groups gathered outside the White House to protest Reagan's nuclear politics. Between these two walls is a carefully decorated middle ground, consisting of a red carpet and, around the gilt-framed image of Reagan, the kind of velveteen rope museums routinely deploy in distancing spectators from masterworks.

On first viewing, the whole assemblage seems comfortably generative. Here is the Great Communicator separated from the *vox populi* by an obvious chasm, his authority and isolation staged in terms of the museum. Extended contact with the installation, however, works to subvert this initial reading, beginning with one's attempt to understand what it means to stand on that red carpet, there to consume the simulacra on either side (the right and the left, if I had it correctly; though of course that too comes apart during the experience as a purely relational network of poses). In a remarkable reading of this text Altieri asks if it does not go much further than a satire on the Reagan presidency, as a site of power, to satirize also the fantasy of clear ideological factions confronting each other as well as the way those factions are always already staged.

Then, indeed, one begins to ask if those figures so angrily opposing Reagan aren't staging, in their threat of mob violence, the very "simulacral structures that Reagan manipulated so well" in legitimizing state power. Further then, if we focused on the man, a clear enough "target" for our satirical laughter, instead of focusing on the exchange economy wherein he was (re)presented to us, wouldn't we neglect to confront the very system of commodification that Haacke clearly wishes to subvert? Wouldn't that subversion also entail recognitions of the portrait tradition (Broodthaers) and its simulacral imitations by the media, or of the museum as a site of power complicit with the White House? The idea that Reagan differs from consumers of elite art only in his more masterful adaptation to transcendent ideas of mastery and mastery's simulacral logic, while the polity remains at the stage of an infantilized mob right out of a West or Coover novel, is perhaps one of the most disturbing effects of "Oil Painting, Homage to Marcel Broodthaers."

Just what, on the other hand, a changed expectation for civil activity *should* be, Haacke's installation cannot say. At any rate, as I have argued throughout this book, the demand for recuperated or even new norms of polity and community has never been a modal convention for satire of the subversive, degenerative kind. These texts do their best work in shouting "Fire!" or in otherwise firebombing the cultural theater where meanings are made. That, if we must have it so, is the cultural work of these fictions.

# Notes

## Chapter 1: Introduction

1. See Northrop Frye, "The Nature of Satire," *University of Toronto Quarterly* 14 (1944): 78. For the statement that satire constitutes "a minor form in modern times" see Alan Wilde, *Horizons of Assent: Modernism, Postmodernism, and the Ironic Imagination* (Baltimore: Johns Hopkins University Press, 1981), 28.

2. See Frederick R. Karl, *American Fictions, 1940–1980: A Comprehensive History and Critical Evaluation* (New York: Harper and Row, 1984), 3, 11. Karl connects the experimentation of these writers with the energies of a Rabelais or a Sterne, and with the "adversary element" of these fictions which are "reflecting the larger culture" even as they are "undermining it" (11; note how near this comes to defining them as satires). Karl's listing is certainly not unique, and one might turn as well to the catalogues of novelists themselves. Donald Barthelme singles out "John Barth, William Gass, John Hawkes, Robert Coover, William Gaddis, Thomas Pynchon" and himself as the mainstream postmodernists "in this country" — and excepting Gass they are all satirists; see "Not-Knowing," *Georgia Review* 39 (1985): 513. For similar attempts to set such lists, see "An Interview with Raymond Federman," *Anything Can Happen: Interviews with Contemporary American Novelists,* ed. Thomas LeClair and Larry McCaffery (Urbana: University of Illinois Press, 1983), 141.

3. Jacques Derrida, *Of Grammatology,* trans. Gayatri Spivak (Baltimore: Johns Hopkins University Press, 1976), 70.

4. Jean-François Lyotard and Jean-Loup Thébaud, *Just Gaming,* trans. Wlad Godzich (Minneapolis: University of Minnesota Press, 1985), 60. Unless otherwise stated, references to this edition are cited parenthetically in the text.

5. For approaches to parody as "inter-art discourse" see Linda Hutcheon, *A Theory*

*of Parody: The Teachings of Twentieth-Century Art Forms* (New York: Methuen, 1985), 42–44; and Margaret Rose, *Parody // Metafiction: An Analysis of Parody as a Critical Mirror to the Writing and Reception of Fiction* (London: Croom Helm, 1979), 45–46. Important earlier studies include: Tuvia Shlonsky, "Literary Parody: Remarks on Its Method and Function," *Proceedings of the 4th Congress of the International Comparative Literature Society,* ed. F. Jost (The Hague: Mouton, 1966), 2: 798; and Northrop Frye, *Anatomy of Criticism: Four Essays* (New York: Atheneum, 1967), 233–34.

In what follows, the distinction I make between "generative" and "degenerative" satire is my own, but this way of conceptualizing satirical work builds, most significantly, from the work of René Girard, in *Violence and the Sacred,* trans. Patrick Gregory (Baltimore: Johns Hopkins University Press, 1977). Girard makes a crucial distinction between the modes of degenerative violence and those of ritual, sacrificial violence, whose generative function is to reaffirm sociocultural norms and boundaries. In *The Satiric Inheritance: Rabelais to Sterne* (Princeton, N.J.: Princeton University Press, 1979), Michael Seidel also deploys that distinction generally to describe the ways that the radical satire seeks to disrupt the transmission, or inheritance, of culture. Otherwise, the distinction is my own.

6. The phrase is Frederick Karl's (266).

7. Thomas Pynchon, *Gravity's Rainbow* (New York: Viking, 1973), 231–36. Unless otherwise stated, further references are to this edition and will be cited parenthetically.

8. The Pulitzer decision was announced on May 7, 1974, the day before Pynchon's birthday. John Leonard gives an excellent — and outraged — summary of the events in "The Last Word," *New York Times Book Review,* 19 May 1974, 1, 19. The judges had excitedly recommended *Gravity's Rainbow,* saying, "No work of fiction published in 1973 begins to compare in scale, originality, and sustained interest with Mr. Pynchon's book." The Pulitzer board, composed largely of newspaper publishers, viewed the book as "turgid" and "obscene"; in an unprecedented stroke they voted to resolve their split with the judges by awarding no prize for fiction in 1974.

9. See Gershom Scholem, *Major Trends in Jewish Mysticism* (New York: Schocken, 1954), 78. For a further discussion of Pynchon's uses of Scholem and other sources in constructing this scene see my *A "Gravity's Rainbow" Companion* (Athens: University of Georgia Press, 1988), 120–24.

10. See Gerard Genette, *Palimpsestes: La Littérature au second degré* (Paris: Éditions du Seuil, 1982), 32–34.

11. See Frye, "The Nature of Satire," 78, who seems to have taken the claim from David Worcester's 1940 study, *The Art of Satire* (reprint, New York: Russell and Russell, 1960), 8. Among critics who have also seconded Worcester's claim, notable instances include: Robert C. Elliott, *The Power of Satire: Magic, Ritual, Art* (Princeton, N.J.: Princeton University Press, 1960), 101; Ernest Jackson Hall, *The Satirical Element in the American Novel* (New York: Haskell House, 1966), 80–81; Ellen Douglass Leyburn, *Satiric Allegory: Mirror of Man* (New Haven: Yale University Press, 1956), 12–13; and James Sutherland, *English Satire* (London: Cambridge University Press, 1958), 21.

12. Among the more recent studies to have repeated the Worcester/Frye claim, see Edward A. and Lillian D. Bloom, *Satire's Persuasive Voice* (Ithaca: Cornell University Press, 1979), 27; Mathew Hodgart, *Satire* (New York: McGraw-Hill, 1970), 247; D. C. Muecke, *The Compass of Irony* (London: Methuen, 1969), 11; and Wilde, *Horizons of Assent*, 28.

13. See Wilde, *Horizons of Assent*, 28; and Hall, *The Satirical Element*, 80.

14. Frye, *The Anatomy of Criticism*, 223. Subsequent references are to this edition and will be cited parenthetically.

15. P. K. Elkin, *The Augustan Defense of Satire* (Oxford: Clarendon Press, 1973), 35 and 28, respectively.

16. Wolfgang Iser, *The Act of Reading: A Theory of Aesthetic Response* (Baltimore: Johns Hopkins University Press, 1978), 11.

17. Two cases in point: Roland Barthes' line-by-line reading of Balzac's "Sarrasine" in *S/Z: An Essay*, trans. Richard Miller (New York: Farrar, Straus and Giroux, 1970), and Gerard Genette's systematic approach to Proust in *Narrative Discourse: An Essay in Method*, trans. Jane E. Lewin (Ithaca: Cornell University Press, 1980). Both studies rule out analyses of production and reception, and of broader historicist concerns.

18. See Gilbert Highet, *The Anatomy of Satire* (Princeton, N.J.: Princeton University Press, 1962), 15–20.

19. Frye, *Anatomy of Criticism*, 366; and Paul Alpers, *To Tell a Story: Narrative Theory and Practice* (Los Angeles: William Andrews Clark Memorial Library [U.C.L.A.], 1973), 29.

20. Stephen Mailloux, *Interpretive Conventions: The Reader in the Study of American Fiction* (Ithaca: Cornell University Press, 1982), 129.

21. Worcester, *The Art of Satire*, 8–9. Subsequent references are to this edition and cited parenthetically in-text.

22. David J. Dooley, *Contemporary Satire* (Toronto: Holt, Rinehart and Winston, 1971), 34. For variations on this claim see Bloom and Bloom, *Satire's Persuasive Voice*, 20; Ian Jack, *Augustan Satire: Intention and Idiom in English Poetry, 1660–1750* (New York: Oxford University Press, 1952), 3; Alvin B. Kernan, *The Plot of Satire* (New Haven: Yale University Press, 1965), 26; Harry Levin, "The Wages of Satire," in *Literature and Society: Selected Papers from the English Institute, 1978*, ed. Edward W. Said (Baltimore: Johns Hopkins University Press, 1980), 3–5; Leyburn, *Satiric Allegory*, 13; Maynard Mack, "The Muse of Satire," *Yale Review* 41 (1951): 84–85; Arthur Pollard, *Satire* (London: Methuen, 1970), 1; and Suzanne Dolores Valle-Killeen, "Introduction," *The Satiric Perspective: A Structural Analysis of Late Medieval, Early Renaissance Satiric Treatises* (New York: Senda Nueva, 1980), 15.

23. See, respectively, Highet, 158; James Sutherland, 5; and Leon Guilhamet, *Satire and the Transformation of Genre* (Philadelphia: University of Pennsylvania Press, 1987), 13.

24. T. S. Eliot, Introduction to Johnson's *"London" and "The Vanity of Human Wishes,"* by Samuel Johnson (London: F. Etchells and H. MacDonald, 1930), 26.

25. Levin, "The Wages of Satire," 3. Subsequent references are given parenthetically in the text.

26. See for example Bloom and Bloom, 20; Leyburn, *Satiric Allegory,* 13; and Patricia Meyer Spacks, "Some Reflections on Satire," *Genre* 1 (1968): 16.

27. Curiously, this conception of the satirist's world-historical purpose often came from critics, like Maynard Mack, who professed to desire only a formalist attention on satiric *art.* Opening his 1951 essay, "The Muse of Satire," with paragraphs of praise for the New Critics who were sloughing off biographical and historical approaches to literature, Mack next says about satire: "what is desperately needed today is inquiry that deals neither with origins or effects, but with artifice" (82). Yet throughout the essay he uses a definition of satire as writing with an extraliterary mission — to reform the world according to some positive model. Later, he simplistically associates the satirist with his literary persona, claiming that he "must be accepted by his audience as a fundamentally virtuous and tolerant man" (86), and thereby reopening the issue of those contextual (here, biographical) concerns he had professed to leave behind.

28. See Ronald Paulson, *The Fictions of Satire* (Baltimore: Johns Hopkins University Press, 1967), 7 and 152, respectively; and Frye, *Anatomy of Criticism,* 223–34.

29. Kernan, *The Plot of Satire,* 16; Paulson, *The Fictions of Satire,* 6–7; and W. O. S. Sutherland, *The Art of the Satirist* (Austin: University of Texas Press, 1965), 18.

30. Seidel, *The Satiric Inheritance,* 6 and 3, respectively.

31. See for example, Harriet Deer and Irving Deer, "Satire as Rhetorical Play," *Boundary 2* 5 (1977): 711–21; Hutcheon, *A Theory of Parody;* and Frank Palmeri, *Satire in Narrative: Petronius, Swift, Gibbon, Melville, and Pynchon* (Austin: University of Texas Press, 1990).

32. Quoted from Frye, *Anatomy of Criticism,* 224; Paulson, 4; Rose, 35; and Hutcheon, *A Theory of Parody,* 43.

33. Iser, 38; and Umberto Eco, *The Role of the Reader: Explorations in the Semiotics of Texts* (Bloomington: Indiana University Press, 1979), 223.

34. Ziva Ben-Porat, "Method in *Madness*: Notes on the Structure of Parody, Based on MAD TV Satires," *Poetics Today* 1 (1979): 247–48; and Hutcheon, *A Theory of Parody,* 43.

35. Worcester, 13; Highet, 26 and 56, respectively.

36. Koenraad Kuiper, "The Nature of Satire," *Poetics* 13 (1984): 462–63.

37. Elliott, 81; and Morton Gurewitch, "European Romantic Irony" (Ph.D. diss., Columbia University, 1957), 13.

38. Elkin, 71–77.

39. The formalist definition persists for example in John W. Tilton, *Cosmic Satire in the Contemporary Novel* (Lewisburg, Pa.: Bucknell University Press, 1977). He quite rightly sees contemporary satire as having "no corrective or utilitarian function. It recognizes no 'arm against fantasy,' for it finds man's ailment incurable" (19). But then he goes on to argue that it does not appear to be satire per se; rather, it is defined as something new — "Cosmic Satire." Tilton continues: "Only incidentally exposing foibles, vices, or follies, the satire is truly cosmic in its ultimate purpose of examining the nature of good and evil."

40. Muecke, 23.

41. Eco, *The Role of the Reader,* 194.

42. Iser, 151.

43. Wyndham Lewis, *Men Without Art* (London: Cassell, 1934), 69.

44. Dooley, 16.

45. The phrase is Ronald Paulson's, from *The Fictions of Satire,* 4, but it appears in a number of other studies, such as: Bloom and Bloom, 21; Leyburn, 13; Mack, 85; W. O. S. Sutherland, 11; and Valle-Killeen, 15.

46. This phrasing is Robert C. Elliott's, 226, but it too is widely echoed, for example in Frye, "The Nature of Satire," 88; Paulson, 17; and George A. Test, *Satire: Spirit and Art* (Tampa: University of South Florida Press, 1991), 27.

47. Wyndham Lewis, *Men Without Art,* 70.

48. John Crowe Ransom, "Ubiquitous Moralists," *Kenyon Review* 3 (1941): 99.

49. John Gardner, *On Moral Fiction* (New York: Basic Books, 1978), 14.

50. See, respectively, Frye, *Anatomy of Criticism,* 223; and Kernan, *The Plot of Satire,* 16.

51. Edward Young, quoted in Elkin, 77; and Wyndham Lewis, *Men Without Art,* 69.

52. Muecke, 119–21.

53. René Wellek, *A History of Modern Criticism,* vol. 2, *The Romantic Age* (New Haven: Yale University Press, 1955), 14.

54. See Wilde, 28; as well as Muecke, 182–85; and Wellek, 12–15.

55. The term "devices" is from Paul A. Trout, "A Theory of Norms in Satire," *Satire Newsletter* 19 (1969): 2–5.

56. On antiphrasis, see Wayne Booth, *A Rhetoric of Irony* (Chicago: University of Chicago Press, 1974), 10; but see also Muecke, 19–20.

57. On the aspect of "judgment" in irony see Catherine Kerbrat-Orecchioni, "L'ironie comme trope," *Poétique* 41 (1980): 108–27; on the reader's evaluative interpretations see Jonathan Culler, *Structuralist Poetics: Structuralism, Linguistics, and the Study of Literature* (Ithaca: Cornell University Press, 1975), 154.

58. Wolfgang Keyser, *The Grotesque in Art and Literature,* trans. Ulrich Weisstein (Bloomington: Indiana University Press, 1957), 68–70.

59. Frye, *Anatomy of Criticism,* 224; but also Leonard D. Feinberg, "Satire: The Inadequacy of Recent Definitions," *Genre* 1 (1968): 36; Kernan, *The Plot of Satire,* 52–53; and Valle-Killeen, 16.

60. Flannery O'Connor, *Wise Blood* (New York: Farrar, Straus, 1952), 15.

61. Kernan, *The Plot of Satire,* 148.

62. Frye, *Anatomy of Criticism,* 227; but see also Hodgart, 24, and Paulson, 72.

63. Mikhail Bakhtin, *The Dialogic Imagination,* ed. Michael Holquist, trans. Caryl Emerson and Michael Holquist (Austin: University of Texas Press, 1981), 158–67; and Julia Kristeva, *Desire in Language,* trans. Leon Roudiez (New York: Columbia University Press, 1980), 75–80.

64. Mary Claire Randolph, "The Structural Design in Formal Verse Satire," *Philological Quarterly* 21 (1942): 368–84; and Frye, *Anatomy of Criticism,* 234–35, and 322.

65. Kernan, *The Plot of Satire,* 102.

66. Seidel, 22–23.

67. See Elliott, 259 and 274, respectively; and Frye, *Anatomy of Criticism,* 236.

## Chapter 2: Late-Modernist Disruptions

1. The phrasing, again, is from Frye's 1944 essay, "The Nature of Satire," 78.

2. Quoted in Brom Weber, "The Mode of 'Black Humor,'" in *The Comic Imagination in American Literature,* ed. Louis D. Rubin, Jr. (New Brunswick, N.J.: Rutgers University Press, 1973), 367.

3. See Jay Martin, *Nathanael West: The Art of His Life* (New York: Farrar, Straus, 1970), 79. Quoting the popular maxim of Horace Greeley, West also invoked a literary commonplace: that of the heliotropic or westward progress of learning and empire. The famous last lines of George Berkeley's "Verses on the Prospect of Planting Arts and Learning in America" (1752) neatly state the main idea West seems to have had in mind:

> Westward the course of Empire takes its way;
> The first four Acts already past,
> A fifth shall close the Drama with the Day;
> Time's noblest offspring is the last.

Berkeley's five-act, millenial "Drama" is an idea with a lengthy pedigree. What's notable is how West also employs, in *Locust,* a five-stage regression in art history, its "close" being those riotous events which make possible Tod's painting, "The Burning of Los Angeles." One last, bitter irony: *Locust* was the fourth "act" before the ignoble accident that closed West's career.

4. West, "Some Notes on Violence," *Contact* 1.3 (1932): 132.

5. Critics arguing for an avant-garde West include Jacques Cabou, "Humour noir et surréalisme dans les romans de Nathanael West," *Études Anglaises* 29 (1976): 430–35; Alan Donovan, "Nathanael West and the Surrealistic Muse," *Kentucky Review* 2 (1968): 82–95; Robert I. Edenbaum, "Dada and Surrealism in the United States: A Literary Instance," *Arts and Society* 5 (1968): 114–25; and David Galloway, "Nathanael West's 'Dream Dump,'" *Critique: Studies in Modern Fiction* 6.1 (1964): 46–64. For the counterargument, against that "too-easy parallelism" between West and the European avant-gardes, see Jay Martin, 82; and Donald Torchiana, "*The Day of the Locust* and the Painter's Eye," *Nathanael West: The Cheaters and the Cheated,* ed. David Madden (Deland, Fla.: Everett/Edwards, 1973), 249–82.

6. The occasion was an April 1931 interview for the *New York World Telegram,* shortly after the novel was published by Moss and Kamin; see A. J. Liebling, "Shed a Tear for Mr. West," *New York World Telegram,* 24 June 1931, 11.

7. Nathanael West, *Two Novels by Nathanael West: "The Dream Life of Balso Snell" and "A Cool Million"* (New York: Noonday Press, 1977), 37. Subsequent citations from *Balso Snell* and *A Cool Million* refer to this edition and are given parenthetically.

8. Brom Weber, 366.

9. In 1946, James Laughlin of New Directions brought out a copy of *Miss Lonely-*

*hearts* as part of his "New Classics Series." The book did surprisingly well, was published also in Great Britain (Grey Walls Press, 1949), and prompted the re-release, in 1949, of *The Day of the Locust* (also in the "New Classics Series"). A *Complete Works* appeared in 1957 (New York: Farrar, Straus and Cudahy; also London: Martin Secker and Warburg), followed in 1962 by the New Directions double edition, *Miss Lonelyhearts / The Day of the Locust,* and in 1975 by a Penguin paperback *Collected Works.* At last count the New Directions double edition had gone through seventeen printings, the Penguin edition, eight.

10. The phrase "moral satire" is West's, from a 1932 letter to M. K. Abernathy, the *Contempo* editor who published excerpts of the work-in-progress; see Martin, *Nathanael West,* 150.

11. Nathanael West, *Miss Lonelyhearts / The Day of the Locust* (New York: New Directions, 1962), 32. Subsequent citations from either novel refer to this edition and are given parenthetically.

12. Compare Max Weber, in *The Protestant Ethic and the Spirit of Capitalism* (available to West in Talcott Parsons's 1930 translation), 182: "In the field of [capitalism's] highest development, in the United States, the pursuit of wealth, stripped of religious and ethical meaning, tends to become associated with purely mundane passions, which often actually give it the character of sport." In this state, Weber continues, the "old ideas and ideals" of Protestantism exist in "mechanized petrification, embellished with a sort of convulsive self-importance. For the last stage of this cultural development, it might well be truly said: 'Specialists without spirit, sensualists without heart; this nullity imagines that it has attained a level of civilization never before achieved.'"

13. This reading is not only consistent with the dialogism of West's satire, which calls all pre-scripted "life stories" into question, but consistent also with West's shift to internal focalization and free indirect discourse in the last episode, "Miss Lonelyhearts has a Religious Experience." That shift underscores the solipsism of the protagonist's "experience." Other readers, however, see Miss Lonelyhearts as a "secular messiah." Typical are Robert Coates, "Messiah of the Lonely Heart," *New Yorker,* 15 April 1933, 59; and Thomas M. Lorch, "Religion and Art in *Miss Lonelyhearts,*" *Renascence* 20 (1967): 3–15. Lorch argues that he meets death "in the fullness of Christian faith, charity, and hope," a modern exemplum of Chrisian messianism (13).

14. On West's use of the letters see Martin, 150–52. For a time West considered subtitling his book "A Novel in the Form of a Comic Strip," then he "abandoned [the subtitle] but retained some of the comic strip technique"; see his "Some Notes on *Miss Lonelyhearts,*" *Contempo,* 15 May 1933, 2. The comic strip idea has nevertheless been widely touted, for example in Nancy Walker Hand, "A Novel in the Form of a Comic Strip: Nathanael West's *Miss Lonelyhearts,*" *The Serif* 5 (1968): 14–21; and James F. Light, *Nathanael West: An Interpretive Study* (Evanston, Ill.: Northwestern University Press, 1971), 104–5.

15. West, "Some Notes on *Miss Lonelyhearts,*" 2.

16. In his 1933 review, Robert Coates (a friend of West's) remarked that the novel paralleled "the symbolism of the fourteen stations of the Cross, for the progression does become a kind of modern Calvary" (59). Martin also mentions the parallel, but

cannot account for the apparent discrepancy (fourteen stations; fifteen episodes) except by proposing the first chapter as a kind of prologue. Yet there is no discrepancy if one remembers that the fourteen stations are ended by the celebrant's ascent to the altar before communion, in effect a final "station" that refocuses attention on the ritual's central symbol, the Crucifix.

17. Frye, *Anatomy of Criticism,* 226–29.

18. The term "chronotope" is Mikhail Bakhtin's shorthand for a useful concept: "Literally, 'time-space.' A unit of analysis for studying texts according to the ratio and nature of the temporal and spatial categories represented. . . . Neither category is privileged; they are utterly interdependent. The chronotope is an optic for reading texts as x-rays of the forces at work in the culture system from which they spring"; see Michael Holquist's glossary entry in Bakhtin's *The Dialogic Imagination,* 425.

19. *The Day of the Locust* went through four manuscript versions and, according to Jay Martin, "every important reference to Tod's prophetic painters was put in during final revision. References to the painters of Decay and Mystery . . . were almost inserted entirely at the last, *when West was supremely conscious of the implications of his book"* (Martin, 315–16; my emphasis).

20. Quoted in Edward Greenfield Schwartz, "The Novels of Nathanael West," *Accent* 17 (1957): 261. But see also Torchiana, who finds Tod Hackett's painting on "a curve of sensibility stretching from Bosch and Breughel to the present," a curve which marks Tod (like West, he argues) as a satiric "exploiter of the fragmentary but eternal ugliness" of human society (278); or see Galloway, who works from the contrast between Tod's "artistic perceptivity" as opposed to Homer's "onanistic apathy" (51), in order to read the painting as "West's most definitive statement of America's violence" (52).

21. Seidel, *The Satiric Inheritance,* 30, 17, respectively.

22. Flannery O'Connor, *The Habit of Being: Letters of Flannery O'Connor,* ed. Sally Fitzgerald (New York: Random House, 1979), 5.

23. Rinehart Publishers owned exclusive rights to O'Connor's first novel, a proviso that went with her acceptance of a Rinehart Prize for short fictions she had written while attending the University of Iowa. John Selby was the Rinehart editor who pushed O'Connor to map the book out, revise less, and finish it. Her letters from this period show a remarkable self-possession. O'Connor stuck to her position, explaining to a former teacher at Iowa: "No one can convince me that I shouldn't rewrite as much as I do" (*Habit of Being,* 14). Eventually Robert Giroux of Farrar, Straus took on the project.

24. Ibid., 27.

25. For O'Connor's bemused but disheartened reactions to early reviews of *Wise Blood,* see for example her letters to Robert Giroux (36) and to the Fitzgeralds (39). She suggested to Giroux that he should send copies of the book to Salvation Army reading rooms: "According to some of the reviews you have sent me, I ought to be in it." Only the review by R. W. B. Lewis saw clearly to the heart of her work. He aptly identifies O'Connor's "grotesque style" as a satirical mode which necessitates "no real plot," and he notes O'Connor's kinship to Nathanael West. Still, Lewis thought he saw a disjunction between the novel's "characters and incidents" and its "remarkably

pure, luminous prose"; see Lewis, "Eccentric's Pilgrimage," *Hudson Review* 6 (1953): 145. This became a common though never clearly stated criticism. Martha Stevens is the scholar who argues for "a classic set of unsolved novelistic problems" in *Wise Blood,* and I have summarized her main objections; see her *The Question of Flannery O'Connor* (Baton Rouge: Louisiana State University Press, 1973). There are earlier versions of her argument in (for example) Jonathan Baumbach, *The Landscape of Nightmare* (New York: New York University Press, 1970); Stuart L. Burns, "The Evolution of *Wise Blood,*" *Modern Fiction Studies* 16 (1970): 147–62; Leon Driskell and Joan T. Brittain, *The Eternal Crossroads: The Art of Flannery O'Connor* (Lexington: University Press of Kentucky, 1971); and Josephine Hendin, *The World of Flannery O'Connor* (Bloomington: Indiana University Press, 1970).

26. *Habit of Being,* 501, 70, and 470, respectively.

27. Ibid., 69 and 272, respectively.

28. The revisions O'Connor made in moving from short stories to full-length novel are well detailed in Burns.

29. *Habit of Being,* 10, 16, and 352, respectively. O'Connor once said that she valued the works of Nikolai Gogol "along with the light" (ibid., 44). O'Connor had read West's *The Day of the Locust* by autumn, 1949, shortly after New Directions re-released the book in its "New Classics" series. That edition was in O'Connor's library; see Arthur F. Kinney, *Flannery O'Connor's Library: Resources of Being* (Athens: University of Georgia Press, 1985), listing no. 612.

30. O'Connor, *Wise Blood,* 97 and 20, respectively; subsequent references are cited parenthetically.

31. I have presented a more detailed stylometric analysis of O'Connor's tropes in a 1983 essay, "Style in *Wise Blood,*" *Genre* 16: 75–97. A census found 105 similes in the text: 25 involved the declension of a character to some bestial level, and 34 more involved the declension of a character to still lower (vegetable or mineral) orders of being. The rest, 46 in all, signify an ascent of inanimate being to higher orders of instinctual or intentional being.

32. Taking a cue from Carl Proffer's 1967 study of Gogol's *Dead Souls,* my 1983 essay (n. 31, above) compared the simile/word ratio for a number of texts, West's included, where the grotesque has a significant function. Excepting Gogol, O'Connor simply uses *more* and *more kinds* of simile than any comparable writer: 1 for every 395 words (Gogol's *Dead Souls,* 1:335). Other standards for comparison: West, *Miss Lonelyhearts,* 1:410; Hawkes, *The Cannibal,* 1:825; and Anderson, *Winesburg, Ohio,* 1:925.

33. Evidently, achieving this separation of the narrator's discourse from that of her characters was no easy task. O'Connor advised a friend, in 1954: "The omniscient narrator is not supposed to use colloquial expressions. I send a good many of my things to Caroline Gordon for her criticism and she is always writing me that I musn't say such things, that the om. nar. never speaks like anyone but Dr. Johnson" (*Habit of Being,* 69). Similarly, five months later she wrote: "In any fiction where the omniscient narrator uses the same language as the characters, there is a loss of tension and a lowering of tone. This is something that it has taken me a long time to learn myself" (ibid., 95).

34. Culler, *Structuralist Poetics,* 135.

35. See for example Derrida's argument, "The Violence of the Letter," in *Of Grammatology.* If the origins of language are in wish-fulfillment, and in the ego's desire to impose difference, then language is the prison-house of this logocentric system. We might thus define the function of the grotesque in conventional (moral) satire as a type of this "violence." For, while the surface features of the text appear to wipe away system through a hysterical condition of non-difference (the grotesque trope), their overarching purpose is to clear the field for a system of moral difference whose strength is now redoubled. Yet the problem for such a satirist, as Seidel argues, is that his moral purpose may be razed by a contamination from his own materials. "The satirist is deeply implicated in satire's degenerative fictions precisely because he thrives as the chronicler of degenerative norms" (*Satiric Inheritance,* 4).

36. See Mikhail Bakhtin, *Rabelais and His World,* trans. Hélène Iswolsky (Cambridge, Mass.: MIT Press, 1968), 310.

37. Bakhtin again: "The object (tenor) transgresses its own confines, ceases to be itself. The limits between the body and the world are erased, leading to a fusion of the one with the other and with surrounding objects" (ibid.). Bakhtin's approach to the subject takes us a good deal beyond Keyser's historicist treatment, but is itself limited by his adherence to a corrective-curative model of its functioning in literary satire.

38. Ibid., 317–18.

39. René Girard, *Violence and the Sacred,* 31.

40. Gaston Bachelard, *The Poetics of Space,* trans. Maria Jolas (Boston: Beacon Press, 1969), 78.

41. O'Connor, *Mystery and Manners: Occasional Prose,* ed. Sally and Robert Fitzgerald (New York: Farrar, Straus and Cudahy, 1962), 68. O'Connor's readings from this period, tallied in Kinney, show how central was this "incarnational" purpose to her work. In Cardinal Newman's *An Essay in Aid of a Grammar of Ascent* she underlined the following passage: "Words which make nonsense, do not make a mystery." And, a few pages further, this: "Belief, on the other hand, being concerned with things concrete, not abstract, which variously excite the mind from their moral and imaginative properties, has for its objects, not only directly what is true, but inclusively what is beautiful, useful, admirable, heroic" (Kinney, item no. 113). Similarly, in her edition of *St. John of the Cross* she marked another passage treating the crucial status of "sensible experiences of divine grace" (Kinney, item no. 149).

42. O'Connor, *Mystery and Manners,* 72.

43. John Hawkes, "Flannery O'Connor's Devil," *Sewanee Review* 70 (1962): 398.

44. O'Connor surely would agree that charity is essential to the Christian idea of redemption. For example, in her copy of *St. John of the Cross* (1932; Kinney, item no. 149), she underlined a passage concerned with the "error" of having "an inordinate desire for sensible experiences of divine grace," when such a desire operates "without good works and [is] unvivified by charity." She continued underlining further on, where St. John is given as the example of "a pure living faith, informed by charity and working by charity, a faith that is the sole proportionate means to a living union with god."

45. The first phrase, "design and debris," is from Papa's remarks to Henri in Hawkes's *Travesty* (New York: New Directions, 1976), 17. Hawkes's other comments are from his "Notes on the Wild Goose Chase," *Massachusetts Review* 3 (1962): 787–88. In English the term "polylogical" maintains its sense not only of "much speaking" but of extravagance tending to folly: the "signes of a Foole" as one old O.E.D. source puts it. But Julia Kristeva's definition is the pertinent one here. The postmodern satire, as "polylogue," laughs from an understanding that meanings are decentered, arbitrary like the linguistic sign itself, and therefore ungraspable, though perhaps audible in the narrative orchestration; see Kristeva, *Desire in Language*, 175–81.

46. "A Trap to Catch Little Birds With: An Interview with John Hawkes," in *A John Hawkes Symposium*, ed. Anthony Santore and Michael Pocalyko (New York: New Directions, 1977), 174.

47. See Guerard's "Introduction" and "Addendum" to *The Cannibal* (New York: New Directions, 1962), xix–xx. Subsequent references to the novel will be given parenthetically.

48. André LeVot, "Du degré zéro du langage a l'heure H de la fiction: sexe, texte, et dramaturgie dans *The Cannibal*," *Études Anglaises* 29.3 (1976): 488–89.

49. "John Hawkes: An Interview" (1964), in *Studies in "Second Skin,"* ed. John Graham (Columbus: Ohio State University Press, 1974), 29.

50. A short list: Robert Scholes, "Metafiction," *Iowa Review* 1 (1970): 100–15; Fredric Jameson, "Metacommentary," *PMLA* 86 (1971): 9–19; and Jean Verrier's "Le récit réfléchi," *Litterature* 5 (1972): 58–68. Among more recent efforts see in particular Rose, *Parody // Metafiction,* and Linda Hutcheon, *Narcissistic Narrative: The Metafictional Paradox* (New York: Methuen, 1984). Hutcheon argues that the reader's interpretive freedom is a key convention of the metafictional mode. The laying bare of diegetic codes enables one to discover "the responsibility, the almost existentialist freedom in responsibility, that metafiction requires of the reader" (30).

51. Some examples: Humbert in his cell at the end of Nabokov's *Lolita*, Oedipa Maas's imprisonment at the close of Pynchon's *The Crying of Lot 49*, Richard Nixon in the death-row cell of Ethel Rosenberg in Coover's *The Public Burning*, and Gagnon held in La Violaine prison in Hawkes's *The Passion Artist*. Sometimes the destructive irony is also thematized as the dismemberment of a character, for example of Homer Simpson at the end of West's *The Day of the Locust*, or Hazel Motes's self-mutilation at the end of O'Connor's *Wise Blood*.

52. See Charles Baxter, "In the Suicide Seat: Reading John Hawkes's *Travesty*," *Georgia Review* 34 (1980): 871–72; and Tony Tanner, "No Instructions How to Read," *New York Times Book Review*, 28 March 1976, 1, 23.

53. *The Passion Artist* (New York: Harper and Row, 1979), 2.

54. Kristeva locates a similar correspondence — abjection of the female, and powerplay of the fascist father — in the satirical writings of Céline; see *Powers of Horror: An Essay in Abjection*, trans. Leon Roudiez (New York: Columbia University Press, 1982), 157–73. Similarly, Deleuze and Guattari identify in Oedipal narrative the one, great legitimizing "myth" or archetype of fascism, with mainstream psychoanalytic practice as a home office for that effort, and branch offices in every semiological system (such as storytelling) that would subordinate desire to the polar rules of plenary

structure and its absence; see their *Anti-Oedipus: Capitalism and Schizophrenia*, trans. Robert Hurley, Mark Seem, and Helen R. Lane (Minneapolis: University of Minnesota Press, 1983).

55. See W. M. Frohock, "John Hawkes' Vision of Violence," *Southwest Review* 50 (1965): 65–79; Donald Greiner, *Comic Terror: The Novels of John Hawkes* (Memphis: Memphis State University Press, 1973); Tony Tanner, "Necessary Landscapes and Luminous Deteriorations: On Hawkes," *Triquarterly* 20 (1970): 145–79; and Thomas Armstrong, "Reader, Critic, and the Form of John Hawkes's *The Cannibal*," *Boundary* 2 5 (1977): 835–37.

56. Wayne Booth, *The Rhetoric of Irony*, 35–37.

57. Respectively, see Patrick O'Donnell, *John Hawkes* (Boston: Twayne, 1983), 14; John Kuehl, *John Hawkes and the Craft of Conflict* (New Brunswick, N.J.: Rutgers University Press, 1974), 10; Frohock, 69; and Kuehl, 42.

58. Here is Hawkes: "I began *The Cannibal* after reading a brief notice in *Time* magazine about an actual cannibal discovered in Bremen, Germany (where I had been, coincidentally, during the war)" ("John Hawkes: An Interview," 147). The statement later cropped up in Webster Schott's "John Hawkes: An American Original," *New York Times Book Review*, 29 May 1966; and in O'Donnell (14). But I have been unable to verify this account. Hawkes says that he began writing the novel over Christmas, 1947, and finished the manuscript nine months later. A thorough check, not only of *Time* but of similar newsmagazines, from 1945 through 1948, uncovered nothing.

59. See Peter Andreas Munch, *Norse Mythology* (New York: Macmillan, 1926), 272–75; Maximillian J. Rudwin, *The Origin of German Carnival Comedy* (New York: G. E. Stechert, 1926), 14–16; and Barbara Swain, *Fools and Folly* (New York: Random House, 1932), 66–69.

60. Rudwin, 44–52.

61. Not only did the Nazi *Reich* begin its death-throes in April of 1945 but in that year Easter fell on April Fool's Day, a coincidence that had occurred just forty-eight times since A.D. 500. It was widely noted at the time. Thomas Pynchon employs it at the close of *Gravity's Rainbow*, with its Easter 1945 setting.


## Chapter 3: What Was Black Humor?


1. Conrad Knickerbocker hailed Black Humor in his review of *Candy*, "Candide as a Co-ed," *New York Times Book Review*, 17 May 1964, 5. See Ihab Hassan, "Laughter in the Dark: The New Voice in American Fiction," *American Scholar* 33 (1964): 636; Conrad Knickerbocker, "Humor with a Mortal Sting," *New York Times Book Review*, 27 September 1964, 3, 60–61; "Black Humor Fictions," *Time*, 12 February 1965, 95–96; Robert Scholes, *The Fabulators* (New York: Oxford University Press, 1967); Burton Feldman, "Anatomy of Black Humor," *Dissent* 15 (1968): 158–60; Phillip Rahv, "On Pornography, Black Humor, Norman Mailer, Etc.," *Partisan Review* (1967), also in his *Literature and the Sixth Sense* (Boston: Houghton Mifflin, 1970), 138–39; and John W.

Aldridge, "Donald Barthelme and the Doggy Life," *Atlantic* (1968), reprinted in his *The Devil in the Fire: Retrospective Essays on American Literature and Culture, 1951–1971* (New York: Harpers, 1972), 261–66.

2. See for example the jacket blurbs on such paperback editions as Pynchon's *V.* (Bantam, 1964), Roth's *Our Gang* (Dell, 1972), and Vonnegut's *God Bless You, Mr. Rosewater* (Dell, 1966) — all of which are still in print at this writing. Every year Black Humor is also the subject of one or two dissertations and a half-dozen or so articles, in which the definitions handed down from the sixties and early seventies reappear with a remarkable resiliency. Some examples: Sandra Ann Hunt, "The Black Humor Novel in American Literature" (Ph.D. diss., University of North Carolina, Chapel Hill, 1977); and Elaine B. Safer, "The Allusive Mode and Black Humor in Barth's *Sot-Weed Factor*," *Studies in the Novel* 13 (1981): 424–38. Safer's essay is part of her longer study *The Contemporary American Comic Epic: The Novels of Barth, Pynchon, Gaddis, and Kesey* (Detroit: Wayne State University Press, 1988). During the late sixties and through the seventies, the major vehicle for scholarly essays of Black Humor was *Critique: Studies in Fiction*. This focus was consistent with the interests of the editor, Max Schulz, whose *Black Humor Fiction of the Sixties: A Pluralistic Definition of Man and His World* (Athens: Ohio University Press, 1973) remains in print, and a key scholarly study of the subject.

3. See, respectively, Walter Blair and Hamlin Hill, *America's Humor* (New York: Oxford University Press, 1978), 498; Frank D. McConnell, *Four Postwar American Novelists: Bellow, Mailer, Barth and Pynchon* (Chicago: University of Chicago Press, 1977), 215; Jerome Klinkowitz, "Final Word on Black Humor," *Contemporary Literature* 15 (1974): 271–76; Sanford Pinsker, "The Graying of Black Humor," *Studies in the Twentieth Century* 9 (1972): 15–34; Schulz, *Black Humor Fiction*, 13; Phillip Rahv, "On Pornography, Black Humor, Norman Mailer, Etc.," *Literature and the Sixth Sense*, 186. The 1973 *Playboy* interview with Kurt Vonnegut is reprinted in his *Wampeters, Foma, and Granfalloons (Opinions)* (New York: Dell, 1976), source of the remark quoted here (257).

4. Vonnegut's remark, quoted above, is typical. In his anthology, *Black Humor* (New York: Bantam, 1965), Bruce Jay Friedman also commented that whatever critical legitimacy one found in the phrase Black Humor, "you can count on it to fizzle after a bit" (x). Donald Barthelme has similarly denied the term's usefulness; and in his essay, "Not-Knowing," the list of alleged "Postmodernists" reads like an extract of the best of those (Barth, Hawkes, Gaddis, and Pynchon) who once gathered under the cognomen "Black Humor" but who were good enough to outlast its hype — more evidence, I believe, that the term was mainly a way of identifying a modal expression or *a temperament*, now called the postmodern. There was, incidentally, just one book that might seem a collaborative project: Terry Southern and Mason Hoffenberg's *Candy*, initially published by Maurice Girodias's Olympia Press in 1958 (his list also included Nabokov's *Lolita* and Burrough's *Naked Lunch*), subsequently released in America by Putnam's (1964). *Candy* was widely received as a send-up of the pornographic novel; there is every indication, however, that the two young writers were simply motivated by the promise of quick profits — certainly not an idea of changing the rules for narrative satire.

5. Scholes, *The Fabulators,* 38–39.

6. Hassan, "Laughter in the Dark," 636.

7. Knickerbocker, "Humor with a Mortal Sting," 3 and 60.

8. Friedman, *Black Humor,* ix; but see also Douglas M. Davis, ed., *The World of Black Humor: An Introductory Anthology of Selections and Criticism* (New York: E. P. Dutton, 1967), 16; as well as Bruce Janoff, "Black Humor: Beyond Satire," *Ohio Review* 14 (1972): 7.

9. Raymond Olderman, *Beyond the Waste Land: A Study of the American Novel in the 1960's* (New Haven: Yale University Press, 1972), 22.

10. George Steiner, *Language and Silence: Essays on Language, Literature and the Inhuman* (New York: Atheneum, 1972), 10.

11. Friedman, *Black Humor,* x.

12. See Alpers, 29; but also Frye, *Anatomy of Criticism,* 366; and Mailloux, 128–30.

13. In *Black Humor Fiction of the Sixties,* Max Schulz mentions Swift, the early Nathanael West, and Evelyn Waugh (12); similarly, in his anthology Douglas Davis singles out "Three Beginnings" of Black Humor in fictions by Kafka, West, and Nabokov, granting at the same time that there are "older, safer precedents" to be found in the works of, for example, Voltaire and Swift (29–30). Brom Weber, who clearly recognized Black Humor as a refraction of the modal conventions associated with previous satires, looked back not only to these antecedents but also to French surrealism, as well as "selections from" Melville, Bierce, Twain, Sherwood Anderson, and others, all of whom "were deliberate practitioners of black humor" (370).

14. See for example Douglas Davis, who claims that "[t]he Black Humorists have restored the novel to relevance" and succeeded in making the novel "again the vehicle of contemporary feeling" (22–23); and Janoff, whose sense of "black humor as a genre" is buttressed by his observation that it is a phenomenon peculiar to the novel as it was being "written within the two decades following World War II." Or see Schulz and Donald Greiner, "Djuna Barnes's *Nightwood* and the American Origins of Black Humor," *Critique* 17 (1976): 1–53; for both the recurrent phrase "black humor fiction" indicates the reception of these writings within a particular subgenre of the novel.

As for connections to the other arts, Douglas Davis considers the Theater of the Absurd, Pop Art, and the New Music (i.e., John Cage) as parallel developments; Schulz considers many of the same; Mathew Winston, in "*Humour noir* and Black Humor," *Veins of Humor,* ed. Harry Levin (Cambridge: Harvard University Press, 1972), 269–84, gives extensive treatment to absurdist drama, especially in light of Esslin's study, *The Theatre of the Absurd.* To such critics, these parallels seemed to underscore the generic integrity of Black Humor. Yet it makes more taxonomic sense to interpret the developments as expressions of a new sensibility, and thus to define Black Humor as a modal shift necessary to that expression.

15. Later in the same year, Gilbert Highet, in his *Anatomy of Satire,* would derive "black humor" from the Greek idea of "black salt," because in a literary context "salt" meant wit and humor; thus "black salt" referred to an especially crude, bitter humor (30).

16. See the 1965 *Time* essay, "Black Humor Fiction," 94. A lone exception is

Winston's 1972 essay. The only scholar to explore the possible relations in any detail, he notes that "virtually all critics who wrote about black humor ignored its French antecedents" (272–73), and then shows that while Breton's *humour noir* was founded on a detached, ironic perspective, American Black Humor seemed to develop from an erasure of that detachment and a disorientation in the midst of grotesque extremes, horror and humor, "threat and amusement" (275). This comparison is, however, based on a too-limiting idea of Breton's *humour*, as I argue below. Brom Weber also touches on the possible Black Humor/*Humour noir* links, but not in as much detail. Still the best introduction to the surrealist context of *Humour noir* is J. H. Matthews, "Intelligence at the Service of Surrealism: Breton's *Anthologie de l'humour noir*," *Books Abroad* 41 (1967): 267–73. A review essay of the final (1966) edition of Breton's *Anthologie de l'humour noir*, this essay (like Breton's work itself) appears to have had little or no influence on American Black Humorists.

17. Frye, "The Nature of Satire," 78; Hassan, "Laughter in the Dark," 637.

18. Janoff, "Black Humor: Beyond Satire," 10. His bibliographical sources for the definition of satire are notable: Frye, *Anatomy of Criticism*; Feinberg, *The Satirist: His Temperament, Motivation, and Influence* (Ames: Iowa State University Press, 1963); and Paulson, *The Fictions of Satire* — formalists all, as I have argued in chapter 1. And his essay is representative of the field: see also Brom Weber (362), who contrasts Black Humor's monstrous and morally uncertain world to that of the great Augustan satirists; Winston (274), who argues that, "unlike satire," Black Humor "does not assume a set of norms"; or Linda Horvay Barnes, *The Dialectics of Black Humor: Process and Product* (Frankfurt: Peter Lang, 1978), who claims the Black Humorists are "beyond satire" because their work "posits no answers" and makes no corrective gestures, for "previous solutions have been frought with illusion" (25).

19. Janoff, 8–10.

20. Schulz, *Black Humor Fiction*, 28.

21. Knickerbocker, "Humor with a Mortal Sting," 60.

22. See Janoff, 12; Scholes, 44–45; Barnes, 25.

23. Aldridge, 261–62.

24. Ibid., 263.

25. Feldman, 158; Aldridge, 263.

26. Roth, *Portnoy's Complaint* (New York: Random House, 1969), 111.

27. For comparable remarks, see Hassan, "Laughter in the Dark," 636; Davis, 22; Aldridge, 262; Olderman, 26; and Janoff, whose comments are representative: "There is a strong analogy between black humor and the psychology of the Jewish joke," with its laughter hinging on "a maximum of suffering and a minimum of hope" (15–16). Later critics have stuck by these early observations. In *The Secret of Humor* (Amsterdam: Rodopi, 1978), Leonard Feinberg defines Black Humor as "aggression against everything," in the manner of "a sick joke" (162–63). And Linda Horvay Barnes seconds Scholes's pronouncement, but takes the analysis considerably farther (25–31).

28. Scholes, *The Fabulators*, 46 and 43, respectively; Aldridge, 262; Klinkowitz, "Final Word on Black Humor," 273.

29. Hassan, "Laughter in the Dark," 636; and Vance Bourjaily, "What Vonnegut Is and Isn't," *New York Times Book Review*, 13 August 1972, 3.

30. Vonnegut, *Playboy* interview, in *Wampeters, Foma, and Granfalloons (Opinions)*, 257. Subsequent citations are given parenthetically.

31. Sigmund Freud, *Jokes and Their Relation to the Unconscious*, vol. 8 of *The Standard Edition of the Complete Psychological Works of Sigmund Freud*, trans. James Strachey (London: Hogarth Press, 1959), 228–29.

32. Kurt Vonnegut, *Cat's Cradle* (New York: Dell, 1970), 111–12; further references are cited parenthetically.

33. Kurt Vonnegut, *Mother Night* (New York: Dell, 1966).

34. Michael Wood, "Dancing in the Dark," *New York Review of Books*, 31 May 1973, 23–25.

35. Conrad Festa, "Vonnegut's Satire," in *Vonnegut in America: An Introduction to the Life and Work of Kurt Vonnegut*, ed. Jerome Klinkowitz and Donald D. Lawler (New York: Dell, 1977), 136 and 139, respectively.

36. Leslie Fiedler, "The Divine Stupidity of Kurt Vonnegut," *Esquire*, September 1970, 196.

37. Thomas Pynchon, *V.* (New York: Bantam, 1964), 92 and 97, respectively.

38. Terry Southern, *The Magic Christian* (New York: Random House, 1960), 10; subsequent references are cited parenthetically.

39. Nelson Algren — never at a loss for superlatives, and thus always good copy for book jackets — was the reviewer who praised *The Magic Christian* as "profoundly satiric" (in a February 27, 1960, review for *The Nation*). But his enthusiasm was matched by others, such as Martin Tucker (for *New Republic*, 29 February 1960) and Edward Kennebeck (for *Commonweal*, 29 April 1960). Among those hailing Southern as an early example of Black Humor writing were Knickerbocker, in "Humor with a Mortal Sting" (3) and in an earlier review of Southern and Hoffman's *Candy*, "Candide as a Co-ed," *New York Times Book Review*, 17 May 1964, 5; as well as Friedman (8), *Time* (94), and Davis (116).

40. Davis, 116.

41. See Jerome Klinkowitz, *Literary Disruptions: The Making of a Post-Contemporary American Fiction* (Urbana: University of Illinois Press, 1980), 192. See also Martin Levin, in a February 21, 1960, review for the *New York Times Book Review: The Magic Christian* is "less a novel than a practical joke — in fact, a marathon of practical jokes committed by a surrealist billionaire"; but because it never gets beyond the practical joke, the "satire . . . floats too far above its luxuriant subject matter to pick out any but the most familiar landmarks" (4). For a similar appraisal, see also John Coleman, in a review for *The Spectator* (13 July 1959) of the British edition published by Andre Deutsch in slightly different form one year before Random House released the American edition. Coleman identified the structural principal of *The Magic Christian* as "sick jokes raised to the power of art by inflation," and argued that its assaults were "a shade too obvious to be really effective" (13).

Klinkowitz's claim that the editors at Random House submitted *The Magic Christian* to a brutal "castration" needs reexamining. On his own admission, the only difference between the Deutsch and Random House editions is chapter 13. The Random House editors objected to a seven-page section in which Southern composed a satire on a U.S. senator who closely resembles Joseph McCarthy. In that section, Grand is disturbed by a senator elected on the basis of anticommunist slogans. His plan is to pay the man to finger the most upstanding Americans as Communists, all of them enumerated on a great list that is, in fact, a blank page. The idea is to observe how long the American populace can be gulled. Grand even sets up public hearings as a stage for the Senator to rant like a madman, all the while expecting cooler heads to step in: "But the men with the jacket never came. And, in fact, no one raised a finger — a finger to topple the rotten egg from the wall" (143). In the British edition, that episode had filled the second half of chapter 13, not "the chapter" itself, as Klinkowitz claims. In its place, the American edition inserts another joke: "Grand had a bit of fun when he engaged a man to smash crackers with a sledgehammer in Times Square." This episode, which carries on for some three pages of smashed sidewalks, gawking pedestrians, and diverted traffic, ridicules a jaded public's hunger for spectacle.

Such a revision was certainly a silly concession to political exigencies, but it had nothing to do with the narrative "climax" of the satire in Southern's novel, as Klinkowitz holds (191). The true climax, dragged on through *The Magic Christian*'s final three chapters, details the sailing of Grand's ship of fools, "The Magic Christian" itself, described as "in terms of public outrage, his [Grand's] *succes d'estime*" (*The Magic Christian*, 117). In this novel, as in the annals of Black Humor, Southern's revision was a minor surrender.

42. Newman, *The Post-Modern Aura*, 77.

43. See Booth, 6; and Wilde, 9. Further references to either of these texts will be cited parenthetically.

44. See Richard Kostelanetz, "The Point Is That Life Doesn't Have Any Point," *New York Times Book Review*, 6 June 1965, 3; and Janoff, "Black Humor: Beyond Satire," 11 and 18, respectively; and Barnes, 31. Compare Hassan, from "Laughter in the Dark": "The ironic attitude lies close to the satiric, [yet in] the latter, the object of attention is not the monstrous, which is irremediable, but rather the follies and vices of men, things merely reprehensible" (637). Comparable definitions appear in Davis, 65; and Friedman, xi.

45. Still, Wilde's move is typical. See for instance Booth, who subscribes to the idea of external targets or "victims" and thus implicitly to the idea of satire's corrective and normative aims (27–31); or Muecke, who links "normative ironies" to the idea and practice of satire (119); and Morton Gurewitch's 1957 dissertation, which holds that "[t]he ironist does not pretend to cure such a universe [which is in his words "permanently out of joint"] or to solve its mysteries. It is satire that solves. The images of vanity, for example, that litter the world's satire are always satisfactorily deflated at the end; but the vanity of vanities that informs the world's irony is beyond liquidation." See Gurewitch, "European Romantic Irony" (Ph.D. diss., Columbia University, 1957), 15.

46. André Breton, *Anthologie de l'humour noir*, ed. Jean-Jacques Pauvert (Paris: Gallimard, 1966), 274. Further references are to this edition, and are cited parenthetically.

47. So the book was received at the time of its American publication. William Styron and Albert Goldman both seconded the appraisal Putnam's placed on its dust jacket: that *Candy* was a satirical "spoof on pornography." Styron went on to point

out some of the specific targets of the authors' ridicule, for example the protective-possessive parent and the schools and religious institutions that serve as institutions for sexual repression. He summed up the review by saying that "*Candy* in its best scenes is wickedly funny to read and morally bracing as only good satire can be" (*New York Review of Books,* 14 May 1964, 8). For similar appraisals, see Goldman's review, *New Republic,* 11 July 1964, 17, and especially Conrad Knickerbocker's "Candide as a Co-ed," *New York Times Book Review,* 17 May 1964, which takes the book as "a marvelous prank" as well as a "sternly moral satire on sexual attitudes." He ends by praising Southern as "the most inventive and corrosive of Black Humorists" (5), the first use of that term in context with Barth, Donleavy, Heller, Purdy, and Pynchon.

48. Vladimir Nabokov, *Lolita* (New York: Berkeley, 1977), 283. Subsequent references are to this edition and are cited parenthetically.

49. Booth, 6. For acclamations of *Lolita* as a Black Humor classic see for example Schulz, 21–23, who noted the morally uncertain stance of Nabokov's parodies as well as how, in *Lolita,* the "dogma of plot" was redefined in its relation to "the independent role of incidents and surface details." Nabokov's widely quoted remark, in *Strong Opinions* (New York: McGraw-Hill, 1973), that "satire is a lesson, parody is a game" (75) should be taken, I think, as a recognition of how limiting he found the traditional definition of satire and of his need to find an alternative terminology.

50. Culler, *Structuralist Poetics,* 193.

51. The celebrity in the Drômes ad is playwright Clare Quilty. Dolores Haze had clipped the page from a magazine and hung it on her bedroom wall at 342 Lawn Street. When Humbert arrives in the household she sees him, perhaps even falls for him, as an ersatz-Quilty, and eventually Lo will of course run off with Quilty himself — the only man she "ever loved" as she will tell Humbert three years later. Finally, in the murder scene it is Quilty, Humbert's doppelganger, who appears smoking a Drômes. As Nabokov has said, "These are the secret points, the subliminal coordinates, by means of which the book is plotted" (*Lolita,* 287).

52. Donald Barthelme, *Snow White* (New York: Atheneum, 1972), 97. Subsequent references are to this edition and are cited parenthetically.

53. Schulz, 17.

54. See for example Greiner, "Djuna Barnes's *Nightwood* and the American Origins of Black Humor"; he accepts Schulz's idea wholesale: "Most of these novelists realize that all versions of reality are valid since life is disordered and fractured"; thus, "the form of the fiction illustrates the multiplicity of reality" (45). In addition, see Barnes, 25; and Winston, 276–77.

55. Susan Sontag, *Against Interpretation* (New York: Delta, 1981), 280.

56. Like many others, Lawrence Alloway, in *American Pop Art* (New York: Macmillan, 1974), dates the formal beginnings of Pop Art to September 1956 and Richard Hamilton's "This is Tomorrow" exhibit at London's Whitechapel Gallery. In America, contemporaneous work by Robert Rauschenberg and Jasper Johns set the stage for further experiments. By 1962, Andy Warhol and Roy Lichtenstein were wholly engaged in such work: Warhol with artifacts like the famous Marilyn photos and the Campbell's Soup cans, Lichtenstein with the comic book images.

57. Lawrence Alloway, *Roy Lichtenstein* (New York: Abbeville, 1983), 34.

58. Alloway, *American Pop Art*, 43.

59. See Harold Rosenberg, *The De-Definition of Art* (New York: Horizon, 1972): "[Since Pop] no influential American art movement has been either overtly or passively hostile to the majority culture. On the contrary, the leading idea . . . has been to exorcise the negative impulses that tormented the earlier vanguard," which could never get over its distaste for the stuff of material culture (218). Similarly, in *After the Wake: An Essay on the Contemporary Avant-Garde* (Oxford: Clarendon Press, 1980), Christopher Butler argues that "the catalyst for a huge expansion of stylistic range and psychological appeal, in all the arts, came in the late 1950s and early 1960s with Pop art" (115). For comparable assessments see also Nicholas Calas, "Why Not Pop Art?" *Art and Literature* 4 (1965): 178–84; and Robert Rosenblum, "Pop Art and Non-Pop Art," *Art and Literature* 5 (1965): 80–93.

60. Iser, 11.

61. Butler, 92.

62. A reproduction of the canvas, alongside its comic book source, appears in Alloway, *Roy Lichtenstein*, 28–29.

63. The words are from Christopher Lasch, *The Culture of Narcissism: American Life in an Age of Diminishing Expectations* (New York: Warner Books, 1979), 48; but see also Morris Dickstein, *Gates of Eden: American Culture in the Sixties* (New York: Basic Books, 1977), 126.

64. Knickerbocker, "Humor with a Mortal Sting," 3; Schulz, 15.

65. In *Literature Against Itself: Literature in Modern Society* (Chicago: University of Chicago Press, 1979), Gerald Graff criticizes Barthelme for failing to develop "a sufficient sense of objective reality" outside the book (226), thus for failing to take an adversary stance toward mass culture (238). Similarly, Christopher Lasch charges that Barthelme, like other Black Humorists, provides no socially "useful" fantasy to challenge the "pathological narcissism" marketed under the rubric of pop culture (52–55). Both seek to preserve the authority of elite culture. See also Robert Morace, "Donald Barthelme's *Snow White*: The Novel, the Critics, and the Culture," *Critique* 26 (1984); even though he takes Lasch and Graff to task for disliking the book, Morace still reads *Snow White* as a "critique of the reductive linguistic democracy of contemporary American mass culture" (1). For similar remarks see Dickstein, 221.

66. James Purdy, *Cabot Wright Begins* (New York: Farrar, Straus and Giroux, 1964), 14. Subsequent references are cited parenthetically.

67. Karl, 322.

68. Webster Schott, "James Purdy: American Dreams," *Nation* 198 (1964): 300.

69. Molly Hite, *Ideas of Order in the Novels of Thomas Pynchon* (Columbus: Ohio State University Press, 1983), 93.

70. Thomas Pynchon, "Introduction," *Slow Learner* (Boston: Little, Brown, 1984), 22.

71. See, for example, Peter Cooper, *Signs and Symptoms: Thomas Pynchon and the Contemporary World* (Berkeley and Los Angeles: University of California Press, 1983), 56; Richard Poirier, "Embattled Underground," *New York Times Book Review*, 1 May 1966, 5; and Tony Tanner, *City of Words: American Fiction, 1950–1970* (New York: Harper and Row, 1971), 167–68.

72. Tony Tanner, *Thomas Pynchon* (London: Methuen, 1982), 56.

73. Thomas Pynchon, *The Crying of Lot 49* (New York: Bantam, 1967), 135. Subsequent references are to this edition and are cited parenthetically.

74. Hite, 71.

75. See Schulz, 63; and Joseph Slade, *Thomas Pynchon* (New York: Warner Books, 1974), 126.

76. See Robert Sklar, "An Anarchist Miracle: The Novels of Thomas Pynchon," in *Pynchon: A Collection of Critical Essays,* ed. Edward Mendelson (Englewood Cliffs, N.J.: Prentice-Hall, 1978), 93–94; and Tanner, *Thomas Pynchon,* 56.

77. For the first instance, see Roger B. Henkle, "Pynchon's Tapestries on the Western Wall," in Mendelson, *Pynchon: A Collection of Critical Essays,* 104–6; for the second, see Frank Kermode, "Decoding the Trystero," also in Mendelson, 165.

78. See N. Katherine Hayles, "'A Metaphor of God Knew How Many Parts': The Engine that Drives *The Crying of Lot 49*," in *New Essays on "The Crying of Lot 49,"* ed. Patrick O'Donnell (New York: Cambridge University Press, 1991), 116 and 121, respectively; and John Johnston, "Toward the Schizo-Text: Paranoia as Semiotic Regime in *The Crying of Lot 49*," also in O'Donnell, 47–48.

79. Still the best on this topic is Anne Mangel's 1971 essay, "Maxwell's Demon, Entropy, Information: *The Crying of Lot 49*," reprinted in *Mindful Pleasures: Essays on Thomas Pynchon,* ed. George Levine and David Leverenz (Boston: Little, Brown, 1975). After pointing out the virtual homology between Boltzmann's equation for entropy and Claude Shannon's for cybernetic noise, she goes on to discuss the further paradox: "the more entropy or disorder in the system, the more information will be needed to describe the system" (95).

80. Hawkes, "Flannery O'Connor's Devil," 398.

81. Hawkes, "A Trap to Catch Little Birds With," 174; and *Travesty,* 14. Further references to the novel are cited parenthetically.

82. Gilles Deleuze, *Logique du sens* (Paris: Editions Minuit, 1972), chapter 12, passim.

83. Comparisons to West and O'Connor are indeed notable. In chapter 2, n. 32 I discussed O'Connor's comparative tropes, which appear with a frequency of occurences per words of text, at a ratio of 1:395, versus 1:410 in *Miss Lonelyhearts.* The ratio in *Travesty*: 1:228. Also, Hawkes's comparative tropes are of a wider range and variety.

84. Baxter, 883. Equally disturbing, however, is Tony Tanner's review, "No Instructions How to Read," *New York Times Book Review,* 28 March 1976; it argues that *Travesty* is so vehemently antirealistic as to supply "no instructions" to a reader desperately in need of them (23). This argument reappears in Charles Baxter's essay, which argues that Henri is a figure for that numbed, passive, unprotesting reader who is putatively acquiescing in the death of literature.

85. See Thomas LeClair, "Robert Coover, *The Public Burning,* and the Art of Excess," *Critique* 23.3 (1982): 5. For further instances of the attack, see Mary McCarthy's essays collected in *Ideas and the Novel* (New York: Harcourt, Brace, and Jovanovich, 1980); Martin Price, *Forms of Life: Character and Moral Imagination in the Novel*

(New Haven: Yale University Press, 1983); and Robert Alter, "The American Political Novel," *New York Times Book Review*, 10 August 1980, 3, 26–27.

## Chapter 4: The Sixties and After

1. Fredric Jameson, *The Political Unconscious: Narrative as a Socially Symbolic Act* (Ithaca: Cornell University Press, 1981), 281.

2. Stephen Vizinczey, "Engineers of a Sham: How Literature Lies about Power," *Harpers*, June 1986, 69.

3. Alter, 3 and 27, respectively. See also Norman Podhoretz, "Uncle Sam and the Phantom," *Saturday Review*, 17 September 1977, 27–28,

4. See Alfred Kazin, "American Writing Now," *New Republic*, 18 October 1980, 27–30; and McCarthy, *Ideas and the Novel*, 6–9, and passim.

5. See Gardner, *On Moral Fiction*, 197–98. The claim that political issues are "too great" for satire comes from Hodgart, 78. In this connection the example of Norman Podhoretz is also instructive. A liberal Democrat throughout the fifties and early sixties, by 1968 he had abandoned his leftist affiliations out of dislike for the (to him) excesses of antiwar and civil rights groups. When the Democrats nominated George McGovern for the presidency in 1972, Podhoretz condemned the party and thereafter his stance in *Commentary*, which he edits, moved increasingly rightward. In the essays collected in *The Bloody Crossroads: Where Literature and Politics Meet* (New York: Simon and Shuster, 1986), he goes so far as to blame thwarted sixties radicals and frustrated McGovernites for unfairly driving Richard Nixon from office. Thus he ignores the general outrage at transgressions of law throughout the executive branch, and this benign view of Nixon surely stood behind Podhoretz's 1977 condemnation of Coover's novel, *The Public Burning*, which is reiterated in the 1984 volume. Podhoretz wants to believe that a novel like Coover's can be criticized on purely formal grounds, on a basis of objective (and realist) criteria where it either stands or falls. But most often that supposed objectivity is mainly used to convey or mask his own political positions. Of late, aside from the work on *Commentary*, he is enmeshed in a wide range of political action groups devoted to rescinding much of the sixties program for civil rights and to rearming the military on a vast scale. These affiliations make him a central figure in the group of neo-conservatives — like former UN Ambassador Jeanne Kirkpatrick, Midge Decter (Podhoretz's wife), Elliott Abrams (formerly assistant secretary of state in the Reagan and Bush administrations), and Irving Kristol (editor of *Encounter*, a magazine begun in the fifties as a publishing front for the anti-communist policies of the CIA) — all of whom are influential in shaping Republican foreign and domestic policy.

6. See Friedman, "Introduction," *Black Humor*, x. For comparable instances, Max Schulz's treatment — in *Black Humor Fiction of the Sixties* — is rather typical. He mentions Friedman's argument, commenting in particular on the "discontinuous and instantaneous universe" offered to us through the media (18). But Schulz does not see these possibilities as challenging or assuming the normative-corrective bent of

traditional satire. Instead they mainly demand formal changes — a less continuous plotting and destabilized characters — which unfold in the context of a "metaphysics of multiplicity" (19), Schulz's terms for a certain comical or even cynical kind of moral relativism.

7. William Stott, *Documentary Expression and Thirties America* (New York: Oxford University Press, 1973), 18 and 24, respectively. Further references are to this edition and will be cited parenthetically.

8. Pollard, *Satire,* 73–74.

9. Howard Zinn, *The Politics of History* (Boston: Beacon Press, 1970), 40.

10. McCarthy, *On the Contrary* (New York: Farrar, Straus and Cudahy, 1961), 257–59.

11. The metafictional novel exposed these realist conventions, particularly the assumption that realist fictions owed mimetic fidelity to "objective" facts of its reference world. Instead, the metafictional novel uncovers the uses of language — the diegetic means — for constructing, sustaining, and endorsing the image of that reference world. John Barth's 1967 essay, "The Literature of Exhaustion," in *Atlantic,* August 1967, 29–34, argues that prognoses of the novel's death rested on the mimetic view, and that the writer could still discover endless fabulative possibility in kinds of diegetic play. For more recent treatments see, for example, Christine Brooke-Rose, *A Rhetoric of the Unreal: Studies in Narrative and Structure, Especially the Fantastic* (London: Cambridge University Press, 1981), particularly chapter 12; and Patricia Waugh, *Metafiction: The Theory and Practice of Self-Conscious Fiction* (New York: Methuen, 1984), 10–20.

12. Hodgart, 61.

13. Kernan, *The Plot of Satire,* 33.

14. Elliott, 258 and 275, respectively.

15. Seidel, *The Satiric Inheritance,* 8. Subsequent references are to this edition and are cited parenthetically.

16. Girard, 82. Subsequent references are cited parenthetically.

17. Mary McCarthy, *The Groves of Academe* (New York: Avon, 1981), 13 and 219, respectively. Further references are to this edition and are cited parenthetically.

18. Still the best study of Himes's fiction and its reception: James Lundquist, *Chester Himes* (New York: Ungar, 1976).

19. Chester Himes, *Pinktoes* (New York: Dell, 1961), 16. Subsequent references are to this edition and are cited parenthetically.

20. Charles Wright, *The Wig: A Mirror Image* (New York: Farrar, Straus and Giroux, 1966), 3. Subsequent references are to this edition and are cited parenthetically.

21. Ishmael Reed, *The Free-Lance Pallbearers* (New York: Avon, 1977), n.p. Subsequent references are to this edition and are cited parenthetically. On Reed and West, see "Ishmael Reed: An Interview," *Interviews with Black Writers,* ed. John O'Brien (New York: Liveright, 1973), 167.

22. Franco LaPolla, "*The Free-Lance Pallbearers;* or, No More Proscenium Arch," *Review of Contemporary Fiction* 4 (1984): 192.

23. Michel Fabre, "*The Free-Lance Pallbearers* ou le langage du pouvoir," *Revue française d'études américaines* 1 (1976): 83–100.

24. Neil Schmitz, "Donald Barthelme and the Emergence of Modern Satire," *Minnesota Review* 1 (1971): 109.

25. See Elliott, 11; Girard, 95.

26. In his interview with John O'Brien (see n. 21, above), Reed has explained the origins of his title: "Yellow Back," for the dime-novel westerns once distinguished by their yellow covers; "Radio" as a way of signifying the transformation of that written genre into something like a jazzed-up oral narration; and "Broke Down" to indicate the shattering of the dime-western's thematic center, its imperialist mythology of conquest and landholding. In addition, *Mumbo Jumbo* mentions a Hoo-Doo "Radio Loa" (or voodoo spirit) that appeared during the First World War: "It loves to hear the static concerning its victims' crimes before it 'eats' them. . . . This particular loa has a Yellow Back to symbolize its radio circuitry . . . a very mean, high-powered loa"; see Reed's *Mumbo Jumbo* (New York: Avon, 1978), 172–73.

27. Reed, *Yellow Back Radio Broke Down* (New York: Avon, 1977), 18. Subsequent references are to this edition and are cited parenthetically.

28. Loop Garoo first appears in Reed's well-known poem from the sixties, "I Am a Cowboy in the Boat of Ra." There he is Loup Garou, from the French for a "werewolf." The name also calls to mind a fifties Hollywood cowboy named Lash Larue, who (like Loop) used to wear black and defend himself with a bullwhip. In *Yellow Back,* Loop routs Drag Gibson's gang with a whip, stripping them of guns, marshalls' stars, and belt-buckles with pinpoint lashings.

29. Irving Howe, "New Black Writers," *Harper's,* December 1969, 141.

30. Kristeva, *Desire in Language,* 80 and 84, respectively.

31. *Mumbo Jumbo,* 73 and 241. Subsequent references are cited parenthetically.

32. Robert Gover, "An Interview with Ishmael Reed," *Black American Literature Forum* 12 (1978): 13–14.

33. Norman Mailer, *Why Are We in Vietnam?* (New York: Putnam's, 1967), 58. Subsequent references are to this edition and are cited parenthetically.

34. Karl, 312; for the jacket blurbs, see Heller, *Catch-22* (New York: Dell, 1962). Text references are to this edition and will be cited parenthetically.

35. Kernan, *The Plot of Satire,* 77–79; Frye, *Anatomy of Criticism,* 160–62.

36. Karl, 312.

37. See for example Bruce Janoff, "Black Humor, Existentialism, and Absurdity: A Generic Confusion," *Arizona Quarterly* 30 (1974). He argues that Yossarian "suddenly learns that there is something more than total ego involvement aimed at self-preservation: he discovers social involvement — in effect the existential ideal of service" (299). Or see Thomas LeClair, "Death and Black Humor," *Critique* 17 (1976), an essay that similarly comments on Yossarian's transformation from "a thanatophobic victim" into "a charitable idealist" who runs "*to* responsibilities" (15).

38. Kurt Vonnegut, *Slaughterhouse-Five; or, The Children's Crusade* (New York: Delacorte, 1969), 193. Subsequent references are to this edition and are cited parenthetically.

39. For instance see Michael Wood's 1973 review essay, "Dancing in the Dark," *New York Review of Books,* 31 May 1973, 23; Festa, 146–47; Olderman's discussion in *Beyond the Wasteland,* 213–16; and Linda Horvay Barnes's chapter on *Slaughterhouse-*

*Five.* Like Olderman, she holds that Vonnegut resolves that dialectical split in moments of pure compassion, moments that exist in "the space between" the despair and the lies (90–92).

40. Barnes, 91; Olderman, 214.

41. Ralph Waldo Emerson, "Nature," in *Ralph Waldo Emerson: Selected Essays, Lectures, and Poems,* ed. Robert D. Richardson (New York: Bantam, 1990), 27.

42. See Richard Drinnon, *Facing West: The Metaphysics of Indian-Hating* (Minneapolis: University of Minnesota Press, 1980).

43. See Karl, 12–13; and McConnell, 100–101.

44. Philip Roth, *Our Gang* (New York: Random House, 1971), 193. Subsequent references are to this edition and are cited parenthetically.

45. Orwell's well-known remarks connect the "present political chaos" (of 1946) with "the decay of language." He goes on: "One can probably bring about some improvement by starting at the verbal end. . . . Political language — and with variations this is true of all political parties, from Conservatives to Anarchists — is designed to make lies sound truthful and murder respectable, and to give the appearance of solidity to pure wind." The passage is often quoted in support of claims about the insidious deceits of political discourse, but equally notable is Orwell's *corrective* aim: to "bring about some improvement" in politics by beginning with language. This is consistent with the normative and curative aims of Roth's satire. Indeed, his second epigraph from Book IV of *Gulliver's Travels* — treating "that Faculty of lying, so perfectly well understood, and so universally practiced among human Creatures" — once more treats the theme of deceit and, in contrasting humankind to the Houyhnhnms, once more points to the curative potential of direct and truthful discourse.

46. Robert Coover, *The Public Burning* (New York: Viking, 1976), 3. Subsequent references are to this edition and are cited parenthetically. Coover's analysis of the documentary and historical texts was wide and thorough. In a review of Louis Nizer's *The Implosion Conspiracy,* for the *New York Times Book Review,* 11 February 1973, he mentions a number of these; scholars pursuing such backgrounds should consult this crucial essay (4, 33). Coover studied the Eisenhower administration and Richard Nixon in particular. For example, Emmet John Hughes's book, *The Ordeal of Power: A Political Memoir of the Eisenhower Years* (New York: Atheneum, 1963), supplied the background for chapter 13, concerned with the cabinet meeting of Thursday, June 18, at which Eisenhower rejected the final clemency appeals; and the influence of Nixon's *Six Crises* (Garden City, N.J.: Doubleday, 1962) is strong throughout, both in epitomizing Nixon's public rhetoric and in supplying Coover with sundry motifs — such as Nixon's sense of a public calling and his thirst to prove himself through constant testing. To date, these sources remain unexplored.

47. See Podhoretz, "Uncle Sam and the Phantom," *Saturday Review,* 17 September 1977, 28. Notable exceptions are the reviews by Thomas R. Edwards, *New York Times Book Review,* 9 August 1977, 9; and Donald Hall, *National Review,* 30 September 1977, 1118. Though he was in error about matters like dates (1953, not 1952), Edwards read the novel as a "vigorous satire" centered on American myths — Alger's self-made men, history as a wonder-working Providence — for which the fictional Richard Nixon is the proving ground and against which he is "constantly testing ver-

sions of himself." And this is why it is appropriate and absurdly right, notes Edwards, that the character should visit Ethel in her death-row cell. Donald Hall gave a perceptive reading of the novel as a satire on American obsessions, for which politics is an ongoing epic theater, and aptly places it in a line of "monstrous, obscene, impossible, valuable fantas[ies]" reaching back at least to Melville. Most reviewers condemned Coover's excesses and ignored his satire; see for instance Celia Betsky's review in *Commonweal*, 28 October 1977, 693.

48. See Walter Clemons, "Shock Treatment," *Newsweek*, 8 August 1977, 75–76. It was Clemons who first linked Coover's novel with the "encyclopedic" tradition illustrated by *Gravity's Rainbow* (his source: Mendelson's 1975 essay on Pynchon). Thomas LeClair's "Robert Coover, *The Public Burning*, and the Art of Excess," *Critique* 23.3 (1982), reads the novel under the rubric of "The Art of Excess," an ingenious category into which he puts the quite different and large-scale books by Gaddis, Pynchon, Joseph McElroy (*Lookout Cartridge*), Don DeLillo (*Ratner's Star*), and John Barth (*Letters*). The main criteria linking them, however, are sheer size (500-plus pages seems the cutoff point), as well as the "large rhetorical risks" these books take in using multimedia allusions and techniques, striving for excessive *quantity* in order to drive home understandings about the alienating *quality* of contemporary culture (6). This much is good, but does not adequately define the modal and generic tensions that give the different fictions their peculiar power. Otherwise LeClair's essay stands alone. Other studies limit themselves to textual explication and the novel's qualities as a subgenre. See for example Louis Gallo, "Nixon and the 'House of Wax': An Emblematic Episode in Coover's *The Public Burning*," *Critique* 23.3 (1982): 43–51; Lois Gordon, *Robert Coover: The Universal Fictionmaking Process* (Carbondale: Southern Illinois University Press, 1983); and Raymond Mazurek, "Metafiction, The Historical Novel, and Coover's *The Public Burning*," *Critique* 23.3 (1982): 29–42.

49. See Susan Strehle, *Fiction in the Quantum Universe* (Chapel Hill: University of North Carolina Press, 1992).

50. Sacvan Bercovitch, *The American Jeremiad* (Madison: University of Wisconsin Press, 1978), 190.

51. See Coover's remarks in "Robert Coover on His Own and Others' Fictions: An Interview," in *Anything Can Happen: Interviews with Contemporary American Novelists*, ed. Tom LeClair and Larry McCaffery (Urbana: University of Illinois Press, 1983), 78. Critics who have interpreted the satire as an argument for the Rosenbergs' innocence include Gordon (60–61) and Podhoretz, in his 1977 review (34).

52. Coover, 1973 review of Nizer, 5. Subsequent references are to this version and are cited parenthetically.

53. Coover, 1973 review of Nizer, 4; and *The Public Burning*, 24, respectively.


## Chapter 5: Encyclopedic Satires

1. See Ronald T. Swigger, "Fictional Encyclopedism and the Cognitive Value of Literature," *Comparative Literature Studies* 12 (1975): 351–66; and Edward Mendelson, "Gravity's Encyclopedia," *Mindful Pleasures: Essays on Thomas Pynchon*, ed. George

Levine and David Leverenz (Boston: Little, Brown, 1975), 161–96. Mendelson's essay is an expanded version of a similar piece, "Encyclopedic Narrative: From Dante to Pynchon," *Modern Language Notes* 91 (1976): 1267–75. Subsequent quotations from Mendelson refer to the longer, 1975 version, and, as with the Swigger essay, will be cited parenthetically.

2. See for example: Speer Morgan, in "*Gravity's Rainbow:* What's the Big Idea?" in *Critical Essays on Thomas Pynchon,* ed. Richard Pearce (Boston: G. K. Hall, 1981), 82–98, acknowledges Mendelson's contribution while preferring to maintain Frye's term, the "Menippean satire"; John Stark, in *Pynchon's Fictions: Thomas Pynchon and the Literature of Information* (Columbus: Ohio State University Press, 1980), summarizes Mendelson on encyclopedic fictions and also leans toward Frye's term, but hedges his bet even further by noting that *Gravity's Rainbow* also "resembles tragedy in many ways" (25–26); Joel Dana Black, in "The Paper Empires and Empirical Fictions of William Gaddis," in *In Recognition of William Gaddis,* ed. John Kuehl and Steven Moore (Syracuse, N.Y.: Syracuse University Press, 1984), applies the concept of fictional encyclopedism in extensive detail; and Molly Hite, in *Ideas of Order in the Novels of Thomas Pynchon* (Columbus: Ohio State University Press, 1983), agrees with Swigger and Mendelson that the "fiendish complexity" of *Gravity's Rainbow,* as well as its "parodic attitude" toward the theories it references, are both qualities of encyclopedic fictions. However, she rightly points out that Pynchon's novel is "thematically committed to incompleteness," and that its resistance to totalizing form challenges the very basis of encyclopedism as Mendelson and Swigger define it.

3. Frye, *Anatomy of Criticism,* 310. Subsequent references are cited parenthetically.

4. Mendelson, 172; the claim is echoed in Swigger, 353.

5. This is a good place to indicate why the long novels of John Barth (*The Sot-Weed Factor, Giles Goat-boy,* and *Letters*) are not included here. They meet few of the formal requirements just spelled out. None of them, for example, has any specific relation to its contemporary surrounding, and they include few or none of the aspects of recent science, statecraft, economy, and art that are essential to the form. Instead, as Linda Hutcheon claims (in *A Theory of Parody,* 72), these fictions are parodic works and not satires in the strict sense meant here. In short, not length alone but the larger pragmatics of form, intent, and reception are what define the encyclopedic satire.

6. The problems with Frye's schema have been widely remarked. In brief, what he calls "genres" most critics (including myself) call "modes," and vice versa. But there is more. In the chapter on genres that leads off *The Fantastic,* Todorov shows that Frye's schema of the four "genres" rests on illogically opposed classificational indices: "introverted/extroverted" (which presents no problem) and "intellectual/personal" (the problem, for it should be either "intellectual/nonintellectual" or "impersonal/personal"). One irony, as Christine Brooke-Rose points out in her excellent summary of these problems (55–56), is that the only "genre" (or mode) unambiguously defined by the schema is the one that was previously unacknowledged but demanded by his theorizing: the "anatomy," as an "extroverted" and "intellectual" form.

7. Jacques Derrida, *Dissemination,* trans. Barbara Johnson (Chicago: University of Chicago Press, 1981), 51–52.

8. Ibid., 52–53.

9. Roland Barthes, *S/Z*, 205–6; Eco, *The Role of the Reader*, 222. Similarly, in *The Act of Reading*, Iser speaks of the "gestalten of memory" on which readers draw while in the process of "consistency-building." In reading for a consistent grasp on the imaginary world, the reader correlates the textual "gestalt-groupings" with those of memory, in a process of selection and matching (124–26).

10. Kristeva, *Desire in Language*, 70. Further references are cited parenthetically.

11. William Gaddis, *The Recognitions* (New York: Avon, 1974), 613. Further references are to this edition and are cited parenthetically.

12. William Gaddis, *J R* (New York: Knopf, 1975), 244. Further references are to this edition and are cited parenthetically.

13. See Guy Debord, *The Society of the Spectacle* (Detroit: Black and Red Press, 1983).

14. A brief onomastic and numerological aside: the Irish surname Gaddis itself invokes a "son of Gad," identifying the author as a nominal descendent of the biblical Jacob's seventh child, the bastard Gad. Jacob fixed on the name, we are told, because it signified "wealth" — the acquisition and maintenance of which is also Gaddis's great subject. Wyatt Gwyon, for instance, is the seventh in a line of wealthy forebears to attend divinity school. And in many ways he anticipates the protagonist in *J R*, Edward (a "guardian of wealth") Bast — who may well be a bastard. Edward is also confronted with the dilemma of deciding whether he will inherit monetary or transcendent "wealth," and he eventually understands that the two are indistinguishable. The numerological allusion to seven will recur (see below).

15. See Steven Moore, *A Reader's Guide to William Gaddis's "The Recognitions"* (Lincoln: University of Nebraska Press, 1982).

16. Ibid., 131.

17. See Max Horkheimer, *Eclipse of Reason* (New York: Seabury Press, 1974), especially chapter 1, "Means and Ends": the "instrumentalization" and, hence, the "neutralization" of reason "deprives it [reason] of any relation to objective content and of its power of judging the latter, and degrades it to an executive agency concerned with the how rather than the what, transforms it to an ever-increasing extent into a mere dull apparatus for registering facts" (55). In *Dialectic of Enlightenment*, trans. J. Cumming (New York: Herder and Herder, 1972), Adorno and Horkheimer will continue to condemn this "instrumentalization" that (to them) is pandemic in the marketing of mass culture — what they aptly termed the *Kulturindustrie* — of postmodernism.

18. Karl Marx and Friedrich Engels, *Marx and Engels: Basic Writings on Politics and Philosophy*, trans. and ed. Lewis S. Feuer (Garden City, N.Y.: Doubleday, 1959), 320.

19. Fredric Jameson, *The Prison-House of Language: A Critical Account of Structuralism and Russian Formalism* (Princeton, N.J.: Princeton University Press, 1972), 180. In what follows, I draw as well on Jean-Joseph Goux, "Numismatique: l'or, le phallus, et la langue," *Tel Quel* 35 (1968): 64–89, and 36 (1968): 54–74.

20. In writing a 1971 dissertation on *The Recognitions*, Peter W. Koenig made extensive use of Gaddis's working notes and manuscript materials. Steven Moore quotes from these papers in his *Reader's Guide* to the novel, referring in particular to Gaddis's

notes about Wyatt. Gaddis commented, for example, that Wyatt's "process of art is the working out of his redemption" (Moore, 18). In addition it is clear that Gaddis conceived of this "process" in the Jungian lexicon of alchemical work, especially Jung's interpretation of alchemy as a process whose aim is the conjunction and synthesis of psychic contraries (see Moore, 16–19). In what follows I develop these references and intentions at greater length.

Also, see Christopher Knight, "Flemish Art and Wyatt's Quest for Redemption in William Gaddis's *The Recognitions*," in Kuehl and Moore, *In Recognition of William Gaddis*, 58–69. Looking at the allusions to Flemish painting and painters, Knight reads Wyatt's art work as a process of "transcendental intuition" which takes him beyond the materialistic contradictions exemplified in counterfeiting, and which ultimately brings him "the possibility, through love, of redemption" (64, 68). Joseph Salemi reads the novel in a similarly upbeat, optimistic way, concluding that Wyatt's growth illustrates how "art is an act of atonement, in that it constellates true significance in the midst of falsity, redeeming that falsity just as the cross redeems sin. In point of fact, Gaddis's position seems to be that genuine art atones not only for false art, but for false life" (56). These interpretations well represent most of the reviews and other scholarly essays. Only Steven Moore asks the question that none of them take up: "Can art indeed be the exemplar of redemption in a novel where, of the three principal artists, two [Wyatt and Sinisterra] are counterfeiters and the third [Stanley] a neurotic Catholic who perishes as a result of his work?" (20). And while Moore does not detail an answer to his question, it is exactly the problem we must pursue in what follows.

21. William Gaddis, "The Rush for Second Place," *Harper's*, April 1981, 35.

22. There are further ironies. Stanley does not "recognize" it, but that low C vibrates at the same frequency as the chugging engine aboard the ship that brought him to Italy, the *Conte di Brescia*. And, as Steven Moore points out (256), that name is clearly meant to recall Adamo di Brescia, the count Dante confines in Hell for counterfeiting. As if this weren't enough to damn his efforts, Stanley plays the fatal note on an organ donated to the chapel at Fenestrula (from *fenestra*: window) by a wealthy American industrialist who, characteristically, got the biggest instrument money could buy, for a chapel too small and fragile to withstand its power.

23. While "Black Humor" did not make its formal debut until the autumn of 1964, a number of critics were quick to point out *The Recognitions* as a most important early example of the mode. See for example Knickerbocker, "Humor with a Mortal Sting," 3; Davis, 13; and Weber, 361. Davis saw *The Recognitions* and Hawkes's *The Cannibal* both "prefiguring" Black Humor in its high (sixties) mode, though he also acknowledged that Gaddis's encyclopedic reach often takes us "quite outside" the boundaries "normally associated with Black Humor" (82). Years later, in a review of *J R*, John Aldridge sought to summarize these developments: "The most authoritative mode in the serious fiction of the Fifties was primarily realistic, and the novel of fabulation and Black Humor — of which *The Recognitions* was later to be identified as a distinguished pioneering example — had not yet come into vogue. . . . Rereading it with the knowledge of all that this movement has taught us about the modern experience

and the opening of new possibilities for the novel, one can see that *The Recognitions* occupies a strikingly unique and primary place in contemporary literature"; see his "The Ongoing Situation," *Saturday Review*, 4 October 1975, 27.

24. See for example Gerard Genette, *Narrative Discourse: An Essay in Method*, trans. Jane E. Lewin (Ithaca: Cornell University Press, 1980). "Order" is the register of differences between the succession of events in the story and their arrangement in the narrative (35); "duration" is the register of "speed" in the narrative, that difference between the elapsed time of the story and the length of its treatment in the narrative (87); while "frequency" is the register of the number of times that one or more story-events are narrated (114). In *J R* the narrative order tends toward synchrony, its dialogues having none but the most conversational means of including analepsis or prolepsis, and its descriptive asides introducing only the swiftest and most insignificant ellipses. Excepting those ellipses, the narrative duration develops no notable differences between story-time and the time of one's reading. And the narrative frequency tends toward the "singulative"—each event told once, then reintroduced only in the most common conversational way.

25. See my reader's guide, *A "Gravity's Rainbow" Companion* (Athens: University of Georgia Press, 1988), 9–11.

26. Gaddis, *J R*, 3; unless indicated in brackets, all ellipsis marks are from the text itself. They do important work in a novel whose theme is the fragmentation necessary to unlimited exchange. Similarly, Gaddis's use of the tiret instead of quotation marks to indicate speech is a carryover from *The Recognitions*, and another important strategy in a text that blurs the proprietary distinctions between phrases.

27. In scene 1 of *The Rhinegold*, the Nibelungs say of their fantastic ring that it is "worthless, except when you *play*," by which Wagner clearly meant play as a kind of serendipitous, indeterminate delight that is opposite the profit-motives of commerce. Like Alberich's, J R's inversion of that dictum winds up the mainspring of Gaddis's plot.

28. The phrase is from Marx's "Critique of the Gotha Programme," and Schepperman has altered only the first two and one-half words, "FROM EACH ACCORD," adding lines to the letters or completing circles to transform them into the bogus Greek phrase (*J R* 20), a joke on the school board that Jack Gibbs will later indirectly acknowledge (407).

29. See *Die Fragmente der Vorosokratiker*, ed. and trans. H. Diels (Dublin/Zurich: Wiedemann, 1952). Jack gives a fair rendering of fragments 57 and 60 and of MS 31B.

30. James's best known work, according to the text, is an opera called "Philoctetes." In Greek mythology, Philoctetes is the young hero exiled to a secluded isle because he entered a sacred garden, where he is bitten by a snake. But his skills as an archer make him valuable during wartime and he is coaxed away from the placid seclusion of his otherwise uninhabited isle by Ulysses, who deceitfully promises worldly gain. Philoctetes' loss or solitude is analogous to the condition of all the artists represented in *J R*. In a 1985 interview Gaddis remarked to a newsman that this "idea has always fascinated me"; see Lloyd Grove, "Harnessing the Power of Babble," *Washington Post*, 23 August 1985, B10.

31. The best known are Juvenal's sixth satire, as well as those sections of *Gulliver's Travels* in which Swift's revulsion for female sexual and excretory functions stands out. But woman as target for the satirist's venom is an old satirical motif, as a number of literary historians have pointed out. See, for example, Frye, *Anatomy of Criticism,* where it is linked to "the Omphale archetype, the man bullied or dominated by women" (228); Highet, *the Anatomy of Satire,* 39 and passim; and Hodgart, 79–107. Hodgart notes that "a later revival of the genre [of misogynistic satire] took place in early twentieth-century America [in attacks on "Momism" in the short stories of Lardner and Thurber], though perhaps that too is a closed chapter" (106).

32. In *The Rhetoric of Irony,* Booth has discussed these difficulties in reconstructing the intent of a satire. It always depends "on a proper use of knowledge or inference about the author and his surroundings," yet the complexities of satirical form often make such a reconstruction "difficult, and it may finally be impossible" (120). More specifically in a narrative fiction, readers must search for what Booth calls "conflicts of belief," those unmistakable differences between "the beliefs expressed" by a character or narrator and the beliefs supposedly held by the narratee or the author himself (73). In a case like *J R,* however, when the narratee and author have seemingly been erased from the text, one cannot draw such inferences.

33. Seidel, *Satiric Inheritance,* 56–58.

34. See for example Edward Mendelson, "Pynchon's Gravity," *Yale Review* 62 (1973): 624–31; Richard Poirier, "Rocket Power," *Saturday Review of the Arts,* March 1973, 59–64; and Tony Tanner, "V and V-2," *London Magazine* 13 (1974): 80–88.

35. In particular Joseph Slade's *Thomas Pynchon;* the collection of essays edited by Levine and Leverenz; William Plater, *The Grim Phoenix: Reconstructing Thomas Pynchon* (Bloomington: Indiana University Press, 1978); Tony Tanner, *Thomas Pynchon;* Molly Hite, *Ideas of Order;* Kathryn Hume, *Pynchon's Mythography: An Approach to "Gravity's Rainbow"* (Carbondale: Southern Illinois University Press, 1987); and Alec McHoul and David Wills, *Writing Pynchon: Strategies in Fictional Analysis* (Urbana: University of Illinois Press, 1989).

36. See for example M. Keith Booker, *Techniques of Subversion in Modern Literature: Transgression, Abjection, and the Carnivalesque* (Gainesville: University of Florida Press, 1991); Theodore Kharpertian, *A Hand to Turn the Time: The Menippean Satires of Thomas Pynchon* (Rutherford, N.J.: Fairleigh Dickinson University Press, 1990); and Alfred MacAdam, "Pynchon as Satirist: To Write, To Mean," *Yale Review* 67 (1978): 555–66.

37. MacAdam, 566. Tanner, for example, details the delights and complexities of Pynchon's heteroglot writing and then locates its normative basis in the "counterforce" of Love: for instance between Roger and Jessica, "based on a real feeling of mutuality, loss of ego, true sensuality" (*Thomas Pynchon,* 87). I argue against that reading of the Roger and Jessica liaison in what follows. Plater, in what has become another all-too-typical reading of the novel, finds similar delights and locates the novel's positive norms in an ethos of "Caring" (175–86), though he also neglects to consider the ways that reading is problematized by the scripted or plotted feel of those moments of empathy he cites.

38. MacAdam, 564–66.

39. Karl, 447.

40. George Puttenham, *The Arte of English Poesie,* ed. G. D. Willcock (Cambridge: Cambridge University Press, 1936), 170.

41. Kathryn Hume, "Views from Above, Views from Below: The Perspectival Subtext of *Gravity's Rainbow,*" *American Literature* 60 (1988): 625–42.

42. Vonnegut, *Slaughterhouse-Five,* 63–64.

43. Genette, quoted in Culler, *Structuralist Poetics,* 210.

44. Hayden White, *Tropics of Discourse: Essays in Cultural Criticism* (Baltimore: Johns Hopkins University Press, 1975), 10.

45. Robert Scholes, *Semiotics and Interpretation* (New Haven: Yale University Press, 1982), 62–63; and Tzvetan Todorov, "The Typology of Detective Fiction," in *The Poetics of Prose,* trans. Richard Howard (Ithaca: Cornell University Press, 1977), 42–51.

46. McHoul and Wills, 53–56.

47. See my *A "Gravity's Rainbow" Companion,* 72.

48. Herman Melville, *Moby Dick; or, The Whale* (Berkeley and Los Angeles: University of California Press, 1979), 125–26.

49. See Milic Capek, *The Philosophical Impact of Contemporary Physics* (New York: Van Nostrand, 1961), 340–44; as well as Ilya Prigogine and Isabelle Stengers, "Postface," *Hermes,* by Michel Serres (Baltimore: Johns Hopkins University Press, 1982), 137–55.

50. Quoted in Capek, 122.

51. Capek, 125; Prigogine and Stengers, 145–46.

52. See for example Friedrich Nietzsche, *The Will to Power,* vol. 9 in *The Complete Works* (London: Foulis, 1913): "The universe is thus . . . a circular movement which has already repeated itself an infinite number of times, and which plays its game for all eternity" (430). Or see Henry Bergson, *Creative Evolution,* trans. A. Mitchell (New York: Modern Library, 1944): "A group of elements which has gone through a state can therefore always find its way back to that state, if not by itself, at least by means of an external cause able to restore everything to its place. This amounts to saying that any state of the group may be repeated as often as desired, and consequently that the group does not grow old" (11). And yet while we are at it, why not define modernist poetics in general according to this ideology of Recurrence and Return? For it is a commonplace to assert that texts are the more modernist as they are more archaic or primitivistic. Some examples: Eliot's regression toward Sanskrit origins as he concludes *The Wasteland;* Pound's work with ancient Chinese ideograms and odes; Lawrence's interest in Etruscan and pre-Columbian Amerindian cultures; Picasso's interest in the cave paintings at Altamira, like Brancusi's in pre-Hellenic sculpture. This list could go on and on. Pynchon's self-conscious use of this poetics; his satirical subversions of it, especially in light of contemporary science; and furthermore his deconstruction of the power relations at stake in it, especially in the logic of the scapegoat operating in popular and elite culture alike, both sustains and thrives upon that logic — these define his postmodernity in the broadest terms.

53. Capek, 345.

54. See Prigogine and Stengers, 146; and, for comparison, *Gravity's Rainbow,* 167, when the spirit of assassinated German foreign minister Walter Rathenau cautions

those attending a seance: "All talk of cause and effect is secular history, and secular history is a diversionary tactic." The incisive questions, he warns, involve "the real nature of control."

55. Michel Serres, *Hermes: Literature, Science, Philosophy,* ed. Josué Harari and David F. Bell (Baltimore: Johns Hopkins University Press, 1982), 150n.

56. See Dwight Eddins, *The Gnostic Pynchon* (Bloomington: Indiana University Press, 1990).

57. Capek, 129–30.

58. Serres, 83.

59. Prigogine and Stengers, 152–55.

60. Michel Beaujour, "The Game of Poetics," *Yale French Studies* 41 (1968): 61–62.


## Chapter 6: Conclusion

1. Jameson, *Postmodernism, Or the Cultural Logic of Late Capitalism* (Durham, N.C.: Duke University Press, 1990), 17.

2. Charles Altieri, "The Powers and Limits of Oppositional Postmodernism," *American Literary History* 2 (1990): 447.

3. See Paul Maltby, *Dissident Postmodernists: Barthelme, Coover, Pynchon* (Philadelphia: University of Pennsylvania Press, 1991).

# Bibliography

Adorno, T. W., and Max Horkheimer. "The Culture Industry." *Dialectic of Englightenment*. Trans. J. Cumming. New York: Herder and Herder, 1972.

Aldridge, John W. "Donald Barthelme and the Doggy Life." *Atlantic,* July 1968. Reprinted in *The Devil in the Fire: Retrospective Essays on American Literature and Culture, 1951–1971*, 261–66. New York: Harpers, 1972.

————. "The Ongoing Situation." *Saturday Review,* 4 October 1975, 27, 29–30.

Alloway, Lawrence. *American Pop Art.* New York: Macmillan, 1974.

————. *Roy Lichtenstein.* New York: Abbeville, 1983.

Alpers, Paul. *To Tell a Story: Narrative Theory and Practice.* Los Angeles: William Andrews Clark Memorial Library (UCLA), 1973.

Alter, Robert. "The American Political Novel." *New York Times Book Review,* 10 August 1980, 3, 26–27.

Altieri, Charles. "The Powers and Limits of Oppositional Postmodernism." *American Literary History* 2 (1990): 443–81.

Arac, Jonathan, ed. *Postmodernism and Politics: New Directions.* Minneapolis: University of Minnesota Press, 1986.

Armstrong, Thomas. "Reader, Critic, and the Form of John Hawkes' *The Cannibal.*" *Boundary* 2 5 (1977): 829–44.

Bachelard, Gaston. *The Poetics of Space.* Trans. Maria Jolas. Boston: Beacon Press, 1969.

Bakhtin, Mikhail. *Rabelais and His World.* Trans. Helene Iswolsky. Cambridge, Mass.: MIT Press, 1968.

————. *The Dialogic Imagination.* Ed. Michael Holquist. Trans. Caryl Emerson and Michael Holquist. Austin: University of Texas Press, 1981.

Bakhtin, Mikhail, and P. M. Medvedev. *The Formal Method in Literary Scholarship: A*

*Critical Introduction to Sociological Poetics.* Trans. Albert J. Wehrle. Cambridge, Mass.: Harvard University Press, 1985.

Barnes, Linda Horvay. *The Dialectics of Black Humor: Process and Product.* Frankfurt: Peter Lang, 1978.

Barthelme, Donald. "After Joyce." *Location* 1.2 (1964): 13–16.

———. *Snow White.* 1967. New York: Atheneum, 1972.

———. *The Dead Father.* 1975. New York: Pocket Books, 1976.

———. "An Interview with Donald Barthelme." In *Anything Can Happen: Interviews with Contemporary American Novelists,* ed. Thomas LeClair and Larry McCaffery, 32–44. Urbana: University of Illinois Press, 1983.

———. "Not-Knowing." *Georgia Review* 39 (1985): 509–22.

Barthes, Roland. *Mythologies.* 1957. Trans. Annette Lavers. New York: Hill and Wang, 1972.

———. *Elements of Semiology.* 1964. Trans. Annette Lavers. New York: Hill and Wang, 1968.

———. *S/Z: An Essay.* 1970. Trans. Richard Miller. New York: Farrar, Straus and Giroux, 1974.

Baudrillard, Jean. *Simulations.* Trans. Paul Foss, Paul Patton, Philip Beichtman. New York: Semiotext(e), 1981.

Baumbach, Jonathan. *The Landscape of Nightmare.* New York: New York University Press, 1970.

Baxter, Charles. "In the Suicide Seat: Reading John Hawkes' *Travesty.*" *Georgia Review* 34 (1980): 871–85.

Beaujour, Michel. "The Game of Poetics." *Yale French Studies* 41 (1968): 61–69.

Bellow, Saul. "Some Notes on Recent American Fiction." 1963. Reprinted in *The World of Black Humor: An Introductory Anthology of Selections and Criticism,* ed. Douglas M. Davis, 329–37. New York: E.P. Dutton, 1967.

Ben-Porat, Ziva. "Method in Madness: Notes on the Structure of Parody, Based on MAD TV Satires." *Poetics Today* 1 (1979): 245–72.

Benstock, Bernard. "On William Gaddis: In Recognition of James Joyce." *Wisconsin Studies in Contemporary Literature* 6 (1965): 177–89.

Bercovitch, Sacvan. *The American Jeremiad.* Madison: University of Wisconsin Press, 1978.

Bergson, Henri. *Creative Evolution.* Trans. A. Mitchell. New York: Modern Library, 1944.

Betsky, Celia. Review of *The Public Burning.* *Commonweal,* 28 October 1977, 693–96.

Black, Joel Dana. "The Paper Empires and Empirical Fictions of William Gaddis." In *In Recognition of William Gaddis,* ed. John Kuehl and Steven Moore, 162–73. Syracuse, N.Y.: Syracuse University Press, 1984.

"Black Humor Fictions." *Time,* 12 February 1965, 95–96.

Blair, Walter, and Hamlin Hill. *America's Humor.* New York: Oxford University Press, 1978.

Bloom, Edward A., and Lillian D. Bloom. *Satire's Persuasive Voice.* Ithaca: Cornell University Press, 1979.

Booker, M. Keith. *Techniques of Subversion in Modern Literature: Transgression, Abjection, and the Carnivalesque.* Gainesville: University of Florida Press, 1991.

Booth, Wayne. *A Rhetoric of Irony.* Chicago: University of Chicago Press, 1974.

Bourjaily, Vance. "What Vonnegut Is and Isn't." *New York Times Book Review,* 13 August 1972, 3, 10.

Breton, André. *Anthologie de l'humour noir.* Ed. Jean-Jacques Pauvert. Paris: Gallimard, 1966.

Brooke-Rose, Christine. *A Rhetoric of the Unreal: Studies in Narrative and Structure, Especially the Fantastic.* London: Cambridge University Press, 1981.

Bruns, Gerald L. "Allegory and Satire: A Rhetorical Meditation." *New Literary History* 11 (1979): 121–32.

Burns, Stuart L. "The Evolution of *Wise Blood.*" *Modern Fiction Studies* 16 (1970): 147–62.

Butler, Christopher. *After the Wake: An Essay on the Contemporary Avant-Garde.* Oxford: Clarendon Press, 1980.

Cabou, Jacques. "Humour noir et surréalisme dans les romans de Nathanael West." *Études anglaises* 29 (1976): 430–35.

Calas, Nicholas. "Why Not Pop Art?" *Art and Literature* 4 (1965): 178–84.

Capek, Milic. *The Philosophical Impact of Contemporary Physics.* New York: Van Nostrand, 1961.

Case, Arthur E. *Four Essays on "Gulliver's Travels."* Princeton, N.J.: Princeton University Press, 1945.

Clark, A. M. *Studies in Literary Modes.* Edinburgh: Oliver and Boyd, 1946.

Clark, John R., and Anna Lydia Motto, eds. *Satire: That Blasted Art.* New York: Putnam, 1973.

Clemons, Walter. "Shock Treatment." *Newsweek,* 8 August 1977, 75–76.

Clerc, Charles, ed. *Approaches to "Gravity's Rainbow."* Columbus: Ohio State University Press, 1983.

Coates, Robert. "Messiah of the Lonely Heart." *New Yorker,* 15 April 1933, 59.

Coleman, John. Review of *The Magic Christian. The Spectator,* 13 July 1959, 13.

Cooper, Peter. *Signs and Symptoms: Thomas Pynchon and the Contemporary World.* Berkeley and Los Angeles: University of California Press, 1983.

Coover, Robert. *The Universal Baseball Association, Inc., J. Henry Waugh, Prop.* New York: Random House, 1968.

——— . Review of Louis Nizer's *The Implosion Conspiracy. New York Times Book Review,* 11 February 1973, 4, 33.

——— . *The Public Burning.* New York: Viking, 1976.

——— . "An Interview with Robert Coover." In *Anything Can Happen: Interviews with Contemporary American Novelists,* ed. Thomas LeClair and and Larry McCaffery, 63–78. Urbana: University of Illinois Press, 1983.

Courtney, E. "Parody and Literary Allusion in Menippean Satire." *Philologus* 106 (1962): 86–100.

Couturier, Maurice, and Regis Durand. *Donald Barthelme.* Contemporary Writers Series. New York: Methuen, 1982.

Culler, Jonathan. *Structuralist Poetics: Structuralism, Linguistics, and the Study of Literature*. Ithaca: Cornell University Press, 1975.

——— . *In Pursuit of Signs: Semiotics, Literature, Deconstruction*. Ithaca: Cornell University Press, 1981.

Dane, Joseph A. "Parody and Satire: A Theoretical Model." *Genre* 13 (1980): 145–59.

Davis, Douglas M., ed. *The World of Black Humor: An Introductory Anthology of Selections and Criticism*. New York: E. P. Dutton, 1967.

Debord, Guy. *The Society of the Spectacle*. Detroit: Black and Red Press, 1983.

Deer, Harriet, and Irving Deer. "Satire as Rhetorical Play." *Boundary 2* 5 (1977): 711–21.

Deleuze, Gilles. *Logique du sens*. Paris: Editions Minuit, 1972.

Deleuze, Gilles, and Félix Guattari. *Anti-Oedipus: Capitalism and Schizophrenia*. Trans. Robert Hurley, Mark Seem, and Helen R. Lane. Minneapolis: University of Minnesota Press, 1983.

——— . *A Thousand Plateaus: Capitalism and Schizophrenia*. Trans. Brian Massumi. Minneapolis: University of Minnesota Press, 1987.

DeLillo, Don. *White Noise*. New York: Viking, 1985.

Derrida, Jacques. *Of Grammatology*. Trans. Gayatri Spivak. Baltimore: Johns Hopkins University Press, 1976.

——— . *Dissemination*. Trans. Barbara Johnson. Chicago: University of Chicago Press, 1981.

Dickstein, Morris. *Gates of Eden: American Culture in the Sixties*. New York: Basic Books, 1977.

Diels, H. *Die Fragmente der Vorosokratiker*. Dublin/Zurich: Wiedemann, 1952.

Donleavy, J. P. *The Ginger Man*. New York: Dell, 1973.

Donovan, Alan. "Nathanael West and the Surrealistic Muse." *Kentucky Review* 2 (1968): 82–95.

Dooley, David J. *Contemporary Satire*. Toronto: Holt, Rinehart and Winston, 1971.

Drinnon, Richard. *Facing West: The Metaphysics of Indian-Hating*. Minneapolis: University of Minnesota Press, 1980.

Driskell, Leon V., and Joan T. Brittain. *The Eternal Crossroads: The Art of Flannery O'Connor*. Lexington: University Press of Kentucky, 1971.

Eco, Umberto. *A Theory of Semiotics*. Bloomington: Indiana University Press, 1976.

——— . *The Role of the Reader: Explorations in the Semiotics of Texts*. Bloomington: Indiana University Press, 1979.

Eddins, Dwight. *The Gnostic Pynchon*. Bloomington: Indiana University Press, 1990.

Eden, Rick A. "Detective Fiction as Satire." *Genre* 16 (1983): 279–95.

Edenbaum, Robert I. "Dada and Surrealism in the United States: A Literary Instance." *Arts and Society* 5 (1968): 114–25.

Edwards, Thomas R. "Real People, Mythic History." *New York Times Book Review*, 14 August 1977, 9, 26.

Efron, Arthur. Untitled response, in "Modern Satire: A Mini-Symposium," ed. George A. Test. *Satire Newsletter* 6.2 (1969): 6–9.

Eliot, T. S. Introduction to *Johnson's "London" and "The Vanity of Human Wishes,"* by

Samuel Johnson. London: F. Etchells and H. MacDonald, 1930.

Elkin, P. K. *The Augustan Defence of Satire*. Oxford: Clarendon Press, 1973.

Elliott, Robert C. *The Power of Satire: Magic, Ritual, Art*. Princeton, N.J.: Princeton University Press, 1960.

Emerson, Ralph Waldo. *Ralph Waldo Emerson: Selected Essays, Lectures, and Poems*. Ed. Robert D. Richardson. New York: Bantam, 1990.

Esslin, Martin. *The Theatre of the Absurd*. 2d ed. Woodstock, N.Y.: Overlook Press, 1973.

Fabre, Michel. "*The Free-Lance Pallbearers* ou le langage du pouvoir." *Revue française d'études américaines* 1 (1976): 83–100.

Fadiman, Clifton. "Humor as a Weapon." *The Center Magazine* (Santa Barbara: Center for the Study of Democratic Institutions) 4.1 (1971): 20–23.

Federman, Raymond. "An Interview with Raymond Federman." In *Anything Can Happen: Interviews with Contemporary American Novelists*, ed. Thomas LeClair and Larry McCaffery, 126–52. Urbana: University of Illinois Press, 1983.

Feinberg, Leonard. *The Satirist: His Temperament, Motivation, and Influence*. Ames: Iowa State University Press, 1963.

———. *Introduction to Satire*. Ames: Iowa State University Press, 1967.

———. "Satire: The Inadequacy of Recent Definitions." *Genre* 1 (1968): 31–37.

———. *The Secret of Humor*. Amsterdam: Rodopi, 1978.

Fekete, John, ed. *Life after Postmodernism: Essays in Value and Culture*. New York: St. Martins, 1987.

Feldman, Burton. "Anatomy of Black Humor." *Dissent* 15 (1968): 158–60.

Festa, Conrad. "Vonnegut's Satire." In *Vonnegut in America: An Introduction to the Life and Work of Kurt Vonnegut*, ed. Jerome Klinkowitz and Donald D. Lawler, 133–49. New York: Dell, 1977.

Fiedler, Leslie A. "The Divine Stupidity of Kurt Vonnegut." *Esquire*, September 1970, 195–97, 199–200.

Field, Andrew. *Nabokov, His Life in Art: A Critical Narrative*. Boston: Little, Brown, 1967.

———. *Nabokov: His Life in Part*. New York: Penguin, 1978.

Fletcher, M. D. "Vidal's *Duluth* as 'Post-Modern' Political Satire." *Thalia* 9 (1986): 10–21.

Flowers, Betty. "Barthelme's *Snow White*: The Reader-Patient Relationship." *Critique* 16 (1975): 33–43.

Fokkema, Douwe Wessel. *Literary History, Modernism, and Postmodernism*. Philadelphia: John Benjamins, 1984.

Foster, Hal. *The Anti-Aesthetic: Essays on Postmodern Culture*. Port Townshend, Wash.: Bay Press, 1983.

Freud, Sigmund. *Jokes and their Relation to the Unconscious*. 1905. Vol. 8 of *The Standard Edition of the Complete Psychological Works of Sigmund Freud*. Trans. James Strachey. London: Hogarth Press, 1959.

Freund, Winfried. *Die literarische Parodie*. Stuttgart: Metzler, 1981.

Friedman, Bruce Jay, ed. *Black Humor*. New York: Bantam, 1965.

Frohock, W. M. "John Hawkes' Vision of Violence." *Southwest Review* 50 (1965): 65–79.

—— . "The Edge of Laughter: Some Modern Fiction and the Grotesque." In *Veins of Humor,* ed. Harry Levin, 243–54. Cambridge: Harvard University Press, 1972.

Frye, Northrop. "The Nature of Satire." *University of Toronto Quarterly* 14 (1944): 76–89.

—— . *Anatomy of Criticism: Four Essays.* 1957. New York: Atheneum, 1967.

Fuhrmann, Manfred. "Narr und Satire." In *Das Komische,* ed. Wolfgang Preisendanz and Rainer Warning, 425–27. Poetik und Hermeneutik, vol. 7. Munich: Wilhelm Fink, 1976.

Gaddis, William. *The Recognitions.* 1955. New York: Avon, 1974.

—— . *J R.* New York: Knopf, 1975.

—— . "The Rush for Second Place." *Harper's,* April 1981, 31–39.

—— . *Carpenter's Gothic.* New York: Viking, 1985.

Gallo, Louis. "Nixon and the 'House of Wax': An Emblematic Episode in Coover's *The Public Burning.*" *Critique: Studies in Modern Fiction* 23.3 (1982): 43–51.

Galloway, David. "Nathanael West's 'Dream Dump.' " *Critique: Studies in Modern Fiction* 6.1 (1964): 46–64.

Gardner, John. *On Moral Fiction.* New York: Basic Books, 1978.

Genette, Gerard. *Narrative Discourse: An Essay in Method.* Trans. Jane E. Lewin. Ithaca: Cornell University Press, 1980.

—— . *Palimpsestes: La littérature au second degré.* Paris: Éditions du Seuil, 1982.

Girard, René. *Violence and the Sacred.* Trans. Patrick Gregory. Baltimore: Johns Hopkins University Press, 1977.

Gitlin, Todd. "Hip-Deep in Postmodernism." *New York Times Book Review,* 6 November 1988, 1, 35–36.

Goldman, Albert. Review of *Candy. New Republic,* 11 July 1964, 17.

Gordon, Lois. *Robert Coover: The Universal Fictionmaking Process.* Carbondale: Southern Illinois University Press, 1983.

Goux, Jean-Joseph. "Numismatique: l'or, le phallus, et la langue." *Tel Quel* 35 (1968): 64–89; 36 (1968): 54–74.

Gover, Robert. "An Interview with Ishmael Reed." *Black American Literature Forum* 12 (1978): 12–19.

Graff, Gerald. *Literature against Itself: Literature in Modern Society.* Chicago: University of Chicago Press, 1979.

Gray, Paul. Review of *The Public Burning. Time,* 8 August 1977, 70–71.

Greiner, Donald J. *Comic Terror: The Novels of John Hawkes.* Memphis: Memphis State University Press, 1973.

—— . "Djuna Barnes' *Nightwood* and the American Origins of Black Humor." *Critique* 17 (1976): 41–53.

Gross, John. "Darkness Risible." *Encounter* 23.4 (1964): 41–43.

Grove, Lloyd. "Harnessing the Power of Babble" [Interview with William Gaddis]. *Washington Post,* 23 August 1985, B10.

Guilhamet, Leon. *Satire and the Transformation of Genre.* Philadelphia: University of Pennsylvania Press, 1987.

Gurewitch, Morton. "European Romantic Irony." Ph.D. diss., Columbia University, 1957.

———. *Comedy: The Irrational Vision*. Ithaca: Cornell University Press, 1975.

Haas, William E. "Some Characteristics of Satire." *Satire Newsletter* 3.1 (1965): 1–3.

Hall, Donald. "Three Million Toothpicks." *National Review,* 30 September 1977, 1118–20.

Hall, Ernest Jackson. *The Satirical Element in the American Novel*. New York: Haskell House, 1966.

Hand, Nancy Walker. "A Novel in the Form of a Comic Strip: Nathanael West's *Miss Lonelyhearts.*" *The Serif* 5 (1968): 14–21.

Harvey, David. *The Condition of Postmodernity: An Enquiry into the Origins of Cultural Change*. Cambridge, Mass.: Basil Blackwell, 1989.

Hassan, Ihab. "Laughter in the Dark: The New Voice in American Fiction." *American Scholar* 33 (1964): 636–40.

———. *The Dismemberment of Orpheus: Toward a Postmodern Literature*. 1971. 2d ed. Madison: University of Wisconsin Press, 1982.

———. "Making Sense: The Trials of Postmodern Discourse." *New Literary History* 18 (1987): 437–59.

Hauck, Richard B. *A Cheerful Nihilism: Confidence and the Absurd in American Humorous Fiction*. Bloomington: Indiana University Press, 1971.

Hawkes, John. *The Cannibal*. 1949. New York: New Directions, 1962.

———. "Notes on Violence." *Audience* 7 (1960): 60.

———. "Flannery O'Connor's Devil." *Sewanee Review* 70 (1962): 395–407.

———. "Notes on *The Wild Goose Chase.*" *Massachusetts Review* 3 (1962): 784–88.

———. "John Hawkes: An Interview." 1964. Reprinted in *Studies in "Second Skin,"* ed. John Graham, 18–32. Columbus: Ohio State University Press, 1974.

———. "Notes on Writing a Novel." *Triquarterly* 30 (1974): 109–26.

———. *Travesty*. New York: New Directions, 1976.

———. " 'A Trap to Catch Little Birds with': An Interview with John Hawkes." In *A John Hawkes Symposium,* ed. Anthony Santore and Michael Pocalyko, 165–84. New York: New Directions, 1977.

———. *The Passion Artist*. New York: Harper and Row, 1979.

———. "Life and Art: An Interview with John Hawkes." *The Review of Contemporary Fiction* 3.3 (1983): 107–27.

Hayles, N. Katherine. "Postmodern Parataxis: Embodied Texts, Weightless Information." *American Literary History* 2 (1990): 394–421.

———. " 'A Metaphor of God Knew How Many Parts': The Engine That Drives *The Crying of Lot 49.*" In *New Essays on "The Crying of Lot 49,"* ed. Patrick O'Donnell, 97–125. New York: Cambridge University Press, 1991.

Heller, Joseph. *Catch-22*. 1961. New York: Dell, 1962.

Hendin, Josephine. *The World of Flannery O'Connor*. Bloomington: Indiana University Press, 1970.

———. *Vulnerable People: A View of American Fiction since 1945*. New York: Oxford University Press, 1978.

Henkle, Roger B. "Pynchon's Tapestries on the Western Wall." In *Pynchon: A*

Collection of Critical Essays, ed. Edward Mendelson, 97–111. Englewood Cliffs, N.J.: Prentice-Hall, 1978.

Hewitt, Douglas. *The Approach to Fiction*. London: Longmans, 1982.

Highet, Gilbert. *The Anatomy of Satire*. Princeton, N.J.: Princeton University Press, 1962.

Hill, Hamlin. "Black Humor: Its Cause and Cure." *Colorado Quarterly* 17 (1968): 57–64.

Himes, Chester. *Pinktoes*. New York: Dell, 1961.

Hite, Molly. *Ideas of Order in the Novels of Thomas Pynchon*. Columbus: Ohio State University Press, 1983.

Hodgart, Matthew. *Satire*. New York: McGraw-Hill, 1970.

Honig, Edwin. *Dark Conceit: The Making of Allegory*. Evanston, Ill.: Northwestern University Press, 1959.

Horkheimer, Max. *Eclipse of Reason*. 1947. New York: Seabury Press, 1974.

Howe, Irving. "New Black Writers." *Harper's Magazine,* December 1969, 130–41.

Hughes, Emmett John. *The Ordeal of Power: A Political Memoir of the Eisenhower Years*. New York: Atheneum, 1963.

Hume, Kathryn. "Robert Coover's Fiction: The Naked and the Mythic." *Novel* 12.2 (1979): 127–48.

———. *Pynchon's Mythography: An Approach to "Gravity's Rainbow."* Carbondale: Southern Illinois University Press, 1987.

———. "Views from Above, Views from Below: The Perspectival Subtext in *Gravity's Rainbow*." *American Literature* 60 (1988): 625–42.

Hunt, Sandra Ann. "The Black Humor Novel in American Literature." Ph.D. diss., University of North Carolina, Chapel Hill, 1977.

Hutcheon, Linda. *Narcissistic Narrative: The Metafictional Paradox*. New York: Methuen, 1984.

———. *A Theory of Parody: The Teachings of Twentieth-Century Art Forms*. New York: Methuen, 1985.

———. *A Poetics of Postmodernism: History, Theory, Fiction*. New York: Routledge, 1988.

Huyssen, Andreas. "Mapping the Postmodern." *New German Critique* 33 (1984): 5–52.

———. *After the Great Divide: Postmodernist Culture*. Bloomington: Indiana University Press, 1986.

Iser, Wolfgang. *The Act of Reading: A Theory of Aesthetic Response*. Baltimore: Johns Hopkins University Press, 1978.

Jack, Ian. *Augustan Satire: Intention and Idiom in English Poetry, 1660–1750*. New York: Oxford University Press, 1952.

Jameson, Fredric. "Metacommentary." *PMLA* 86 (1971): 9–19.

———. *The Prison-House of Language: A Critical Account of Structuralism and Russian Formalism*. Princeton, N.J.: Princeton University Press, 1972.

———. *Fables of Aggression: Wyndham Lewis, the Modernist as Fascist*. Berkeley and Los Angeles: University of California Press, 1979.

——— . *The Political Unconscious: Narrative as a Socially Symbolic Act.* Ithaca: Cornell University Press, 1981.

——— . "The Politics of Theory: Ideological Positions in the Postmodernism Debate." *New German Critique* 33 (1984): 53–65.

——— . "Postmodernism, or The Cultural Logic of Late Capitalism." *New Left Review* 146 (1984): 53–92.

——— . *Postmodernism, Or the Cultural Logic of Late Capitalism.* Durham, N.C.: Duke University Press, 1990.

Janoff, Bruce. "Black Humor: Beyond Satire." *Ohio Review* 14 (1972): 5–20.

——— . "Black Humor, Existentialism, and Absurdity: A Generic Confusion." *Arizona Quarterly* 30 (1974): 294–304.

Jencks, Charles. *What Is Postmodernism?* New York: St. Martin's Press, 1986.

Jensen, H. James, and Melvin R. Zirker, Jr., eds. *The Satirist's Art.* Bloomington: Indiana University Press, 1972.

Johnston, John. "Toward the Schizo-Text: Paranoia as Semiotic Regime in *The Crying of Lot 49*." In *New Essays on "The Crying of Lot 49,"* ed. Patrick O'Donnell, 47–78. New York: Cambridge University Press, 1991.

Josipovici, G. D. "*Lolita*: Parody and the Pursuit of Beauty." *Critical Quarterly* 6 (1964): 35–48.

Karl, Frederick R. *American Fictions, 1940–1980: A Comprehensive History and Critical Evaluation.* New York: Harper and Row, 1984.

Karrer, Wolfgang. *Parodie, Travestie, Pastiche.* Munich: Wilhelm Fink, 1977.

Kazin, Alfred. "American Writing Now." *New Republic,* 18 October 1980, 27–30.

Kerbrat-Orecchioni, Catherine. "L'ironie comme trope." *Poétique* 41 (1980): 108–27.

Kermode, Frank. *The Sense of an Ending: Studies in the Theory of Fiction.* New York: Oxford University Press, 1966.

——— . "Decoding the Trystero." In *Pynchon: A Collection of Critical Essays,* ed. Edward Mendelson, 162–66. Englewood Cliffs, N.J.: Prentice-Hall, 1978.

Kernan, Alvin B. *The Cankered Muse: Satire of the English Renaissance.* New Haven: Yale University Press, 1959.

——— . *The Plot of Satire.* New Haven: Yale University Press, 1965.

Keyser, Wolfgang. *The Grotesque in Art and Literature.* Trans. Ulrich Weisstein. Bloomington: Indiana University Press, 1957.

Kharpertian, Theodore D. *A Hand to Turn the Time: The Menippean Satires of Thomas Pynchon.* Rutherford, N.J.: Fairleigh Dickinson University Press, 1990.

Kinney, Arthur F. *Flannery O'Connor's Library: Resources of Being.* Athens: University of Georgia Press, 1985.

Klinkowitz, Jerome. "Final Word on Black Humor." *Contemporary Literature* 15 (1974): 271–76.

——— . *Literary Disruptions: The Making of a Post-Contemporary American Fiction.* Urbana: University of Illinois Press, 1980.

——— . *Rosenberg / Barthes / Hassan: The Postmodern Habit of Thought.* Athens: University of Georgia Press, 1988.

——— . *Donald Barthelme: An Exhibition.* Durham, N.C.: Duke University Press, 1991.

Klinkowitz, Jerome, and Donald L. Lawler, eds. *Vonnegut in America: An Introduction to the Life and Work of Kurt Vonnegut.* New York: Dell, 1977.

Klinkowitz, Jerome, and John Somer, eds. *The Vonnegut Statement: Essays on the Life and Work of Kurt Vonnegut, Jr.* New York: Delacorte, 1973.

Knickerbocker, Conrad. "Candide as a Co-ed." *New York Times Book Review,* 17 May 1964, 5.

————. "Humor with a Mortal Sting." *New York Times Book Review,* 27 September 1964, 3, 60–61.

Knight, Christopher. "Flemish Art and Wyatt's Quest for Redemption in William Gaddis's *The Recognitions.*" In *In Recognition of William Gaddis,* ed. John Kuehl and Steven Moore, 58–69. Syracuse, N.Y.: Syracuse University Press, 1984.

Kostelanetz, Richard. "The Point Is That Life Doesn't Have Any Point." *New York Times Book Review,* 6 June 1965, 3, 28–30.

Kristeva, Julia. *Desire in Language.* Trans. Leon Roudiez. New York: Columbia University Press, 1980.

————. *Powers of Horror: An Essay on Abjection.* Trans. Leon Roudiez. New York: Columbia University Press, 1982.

Kroker, Arthur, and David Cook. *The Postmodern Scene: Excremental Culture and Hyper-Aesthetics.* New York: St. Martin's Press, 1986.

Kuehl, John. *John Hawkes and the Craft of Conflict.* New Brunswick, N.J.: Rutgers University Press, 1974.

————. *Alternate Worlds: A Study of Postmodern Anti-Realist Fiction.* New York: New York University Press, 1989.

Kuehl, John, and Steven Moore, eds. *In Recognition of William Gaddis.* Syracuse, N.Y.: Syracuse University Press, 1984.

Kuiper, Koenraad. "The Nature of Satire." *Poetics* 13 (1984): 459–73.

Kundera, Milan. " 'Man Thinks, God Laughs.' " *New York Review of Books,* 13 June 1985, 11.

LaPolla, Franco. "*The Free-Lance Pallbearers;* or, No More Proscenium Arch." *Review of Contemporary Fiction* 4 (1984): 188–94.

Lasch, Christopher. *The Culture of Narcissism: American Life in an Age of Diminishing Expectations.* New York: Warner Books, 1979.

Lawson, Hilary. *Reflexivity: The Postmodern Predicament.* La Salle, Ill.: Open Court, 1985.

LeClair, Thomas. "Death and Black Humor." *Critique* 17 (1976): 5–40.

————. "Robert Coover, *The Public Burning,* and the Art of Excess." *Critique* 23.3 (1982): 5–28.

————. *The Art of Excess: Mastery in Contemporary American Fiction.* Urbana: University of Illinois Press, 1989.

LeClair, Thomas, and Larry McCaffery, eds. *Anything Can Happen: Interviews with Contemporary American Novelists.* Urbana: University of Illinois Press, 1983.

Leland, John. "Remarks Re-Marked, Barthelme: What Curios of Signs!" *Boundary 2* 5 (1977): 795–811.

Leonard, John. "The Last Word." *New York Times Book Review,* 19 May 1974, 1, 19.

Leverence, John. "Gaddis Anagnorisis." In *In Recognition of William Gaddis,* ed. John Kuehl and Steven Moore, 32–45. Syracuse, N.Y.: Syracuse University Press, 1984.

Levin, Harry. "The Wages of Satire." In *Literature and Society: Selected Papers from the English Institute, 1978,* ed. Edward W. Said, 1–14. Baltimore: Johns Hopkins University Press, 1980.

———, ed. *Veins of Humor.* Cambridge: Harvard University Press, 1972.

Levin, Martin. Review of *The Magic Christian. New York Times Book Review,* 21 February 1969, 4.

Levine, George, and David Leverenz, eds. *Mindful Pleasures: Essays on Thomas Pynchon.* Boston: Little, Brown, 1976.

LeVot, Andre. "Du degré zéro du langage a l'heure H de la fiction: sexe, texte, et dramaturgie dans *The Cannibal.*" *Études anglaises* 29.3 (1976): 487–98.

Lewis, R. W. B. "Eccentric's Pilgrimage." *Hudson Review* 6 (1953): 144–45.

Lewis, Wyndham. *Men Without Art.* London: Casell, 1934.

———. "The Greatest Satire is Nonmoral." In *Satire: Modern Essays in Criticism,* ed. Ronald Paulson, 66–79. Englewood Cliffs, N.J.: Prentice-Hall, 1971.

Leyburn, Ellen Douglass. *Satiric Allegory: Mirror of Man.* New Haven: Yale University Press, 1956.

———. Untitled response, in "Modern Satire: A Mini-Symposium," ed. George A. Test. *Satire Newsletter* 6.2 (1969): 1.

Lhamon, W. T., Jr. "The Most Irresponsible Bastard." *New Republic* 168 (1973): 24–28.

Liebling, A. J. "Shed a Tear for Mr. West." *New York World Telegram,* 24 June 1931, 11.

Light, James F. *Nathanael West: An Interpretive Study.* Evanston, Ill.: Northwestern University Press, 1971.

Lodge, David. *The Modes of Modern Writing: Metaphor, Metonymy, and the Typology of Modern Literature.* Ithaca: Cornell University Press, 1977.

Lorch, Thomas M. "Religion and Art in *Miss Lonelyhearts.*" *Renascence* 20 (1967): 3–15.

Lundquist, James. *Chester Himes.* New York: Ungar, 1976.

Lyotard, Jean-François. *The Postmodern Condition: A Report on Knowledge.* 1979. Trans. Geoff Bennington and Brian Massumi. Minneapolis: University of Minnesota Press, 1984.

Lyotard, Jean-François, and Jean Loup Thébaud. *Just Gaming.* Trans. Wlad Godzich. Theory and History of Literature, vol. 20. Minneapolis: University of Minnesota Press, 1985.

MacAdam, Alfred. "Pynchon as Satirist: To Write, To Mean." *Yale Review* 67 (1978): 555–66.

Mack, Maynard. "The Muse of Satire." *Yale Review* 41 (1951): 80–92.

Mailer, Norman. *The White Negro: Superficial Reflections on the Hipster.* San Francisco: City Lights, 1958.

———. *Why Are We in Vietnam?* New York: Holt, Rinehart and Winston, 1977.

Mailloux, Stephen. *Interpretive Conventions: The Reader in the Study of American Fiction.* Ithaca: Cornell University Press, 1982.

Maltby, Paul. *Dissident Postmodernists: Barthelme, Coover, Pynchon.* Philadelphia: University of Pennsylvania Press, 1991.

Mangel, Anne. "Maxwell's Demon, Entropy, Information: *The Crying of Lot 49.*" In *Mindful Pleasures: Essays on Thomas Pynchon,* ed. George Levine and David Leverenz, 87–100. Boston: Little, Brown, 1976.

Martin, Jay. *Nathanael West: The Art of His Life.* New York: Farrar, Straus, 1970.

——— , ed. *Nathanael West: A Collection of Critical Essays.* Englewood Cliffs, N.J.: Prentice-Hall, 1971.

Marx, Karl, and Friedrich Engels. *Marx and Engels: Basic Writings on Politics and Philosophy.* Ed. Lewis S. Feuer. Garden City, N.Y.: Doubleday, 1959.

Matanle, Stephen. "Love and Strife in William Gaddis's *J R.*" In *In Recognition of William Gaddis,* ed. John Kuehl and Steven Moore, 106–19. Syracuse, N.Y.: Syracuse University Press, 1984.

Matthews, J. H. "Intelligence at the Service of Surrealism: Breton's *Anthologie de l'humour noir.*" *Books Abroad* 41 (1967): 267–73.

Mazurek, Raymond A. "Metafiction, the Historical Novel, and Coover's *The Public Burning.*" *Critique* 23.3 (1982): 29–42.

McCaffery, Larry. "Barthelme's *Snow White*: The Aesthetics of Trash." *Critique* 16.2 (1975): 19–32.

——— . "Robert Coover on His Own and Other Fictions: An Interview." In *Anything Can Happen: Interviews with Contemporary American Novelists,* ed. Thomas LeClair and Larry McCaffery, 63–78. Urbana: University of Illinois Press, 1983.

McCarthy, Mary. *The Groves of Academe.* 1952. New York: Avon, 1981.

——— . *On the Contrary.* New York: Farrar, Straus and Cudahy, 1961.

——— . *Ideas and the Novel.* New York: Harcourt, Brace and Jovanovich, 1980.

McConnell, Frank D. *Four Postwar American Novelists: Bellow, Mailer, Barth and Pynchon.* Chicago: University of Chicago Press, 1977.

McHale, Brian. *Postmodernist Fiction.* New York: Methuen, 1987.

McHoul, Alec, and David Wills. *Writing Pynchon: Strategies in Fictional Analysis.* Urbana: University of Illinois Press, 1990.

Melville, Herman. *Moby Dick; or, The Whale.* Berkeley and Los Angeles: University of California Press, 1979.

Mendelson, Edward. "Pynchon's Gravity." *Yale Review* 62 (1973): 624–31.

——— . "Encyclopedic Narrative: From Dante to Pynchon." *Modern Language Notes* 91 (1976): 1267–75.

——— . "Gravity's Encyclopedia." In *Mindful Pleasures: Essays on Thomas Pynchon,* ed. George Levine and David Leverenz, 161–96. Boston: Little, Brown, 1976.

——— , ed. *Pynchon: A Collection of Critical Essays.* Englewood Cliffs, N.J.: Prentice-Hall, 1978.

Miner, Earl. "In Satire's Falling City." In *The Satirist's Art,* ed. H. James Jensen and and R. Zirker, 3–27. Bloomington: Indiana University Press, 1972.

Moore, Steven. *A Reader's Guide to William Gaddis's "The Recognitions."* Lincoln: University of Nebraska Press, 1982.

——— . *William Gaddis.* Boston: Twayne, 1989.

Morace, Robert A. "Donald Barthelme's *Snow White*: The Novel, the Critics, and the Culture." *Critique* 26 (1984): 1–10.

Morgan, Speer. *"Gravity's Rainbow*: What's the Big Idea?" In *Critical Essays on Thomas Pynchon,* ed. Richard Pearce, 82–98. Boston: G. K. Hall, 1981.

Muecke, D. C. *The Compass of Irony.* London: Methuen, 1969.

Munch, Peter Andreas. *Norse Mythology.* New York: Macmillan, 1926.

Muste, John M. Untitled response, in "Satire: A Mini-Symposium," ed. George A. Test. *Satire Newsletter* 6.2 (1969): 2–4.

Nabokov, Vladimir. *Lolita.* 1955. New York: Berkeley, 1977.

———. *Strong Opinions.* New York: McGraw-Hill, 1973.

Newman, Charles. *The Post-Modern Aura: The Act of Fiction in an Age of Inflation.* Evanston, Ill.: Northwestern University Press, 1985.

Nietzsche, Friedrich. *The Will to Power.* Vol. 9 of *The Complete Works of Friedrich Nietzsche.* London: Foulis, 1913.

Nixon, Richard. *Six Crises.* Garden City, N.J.: Doubleday, 1962.

O'Brien, John. "Ishmael Reed: An Interview." In *Interviews with Black Writers,* ed. John O'Brien. New York: Liveright, 1973.

O'Connor, Flannery. *Wise Blood.* New York: Farrar, Straus, 1952.

———. *Mystery and Manners: Occasional Prose.* Ed. Sally and Robert Fitzgerald. New York: Farrar, Straus and Cudahy, 1962.

———. *Three by Flannery O'Connor.* New York: Signet, 1962.

———. *The Habit of Being: Letters of Flannery O'Connor.* Ed. Sally Fitzgerald. New York: Random House, 1979.

O'Donnell, Patrick. *John Hawkes.* Boston: Twayne, 1983.

———, ed. *New Essays on "The Crying of Lot 49."* New York: Cambridge University Press, 1991.

Olderman, Raymond. *Beyond the Wasteland: A Study of the American Novel in the 1960's.* New Haven: Yale University Press, 1972.

Palmeri, Frank. *Satire in Narrative: Petronius, Swift, Gibbon, Melville, and Pynchon.* Austin: University of Texas Press, 1990.

Pannenborg, Willem August. *Satirische schrijvers: karakter en temperament.* Assen: Van Gorcum, 1953.

Paulson, Ronald. *The Fictions of Satire.* Baltimore: Johns Hopkins University Press, 1967.

———, ed. *Satire: Modern Essays in Criticism.* Englewood Cliffs, N.J.: Prentice-Hall, 1971.

Petillon, Pierre-Yves. "Thomas Pynchon et l'espace aleatoire." *Critique* 34 (1978): 1107–42.

Pinsker, Sanford. "The Graying of Black Humor." *Studies in the Twentieth Century* 9 (1972): 15–34.

Plater, William. *The Grim Phoenix: Reconstructing Thomas Pynchon.* Bloomington: Indiana University Press, 1978.

Podhoretz, Norman. "Uncle Sam and the Phantom." *Saturday Review,* 17 September 1977, 27–28, 34.

————. *The Bloody Crossroads: Where Literature and Politics Meet.* New York: Simon and Schuster, 1986.

Poirier, Richard. "Embattled Underground." *New York Times Book Review,* 1 May 1966, 5, 42–43.

————. "Rocket Power." *Saturday Review,* March 1973, 59–64.

————. "The Importance of Thomas Pynchon." In *Mindful Pleasures: Essays on Thomas Pynchon,* ed. George Levine and David Leverenz, 15–29. Boston: Little, Brown, 1976.

Pollard, Arthur. *Satire.* London: Methuen, 1970.

Preisendanz, Wolfgang, and Rainer Warning, eds. *Das Komische.* Poetik und Hermeneutik, vol. 7. Munich: Wilhelm Fink, 1976.

Price, Martin. *Forms of Life: Character and Moral Imagination in the Novel.* New Haven: Yale University Press, 1983.

Prigogine, Ilya, and Isabelle Stengers. "Postface: Dynamics from Leibniz to Lucretius." In *Hermes: Literature, Science, Philosophy,* by Michel Serres, 135–57. Ed. Josué Harari and David F. Bell. Baltimore: Johns Hopkins University Press, 1982.

Purdy, James. *Cabot Wright Begins.* New York: Farrar, Straus and Giroux, 1964.

Puttenham, George. *The Arte of English Poesie.* Ed. G. D. Willcock. Cambridge: Cambridge University Press, 1936.

Pynchon, Thomas. *V.* 1963. New York: Bantam, 1964.

————. *The Crying of Lot 49.* 1966. New York: Bantam, 1967.

————. *Gravity's Rainbow.* New York: Viking, 1973.

————. *Slow Learner: Early Short Stories.* Boston: Little, Brown, 1984.

————. *Vineland.* Boston: Little, Brown, 1990.

Quintana, Ricardo. "Situational Satire: A Commentary on the Method of Swift." *University of Toronto Quarterly* 18 (1948): 130–36.

Rahv, Philip. "On Pornography, Black Humor, Norman Mailer, Etc." *Literature and the Sixth Sense.* Boston: Houghton Mifflin, 1970.

Randolph, Mary Claire. "The Structural Design of Formal Verse Satire." *Philological Quarterly* 21 (1942): 368–84.

Ransom, John Crowe. "Ubiquitous Moralists." *Kenyon Review* 3 (1941): 95–100.

Reed, Ishmael. *The Free-Lance Pallbearers.* New York, Avon, 1977.

————. *Yellow Back Radio Broke Down.* New York: Avon, 1977.

————. *Mumbo Jumbo.* New York: Avon, 1978.

Reid, Randall. *The Fiction of Nathanael West.* Chicago: University of Chicago Press, 1967.

Riewald, J. G. "Parody as Criticism." *Neophilologus* 50 (1966): 125–48.

Riffaterre, Michael. "The Poetic Functions of Intertextual Humor." *Romantic Review* 65 (1974): 278–93.

Rose, Margaret. *Parody // Metafiction: An Analysis of Parody as a Critical Mirror to the Writing and Reception of Fiction.* London: Croom Helm, 1979.

Rosenberg, Harold. *The De-Definition of Art.* New York: Horizon, 1972.

Rosenblum, Michael. "Pope's Illusive Temple of Infamy." In *The Satirist's Art,* ed.

H. James Jensen and Melvin R. Zirker, 28–54. Bloomington: Indiana University Press, 1972.

Rosenblum, Robert. "Pop Art and Non-Pop Art." *Art and Literature* 5 (1965): 80–93.

Rosenheim, Edward W. *Swift and the Satirist's Art.* Chicago: University of Chicago Press, 1963.

Roth, Philip. *Portnoy's Complaint.* New York: Random House, 1969.

———. *Our Gang.* New York: Random House, 1971.

Rourke, Constance. *American Humor: A Study of the National Character.* 1931. Garden City, N.Y.: Doubleday-Anchor, 1962.

Rovit, Earl. Untitled response, in "Satire: A Mini-Symposium," ed. George A. Test. *Satire Newsletter* 6.2 (1969): 16–18.

Rudwin, Maximillian J. *The Origin of German Carnival Comedy.* New York: G. E. Stechert, 1926.

Russell, Charles. *Poets, Prophets, and Revolutionaries: The Literary Avant-Garde from Rimbaud through Postmodernism.* New York: Oxford University Press, 1985.

Sacks, Sheldon. *Fiction and the Shape of Belief.* Berkeley and Los Angeles: University of California Press, 1964.

Safer, Elaine B. "The Allusive Mode and Black Humor in Barth's *Giles Goat-Boy* and Pynchon's *Gravity's Rainbow.*" *Renascence* 32 (1980): 89–104.

———. "The Allusive Mode and Black Humor in Barth's *Sot-Weed Factor.*" *Studies in the Novel* 13 (1981): 424–38.

———. "The Allusive Mode, the Absurd, and Black Humor in William Gaddis's *The Recognitions.*" *Studies in American Humor* 1.2 (1982): 103–18.

———. *The Contemporary American Comic Epic: The Novels of Barth, Pynchon, Gaddis, and Kesey.* Detroit: Wayne State University Press, 1988.

Sale, Roger. *Fairy Tales and After: From Snow White to E. B. White.* Cambridge: Harvard University Press, 1978.

Salemi, Joseph S. "To Soar in Atonement: Art as Expiation in William Gaddis's *The Recognitions.*" In *In Recognition of William Gaddis,* ed. John Kuehl and Steven Moore, 46–57. Syracuse, N.Y.: Syracuse University Press, 1984.

Schaub, Thomas. *Pynchon: The Voice of Ambiguity.* Urbana: University of Illinois Press, 1981.

Schlegel, Friedrich. *Literary Notebooks, 1797–1801.* Ed. Hans Eichner. Toronto: University of Toronto Press, 1957.

Schmitz, Neil. "Donald Barthelme and the Emergence of Modern Satire." *Minnesota Review* 1 (1971): 109–18.

Scholem, Gershom. *Major Trends in Jewish Mysticism.* 1941. New York: Schocken, 1954.

Scholes, Robert. *The Fabulators.* New York: Oxford University Press, 1967.

———. "Metafiction." *Iowa Review* 1 (1970): 100–15.

———. *Semiotics and Interpretation.* New Haven: Yale University Press, 1982.

Schott, Webster. "James Purdy: American Dreams." *Nation* 198 (1964): 300–302.

———. "John Hawkes: An American Original." *New York Times Book Review,* 29 May 1966, 4.

Schriber, Mary Sue. "Bringing Chaos to Order: The Novel Tradition and Kurt Vonnegut Jr." *Genre* 10 (1977): 283–97.

Schulz, Max F. *Black Humor Fiction of the Sixties: A Pluralistic Definition of Man and His World.* Athens: Ohio University Press, 1973.

Schwartz, Edward Greenfield. "The Novels of Nathanael West." *Accent* 17 (1957): 251–62.

Seidel, Michael. "Satiric Theory and the Degeneration of the State." Ph.D. diss., University of California, Los Angeles, 1970.

———. *The Satiric Inheritance: Rabelais to Sterne.* Princeton, N.J.: Princeton University Press, 1979.

Serres, Michel. *Hermes: Literature, Science, Philosophy.* Ed. Josué Harari and David F. Bell. Baltimore: Johns Hopkins University Press, 1982.

Shlonsky, Tuvia. "Literary Parody: Remarks on Its Method and Function." In *Proceedings of the 4th Congress of the International Comparative Literature Society.* Ed. F. Jost, 2:787–801. The Hague: Mouton, 1966.

Sklar, Robert. "An Anarchist Miracle: The Novels of Thomas Pynchon." In *Pynchon: A Collection of Critical Essays,* ed. Edward Mendelson, 87–96. Englewood Cliffs, N.J.: Prentice-Hall, 1978.

Slade, Joseph. *Thomas Pynchon.* New York: Warner Books, 1974.

Smith, Barbara Hernnstein. "Value without Truth-Value." In *Life After Postmodernism: Essays in Value and Culture,* ed. John Fekete, 1–21. New York: St. Martin's, 1987.

Snyder, John. *Prospects of Power: Tragedy, Satire, the Essay, and the Theory of Genre.* Lexington: University Press of Kentucky, 1991.

Sontag, Susan. *Against Interpretation.* 1966. New York: Delta, 1981.

Sorrentino, Gilbert. *Imaginative Qualities of Actual Things.* New York: Random House, 1971.

Southern, Terry. *The Magic Christian.* London: Andre Deutsch, 1959.

———. *The Magic Christian.* 1959. New York: Random House, 1960.

Southern, Terry, and Mason Hoffenberg. *Candy.* 1958. New York: Penguin, 1985.

Spacks, Patricia M. "Some Reflections on Satire." *Genre* 1 (1968): 13–30.

———. "The Uncertainties of Satire." *Modern Language Quarterly* 40 (1979): 403–11.

Stark, John. *Pynchon's Fictions: Thomas Pynchon and the Literature of Information.* Columbus: Ohio State University Press, 1980.

Starobinski, Jean. "Le discours maniaque." In *Das Komische,* ed. Wolfgang Preisendanz and Rainer Warning, 383–84. Poetik und Hermeneutik, vol. 7. Munich: Wilhelm Fink, 1976.

Steiner, George. *Language and Silence: Essays on Language, Literature and the Inhuman.* New York: Atheneum, 1972.

Stevens, Martha. *The Question of Flannery O'Connor.* Baton Rouge: Louisiana State University Press, 1973.

Stevick, Philip. "Novel and Anatomy: Notes toward an Amplification of Frye." *Criticism* 10 (1968): 153–65.

Stott, William. *Documentary Expression and Thirties America*. New York: Oxford University Press, 1973.

———. "Donald Barthelme and the Death of Fiction." In *Prospects: An Annual of American Cultural Studies,* ed. Jack Salzman, 1:369–86. New York: Burt Franklin, 1975.

Strehle, Susan. *Fiction in the Quantum Universe*. Chapel Hill: University of North Carolina Press, 1992.

Styron, William. Review of *Candy*. *New York Times Book Review,* 14 May 1964, 8.

Sutherland, James. *English Satire*. London: Cambridge University Press, 1958.

Sutherland, W. O. S., Jr. *The Art of the Satirist*. Austin: University of Texas Press, 1965.

Swain, Barbara. *Fools and Folly*. New York: Random House, 1932.

Swigger, Ronald T. "Fictional Encyclopedism and the Cognitive Value of Literture." *Comparative Literature Studies* 12 (1975): 351–66.

Tanner, Tony. "Necessary Landscapes and Luminous Deteriorations: On Hawkes." *Triquarterly* 20 (1970): 145–79.

———. *City of Words: American Fiction, 1950–1970*. New York: Harper and Row, 1971.

———. "V and V-2." *London Magazine* 13 (1974): 80–88.

———. "No Instructions How to Read." *New York Times Book Review,* 28 March 1976, 1, 23.

———. *Thomas Pynchon*. Contemporary Writers Series. London: Methuen, 1982.

Test, George A., ed. "Modern Satire: A Mini-Symposium." *Satire Newsletter* 6:2 (1969): 1–18.

———. *Satire: Spirit and Art*. Tampa: University of South Florida Press, 1991.

Thiher, Allen. *Words in Reflection: Modern Language Theory and Postmodern Fiction*. Chicago: University of Chicago Press, 1984.

Thorburn, David. "A Dissent on Pynchon." *Commentary* 56 (1973): 314–18.

Tilton, John W. *Cosmic Satire in the Contemporary Novel*. Lewisburg, Pa.: Bucknell University Press, 1977.

Todorov, Tzvetan. *The Fantastic: A Structural Approach to a Literary Genre*. Trans. Richard Howard. Ithaca: Cornell University Press, 1975.

Tompkins, Jane. *Sensational Designs: The Cultural Work of American Fiction, 1790–1860*. New York: Oxford University Press, 1985.

Torchiana, Donald. "*The Day of the Locust* and the Painter's Eye." In *Nathanael West: The Cheaters and the Cheated,* ed. David Madden, 249–82. Deland, Fl.: Everett/ Edwards, 1973.

Towers, Robert. "Nixon's Seventh Crisis." *New York Review of Books,* 29 September 1977, 8–10.

Trout, Paul A. "A Theory of Norms in Satire." *Satire Newsletter* 6.1 (1969): 2–5.

Tschizewskij, Dimitri. "Satire oder Groteske." In *Das Komische,* ed. Wolfgang Preisendanz and Rainer Warning, 269–78. Poetic und Hermeneutik, vol. 7. Munich: Wilhelm Fink, 1976.

Tuveson, Ernest. "Swift: The View from within the Satire." In *The Satirist's Art,* ed.

H. James Jensen and Melvin Zirker, 55–85. Bloomington: Indiana University Press, 1972.

Tyler, Stephen A. *The Unspeakable: Discourse, Dialogue, and Rhetoric in the Postmodern World*. Madison: University of Wisconsin Press, 1987.

Valle-Killeen, Suzanne Dolores. "Introduction." *The Satiric Perspective: A Structural Analysis of Late Medieval, Early Renaissance Satiric Treatises*. New York: Senda Nueva, 1980.

Verrier, Jean. "Le récit réfléchi." *Littérature* 5 (1972): 58–68.

Verweyen, Theodor. *Eine Theorie der Parodie*. Munich: Wilhelm Fink, 1973.

Vizinczey, Stephen. "Engineers of a Sham: How Literature Lies about Power." *Harper's*, June 1986, 69–73.

Vonnegut, Kurt, Jr. *Mother Night*. 1961. New York: Dell, 1966.

———. *Cat's Cradle*. 1963. New York: Dell, 1970.

———. *God Bless You, Mr. Rosewater; or, Pearls before Swine*. 1965. New York: Dell, 1966.

———. *Slaughterhouse-Five; or, The Children's Crusade*. New York: Delacorte, 1969.

———. *Wampeters, Foma, and Granfalloons (Opinions)*. 1974. New York: Dell, 1976.

Wadlington, Warwick. *The Confidence Game in American Literature*. Princeton, N.J.: Princeton University Press, 1975.

Waldmeir, Joseph J. "Only an Occasional Rutabaga: American Fiction Since 1945." *Modern Fictions Studies* 15 (1970): 467–81.

Waugh, Patricia. *Metafiction: The Theory and Practice of Self-Conscious Fiction*. New York: Methuen, 1984.

Weber, Brom. "The Mode of 'Black Humor.'" In *The Comic Imagination in American Literature*, ed. Louis D. Rubin, Jr., 361–71. New Brunswick, N.J.: Rutgers University Press, 1973.

Weber, Max. *The Protestant Ethic and the Spirit of Capitalism*. Trans. Talcott Parsons. 1930. New York: Charles Scribner's Sons, 1958.

Weisenburger, Steven. "Style in *Wise Blood*." *Genre* 16 (1983): 74–97.

———. *A "Gravity's Rainbow" Companion*. Athens: University of Georgia Press, 1988.

———. "Barth and Black Humor." *The Review of Contemporary Fiction* 10.2 (1990): 50–56.

Weisgerber, Jean. "The Use of Quotation in Recent Literature." *Comparative Literature* 22 (1970): 36–45.

Weisstein, Ulrich. "Parody, Travesty, and Burlesque: Imitations with a Vengeance." In *Proceedings of the 4th Congress of the International Comparative Literature Association*, ed. F. Jost, 2:802–11. The Hague: Mouton, 1966.

Wellek, René. *A History of Modern Criticism*. Vol. 2, *The Romantic Age*. New Haven: Yale University Press, 1955.

West, Nathanael. *Two Novels by Nathanael West: "The Dream Life of Balso Snell" and "A Cool Million."* 1931 and 1934. New York: Noonday Press, 1977.

———. "Some Notes on Violence." *Contact* 1.3 (1932): 132–33.

———. *Miss Lonelyhearts / The Day of the Locust*. 1933 and 1939. New York: New Directions, 1962.

————. "Some Notes on *Miss Lonelyhearts*." *Contempo*, 15 May 1933, 1–3.

White, Hayden. *Tropics of Discourse: Essays in Cultural Criticism*. Baltimore: Johns Hopkins University Press, 1975.

————. *The Content of the Form: Narrative Discourse and Historical Representation*. Baltimore: Johns Hopkins University Press, 1987.

Wilde, Alan. *Horizons of Assent: Modernism, Postmodernism, and the Ironic Imagination*. Baltimore: Johns Hopkins University Press, 1981.

————. *Middle Grounds: Studies in Contemporary Fiction*. Philadelphia: University of Pennsylvania Press, 1987.

Winston, Mathew. "*Humour noir* and Black Humor." In *Veins of Humor*, ed. Harry Levin, 269–84. Cambridge: Harvard University Press, 1972.

Wood, Michael. "Rocketing to the Apocalpyse." *New York Review of Books*, 22 March 1973, 22–23.

————. "Dancing in the Dark." *New York Review of Books*, 31 May 1973, 23–25.

Worcester, David. *The Art of Satire*. 1940. New York: Russell and Russell, 1960.

Wright, Charles. *The Wig: A Mirror Image*. New York: Farrar, Straus and Giroux, 1966.

Zall, Paul. Untitled response, in "Satire: A Mini-Symposium," ed. George A. Test. *Satire Newsletter* 6.2 (1969): 4–6.

Zinn, Howard. *The Politics of History*. Boston: Beacon Press, 1970.

# Index

Aldridge, John, 87–89
Alger, Horatio, Jr.: parody of, 37–38,
    154, 158, 162, 180, 286 (n. 47)
Allen, Woody, 90
Alter, Robert, 9, 137, 140
Altieri, Charles, 258–59
*Atlantic*, 80
Austen, Jane, 151

Bachelard, Gaston, 59
Bakhtin, Mikhail: on carnival, 96; on
    dialogism and novel, 11–12; on
    Menippean satire, 25, 205–6
Baldwin, James, 151; *Native Son*, 158
Barth, John, 82, 206
Barthelme, Donald: as antirealist, 65,
    164, 165; as Black Humorist, 82,
    121, 137; *Snow White*, 35, 88, 110-ll,
    114–16, 148, 223
Barthes, Roland, 4, 26, 28, 63, 217;
    *Mythologies*, 110
Baudrillard, Jean, 6
Beaujour, Michel, 255
Bellow, Saul, 9
Bercovitch, Sacvan, 191

Bergson, Henri, 172
Black Humor, 28, 31, 140, 221, 239;
    beyond satire, 2, 22, 81, 82–89; and
    "Camp" aesthetic, 111, 113;
    definitions of, 2, 11, 82, 89, 131,
    133, 276 (nn. 13, 14); and
    degenerative satire, 100–101, 178;
    and documentary, 20, 83–84; and
    gallows humor, 90–91, and
    generative satire, 87; and irony, 99–
    100, 279 (n. 44); and jokes, 81–94,
    126, 175, 277 (n. 27), 278 (n. 41);
    and politics, 81, 137; and Pop Art,
    111–13, 280 (n. 56), 281 (n. 59); and
    postmodernism, 81, 85
Booth, Wayne, 99, 108, 258
*Breakfast of Champions* (Vonnegut),
    92, 93
Bruce, Lenny, 90
Burroughs, William, 82

*Candy* (Southern), 82, 101–2, 106, 152
*Cannibal, The* (Hawkes), 6, 12, 25, 27,
    35, 65–79, 96, 109, 131, 136, 142,
    146, 157, 172

Capek, Milic, 250
Caputo, Philip, 170
Carnival, 25–26
*Carpenter's Gothic* (Gaddis), 260
*Catch-22* (Heller), 94, 121, 170–75
*Cat's Cradle* (Vonnegut), 91–92
Chesterton, G. K., 9
Cleaver, Eldridge, 155
*Cool Million, A,* (West), 37, 157, 158
Coover, Robert, 50, 121, 137, 165, 207,
    260; *The Public Burning*, 9, 12, 18,
    25, 74, 79, 109, 141, 143, 144, 146,
    186, 189–98, 199, 207, 209, 217
*Crying of Lot 49, The* (Pynchon),
    122–30, 131, 142, 231–32, 239
Culler, Jonathan, 61, 109

Dadaism, 34
*Day of the Locust, The* (West), 25, 27,
    33–34, 41–49, 146, 172
Debord, Guy, 209
Deconstructionism, 3, 4, 18, 203–4
Deleuze, Gilles, 133; and Felix
    Guattari, 4, 255–56
DeLillo, Don, 260
Derrida, Jacques, 4, 203–4
*Dissent*, 80
Doctorow, E. L., 190
Documentary forms: satire compared
    to, 20, 142–44
Donleavy, J. P., 65, 82, 137; *Ginger
    Man*, 95–96
Dooley, David J., 21
*Dream Life of Balso Snell, The* (West),
    35–37, 93
Dryden, John, 9, 25; "Absalom and
    Achitophel," 144, 186
Dullness: as satirical figure, 26, 34

Eco, Umberto, 18, 20, 204
Eddins, Dwight, 252–53
Eliot, T. S., 16, 27, 209, 216;
    "Gerontion," 213; *Waste Land, The*,
    77, 78–79
Elkin, P. K., 10, 19, 21

Elliott, Robert C., 16, 28, 144, 145, 162
Ellison, Ralph, 151, 158, 159
Empedocles, 228–29
Encyclopedic satire, 28, 200–210, 237,
    288 (n. 2)
Entropy: as satirical trope, 212, 222,
    230, 232, 282 (n. 79)

Faulkner, William: "The Bear," 179,
    181, 182, 184–85; *Sound and the
    Fury, The*, 210
Feldman, Burton, 87, 89
Fiedler, Leslie, 94
Fitzgerald, F. Scott, 141
Foster, Hal, 258
*Free-Lance Pallbearers, The* (Reed), 12,
    27, 142, 157–62, 169, 185
Freud, Sigmund, 91–92
Friedman, Bruce Jay, 82, 86, 88, 121
*Frolic of his Own, A* (Gaddis), 260
Frye, Northrop, 14, 16, 24, 28, 42, 147,
    200, 206; *Anatomy of Criticism, The*,
    10, 201–2; "The Nature of Satire,"
    1, 9

Gaddis, William, 28, 65, 82, 121, 137,
    191, 260; *Carpenter's Gothic*, 260;
    *Frolic of His Own, A*, 260; *J R*, 6, 12,
    142, 144, 171, 205–8, 222–37;
    *Recognitions, The*, 35, 208–21
Gardner, John: on moral fictions, 9,
    137; on politics and fiction,
    140–41, 258
Genette, Gerard, 179, 243
Genres: satire and theories of, 13,
    50, 113
Gibbs, Josiah Willard, 212, 230
Gide, André, 209, 215
*Ginger Man, The* (Donleavy), 95–96
Girard, René, 55, 145–48, 161, 197
Goux, Jean-Joseph, 217
*Gravity's Rainbow* (Pynchon), 6–8, 12,
    25, 27, 31, 35, 50, 74, 79, 94, 136,
    141, 146, 186, 205–7, 217, 223,
    224, 237–56

Gregory, Dick, 90
Greimas, A. J., 217, 221, 245
Grotesque, the: and satire, 23–24, 51,
    147, 191, 270 (n. 25); and similes,
    53–55, 62, 63, 133–35, 271 (nn. 31,
    32), 282 (n. 83)
Guerard, Albert J., 65
Gurewitch, Morton, 20

Haacke, Hans, 260
Hassan, Ihab, 3, 82, 85
Hawkes, John: and Black Humor, 82,
    121; Cannibal, The, 6, 12, 25, 27, 35,
    65–79, 96, 109, 131, 136, 142, 146,
    157, 172; and degenerative satire,
    28, 137, 140, 178, 260; on Flannery
    O'Connor, 62, 64; Travesty, 122,
    130–37, 148, 172
Hayles, N. Katherine, 128
Heller, Joseph, 82, 121, 137; Catch-22,
    94, 170–75
Hemingway, Ernest, 141, 181, 185
Herr, Michael, 170
Highet, Gilbert, 13, 19
Himes, Chester, 151; Pinktoes, 151–54
Hite, Molly, 125
Hofstadter, Richard, 166
Holzer, Jenny, 260
Horkheimer, Max, 79
Howe, Irving, 163
Hume, Kathryn, 242
Hutcheon, Linda, 17
Huyssen, Andreas, 3
Hysteria: as satirical trope, 33, 49,
    54–55, 56, 134, 179, 208
Hysteron proteron: as trope, 241–48,
    252. See also Regression

Irony, 23, 279 (n. 44); general, 22, 24,
    99–100; specific, 22–24, 99
Iser, Wolfgang, 18, 112

Jack, Ian, 10
Jakobson, Roman, 63
Jameson, Fredric, 139–40, 168, 217,

    222; on postmodernism,
    257–58, 259
Johnson, Lyndon, 154, 157, 158, 186
Johnson, Samuel, 16, 53
Johnston, John, 128
Jokes, 175, 188–89. See also
    Black Humor
J R (Gaddis), 6, 12, 144, 171, 205–8,
    222–37

Karl, Frederick, 2, 119, 171, 173, 239
Kazin, Alfred, 137, 141
Kennedy, John F., 82, 186
Kernan, Alvin B., 9, 25, 26, 144, 173
Kesey, Ken, 175
Keyser, Wolfgang, 23–24
Klinkowitz, Jerome, 88
Knickerbocker, Conrad, 82, 86,
    87, 137
Kristeva, Julia, 205–6
Kruger, Barbara, 260
Kuiper, Koenraad, 19

Last Days of Louisiana Red, The (Reed),
    169, 185–86
LeClair, Thomas, 137, 204, 206
LeVot, André, 71
Lewis, Sinclair, 32
Lewis, Wyndham, 9, 21, 22, 216; Men
    without Art, 6
Lichtenstein, Roy, 112–13
Lolita (Nabokov), 12, 102–10, 131,
    148, 152
Lorentz, Pare, 142
Lyotard, Jean-Françoise, 3, 4, 6, 237;
    Just Gaming, 4

MacAdam, Alfred, 238
Magic Christian, The (Southern), 95,
    96–98
Mailer, Norman, 162; Why Are We in
    Vietnam?, 169–70, 178–85
Mailloux, Stephen, 13
Malcolm X, 155, 240
Maltby, Paul, 259

Mann, Thomas, 209
Marquand, J. P., 32
Martin, Jay, 44
Marx, Karl, 216, 228
McCarthy, Mary, 32, 137, 141, 143, 151, 259; *Groves of Academe, The,* 148–51, 189
McHale, Brian, 3
McHoul, Alec, and David Wills, 245
Melville, Herman, 191; *Moby Dick,* 238, 250
Mendelson, Edward, 200–201, 206
Menippean satire, 25, 164, 202, 205–6
Metafiction, 5, 70, 284 (n. 11)
*Miss Lonelyhearts* (West), 38–41, 54, 93, 146, 148
Modes: satire and theories of, 13–14, 50
Moore, Steven, 213
Muecke, D. C., 20, 22
*Mumbo Jumbo* (Reed), 157, 164–69
Munch, Peter Andreas, 77

Nabokov, Vladimir, 65, 82, 121, 140; *Lolita,* 12, 79, 102–10, 131, 148, 152
Newman, Charles, 258
Nietzsche, Friedrich, 4
Nixon, Richard: as fictional character, 18, 158, 185, 190–97, 283 (n. 5), 286 (nn. 46, 47)
Nizer, Louis, 192, 197

O'Brien, Tim, 170, 175
O'Connor, Flannery, 22–23, 24–25, 65, 137, 141; *Wise Blood,* 9, 27, 35, 49–64, 146
Oedipal myth: satire of, 74–75, 273 (n. 54)
Olderman, Raymond, 83
Orwell, George, 187
*Our Gang* (Roth), 151, 186–89

Parody, 5, 10, 17, 18, 144, 179, 257–58, 263 (n. 5), 288 (n. 5)
*Partisan Review,* 80

Pastiche, 257
Paulson, Ronald, 9, 16, 17
Perry, Bliss, 9
Petronius, 14, 26, 172, 200
*Pinktoes* (Himes), 151–54
Podhoretz, Norman, 141, 258, 283 (n. 5)
Pope, Alexander, 9, 25, 26; *Dunciad, The,* 26, 186
Postmodernism, 3–5, 29, 273 (n. 45), 275 (n. 4)
Pound, Ezra, 216, 222
Price, Martin, 137
Price, Richard, 9
Prigogine, Ilya, 250–51, 253
*Progression d'effet:* as technique, 239–40
Propaganda: satire as, 15, 16, 266 (n. 27)
*Public Burning, The* (Coover), 9, 12, 18, 25, 74, 79, 109, 141, 143, 144, 146, 186, 189–98, 199, 207, 209, 217
Pulitzer Prize, 7, 140, 238, 264 (n. 8)
Purdy, James, 82, 121, 185, 259; *Cabot Wright Begins,* 27, 116–21, 122, 148
Puttenham, George, 241
Pynchon, Thomas: as Black Humorist, 82, 121; *Crying of Lot 49, The,* 122–30, 131, 142, 231–32, 239; and degenerative satire, 65, 137, 140, 178; *Gravity's Rainbow,* 6–8, 12, 25, 27, 31, 35, 50, 74, 79, 94, 136, 141, 146, 186, 205–7, 217, 223, 224, 237–56; and Menippean satire, 164, 165; *V.,* 94; *Vineland,* 260

Rabelais, François, 14, 26
Rahv, Philip, 87
Ransom, John Crowe, 21
*Recognitions, The* (Gaddis), 35, 208–21
Reed, Ishmael, 141, 144, 260; *Free-Lance Pallbearers, The,* 12, 27, 142, 157–62, 169, 185; *Last Days of Louisiana Red, The,* 169, 185–86; *Mumbo Jumbo,* 157, 164–69; *Yellow*

*Back Radio Broke Down,* 157, 162–64, 166

Regression: as satirical trope, 36, 43–44, 78, 268 (n. 3), 293 (n. 52). *See also* Hysteron proteron

Rose, Margaret, 17

Rosenberg, Julius and Ethel, 150, 190, 192–97

Roth, Philip: *Our Gang,* 151, 186–89; *Portnoy's Complaint,* 89

Ruby, Jack, 82–83

Sale, Roger, 114

Satire: degenerative mode of, 3, 5–6, 14, 27, 28, 55, 62, 70, 123, 136, 140, 144–48, 194, 197, 200, 202, 230, 242, 260, 264 (n. 5), 272 (n. 35); formalist theories of, 1, 9–10, 12, 14–23, 146–47, 266 (n. 39); generative mode of, 1, 11, 27, 145, 193, 202, 264 (n. 5); and misogyny, 236–37, 292 (n. 31); and *satura,* 5, 147. *See also* Black Humor; Menippean satire

Scholes, Robert, 82, 243; *Fabulators, The,* 80

Schulz, Max, 86–87, 113

Seidel, Michael, 17, 26, 48, 123, 144–45, 259

Serres, Michel, 251

Sherman, Cindy, 260

*Slaughterhouse-Five* (Vonnegut), 170, 175–78, 242

*Snow White* (Barthelme), 35, 88, 110–11, 114–16, 148, 223

Sontag, Susan, 111–12

Southern, Terry, 82, 121, 137; *Candy,* 82, 101–2, 106, 152; *Magic Christian, The,* 32, 95, 96–98

Steinbeck, John, 143

Steiner, George, 83, 223

Sterne, Laurence, 202

Stevick, Philip, 201

Stone, Robert, 170, 175

Stott, William, 142–43

Surrealism, 33, 34, 268 (n. 5), 277 (n. 16)

Swift, Jonathan, 16–17, 93; *Gulliver's Travels,* 143, 209

Swigger, Ronald T., 200–201, 205

Tanner, Tony, 122

Thackeray, William M., 151

Thébaud, Jean-Loup, 5

*Time,* 80, 91, 95

Todorov, Tzvetan, 243–44

*Travesty* (Hawkes), 122, 130–37, 148, 172

Twain, Mark, 29

*V.* (Pynchon), 94

Vidal, Gore, 260

Vietnam War, 170–71, 175, 177, 178, 186

*Vineland* (Pynchon), 260

Vonnegut, Kurt, 25, 27, 50, 82, 121, 137, 259; *Breakfast of Champions,* 92, 93; *Cat's Cradle,* 91–92; *Slaughterhouse-Five,* 170, 175–78, 242

Wagner, Richard: and *Ring* cycle, 213, 224–27

Walker, Alice, 157

Warren, Robert Penn, 141

Washington, Booker T., 158

Wellek, René, 22

West, Nathanael, 33–49, 65, 120, 122, 137, 140, 141, 156, 157, 162, 178, 180, 185, 222; *Cool Million, A,* 37, 157, 158; *Day of the Locust, The,* 25, 27, 33–34, 41–49, 142, 146, 172; *Dream Life of Balso Snell, The,* 35–37, 93; *Miss Lonelyhearts,* 38–41, 54, 93, 146, 148

White, Hayden, 243

*Why Are We in Vietnam?* (Mailer), 169–70, 170–85

*Wig, The* (Wright), 154–56, 158

Wilde, Alan, 2, 3, 99

Wilson, Edmund, 47

*Wise Blood* (O'Connor), 9, 27, 35,
 49–64, 146

Wolfe, Tom, 260

Wood, Michael, 93

Worcester, David, 9, 10, 15, 19

Wright, Charles: *Wig, The,* 154–56, 158

Wycherly, William, 153

*Yellow Back Radio Broke Down* (Reed),
 157, 162–64, 166

Zinn, Howard, 143